The Rise of the Public in Enlightenment Europe

James Melton's lucid and accessible study examines the rise of 'the public' in eighteenth-century Europe. A work of comparative synthesis focussing on England, France and the German-speaking territories, this is the first book-length, critical reassessment of what Habermas termed the 'bourgeois public sphere'. During the Enlightenment the public assumed a new significance as governments came to recognize the power of public opinion in political life; the expansion of print culture created new reading publics and transformed how and what people read; authors and authorship acquired new status, while the growth of commercialized theatres transferred monopoly over the stage from the court to the audience; and salons, coffeehouses, taverns, and Masonic lodges fostered new practices of sociability. Spanning a variety of disciplines, this important addition to New Approaches in European History will be of great interest to students of social and political history, literary studies, political theory, and the history of women.

JAMES VAN HORN MELTON is Chair of the Department of History at Emory University. He is author of *Absolutism and the Eighteenth-Century Origins of Compulsory Schooling in Prussia and Austria* (Cambridge, 1988), co-translator (with Howard Kaminsky) of Otto Brunner's *Land and Lordship: Structures of Governance in Medieval Austria* (Philadelphia, 1992), and co-editor (with Hartmut Lehmann) of *Paths of Continuity: Central European Historiography from the 1930s to the 1950s* (Cambridge, 1994).

NEW APPROACHES TO EUROPEAN HISTORY

Series editors
WILLIAM BEIK   *Emory University*
T. C. W. BLANNING   *Sidney Sussex College, Cambridge*

New Approaches to European History is an important textbook series, which provides concise but authoritative surveys of major themes and problems in European history since the Renaissance. Written at a level and length accessible to advanced school students and undergraduates, each book in the series addresses topics or themes that students of European history encounter daily: the series embraces both some of the more 'traditional' subjects of study, and those cultural and social issues to which increasing numbers of school and college courses are devoted. A particular effort is made to consider the wider international implications of the subject under scrutiny.

To aid the student reader scholarly apparatus and annotation is light, but each work has full supplementary bibliographies and notes for further reading: where appropriate chronologies, maps, diagrams and other illustrative material are also provided.

For a list of titles published in the series, please see end of book.

The Rise of the Public in Enlightenment Europe

James Van Horn Melton

Emory University

CAMBRIDGE
UNIVERSITY PRESS

CAMBRIDGE UNIVERSITY PRESS
Cambridge, New York, Melbourne, Madrid, Cape Town, Singapore, São Paulo, Delhi

Cambridge University Press
The Edinburgh Building, Cambridge CB2 8RU, UK

Published in the United States of America by Cambridge University Press, New York

www.cambridge.org
Information on this title: www.cambridge.org/9780521469692

First published 2001
Fourth printing 2008

Printed in the United Kingdom at the University Press, Cambridge

A catalogue record for this publication is available from the British Library.

Library of Congress cataloguing in publication data
Melton, James Van Horn, 1952–
The rise of the public in Enlightenment Europe / James
Van Horn Melton.
    p.   cm. – (New approaches to European history; 22)
Includes bibliographical references and index.
ISBN 0 521 46573 7 – ISBN 0 521 46969 4 (pbk.)
1. Enlightenment – Europe.   2. Europe – Social life and customs –
18th century.   3. Europe – Intellectual life – 18th century.   4. Civil society –
Europe – History – 18th century.   5. Printing – Social aspects – Europe –
18th century.   I. Title.   II. Series.
D286 .M44   2001
940.2′8 – dc21   2001025456

ISBN 978-0-521-46573-7 hardback
ISBN 978-0-521-46969-4 paperback

To Barbara, Sarah, and Peter

Contents

List of tables

Acknowledgments

It is a special pleasure to acknowledge my debt to the *Max-Planck-Institut für Geschichte* in Göttingen, where I completed much of the research for this book as a visiting fellow during the summers of 1993, 1995, and 1997. I am grateful to Gerhard Oexle and especially to Jürgen Schlumbohm for serving as sponsors during my terms at the Institute. Hans Erich Bödecker and Rudolf Vierhaus also gave generously of their time and ideas, and I hope that Hartmut Lehmann, the Institute's director, knows how much his friendship and support have meant to me over the years. I would also like to thank my fellow participants in the seminar on Women and Political Thought in Tudor-Stuart England, led by Barbara Harris at the Folger Shakespeare Library in the fall semester of 1994, where some of the ideas in this book germinated.

A grant from the University Research Council of Emory University during the fall semester of 1995 released me from my teaching duties and made it possible for me to write drafts of several chapters. A sabbatical leave granted by Emory's College of Arts and Sciences in the fall of 1998 enabled me to finish much of what remained. I am grateful to my home institution for its support, and to Patsy Stockbridge in the Department of History for her help in preparing the final version of the manuscript. I also wish to acknowledge the able assistance of Johanna Rickman in helping to track down lost citations and references.

I would also like to thank professional colleagues inside and outside the field who took time to read various parts of the manuscript. Where they did not succeed in purging it of factual errors or interpretive lapses, it was not from want of trying. Especially deserving of my thanks are Thomas E. Kaiser, who over the years has been an unfailing source of intellectual stimulation and insight, and Elise Wirtschafter, who took time away from a Guggenheim fellowship to read and comment on the manuscript in full. I owe a substantial debt to Dena Goodman, whose work has helped guide my thinking about Enlightenment salons and refined my understanding of Jürgen Habermas. Her close reading of the introduction and chapter 6 raised questions I may not have answered, but her criticisms did save me from error at various points in the manuscript. I am also grateful to Paul Monod for his detailed comments on the first two chapters, and to Howard Kaminsky and Gary Kates for their critiques of chapters 3 and 4. At Emory my thanks go to members of the German Studies Roundtable and the Vann Seminar in Premodern History, to whom I presented papers related to this project. My Emory colleagues Walter Adamson, Martina Brownley, Geoff Clark, and John Sitter also read parts of the manuscript and encouraged the book along in different ways. Mark Bauerlein provided a close reading of several chapters and did his best to polish my prose. At Emory I also learned much from graduate students I have taught over the past decade in my seminar on the public sphere, who pressed me to refine my ideas at critical points.

William Beik and Timothy Blanning originally invited me to contribute this volume to the series for which they serve as general editors. I am deeply grateful to them for their patience, encouragement, and suggestions, as well as to my editors at Cambridge University Press, Elizabeth Howard and Sophie Read. The constant support I have enjoyed from my parents, Herman and Helen, and my brothers, Edgar and William, has meant much to me. My deepest debt is to Barbara, for the joy she has given her husband, and to Sarah and Peter, for the pleasure and pride they have brought their father. I dedicate this book to the three of them.

Introduction
What is the public sphere?

"Public" has a long history.[1] In Roman antiquity the adjective *publicus* could refer to a collective body of citizens or subjects (as in *res publica*) and its property. The Romans also contrasted *publicus* with the domain of the private household to denote public spaces like streets, squares, or theaters. *Publicum*, the noun form, had a more specifically political meaning and referred to the area, property, or income of the state. This association of public with the state gained renewed currency in early modern Europe, the classic age of dynastic state-building, and this link persists today: candidates run for public office, state agencies are housed in public buildings, state parks are public property.

Yet there is another, more recent meaning of *public*. We use it in the sense of audience, as in speaking of the public for a book, a concert, a play, or an art exhibition. Reading public, music public, theater public – such usages began to appear in the seventeenth century and had become common by the eighteenth. Unlike earlier meanings, these were unrelated to the exercise of state authority. They referred rather to publics whose members were private individuals rendering judgment on what they read, observed, or otherwise experienced. A burgeoning print culture provided one medium through which these publics made their opinions known; new or expanding arenas of sociability like coffeehouses, salons, and masonic lodges were another. These publics arose in the context of an expanding culture of consumption where cultural products were available to those who could pay for them, regardless of formal rank. The commodification of literature wrought by the popularity of the eighteenth-century novel, the cultural amenities available to patrons of fashionable resorts like Bath in England or Bad Pyrmont in Germany, the evolution of theaters from courtly into commercial institutions, the entertainment districts lining the boulevards of Paris or clustered in the pleasure gardens

---

[1] On the history of the term "public," see Lucian Hölscher, "Öffentlichkeit," in *Geschichtliche Grundbegriffe: Historisches Lexikon zur politisch-sozialen Sprache in Deutschland*, ed. Otto Brunner, Werner Conze, and Reinhart Koselleck, vol. IV (Stuttgart, 1978), 413–67.

of London's Ranelagh and Vienna's Prater, all exemplified the expanding networks of print and sociability characteristic of the eighteenth-century Enlightenment. They heralded the arrival of "the public" as a cultural and political arbiter, an entity to which contemporaries increasingly came to refer as a sovereign tribunal. Friedrich Schiller wrote in 1782 that "the public is everything to me, my school, my sovereign, my trusted friend. I shall submit to this and to no other tribunal." London's *Theatrical Guardian* affirmed the public's sovereignty over the stage when it declared in 1791 that "the public is the only jury before the merits of an actor or an actress are to be tried, and when the endeavors of a performer are stampt by them with the seal of sanction and applause, from that there should be no appeal." In 1747 the French art critic La Font de Saint-Yenne, the first to call for the establishment of a public museum in the Louvre, justified his proposal on the grounds that "it is only in the mouths of those firm and equitable men who compose the Public . . . that we can find the language of truth." In the political realm "public opinion" acquired agency and legitimacy, even in the eyes of a theoretically absolute sovereign like Louis XVI, who wrote that "I must always consult public opinion; it is never wrong."[2]

Focussing on England, France, and the German-speaking lands, this book is about the growing importance of "the public" in eighteenth-century life. Chapters 1 and 2 examine the political dimensions of this process, and serve as case studies of the importance that "public opinion" acquired in Enlightenment political culture. The succeeding three chapters on the evolution of reading, writing, and the stage investigate the possibilities as well as the dilemmas posed by the expanding audience for literary and theatrical works. Finally, Chapter 6 on salons, Chapter 7 on taverns and coffeehouses, and Chapter 8 on freemasonry, examine the new modes of sociability that accompanied the rise of the public in Enlightenment Europe. This book is necessarily selective in the kinds of publics it examines. I have not looked at other areas, such as painting or concert life, where contemporaries also accorded "the public" a new significance and wrestled with the question of how to shape or even define it.[3]

[2] Quotes taken from Friedrich Schiller, *Sämtliche Werke*, ed. G. Fricke and H. Göpfert (Munich, 1959), V:856; Leo Hughes, *The Drama's Patrons: A Study of the Eighteenth-Century London Audience* (Austin and London, 1971), 5; Thomas E. Crow, *Painters and Public Life in Eighteenth-Century Paris* (New Haven and London, 1985), 6; John Hardman, *French Politics 1774–1789: From the Accession of Louis XVI to the Fall of the Bastille* (London and New York, 1995), 232. On public opinion as "tribunal" see Mona Ozouf, "'Public Opinion' at the End of the Old Regime," *Journal of Modern History* 60 (1988), 9–13.

[3] These subjects have been examined recently in several stimulating works. On painting and the public sphere in the eighteenth century, see Crow, *Painters and Public Life*, as well as David H. Solkin, *Painting for Money: The Visual Arts and the Public Sphere in Eighteenth-Century England* (New Haven and London, 1992). On musical publics, see James

Nor, on the whole, does this work explore the public spheres of plebeian popular protest and sociability that social historians have done so much to illuminate.[4] To do so would entail writing a completely different book, and for the most part the public sphere treated here was inhabited by men and women with sufficient property and education to enjoy regular access to newspapers, novels, and other products of eighteenth-century print culture.

As a comparative work of synthesis, this book builds on a body of French, German, and Anglo-American scholarship that has grown enormously over the past two decades. Inspiring much of this scholarship is the work of the German philosopher and cultural theorist Jürgen Habermas. Habermas's *Structural Transformation of the Public Sphere* was published in 1962, and in a few years became one of the most widely discussed works of social and political theory on the West German intellectual scene.[5]

H. Johnson's *Listening in Paris: A Cultural History* (Berkeley, 1995), and John Brewer's *The Pleasures of the Imagination: English Culture in the Eighteenth Century* (London, 1997), chapters 10 and 14.

[4] The works of George Rudé and above all E. P. Thompson were pathbreaking in this field. See Rudé, *The Crowd in History: A Study of Popular Disturbances in France and England, 1730–1848* (New York, 1964); Rudé, *Paris and London in the Eighteenth Century: Studies in Popular Protest* (New York, 1971). For Thompson, see his *Making of the English Working Class* (London, 1964), as well as the essays republished in his *Customs in Common: Studies in Traditional Popular Culture* (New York, 1993). On urban popular protest, see also William Beik, *Urban Protest in Seventeenth-Century France: The Culture of Retribution* (Cambridge, 1997); Günther Lottes, *Politische Aufklärung und plebejisches Publikum: Zur Theorie und Praxis des englischen Radikalismus im späten 18. Jahrhundert* (Munich, 1979); Andreas Griessinger, *Das symbolische Kapital der Ehre: Streikbewegungen und kollektives Bewusstsein deutscher Handwerksgesellen im 18. Jahrhundert* (Frankfurt am Main, 1981). On both rural and urban contexts see Andreas Würgler, *Unruhen und Öffentlichkeit: Städtische und ländliche Protestbewegungen im 18. Jahrhundert* (Tübingen, 1995).

[5] Jürgen Habermas, *Strukturwandel der Öffentlichkeit: Untersuchungen zur einen Kategorie der bürgerlichen Gesellschaft* (Darmstadt and Neuwied, 1962). Habermas's book acquired an almost canonical status on the German New Left and was an important theoretical text for the German student movement of the 1960s. Its early reception can be understood in the context of German domestic politics of the period, above all disenchantment with the advent in 1966 of the so-called Grand Coalition between the two leading German parties, the Social Democrats (SPD) and the Christian Democratic Union (CDU). The SPD–CDU coalition convinced many on the left that they had no oppositional voice in the German parliament, and that any authentic opposition had to situate itself outside existing governmental structures. Also important for the reception of Habermas's book was the media campaign waged against the German student movement by the Springer publishing house in the *Bildzeitung*, the sensationalist right-wing tabloid. The critique of the mass media developed by Habermas in his *Structural Transformation* resonated on the German New Left, because it seemed to provide a strategy for creating an autonomous, extraparliamentary sphere of political action outside the bureaucratic institutions of the state and immune to the manipulated consent of monopolized mass media. Habermas, however, grew increasingly uneasy with the violent drift he detected on the student left, and by the summer of 1968, as the German SDS became increasingly radicalized (and to Habermas, uncritically utopian), the break between Habermas and the radical left was open. For the debate between Habermas and the German SDS see Habermas, "Die Scheinrevolution und ihre Kinder," and Oskar Negt, "Einleitung," in *Die Linke Antwortet*

Its impact outside of the German-speaking world was belated, however, since French and English translations did not appear until 1978 and 1989 respectively. Hence in Anglo-American scholarship the book long enjoyed a kind of cult status, the exclusive preserve of a relatively small group of scholars able to read the German original. The publication of the 1978 French translation paved the way for its broader reception until finally, almost thirty years after it first came out, it appeared in English.[6]

Although *The Structural Transformation of the Public Sphere* is Habermas's most historical work, it addresses a question that would be central to his concerns as a philosopher: what are the conditions under which rational, critical, and genuinely open discussion of public issues becomes possible? For historical and theoretical insight he turns to the late seventeenth and eighteenth centuries, when the ideal of what Habermas calls the "bourgeois public sphere" arose in its classic form.[7] Habermas understood this public sphere above all as a realm of communication marked by new arenas of debate, more open and accessible forms of urban public space and sociability, and an explosion of print culture in the form of newspapers, political journalism, novels, and criticism. He acknowledged that the presumed openness and egalitarianism of the bourgeois public sphere were, from its inception, belied by class interest, and that in the nineteenth and twentieth centuries it would lose its critical function as it became absorbed into mass-consumer culture. Yet he still believed that the norms of the public sphere could be salvaged and remain a model for open, critical, and rational debate.

Habermas's bourgeois public sphere was the historical product of two long-term developments. The first was the rise of modern nation-states dating from the late Middle Ages, a process that went hand in hand with the emergence of society as a realm distinct from the state. The modern

---

Jürgen Habermas (Frankfurt am Main, 1968), 5–32. On the general political context see Robert C. Holub, *Jürgen Habermas: Critic in the Public Sphere* (London and New York, 1991), 78–98.

[6] The French edition was published as *L'espace public: Archéologie de la publicité comme dimension constitutive de la société bourgeoise*, trans. Marc B. de Launay (Paris, 1978). The English translation: *The Structural Transformation of the Public Sphere: An Inquiry into a Category of Bourgeois Society*, trans. Thomas Burger (Cambridge, Mass., 1989).

[7] For a discussion of Habermas's concept of the public sphere, a good place to begin is Craig Calhoun, "Introduction: Habermas and the Public Sphere," in Calhoun, ed., *Habermas and the Public Sphere* (Cambridge, Mass. and London, 1992). Insightful analyses can also be found in Dena Goodman, "Public Sphere and Private Life: Toward a Synthesis of Current Historiographical Approaches to the Old Regime," *History and Theory* 31 (1992); Margaret Jacob, "The Mental Landscape of the Public Sphere: A European Perspective," *Eighteenth Century Studies* 28 (1994); and Anthony J. La Vopa, "Conceiving a Public: Ideas and Society in Eighteenth-Century Europe," *Journal of Modern History* 64 (1992).

state, with its monopoly of force and violence, would become the sphere of public power, while society came to be understood as a realm of private interest and activity. The Middle Ages had known no such distinction, for the medieval "state" did not exercise anything like sovereignty in the modern sense. The administrative, military, judicial, and fiscal functions we associate with the modern state were instead exercised at various levels by seigneurs, towns, the church, guilds, and other "private" individuals or corporations. Seigneurs, for example, were not merely private landowners, since their rights of property included rights of administration and jurisdiction over their peasants. The relationship between seigneurs and their peasants was thus both political and social in nature. But as territorial states consolidated their authority during the early modern period, they steadily absorbed many of the political functions that had previously been exercised as rights of lordship by nobles, towns, ecclesiastical corporations, and so forth. These powers were now carried out by a sovereign state whose authority was more sharply defined *vis-à-vis* its subjects. This consolidation of state authority was most visible in the absolutist regimes of the seventeenth and eighteenth centuries, where sovereignty found symbolic expression in what Habermas calls the "representative publicness" of court ritual and display. The pomp and grandeur of the absolutist court sought to underscore the distance between sovereign and subject and focus attention on the ruler as the sole embodiment of public authority. But just as court ceremonies were meaningless without an audience to observe them, so did the absolute monarchy's claims of *public* authority presuppose a *private* body of subjects under royal rule. In making the state the locus of sovereign power, absolutism also created *society* as a private realm distinct from it. It was within this private social realm, the embryo form of modern "civil society," that the bourgeois public sphere would emerge.

The rise of capitalism, the second development framing the formation of the bourgeois public sphere, further disjoined state and society. Society, though subject politically to the state, acquired growing autonomy and self-awareness through the integrating forces of mercantile capitalism. The expansion of national and international markets hastened the flow of information as well as the circulation of goods, as communication networks grew wider and denser through improvements in transportation, the growth of postal services, and the newspapers and commercial sheets circulating in response to the heightened demand for information relevant to foreign and domestic markets. Although governments themselves promoted these developments in the interest of fostering trade and enhancing revenue, the social and economic integration created by expanding networks of communication and exchange reinforced the growing

independence of society. In the eighteenth century this new sense of autonomy found expression in the emerging science of political economy,
with its idea of market society as an autonomous sphere of exchange subject to its own laws. It reached fruition in the early nineteenth century
in the Hegelian antithesis of state and society, which distinguished between a political realm dominated by the state and a private one in which
individuals associated freely and pursued their own interests.[8]

At the same time, argues Habermas, as the market replaced the household as the primary locus of production and exchange, the sphere of
family and household changed accordingly. The eighteenth century saw
the emergence of the new, bourgeois conception of the family as a sphere
of intimacy and affection. Aristotle's classical model of the household had
viewed it as a sphere of coercion and necessity, inferior to the freedom
exercised by the male citizen in the polis. The Aristotelian household
was coercive owing to the absolute authority exercised by the patriarch
over the women, children, and slaves who made up the household. It was
a sphere of necessity since its chief function was to provide basic needs,
namely biological reproduction and the production of goods, which in
turn provided the male citizen with the leisure and independence necessary for his full participation in the political life of the polis. In the Middle
Ages the noble household retained a similarly broad range of functions,
since the rights of property comprised in noble lordship included dominion over one's peasants. The noble household was a unit of production
but also a sphere of domination.

In the early modern period, however, capitalism and the rise of the
state began to strip the household of these older functions. As the market
replaced the household as the primary site for the production of goods,
and as the territorial state increasingly absorbed administrative and judicial functions once exercised by the household, the household was increasingly privatized. Although losing many of its coercive and productive
functions, it also gained greater autonomy *vis-à-vis* the state and the world
of labor. What resulted was the new model of the bourgeois family, for
which the domestic sphere was primarily as a sphere not of production
and domination but of intimacy and affection. Private and thus shielded
from outside intrusion, a refuge from the coercion of the state and the
necessities of labor, the bourgeois family was conceived as an enclave of
humanity distinct from the hierarchies of birth and power that governed

---

[8] On this process see more recently Marvin B. Becker, *The Emergence of Civil Society
in the Eighteenth Century: A Privileged Moment in the History of England, Scotland, and
France* (Bloomington and Indianapolis, 1994). Habermas's own analysis draws on the
theoretical insights of the Austrian medievalist Otto Brunner. See Brunner, *Land and
Lordship: Structures of Governance in Medieval Austria*, translated with an introduction by
Howard Kaminsky and James Van Horn Melton (Philadelphia, 1992), especially ch. 2.

social and political relationships outside it. Its ideals of companionate marriage prescribed bonds between husband and wife that were emotional and not simply economic in nature. It deemed children as objects of love and nurturing, with the family as a nursery for the acquisition of moral education.

Habermas recognized that these ideals were to some extent an ideological construct. More recent historians of marriage and the family have been relentless in highlighting the gendered dimensions of "bourgeois domesticity," and the eighteenth century no doubt had its share of tyrannical middle-class fathers ruling over dysfunctional middle-class families.[9] Coming out of a Marxist tradition that was still relatively unconcerned with matters of gender, Habermas at any rate focussed instead on property relations as the main source of inconsistency in bourgeois ideals of the family. On the one hand, argues Habermas, the norms of intimacy and love that developed within the privacy and autonomy of the bourgeois household were universal ideals, human qualities that transcended rank and class. On the other hand, because the protected sphere of the bourgeois family owed its relative autonomy to the possession of property, the exclusion of the unpropertied belied the universality of bourgeois domestic ideology. This contradiction would later emerge in the tension between the bourgeois public sphere's universal ideals of openness, inclusion, and equality, and its *de facto* exclusion of those who lacked the property and education to participate in it.

Still, Habermas refused to dismiss the norms of the bourgeois family as an ideological fiction. Their universality provided the moral basis for the ideal of a socially transcendent public that would challenge the legitimacy of the hierarchical, asymmetrical relationships on which the social and political order of the Old Regime was based. Originating in the privacy and "interiority" of the bourgeois family, these norms entered the broader public arena through the eighteenth-century literary market. This literary public sphere, at least in the beginning, was fundamentally a-political. Exemplified by periodicals like the moral weeklies of Addison and Steele and later by the sentimental novels of Samuel Richardson, Jean-Jacques Rousseau, and the young Johann Wolfgang von Goethe, it mapped out an autonomous private realm through its preoccupation with the world of family, love, courtship, and sociability. The literary public sphere developed in tandem with institutions of sociability like coffeehouses, reading clubs, and salons. As an arena

---

[9] Lynn Hunt has observed that French novels of the mid-eighteenth century "portrayed a family world in disarray, whether in novels by women in which wives confronted the abuses of husbands or in novels by men in which tyrannical fathers were opposed by rebellious or sacrilegious sons." *The Family Romance of the French Revolution* (Berkeley and Los Angeles, 1992), 23.

where private individuals engaged in rational and critical discussion, it soon moved beyond a non-political literary world and extended its purview to political matters. Habermas views this process as having occurred first in England, where he finds evidence of a politicized public sphere already in the late seventeenth and early eighteenth centuries. Variants then developed on the continent, epitomized by the publication of the *Encyclopédie* in France (1751–72) and the emergence of political journalism in the territories of the Holy Roman Empire during the 1770s. By the eve of the French Revolution, enlightened journalists and critics throughout Europe had assumed the mantle of "public opinion" (*opinion publique* in France, *Publizität* or *öffentliche Meinung* in Germany) in demanding a fundamental transformation of the old order.

The bourgeois public sphere, then, arose within the private domain of the family but would ultimately acquire a political charge. As a realm of discourse and debate, argues Habermas, the public sphere rested on three assumptions. First, the dictates of reason and not the authority or identity of the speaker (or writer) were held to be the sole arbiter in debate. As a realm of communication that claimed to disregard status, the public sphere was in principle inclusive: membership was not based on rank, though it did presume education since full participation depended on one's ability to engage ideas presented in books, periodicals, and other products of print culture. Second, nothing was immune to criticism. In its mature form, the public sphere claimed the right to subject everything to scrutiny – art, music, and the world of letters, but also religious beliefs, the actions of government, or the privileges of elites. Hence for Habermas the public sphere was inherently oppositional in its thrust, since its critical range extended inexorably to individuals and institutions traditionally exempt from scrutiny. Finally, the bourgeois public sphere was hostile to secrecy. Publicity was a cardinal principle of the public sphere, and it ran counter to the absolutist notion of politics as an *arcanum*, a "secret" or "mystery" to which none but rulers and their ministers should be privy. The Prussian King Frederick II affirmed the absolutist principle of secrecy in a decree from 1784:

A private person has no right to pass *public* and perhaps even disapproving judgment on the actions, procedures, laws, regulations, and ordinances of sovereigns and courts, their officials, assemblies, and courts of law, or to promulgate or publish in print pertinent reports that he manages to obtain. For a private person is not at all capable of making such judgment, because he lacks complete knowledge of circumstances and motives.[10]

[10] Quoted in Habermas, *Structural Transformation of the Public Sphere*, 25. On secrecy and absolutism see Andreas Gestrich, *Absolutismus und Öffentlichkeit: Politische Kommunikation in Deutschland zu Beginn des 18. Jahrhunderts* (Göttingen, 1994), 34–74.

For Frederick, the affairs of government were necessarily opaque and incomprehensible to everyone outside the king and his inner circle (he himself went so far as to arrange the abduction and beatings of foreign journalists who thought otherwise). The ideology of the public sphere, on the other hand, assumed that private persons could deliberate ratio- nally on public affairs and that indeed, the collective judgments of "public opinion" could make government more rational. But for public opinion to be rational it had to be informed, and an informed public opinion depended on a greater degree of transparency in government. It also re- quired that debate on public affairs be open and relatively unconstrained by censorship. *[margin note: rational needs to be informed]*

These norms, argues Habermas, found mature expression in the crit- ical spirit of the late Enlightenment (here he especially emphasizes the importance of Immanuel Kant's moral philosophy) and challenges to the traditional order unleashed by the French Revolution. They would be- come basic tenets of nineteenth-century liberalism and its ideal of civil society as a sphere of freedom. For Habermas, however, the "heroic" age of the liberal-bourgeois public sphere was relatively brief and ultimately fell victim to the social and political transformations of the nineteenth cen- tury. The impoverished masses of early industrialism, lacking the property and the education on which participation in the bourgeois public sphere was premised, highlighted the limits of its universal claims. Moreover, the ideals of the bourgeois public sphere presupposed a separation of state and society that proved increasingly untenable during the course of the nineteenth century. This separation was undermined on one side by the socially interventionist welfare state, and on the other by the growing power of corporations and unions that were ostensibly "private" but in- creasingly assumed a quasi-public character. As the boundaries between state and society eroded, the privacy of the family was steadily invaded by the intrusion of the state and quasi-public institutions. As the family lost its remnants of autonomy, it was reduced to a passive domestic domain subject to intrusion by outside forces and vulnerable to the manipulative forces of the mass media and the "culture industry." Just as the family shrank into an arena of passive consumption, so too did the public sphere lose its critical edge and surrender to the dominion of advertising, public relations, and mass-consumer culture.

Here Habermas's apparent pessimism followed in the tradition of Theodor Adorno and Max Horkheimer, his Marxist mentors who like- wise emphasized the role of late-capitalist mass culture in fostering passive conformity and assent. Yet Habermas had somewhat more faith in the enduring critical potential of the bourgeois public sphere and the Enlight- enment ideals on which it was based. In their *Dialectic of Enlightenment* (1947), published amidst the rubble of war and genocide, Adorno and

Horkheimer had focussed on the darker side of Enlightenment rationality as a source of technocratic control and domination. Fifteen years later Habermas was more inclined to emphasize the democratic, emancipatory potential of the Enlightenment. Although recognizing that the public sphere of the Enlightenment had failed to live up to its own norms, he nevertheless believed it offered a model of open, critical debate whose moral promise transcended its ideological origins.

If historians, and especially historians of eighteenth-century Europe, have engaged the insights of Habermas's book with special vigor, this is in large part due to its ability to integrate seemingly disparate approaches to the field. The public sphere linked the private and the public. Its discursive range extended from the domestic realm to the literary marketplace, modes and institutions of sociability, and arenas of political debate. By exploring the public significance of private discourse and sociability, Habermas's model connects the social with the political. It encourages historians to link, say, discourses on family and marriage with those on government, or the communicative practices of reading societies and salons with social and political structures. For these reasons the quantity and range of scholarship inspired by Habermas's book has been broad, extending from intellectual and cultural history to the history of politics and institutions.

That said, it is also clear that important aspects of his interpretation must be modified and in some cases jettisoned outright. One is its chronology. It is difficult to sustain Habermas's view that the eighteenth-century public sphere of debate and criticism emerged first in the literary realm and was only later politicized. In England, political journalism was flourishing well before the sentimental novels and moral weeklies that Habermas associates with the literary public sphere had become popular, and in France the idea of "public opinion" as a sovereign political tribunal was already being articulated in religious controversies of the 1720s and 1730s.[11] This is not to deny the political significance of seemingly non-political literary practices, but rather to question the temporal priority Habermas assigned them.

More fundamentally, Habermas's model employs a rather conventional Marxist framework that most historians today would find dated. Few, for example, would assign the bourgeoisie of the Old Regime the kind of social cohesion and class consciousness that Habermas does. His emphasis on the bourgeois character of the public sphere works best for England,

---

[11] On problems with Habermas's chronology in the German context, see Gestrich, *Absolutismus und Öffentlichkeit*, 28–33.

where historians have in recent decades rediscovered the importance of the "middling sort" in eighteenth-century English social and cultural life. It is also true that participation in the eighteenth-century public sphere presupposed a relatively high level of literacy and education, which was most commonly the possession of those with sufficient property to afford it. But the fact that the propertied dominated the public sphere did not make it bourgeois. The readers of eighteenth-century novels and periodicals, the people who belonged to reading societies and masonic lodges, attended theaters, or sat in coffeehouses, included substantial numbers of nobles. And in France and the German-speaking lands at least, those members of the middle class who participated most actively in the culture of the public sphere were generally not the rising, economically dynamic bourgeoisie of Marxist lore. Most middle-class men of letters in France came from professional backgrounds, and their income derived not from manufacturing or commerce but from offices received or purchased from the crown. Similarly, middle-class German men of letters tended to be university professors, territorial officials, or pastors – professions tied more to a princely absolutist milieu than a commercial or manufacturing one. In this book, therefore, I have preferred the term "Enlightened" to "bourgeois" public sphere. The former conveys the historical specificity of the public sphere examined here in that it refers not just to any public realm, but to one arising out of conditions specific to the late seventeenth and early eighteenth centuries.

Beyond the fact that nobles as well as members of the middle classes participated in the institutions and practices of the Enlightened public sphere, calling the public sphere bourgeois poses other problems.[12] It implies a certain teleology, at least in the context of the eighteenth century, by conjuring up images of a class struggling to burst the bonds in which absolutism and a feudal order had shackled it. In the process it assigns the public sphere a role that was implicitly oppositional and thus implacably hostile to the traditional society and institutions of the Old Regime. There is no question that the Enlightened public sphere had oppositional (or what Habermas would call emancipatory) features. It fostered more inclusive practices of sociability, and by widening the sphere of discussion and debate it did have the potential to challenge the prerogatives of traditionally dominant institutions and elites. But to focus solely on the subversive dimensions of the Enlightened public sphere overlooks the resilience and adaptability of Old Regime society and institutions, which

---

[12] For a discussion of this problem see the exchange between Keith Baker and Roger Chartier in "Dialogue sur l'espace public: Keith Michael Baker, Roger Chartier," *Politix: Travaux de science politique* 26 (1994), 10–13.

were quite capable of recognizing the communicative potential of the public sphere. Not just oppositional groups but also the crown and other traditional institutions appealed to "public opinion" to mobilize support. Moreover, if the practices of sociability nurtured in salons or masonic lodges tended to dissolve boundaries that had traditionally distinguished noble from bourgeois, the impact was not necessarily subversive. To the contrary, one might just as easily see the social intermingling of noble and bourgeois as having contributed to a process of social integration, fusing the propertied classes of society into a new elite by creating new criteria for social distinction and exclusion based on education and taste. In this respect the Enlightened public sphere betrayed a fundamental paradox: while bridging the social and cultural divide separating noble and non-noble, it simultaneously widened the distance between propertied and plebeian.

In a general sense Habermas was aware of this paradox, which he attributed to the tension between the public sphere's universal ideal of humanity and the system of property relations in which it was embedded. Yet despite his apparent recognition that the public sphere never really lived up to its own norms, those who have charged him with idealizing the public sphere have a point.[13] Part of Habermas's problem is that he takes his history from Marx but his moral philosophy from Kant, and it is sometimes difficult to know which hat he is wearing. Habermas the Marxist describes the public sphere as a process of bourgeois class formation; Habermas the Kantian enshrines it as a normative theory of communication. Habermas the Marxist identifies the public sphere with capitalist social relations; Habermas the Kantian adopts its norms as a moral imperative. Habermas the Marxist sees the public sphere as having been compromised by its bourgeois origins; Habermas the Kantian views it nostalgically as a kind of pure, prelapsarian condition only later corrupted by capitalist sin.

But if, as Habermas sees it, capitalism was the public sphere's pallbearer, it was also its midwife. Capitalist market relations pervaded the Enlightened public sphere, which evolved hand in hand with

---

[13] For an early critique see Oskar Negt and Alexander Kluge, *Public Sphere and Experience: Toward an Analysis of the Bourgeois and Proletarian Public Sphere*, trans. Peter Labanyi *et al.* (Minneapolis and London, 1993), which originally appeared in German as *Öffentlichkeit und Erfahrung: Zur Organisationsanalyse von bürgerlicher und proletarischer Öffentlichkeit* (Frankfurt am Main, 1972). See more recently, Geoff Eley, "Nations, Publics, and Political Cultures: Placing Habermas in the Nineteenth Century," in Calhoun, ed., *Habermas and the Public Sphere,* who notes the failure of Habermas to explore sufficiently the existence of competing "counter-public" spheres (e.g., working-class publics).

commercialized forms of leisure and cultural consumption.[14] T
velopments in print culture that Habermas identifies with the
sphere, such as the growth of reading and writing publics, the rise of
novels, newspapers and political journalism, or the emergence of literary
criticism, were inseparable from the commercialization of letters. Similarly, the proliferation of public spaces where people socialized or sought
entertainment – coffeehouses, pleasure gardens, public theaters, and the
like – was marked by the kind of "culture-consumption" that Habermas associates with a later era. Accordingly, I have described some of
the cultural tensions created by this process of commercialization and
viewed them not as a later excrescence but as a constitutive part of the
Enlightenment public sphere.

Habermas has also been criticized for ignoring the question of gender.
The feminist critic Joan Landes has insisted that the norms of the public sphere were intrinsically masculinist, resting on gendered distinctions
between a (male) public realm and a (female) private one.[15] She views
the French Revolution as having marked the triumph of this masculinist
discourse by enshrining in law a distinction between the public-political
world as a natural male preserve and a private domestic sphere where
women fulfilled their natural roles as wives and mothers. Revolutionary
legislation did in fact withhold voting rights from women, and in the
Terror political organizations like the Society of Revolutionary Republican Women were indeed suppressed. Hence Landes concludes that
the public sphere, far from emancipating women, perpetuated a pub-
lic/private dichotomy that sanctioned their political subordination.

[14] On the eighteenth century as a consumer revolution, see John Brewer, Neil McKendrick,
and J. H. Plumb, eds., *The Birth of a Consumer Society: The Commercialization of Eighteenth-
Century England* (London, 1982); Colin Campbell, *The Romantic Ethic and the Spirit of
Modern Consumerism* (Oxford, 1987), 17–35; Daniel Roche, *The History of Everyday
Things: The Birth of Consumption in France, 1600–1800,* trans. Brian Pearce (Cambridge,
2000), 54–80, 221–49. On the public sphere as a site for the development of a consumer
culture, see Colin Jones, "The Great Chain of Buying: Medical Advertisement, the
Bourgeois Public Sphere and the Origins of the French Revolution," *American Historical
Review* 101 (1996).

[15] Landes, *Women and the Public Sphere in the Age of the French Revolution*; Landes, "The Public and the Private Sphere," in Johanna Meehan, ed., *Feminists Read Habermas: Gendering
the Subject of Discourse* (New York and London, 1995), 91–116; Landes, "Introduction,"
in *Feminism, the Public and the Private* (Oxford and New York, 1998). For other works
emphasizing the gendered nature of the public sphere, see, for example, Nancy Fraser,
"What's Critical about Critical Theory? The Case of Habermas and Gender," in Seyla
Benhabib and Drucilla Cornell, eds., *Feminism As Critique: On the Politics of Gender* (Minneapolis, 1987), and, "Rethinking the Public Sphere: A Contribution to the Critique of
Actually Existing Democracy," in Calhoun, ed., *Habermas and the Public Sphere*; and
Isabel V. Hull, *Sexuality, State, and Civil Society in Germany, 1700–1815* (Ithaca, 1996),
206–7.

Landes's critique was strongly argued and helped stimulate debate on the place of women in the eighteenth-century public sphere. But her view of the public sphere as necessarily masculinist has not, on the whole, won widespread assent. For one thing, such an argument tends to undermine its own premises: in claiming that Habermas's public sphere was by its very nature exclusionary, it implicitly invokes the standards of inclusiveness and universality that the ideology of the public sphere proclaimed.[16] Others have observed that Landes not only ignores Enlightenment writers like the French philosopher Condorcet, whose universalistic conception of humanity envisioned a society in which women would exercise the same political rights as men; her critique also rests on a fundamental misreading of Habermas.[17] The public sphere was not the sphere of political power, as Landes seems to assume, but a private social realm. Women did not of course gain political rights in eighteenth-century Europe – nor, for that matter, did most men. But as a sphere of sociability and discussion distinct from the realm of state power, the public sphere was characterized by a high degree of female participation. As readers and authors, as a conspicuous and sometimes dominant presence in theater audiences, salons, and debating societies, women had a role and visibility without which many practices and institutions of the public sphere would have been inconceivable. Legitimizing their participation were Enlightenment notions of sociability that considered the mingling of the sexes crucial to the progress of civil society. "It is not therefore arts, sciences, and learning, but the company of the other sex, that forms the manners and renders the man agreeable," wrote the Scottish physician William Alexander in affirming the historical role of women as a civilizing agent. Theodor Gottlieb von Hippel's *On Improving the Status of Women* (1792), a work that condemned the French Revolution for failing to grant political rights to women, asked rhetorically: "Where are those private social groups that can exist for any period of time without the company of women?"[18] In this

---

[16] Habermas makes this point in the preface to the 1990 German edition of his book, in response to Carole Pateman's feminist critique of contractual social and political theories in *The Sexual Contract* (Stanford, 1988).

[17] On this point see Goodman, "Public Sphere and Private Life," 14–20. See also Keith Baker, "Defining the Public Sphere in Eighteenth-Century France: Variations on a Theme by Habermas," in Calhoun, ed., *Habermas and the Public* Sphere, 202–3; Daniel Gordon, "Philosophy, Sociology, and Gender in the Enlightenment Conception of Public Opinion," *French Historical Studies* 17 (1992), 899–900; Lawrence E. Klein, "Gender and the Public/Private Distinction in the Eighteenth Century," *Eighteenth Century Studies* 29 (1995), 97–109.

[18] William Alexander, *The History of Women from the Earliest Antiquity, to the Present Time*, 3rd ed. (London, 1782), I:iv–v, as quoted in Sylvana Tomaselli, "The Enlightenment Debate on Women," *History Workshop Journal* 20 (1985), 121; Theodor Gottlieb von Hippel, *On Improving the Status of Women*, translated and edited with an introduction by Timothy F. Sellner (Detroit, 1979), 170.

book I have tried to do justice to women's participation in the Enlightened public sphere, while also recognizing that the norms sanctioning this participation were often ambiguous. The belief that civil society depended on women as a moral and civilizing force rested on notions of sexual difference that could justify banishing them from the political arena. But in sanctioning women's activities as readers, writers, and sociable beings, it also gave them tools and venues for challenging that exclusion. Moreover, the domestic sphere to which propertied women of the eighteenth century were supposedly consigned was much more porous and public than the modern-day stereotype of "bourgeois domesticity" would have us believe. Their households were places where women read, wrote, entertained friends and relatives, and discussed politics, religion, and literary works in salons or at dinner parties. These households were, in short, part of social and communicative networks that did not sever but connected the public and the private realms.[19]

The legacy of the public sphere, then, was ambiguous. It was neither inexorably emancipatory nor inherently repressive, and if it was not irredeemably masculinist, neither was it unqualifiedly feminist. The ambiguities of the eighteenth-century public sphere are still with us, which explains why Habermas's *Structural Transformation of the Public Sphere* continues to engage scholars in fields ranging from history, literary criticism, and music to sociology, feminist theory, and political science. In our day, the computer and the internet have wrought a revolution in communications riven with the same contradiction that marked the Enlightened public sphere – expanded networks of information on the one hand, but also a growing gap between those who enjoy access to it and those who do not. And overall, the boundaries between the public and the private seem today even more unstable and elusive than they did when Habermas published his book almost forty years ago. The problem of just where to locate those boundaries pervades our political discourse, be it in the jeremiads of cultural critics who bemoan our notorious preoccupation with the private lives of public figures, debates over the legality of abortion or the public financing of election campaigns, postmodernist manifestoes that criticize the very idea of "the public" as a strategy for marginalizing minorities, or in the fears spawned by a global capitalism that seems ever more immune to public control and accountability. For these reasons, what the philosopher John Dewey called "the public and its problems" will continue to provoke analysis and debate.

---

[19] Amanda Vickery makes this valuable point in her "Golden Age to Separate Spheres? A Review of the Categories and Chronology of English Women's History," *Historical Journal* 36 (1993), and in her recent study, *The Gentleman's Daughter: Women's Lives in Georgian England* (New Haven and London, 1998), 9.

Part I

Politics and the rise of "public opinion":
the cases of England and France

1 The peculiarities of the English

Foundations of English exceptionalism

"For a long time, and especially since the beginning of this century, there has been no country where more has been written about political affairs than England."[1] August Ludwig Schlözer, the German historian and journalist who made this claim in 1776, was well acquainted with English political culture. As a professor at the University of Göttingen, which was located in the territory of Hanover and founded by George II, Schlözer was himself a subject of the German dynasty that had ruled Britain since 1714. A convinced Anglophile and an ardent admirer of British political institutions, Schlözer considered the rebellious American colonists selfish ingrates.

But if Schlözer was anything but an impartial observer, he was right to consider English political culture unique in fundamental ways. Its relatively free press, party structure, and parliamentary system fostered a degree of political contestation – outside as well as within formal institutions of government – that had no counterpart among the major states of the continent. The vibrancy of England's political public sphere grew out of the turbulent struggles of the English Revolution, a period when censorship all but collapsed, political pamphlets flooded the publishing market, popular petitions and the circulation of parliamentary speeches proliferated, and coffeehouses arose as venues of political discussion. Despite the restoration of the Stuart dynasty in 1660, the Exclusion Crisis of 1679–81 (so named after efforts in parliament to exclude Charles II's heir, the Catholic James II, from the succession) was marked by a resurgence of political activism at all levels. Mark Knights has estimated that the crisis generated between 5 and 10 million printed pamphlets within a three-year period, a time also when thousands of English subjects signed petitions and counter-petitions (or "addresses") supporting or opposing

[1] *Briefwechsel meist historischen und politischen Inhalts*, 1 (1776), 373.

James II's exclusion.[2] The crisis would occasion the birth of England's party system, as well as fundamental debates over which institutions or groups truly represented the will of the nation.

England's incipient public sphere was institutionalized in the decade that followed the Glorious Revolution of 1688–89, which deposed James II and brought William and Mary to the throne. Critical to this process of institutionalization was parliament's failure in 1695 to renew the Licensing Act of 1662, which had provided the basis for the crown's censorship powers and regulation of the book trade. Under the Licensing Act censorship had been exercised by various authorities, including the two secretaries of state (historical and political works), the lord chancellor (law), the earl marshall (heraldry), the archbishop of Canterbury and the bishop of London (theology), and the chancellors of Oxford and Cambridge (philosophy and medicine). In addition to requiring governmental inspection of every cargo of books, pamphlets, and newspapers from abroad, the Licensing Act had limited the number of printing houses to twenty. As Lois Schwoerer and Paul Monod have each shown, the lapse of the Licensing Act in 1695 was not the result of any principled commitment to freedom of the press on the part of parliament. It stemmed rather from the impossibility of enforcing censorship in a period that was so highly politicized, and neither Whigs nor Tories were willing to accept censorship when either was out of power. At any rate, the lapse of the Licensing Act in 1695 effectively dismantled the machinery of Stuart censorship. Equally important, it also removed all limits on the number of printers licensed to publish and sell newspapers, books, and periodicals. The result was a proliferation of publishing firms, the number of which had risen to seventy-five in London and twenty-eight in the provinces by 1724. The British press became among the freest in Europe, with a vibrant market of political journals, pamphlets, and newspapers.

Also crucial for the institutionalization of a political public sphere was the Triennial Act of 1694. While the Stuarts had preferred either not to summon parliament or to allow years to pass without calling general elections, the Triennial Act mandated that elections were to be held at least every three years. The effects were immediate and dramatic: between 1694 and 1716, when the Triennial Act was in effect, ten general elections were held (four alone between 1692 and 1702). More than two decades of incessant electioneering mobilized a substantial segment of the population that over time became accustomed to public participation

[2] Mark Knights, *Politics and Opinion in Crisis, 1678–81* (Cambridge, 1994), 168, 227–305. On popular radicalism in the English Revolution, the classic study is Christopher Hill, *The World Turned Upside Down: Radical Ideas during the English Revolution* (London, 1972), 17.

in the political affairs of the nation. In this overheated political climate, Whig and Tory leaders developed well-oiled propaganda machines enlisting newspapers and journals under their respective banners. Political clubs and party organizations gathered regularly in London's vast network of coffeehouses and taverns to plot strategy or celebrate election victories and politically fraught anniversaries (for example, the birthday of William III for Whigs, or Restoration Day for Tories). The frequency of elections kept party rivalries at a high pitch. Daniel Defoe noted that "the certainty of a new election in three years is an unhappy occasion of keeping alive the divisions and party strife among the people, which otherwise would have died of course."[3]

In this highly partisan atmosphere, the two parties developed their own distinctive ideologies and political styles. Tories came to stand for High Church Anglicanism, the monarchical principle of hereditary succession, opposition to standing armies and continental entanglements, and on the party's fringes, Jacobitism (i.e., support for the restoration of the exiled Stuart pretender). Whigs associated themselves with the Protestant succession, fierce opposition to the Jacobites, and toleration for Protestant dissenters. War, a phenomenon whose role in the expansion of a political public sphere both then and later cannot be overestimated, further intensified the political climate. The enormous fiscal demands occasioned by Britain's struggle with France during the War of the Spanish Succession (1701–14) forced the crown to summon parliament every year, making partisan debates and maneuvering an almost daily fixture of parliamentary life. Issues of war and peace were hotly contested, and although newspaper reporting on parliamentary debates remained prohibited up to 1771, both parties employed the press to publicize their positions. All of this served to draw a broader public into debates over national issues, politicizing and at the same time educating it.

It used to be fashionable to discount the modernity of eighteenth-century British politics. This agnosticism developed in reaction to traditional Whig narratives, which had viewed the eighteenth century as yet another phase in the nation's triumphant progress toward constitutional liberty and world empire. Revisionists like Sir Lewis Namier minimized those very features of eighteenth-century British politics – parties, elections, constitutional struggles – that Whig historians had deemed so glorious and unique. Namier instead highlighted the aristocratic, oligarchical features of Hanoverian politics and the dominance exercised in parliament by a relatively small number of powerful families. Pointing to the narrowness of the franchise, a supposedly apathethic electorate, and

---

[3] Quoted in J. A. Downie, *Robert Harley and the Press: Propaganda and Public Opinion in the Age of Swift and Defoe* (Cambridge, 1979), 1.

the continued influence of the crown in parliament, Namier's interpretation downplayed the significance of ideological and electoral conflict. In the 1980s, a second wave of revisionism raised more doubts about the modern and "progressive" dimensions of Hanoverian political culture. J. C. D. Clark, the most outspoken representative of this trend, portrayed eighteenth-century England as a profoundly traditional social and political order in which the crown, the Anglican church, and the aristocracy continued to hold sway up to the Reform Bill of 1832. Rejecting Whiggish notions of English exceptionalism, Clark concluded that England was not essentially different from the absolutist regimes of the continent.

It is true that in the decades following the accession of the Hanoverian dynasty (1714), British politics became in some respects less vibrant and open. The relative stability that marked the ascendancy of the Whigs under George I (1714–27) and George II (1727–60) rested to a great extent on the oligarchical control and patronage exercised by the crown and a handful of aristocratic politicians. Tainted by its association with the failed Jacobite uprising of 1715, the Tory party sank into an electoral decline that guaranteed one-party rule up to the accession of George III in 1760. Moreover, the repeal of the Triennial Act in 1716 prolonged the life of parliament from three years to seven and thereby sharply reduced the frequency of parliamentary elections. The intent, if not the effect, was to heighten the political influence of local patrons, dilute the impact of voter initiative, and weaken the effect of popular participation. The extent to which the measure discouraged electoral challenges to incumbents is attested to by a sharp decline in the number of contested seats between 1705, when 65 percent of the counties represented in parliament had contested elections, and 1765, when only 7.5 percent did.[4]

Another sign of the shrinking popular base of electoral politics after 1714 was a decline in the size of the voting franchise relative to the population as a whole. In 1715 the electorate in England and Wales may have totaled some 300,000 voters, or 23.4 percent of adult males. By the late eighteenth century this franchise had increased by 40,000, but since the corresponding population had grown at an even faster rate the proportion of adult males who could vote had declined in real terms to 17.2 percent.[5] Much of this decline reflected the lack of any systematic enfranchisement of Britain's growing urban population. Of the sixty-eight English towns having populations of 2,500 or more in 1700, seventeen were unrepresented in parliament. Rapid urbanization further heightened

[4] John Brewer, *Party Ideology and Popular Politics at the Accession of George III* (Cambridge, 1976), 6.

[5] H. T. Dickinson, *The Politics of the People in Eighteenth-Century Britain* (New York, 1995), 32.

the disparity, as the number of towns having no parliamentary representation rose to forty in 1750. Critics routinely contrasted these unrepresented urban centers with the rural, sparsely populated "rotten boroughs" that sent one or more representatives to parliament.

Finally, even though the British crown was ostensibly more limited in its powers than most of its continental counterparts, it retained considerable influence in parliament through the pensions and patronage at its disposal. The crown and its ministers could improve the prospects of a parliamentary supporter by supplying offices, commissions, and contracts that the MP could in turn distribute to politically influential supporters. During the ministry of Sir Robert Walpole (1721–42), the high water-mark of "Whig oligarchy," almost every job at court and in the civil service, armed forces, and church was controlled by the ministry. With this kind of patronage, governments could and did build formidable political machines. A conservative estimate holds that under the Walpole regime, for example, 27 percent of all MPs were ministerial clients.[6]

Longer parliaments, Tory electoral decline, a contracting electorate, underrepresented urban constituencies, the crown's ability to control parliament through patronage and preferments – these explain why scholars like Namier and Clark could look so skeptically on the pieties of Whig historiography. Their work remains a salutary warning against the dangers of transposing modern notions of representative government onto the eighteenth century. There is no question that, in the last analysis, Hanoverian Britain was governed by a narrow oligarchy of wealth and birth. In 1754, 294 out of 558 members of parliament were the sons of MPs and around 400 were relatives of other past or present members. In the early 1800s one out of four members was married to the daughter of an MP, and in 1807 more than 234 MPs representing constituencies in England, Wales, and Scotland owed their seats to some form of aristocratic patronage.[7]

Yet the fact that Hanoverian government was dominated by an oligarchy did not mean that this political elite was impervious to the opinions of those it governed. Scholars have increasingly challenged Namierite interpretations in emphasizing the continued vitality of electoral politics in Hanoverian Britain. Linda Colley showed, for example, that Tory opposition to post-1714 Whig hegemony was by no means as weak and disorganized as was once believed, while Nicolas Rogers and Frank O'Gorman have questioned the stereotype of a pliant and lethargic electorate. Rogers noted that in urban constituencies having at least 1,000 voters, seats were

[6] Linda Colley, *In Defiance of Oligarchy: The Tory Party 1714–60* (Cambridge, 1982), 232.
[7] Frank O'Gorman, *The Long Eighteenth Century: British Political and Social History 1688–1832* (London, 1997), 107; Linda Colley, *Britons: Forging the Nation 1707–1837* (New Haven and London, 1992), 154–55.

contested more often after 1714 than they had ever been.[8] Finding a similarly high number of contested elections, O'Gorman argued that the "unreformed" Hanoverian electorate was more socially inclusive than is often assumed. Analyzing the occupations of voters in six constituencies between 1768 and 1831, O'Gorman broke down the electorate into the following groups and percentages:

> Gentry and professionals 13.6 percent
> Merchants and manufacturers 5.8 percent
> Tradesmen (retailers) 20.5 percent
> Skilled artisans 39.5 percent
> Unskilled laborers 14.2 percent
> Agricultural occupations 6.4 percent

Clearly this was not an electorate based on universal male suffrage (though something approaching it could be found in some constituencies), but neither was it as narrowly based as it is sometimes portrayed.[9]

However broad or narrow the franchise, the rituals of electoral politics drew large numbers of people into its orbit. British elections may have ultimately served to sustain the power of a parliamentary elite, but their effective conduct and management depended on the loyalty and work of local clients and canvassers from much more modest social backgrounds. To the extent, moreover, that elections provided a conduit for propaganda on behalf of a candidate or party, they generated a steady flow of information and communication between political elites and those they governed. Candidates used the press extensively to advertise rallies or publish addresses to constituents. In 1768 a candidate in Essex distributed 33,700 pamphlets, broadsides, and ballads, and in the Middlesex election of that year John Wilkes circulated 40,000 handbills among a constituency of 3,500 voters.[10] Both during and between campaigns, those standing for election were expected to engage in regular, face-to-face contact with their constituents. If the common people were deferential – an assumption that E.P. Thompson did much to revise[11] – a sense of reciprocity informed their deference. They expected a candidate to be accessible, approachable, and to seek their support in person. In 1733 William Hay, an election agent for the duke of Newcastle, warned the duke that one of his parliamentary clients might lose the upcoming election owing to his

---

[8] Nicolas Rogers, *Whigs and Cities: Popular Politics in the Age of Walpole and Pitt* (Oxford, 1989), 390–91.

[9] Rogers, *Whigs and Cities*, 390–91; Frank O'Gorman, *Voters, Patrons, and Parties: The Unreformed Electoral System of Hanoverian England 1734–1832* (Oxford, 1989), 199–233.

[10] Dickinson, *Politics of the People*, 45.

[11] See, for example, his classic *Making of the English Working Class* (London, 1963), and *Whigs and Hunters: The Origin of the Black Act* (New York, 1975).

failure to cultivate his constituents in person: "He has not been around the Town since he went with your Grace, nor I believe asked a single man for his vote: and I am firmly persuaded that half the voters that have been lost have been lost by this unpardonable negligence: the people are affronted by it." In 1784 an election agent for Sir William Milner, who was campaigning for a seat from York, privately criticized the candidate for his unapproachability: "He has, I fear, too cold and ungracious a manner to make great or lasting conquests over the affections of a populace, that must be at least treated as equals – and *pro hac vice* [for that matter] as superiors. The hearty shake, and the familiar bit of conversation must be attended to."[12]

As highly visible and often prolonged affairs, electoral rituals subjected candidates to sustained public scrutiny. By bringing constituents together in various informal venues, they also fostered discussion and the exchange of political gossip and information. "Treating," the common practice whereby candidates feted voters with alcohol, food, and even accommodation at local inns and taverns, was a perquisite of electoral participation and an important arena of sociability during and between campaigns. On the days leading up to an election, voters – usually at a candidate's expense – drank, supped, or breakfasted together. On polling days they often marched to the hustings in procession, and after the votes had been tallied they attended celebration dinners hosted by the candidate. After Charles James Fox's successful campaign for his Westminster seat in 1784, his managers staged five celebration dinners each attended by 700–1000 supporters.[13] These were all occasions for discussing the merits and flaws of a candidate or his opponent, and for debating issues of local or national importance.

Hence focussing too narrowly on rotten boroughs or restrictive franchises misses the significance of Hanoverian elections. They generated a regular and sustained flow of political information between rulers and ruled, as well as periodic, face-to-face contact. All of this gave Hanoverian politics a measure of public exposure and transparency that simply did not exist in the absolutist states of France, Germany, or Austria. A more prosaic feature of Hanoverian political culture, namely the rise of organized lobbies, also stimulated the circulation of information throughout the public sphere. While some in the eighteenth century, like today, tended to see lobbies as a source of corruption and secret influence, organized interest groups were as much a part of Britain's expanding public sphere as its newspapers, journals, and coffeehouses. Commercial and manufacturing lobbies proliferated in eighteenth-century Britain, partly

---

[12] Above quotes taken from Dickinson, *Politics of the People*, 30–31.
[13] *Ibid.*, 47.

as the product of a burgeoning capitalist economy, partly as a response to the government's increased reliance on excise taxes to finance its military needs. Government attempts to impose uniform duties on commodities ranging from beer and spirits to candles and carriages led manufacturers of the affected commodities to join together to push for the repeal or lowering of the excise. During the course of the century trade organizations were formed that levied dues on their members to defray the expenses of lobbyists who then pressed their case before parliamentary committees. Regional manufacturing associations such as the Midland Association of Ironmasters and the West Riding Committee of Worsted Manufacturers became powerful lobbying interests. The expansion of Britain's overseas empire spawned commercial lobbies as well, such as the Virginia Merchants and the Society of West Indian Merchants.

By the end of the century, parliamentary lobbying had become standard among commercial and manufacturing interests, which broadened the public sphere in several respects. For one, lobbies were an important source of the statistical data and reports that made their way into the public domain via petitions to parliament and the press. Government officials, especially those concerned with colonial affairs, found lobbies to be a useful source of statistics and specialized information on matters of trade and commerce. Conversely, lobbyists played a key role in opening up the political domain to public scrutiny by pressuring the government to release official documents relevant to their particular trade or business. Hence, while lobbies undoubtably increased the influence of vested interests in government, they also served to make government more transparent by generating and obtaining statistical data and reports. Lobbyists, like those who agitated for parliamentary reform later in the century, became adept at employing newspapers and pamphlets to influence opinion inside and outside parliament. The Excise Crisis of 1733, which was provoked by the Walpole ministry's attempt to introduce taxes on wine and tobacco, was a harbinger of how potent the combination of lobbies and the press would become. Here representatives of the affected trades published their protests in pamphlets, handbills, and printed sheets of statistics, all designed to influence opinion both inside and outside parliament. By the second half of the eighteenth century, trade and manufacturing groups were regularly relying on local and national newspapers to push for the passage of new bills or the repeal of old ones. In the process, the growth of lobbies broadened the stage of extraparliamentary political action and debate by transforming local interests into national ones. When, say, a General Chamber of Manufacturers was formed in 1785 to influence the fiscal policies of the Pitt ministry, the political consciousness of local manufacturers was expanded as they became integrated into a broader community of interest.

Politics and the press

The aristocratic elite that dominated parliament during the era of Whig ascendancy (1714–60) was not a monolith. It was divided by intense personal rivalries and ideological fissures, many of them predating the Hanoverian accession, which provided a wedge through which dissident political voices could mobilize an extraparliamentary public in moments of crisis.

During the 1720s and 1730s, the emergence of a "Country" or "Patriot" opposition to the Walpole ministry was the chief manifestation of these divisions. Articulated by dissident radical Whigs in league with a Tory party now effectively consigned to the political backbenches, this opposition criticized the domination of parliament by the court and its ministers. Several opposition demands, such as shorter parliaments, the replacement of the standing army with a citizen militia, the curtailment of crown patronage, and the elimination of rotten boroughs, became fixtures of later eighteenth-century political radicalism. In other respects the Country opposition looked more to the past than to the future. Much of its Tory support, for example, lay in a declining petty squirearchy, whose economic position had been undermined by taxes on land levied to fight France during the War of the Spanish Succession (1701–14). But if disaffected segments of the landed gentry constituted the hard core of the Tories' political base, the party's exclusion from court and high office also made it the natural ally of an urban constituency that felt politically excluded and underrepresented. With no patronage at their disposal and little chance of toppling Walpole's Whig machine through electoral means, Tory leaders like Lord Bolingbroke appealed "out-of-doors" – i.e., beyond parliament – to disaffected urban groups who saw the Walpole regime as dominated by a corrupt clique of stock-jobbers and financiers. Implicit in this strategy was the conviction that parliament had grown too corrupt, too vulnerable to manipulation by agents of the crown, to serve as the voice of the nation; one had to appeal beyond formal institutions of power to an extraparliamentary public capable of forcing reform upon a recalcitrant government.

Here Bolingbroke and his Country allies employed the tools of political journalism to mobilize an extraparliamentary opposition. One of their weapons was *The Craftsman* (1726–46), the most famous and best-selling opposition paper of the Walpole era. Subjecting Walpole and his government to an endless stream of invective, *The Craftsman* enjoyed at the height of its popularity a print run of some 10,000–12,000 copies per issue. It lashed out at the land tax, stock speculators, the standing army, long parliaments, and the corrupt consequences of "Robinocracy" – the term it applied to Sir Robert Walpole's ministry. The paper above all denounced the insidiousness of ministerial secrecy and demanded greater publicity and openness in government. *The Craftsman* took its title from its avowed aim of exposing the "craftiness" that permeated the politics of the day: "It shall therefore be my chief business," wrote Bolingbroke in the inaugural issue, "to unravel the dark secrets of *Political Craft*, and trace it through all of its various Windings and intricate Recesses."[14] This language of exposure and publicity fills the pages of *The Craftsman*: "We have trac'd *Corruption* through all its dark lurking Holes, and set its Deformity in a true Light. We have pleaded the cause of *publick Virtue*, against the Misrepresentation of Those, who have endeavor'd to bring it into Contempt."[15] The rhetoric and tactics of the Country opposition did much to broaden the sphere of political debate beyond the world of the court and parliament. During the Excise Crisis of 1733, papers like *The Craftsman* showed how the power of the press could be put to effective political use by helping to mobilize extraparliamentary agitation against Walpole's scheme to tax wine and tobacco. The opposition also refined other extraparliamentary tactics during this period, such as petition campaigns and the formation of electoral clubs and societies that instructed their MPs how to vote on a particular issue. These techniques would later become a staple of British radical politics, and it is no accident that the term "publick opinion" – hitherto rare in English usage – began to gain currency during the 1730s.

Still, Bolingbroke and the Country opposition of the 1720s and 1730s never succeeded in sustaining mass support for a comprehensive program of political reform. One obstacle was the inherent conservatism of the Tory party, whose bedrock Anglicanism and hostility to religious non-conformity cut off the party from a potential source of political dissidence. Moreover, the oppositional tactics crafted by Bolingbroke and his allies functioned as instruments of factions within the political elite, even if these tools would later be adapted more broadly by popular radicals like John Wilkes. They were designed to arouse or manipulate opinion from above, not express it from below. What emerged during the latter half of the eighteenth century was an extraparliamentary sphere of political action that was increasingly national in its focus, more autonomous *vis-à-vis* political elites, and organized from below. The continued growth of political journalism encouraged these developments. During the decades that followed parliament's decision in 1695 not to renew the Licensing Act, London became renowned for the number, variety, and circulation of its newspapers. Its first daily paper, the *Daily Courant*, began publication

---

[14] *The Craftsman*, 1 (1726), 6.
[15] *Ibid.*, dedication.

Table 1 *London newspapers, 1746–1790*

	1746	1770	1783	1790
Dailies	6	5	9	14
Bi-, Tri-weeklies	6	10	7	
Weeklies	6	4	–	2
Total	18	19	–	16

Source: Bob Harris, *Politics and the Rise of the Press: Britain and France, 1620–1800* (London and New York, 1996), 10.

in 1702, although the most widely circulated London paper of the period was the tri-weekly *Post-Man* with an average circulation in August 1712 of 3,812 copies. By the late 1720s, weeklies like the *London Journal* and the *Craftsman* were selling about 10,000 copies per issue. In 1746 the city had eighteen newspapers, including six dailies, six tri-weeklies, and six weeklies. Table 1 above gives a quantitative profile of London newspapers during subsequent years of the century. Provincial newspapers also grew in number. Norwich was the first provincial town to have its own newspaper (1701), followed by Bristol (1702), Exeter (1704), Shrewsbury (1705), Yarmouth (1708), and Worcester (1709). In 1735 some twenty-five provincial newspapers were being published in England, and by 1782 the number had doubled.

As British political journalism expanded, so did the number of those for whom the reading of news became a habit. This rise in readership is evident from figures based on the stamp duty levied on newspapers beginning from 1713 to 1801:[16]

1713	2.5 m
1750	7.3 m
1760	9.4 m
1775	12.6 m
1801	16 m

Although it is not possible statistically to determine with any precision the social status of newspaper buyers, the bulk of this expanding readership most likely came from the middling and upper ranks of society. The price of newspapers, which rose from an average of 2d in 1725 to 6d in 1797, would have made them unaffordable to those below the level of skilled artisans. Not that one necessarily had to buy newspapers in order

[16] Bob Harris, *Politics and the Rise of the Press: Britain and France, 1620–1800* (London and New York, 1996), 12.

to read them: they were readily available, for example, in the London coffeehouses that had become so abundant by 1700. But it was not simply cost but also demand that made newspaper reading primarily a middle- and upper-class pastime. The financial and commercial revolutions of the early eighteenth century, and above all Britain's development as a colonial power, made newspapers and commercial sheets an indispensable source of information for investors whose economic interests were directly affected by the vicissitudes of war and colonial trade.

Wars in particular fueled a demand for information. To a considerable extent, the precocious development of a political public sphere in Britain was the handmaiden of colonialism and the wars it engendered. More than any other kind of event, war aroused public opinion and stimulated the growth of political journalism. A London pamphlet published in 1760 noted the "inundation of political pamphlets, which flows with such a rapid course from the press, whenever we are engaged in a war."[17] The economic stakes of war were high for Britain, with its far-flung empire and a volume of overseas trade that grew in annual value from £10.4 million in 1700–09 to £28.6 million in 1765–74.[18] Intensifying the impact of war was the broad segment of society that invested in Britain's colonial project. In Bristol during the first three-quarters of the century, for example, investors in overseas trade included grocers, bakers, apothecaries, tobacconists, and widows. Because colonial issues were paramount in every war fought by Britain during the eighteenth century, the conduct and outcome of these conflicts directly affected the material interests of large numbers of British subjects.

Not surprisingly, military success became an important index of a government's legitimacy and efficacy. The economic stakes of war fueled patriotic sentiment, and the fact that Britain's chief military and imperial rival was Catholic France also brought deep-seated Protestant sympathies into play. Leopold von Ranke's nineteenth-century insistence on "the primacy of foreign policy" is no longer in fashion among historians, but one could in fact argue that military and diplomatic events triggered almost every domestic crisis and political *cause célèbre* in eighteenth-century Britain. In 1742 it was not the machinations of the Country opposition that brought down the Walpole government but popular outrage, inflamed by the press, over the Walpole's ministry's perceived failure to prosecute war against Spain with sufficient vigor. Britain's participation in the War of the Austrian Succession (1740–48), which aroused suspicions

---

[17] Israel Maudit, *Considerations on the Present State of Affairs in Germany* (London, 1760), as quoted in Manfred Schlenke, *England und das friderizianische Preussen 1740–1763: Ein Beitrag zum Verhältnis von Politik und öffentlicher Meinung in England des 18. Jahrhunderts* (Freiburg and Munich, 1963), 55.

[18] O'Gorman, *The Long Eighteenth Century*, 177.

that the crown was sacrificing British interests to its own Hanoverian ones, sparked another vociferous press campaign, and the subsequent popularity of William Pitt the Elder rested largely on Britain's military successes during the Seven Years' War (1756–63). Issues of war and peace were also the occasion for John Wilkes's rise to national political prominence in 1763. His notorious attack on George III in the 45th issue of the *North Briton* followed the government's ratification of the Treaty of Paris, which Wilkes denounced as a betrayal of British interests. Later on, the disastrous and divisive American War of Independence provided an important impetus to the campaign for parliamentary reform launched by Christopher Wyvill's Association movement.

Hence Britain's engagement in almost constant warfare between 1739 and 1782 meant that the press, for most British subjects the chief source of information on military and diplomatic affairs, assumed an ever-larger role in political life. A London pamphlet from 1761 claimed that "the political principles of most Englishmen are entirely under the influence of pamphlets and newspapers."[19] By the 1760s, an increasingly aggressive press had provoked fears among some observers that its independent role threatened the delicate balance between monarchy, aristocracy, and democracy on which the British constitution was putatively based. These critics feared that the press, as a self-appointed "fourth estate," was usurping the traditional role of the House of Commons as the appropriate arena for canvassing and articulating the opinions of the nation. In his *Political Considerations on the Present Crisis* (London, 1762), J. Marriott observed:

Every act... other than by way of petition to parliament, and through the constitutional channel up to the throne, does greatly tend to distress government in critical times. In such times it is very dangerous to create and introduce a fourth estate, as it were, of a democratical kind into the constitution, and which is therefore more liable in its nature to be played off as an engine against government by the arts of any able set of men who have a private interest in inflaming others not quite so wise as themselves.[20]

Such fears were rooted in an older constitutional discourse that viewed the political stage as a relatively narrow arena circumscribed by the institutions of crown, Lords, and Commons. These concerns reflected the

---

[19] *A Letter from a British Officer Now in Germany* (London, 1761), as quoted in Schlenke, *England und das friderizianische Preussen*, 74–75.

[20] Quoted in Eckhart Hellmuth, "The Palladium of All Other English Liberties: Reflections on the Liberty of the Press in England during the 1760s and 1770s," in Hellmuth, ed., *The Transformation of Political Culture: England and Germany in the Late Eighteenth Century* (Oxford, 1991), 486. On criticisms of the press as a fourth estate see J. A. W. Gunn, *Beyond Liberty and Property: The Process of Self-Recognition in Eighteenth-Century Political Thought* (Kingston and Montreal, 1983), 273.

belief, widely shared by most Whigs and Tories up to the early 1770s, that journalistic reporting of all substantive proceedings and debates in parliament should be prohibited. Accordingly, up until 1771 it was deemed a violation of parliamentary privilege for newspapers to publish debates and speeches beyond the king's address to Lords and Commons at the opening of a session. Printers who violated this provision were fined or even jailed.

Neither the crown nor members of parliament were defenseless in the face of a hostile press. Although the lapse of the Licensing Act had effectively eliminated prepublication censorship, limits on press freedom continued to exist. In 1707 fears of Jacobite conspiracy had led parliament to approve a statute making it high treason to attack the principle that only a Protestant could succeed to the throne. The statute was enforced in 1719, when the Jacobite John Mathews was hung for publishing a pamphlet calling for the restoration of the Stuarts. The Stamp Tax of 1712, the prototype for the infamous American Stamp Act of 1763, was also designed to winnow out anti-government pamphlets and newspapers. The 1712 tax and its successors were not especially effective. Printers were often able to evade the measure by publishing in formats different from those specified by a stamp tax. Where the tax was successfully imposed, however, it did render smaller papers financially more vulnerable and hence more susceptible to governmental bribes and subsidies.

A more significant curb on the press were Britain's libel laws, which broadly applied not only to slanderous works but to any publication deemed injurious to the public peace. Under this definition any attack on parliament, the king, or his ministers could be construed as seditious and subject to libel litigation. A large number of prosecutions for seditious libel occurred during George I's reign and were directed mostly at Jacobite tracts. Walpole's administration successfully prosecuted numerous cases of libel against publishers of papers like *The Craftsman*, and under George III seventy prosecutions for seditious libel were carried out between 1760 and 1790.[21] Even when unsuccessful, libel prosecutions could take a financial toll on those targeted. Larger opposition papers with solid financial backing were able to absorb the costs of government harassment, but smaller papers were more vulnerable and the threat of libel proceedings doubtless created self-imposed limits on press criticism.

Government prosecution or harassment of course ran the risk of adding to the notoriety of a paper and thereby increasing sales. A critic of *The Craftsman* claimed that its editors deliberately "write something every now and then for which they hope [to be prosecuted], otherwise the

---

[21] Arthur Aspinall, *Politics and the Press in England* (London, 1949), 41.

Paper is supposed to have lost its Poignancy."[22] Government crackdowns on hostile journalists could also backfire politically, as shown by the ham-fisted attempts of the Grenville ministry to muzzle John Wilkes in 1763. For these reasons, the crown and its ministers usually found it more effective to employ the same journalistic weapons as their critics. Instead of seeking to stifle press criticism through arrests and harassment, governments preferred to subsidize the publication of newspapers and pamphlets that presented government policies in a favorable light. Sir Robert Harley, secretary of state and chancellor of the exchequer during Queen Anne's reign (1702–14), had pioneered the use of the press as a government tool. In 1704 Harley began subsidizing Defoe's *Review* as a mouthpiece for his ministry, and his journalistic payroll came to include Jonathan Swift, Richard Steele, and an array of lesser writers. Walpole spent an average of between £5,000 and £10,000 annually on press subsidies, prompting *The Craftsman* to complain disingenuously that "we have seen some great Men stoop so low, as to colloque with common *News-Writers* and *Journalists*, in order to obstruct all avenues to Truth, and induce them, by Bribes, to serve their corrupt Purposes with fictitious Intelligence and false *Representations*."[23] The Westminster election of 1749, when the court party financed the circulation of 227,500 electoral letters and broadsheets in support of its candidate, illustrates the extent to which the government sought to exploit the political potential of print. Lord Bute, one of Wilkes's favorite ministerial whipping boys, counteracted the journalistic gibes of his critics by financing the publication of two newspapers and hiring a network of coffeehouse spies to sound out public opinion. Similarly, during the War of American Independence, the North ministry employed the pens of writers such as Samuel Johnson to parry the attacks of anti-war pamphleteers and journalists.

Radicalism and extraparliamentary politics after 1760

The 1760s were a watershed in the emergence of extraparliamentary opinion and activity as an autonomous force in British politics. This new departure was partly the culmination of more than two decades of warfare, which by spurring the growth of the press and stimulating public interest in national affairs had enlarged the extraparliamentary political arena. It was also the product of the shifting party alignments that followed the accession of George III in 1760. In line with his desire to

---

[22] *Liberty and the Craftsman: A Project for Improving the Country Journal* (London, 1730), 4, as cited in Michael Harris, *London Newspapers in the Age of Walpole: A Study of the Origins of the Modern English Press* (London and Toronto, 1987), 150.

[23] *The Craftsman* 2, December 9 (1726), 12.

be a "patriot king" who governed above party, George III brought Tories into his new ministry and thereby ended almost a half-century of the
party's exclusion from government. The effect was ironically to destroy
the Tories as a cohesive political force, for political rehabilitation stripped
them of their decades-old identity as the party of the Country opposition.
The Whig–Tory framework that had traditionally defined parliamentary
contestation now dissolved into a handful of shifting factions and yielded
a succession of weak and divided governments. With the Tories no longer
compelled to appeal out-of-doors as compensation for their banishment
from government, dissident political voices outside of parliament lost a
traditional sponsor within Britain's political elite and were thus thrown
back on their own resources. In the course of the decade, this extraparliamentary opposition developed its own identity as an autonomous force
demanding radical constitutional reforms.

It consisted largely of disaffected elements within the middle and lower-
middle classes of London and other urban centers. The high levels of taxation occasioned by the Seven Years War and later by the war in North
America highlighted the discrepancy between the financial contributions
of these urban groups on the one hand, and their inadequate representation in parliament on the other. These small tradesmen, merchants,
professionals, and manufacturers had come to believe that because they
bore a disproportionate share of the fiscal burdens of war, government
should be more responsive to their interests and opinions. Nurturing their
growing sense of social and political autonomy was the dense network of
clubs, masonic lodges, patriotic societies, trade associations, and other
mutual-aid organizations that had proliferated in urban England during
the previous two decades. Unlike the political clubs of the Restoration and
early eighteenth century, which had been linked closely to the two major
parties and mostly run by aristocratic politicians, these associations developed independently of party leadership and initiative. Beyond providing
conviviality and an outlet for charitable activities, they supplied moral
and economic support to members faced with sudden illness, unemploy-
ment, or debt. As such, they provided a social and economic cushion
to a middle and lower-middle class ever more dependent on credit and
vulnerable to the vicissitudes of Britain's expanding but volatile market
economy.[24]

The Wilkes affair was the *cause célèbre* that galvanized this extraparliamentary public and politicized its associational networks. The son of a

---

[24] See John Brewer, "Commercialization and Politics," in Neil McKendrick, John Brewer,
and J. H. Plumb, eds., *The Birth of a Consumer Society: The Commercialization of Eighteenth-
Century England* (Bloomington, 1982), 217–20.

distiller, John Wilkes was a rakish figure whose political career had been rather undistinguished prior to 1762. Elected as a Whig MP in 1757 and initially a client of the Newcastle–Pitt ministry, Wilkes began his career as a political radical in 1762 after launching his own political newspaper, *The North Briton*. By this time he had joined the opposition to the ministry of George III's favorite, Lord Bute. Wilkes supported Pitt's call for a continuation of the Seven Years War and condemned the government's peace negotiations as a sell-out of British economic and political interests. Wilkes's attacks, which included scandalous innuendoes regarding Lord Bute's relations with the king's mother, culminated in the famous 45th issue of the *North Briton* that condemned the Treaty of Paris and appeared to impugn the king's honesty. Outraged by this personal attack on the crown, the new Grenville ministry responded by arresting Wilkes and forty-eight others (mostly printers and booksellers) it held responsible for the publication. Although the court responsible for adjudicating the case soon released Wilkes on the grounds that his arrest had violated his parliamentary privileges, Wilkes now took the offensive and condemned the government's actions as those of a corrupt and arbitrary regime intent on undermining press liberties and violating the rights of British subjects. The House of Commons retaliated by voting that No. 45 constituted seditious libel, and Wilkes evaded arrest only by fleeing to Paris. By late 1763, when the galleries at London's Drury Lane Theater greeted an appearance by George III with cries of "Wilkes and Liberty" and an angry London crowd prevented the common hangman from carrying out a parliamentary decree ordering the public burning of *North Briton* 45, Wilkes had clearly become a popular hero.

Pro-Wilkite sentiment waned during his exile, but it revived in 1768 when Wilkes returned to England to seek a seat in the general election of that year. Despite his victory he was imprisoned for his previous libel conviction, and when he resumed his attacks on the government following his release he was expelled from parliament. When a new election was held for his Middlesex seat and he won again, he was once more expelled and replaced by his defeated rival. These parliamentary reprisals only enhanced his popularity among the small merchants, manufacturers, retailers, and tradesmen for whom Wilkes had become a symbol of their own political exclusion. These groups rallied to his cause, mobilizing their clubs and societies on his behalf and creating new ones to raise money for him. Wilkite clubs staged street demonstrations to protest his arrest, tavern celebrations marked his birthday and election victories, and letter-writing campaigns in the press were organized in support of his cause. Wilkes's supporters also employed novel marketing techniques that anticipated the modern, commercialized political campaign. In visible displays of solidarity, they purchased Wilkite paraphernalia ranging from punch bowls and engravings to badges, pipes, and mugs. Wilkes's phenomenal popularity ultimately catapulted him to the office of lord mayor of London in 1774 and to a seat in the Commons later that year. Throughout the 1770s he remained a spokesman for parliamentary reform and freedom of the press, although by the end of the decade leadership of the cause had passed to Christopher Wyvill and other radical activists.

Scholars now tend to emphasize the continuities between the Wilkite phenomenon and earlier opposition movements and themes. Kathleen Wilson, for example, has described how the popular adulation inspired by Admiral Edward Vernon's naval victory over the Spanish in 1740 foreshadowed the Wilkes cult. As a critic of Walpole's foreign policy, Vernon had become a rallying point for popular opposition to the regime and its alleged incompetence in protecting British colonial interests. For years afterward, Vernon's profile – like that of Wilkes after 1763 – adorned innumerable tavern signs throughout England, and Mt. Vernon, George Washington's Virginia home built by his half-brother in 1743, was named in the vice-admiral's honor. There were other continuities. The themes of popular sovereignty and resistance to tyranny invoked by Wilkite radicals can be traced back to radical Whig discourse of the late seventeenth century, and Wilkite demands for shorter parliaments and the curtailment of crown patronage had been common fare of the Country opposition to Walpole. One hears echoes of Bolingbroke's *Craftsman* in Wilkes's language of exposure and publicity, and both hailed the illuminative glare of the press as a necessary antidote to government secrecy. As Wilkes wrote in the first issue of his *North Briton* (1762),

The liberty of the press is the birth-right of a Briton, and is justly esteemed the firmest bulwark of the liberties of this country. It has been the terror of all bad ministers for their dark and dangerous designs, or their weakness, inability, and duplicity, have thus been detected and shewn to the public, generally in too strong and just colors for them to bear up against the odium of mankind ... A wicked and corrupt administration must naturally dread this appeal to the world, and will be for keeping all the means of information equally from the prince, parliament, and people.

Here Wilkes and his followers in fact went beyond earlier appeals for greater transparency in government by insisting on the right of newspapers and periodicals to provide detailed accounts of parliamentary debates. In 1768, amid the intensified public interest aroused by Wilkes's return to England and his parliamentary campaign, pro-Wilkes newspapers repeatedly defied the ban on parliamentary reporting. Their efforts were successful, and after 1771 parliament made no further attempts to prosecute newspapers violating the prohibition.

Indeed, despite continuities with earlier discourses of opposition and protest, the Wilkite movement marked a radical departure in the role it assigned to public opinion. Unlike the older Country opposition, which was chiefly concerned with making parliament more independent from the crown, Wilkes and his radical successors were more interested in making parliament more dependent on the opinions of those who elected it. Wilkes's impassioned appeals to public opinion were a tactical necessity: as a parliamentary pariah who could expect aid from neither king nor Commons, public opinion was his last refuge. But in the 1770s, even after Wilkes's personal crusade had prevailed, radicals developed a more coherent constitutional program designed to forge formal and direct lines of influence between parliament and public opinion. The appeal to public opinion, and the search for a means of guaranteeing its political influence, were to be a defining feature of British radicalism in the later eighteenth century.

As had been true of the Wilkite movement, many of the substantive features of this campaign were not new. Eliminating rotten boroughs and increasing the number of parliamentary seats for the more populous counties reiterated long-standing proposals for reform. Though controversial, radical demands for annual elections as a means of making Commons more responsive to the will of the electorate were also an extension of older Country demands for a return to triennial parliaments. Even calls by James Burgh and other radicals for a sweeping extension of the voting franchise had precedents in early radical Whig thought. What was new was the *means* through which radicals hoped to implement these changes. Led by Christopher Wyvill, a former clergyman of gentry background, the Association movement originated in Yorkshire in 1779 and in the following year spread to metropolitan London and to counties throughout England. Fueling the movement was growing disenchantment with the government's conduct of the American war, which deepened older suspicions about court conspiracies and ministerial secrecy. Wyvill's program called for the creation of a coordinated network of county associations to petition parliament for electoral reforms. By early 1780 the movement had organized petitions from thirty-eight counties and boroughs, delegates from which met later that year in London to coordinate their activities as a body. Supporters also waged a publicity campaign in circular letters and newspapers to canvass local support for the movement, and they enjoined voters to withhold support for any parliamentary candidate who did not pledge to support political reform if elected.

Hence Wyvill's movement sought not only to mobilize public opinion, but to institutionalize it as an autonomous agent of reform. Wyvill steadfastly resisted efforts by the Rockingham opposition in parliament to coopt the movement, although Charles James Fox and his supporters did succeed in infiltrating the Westminster association as part of their successful campaign for Fox's election in 1780. London offshoots of the movement, notably John Cartwright's Society for Constitutional Information, pushed Wyvill's efforts to organize extraparliamentary opinion in even more radical directions. As envisioned by Cartwright's fellow radical John Jebb, a permanent, national association of delegates elected by universal suffrage would function as a kind of "counter-parliament" (some radicals in fact spoke of an "out-of-doors Parliament") to pressure the government into implementing electoral reform.[25] Unlike Wyvill, Jebb viewed his proposed association not merely as a petitioning body but as the rival of a corrupt parliament that had to be forced from without to reform itself.

Calls for universal suffrage frightened moderates in the movement, most of whom were relatively prosperous merchants, shopkeepers, manufacturers, and professional men who feared the consequences of enfranchising the unpropertied and uneducated. As was usually the case in the eighteenth century, those who identified themselves with the beneficent voice of public opinion were careful to distinguish themselves from the hoi polloi. In the summer of 1780 the outbreak of the most violent mob action in eighteenth-century London, the anti-Catholic Gordon riots (named after Lord George Gordon, the leader of the virulently anti-Catholic Protestant Association) deepened anxieties about the consequences of enfranchising the unpropertied. All of this served to weaken middle-class support for Wyvill's movement, and the return of peace after 1783 further diluted the disaffection that had stimulated calls for parliamentary reform. With the defeat in the Commons of Pitt the Younger's efforts in 1783 and 1785 to disenfranchise rotten boroughs, the movement seemed to have little to show for its efforts.

Yet British political culture had in fact experienced a fundamental transformation by the 1780s. Not only had the term "public opinion" become common currency in political discourse, but many in parliament had come to see themselves as beholden to it. The change was evident in politicians like Fox, who in 1770 had denied the value of consulting extraparliamentary opinion but in 1783 argued that no minister should be retained who acted independently of it.[26] Outside parliament, the remarkable proliferation of middle-class debating societies during the 1780s points to the extent to which this public had acquired political self-consciousness. By 1780, London had some thirty-five debating clubs

[25] See Gunn, *Beyond Liberty and Property*, 83.
[26] *Ibid.*, 281.

where attendance ranged from 400 to 1,200 people. Some of these societies were radical in their politics and provided a venue for debates on
constitutional reform. Others, less overtly political, debated matters of
marriage, courtship, and romantic love. Significantly, all were commercial ventures staged in rented halls and advertised in the press – testimony
to the commercialized political culture wrought by the pro-Wilkes agitation of the 1760s and 1770s. In the case of the debating societies, this
commercialization had the effect of encouraging women as well as men to
attend as paying customers. In April of 1780 the *London Courant* advertised a debate in Oratorical Hall on the questions, "Has not the conduct
of opposition been uniformly consistent with public utility these ten years
past? and, Is it true, that the people of Ireland have grounded their claims
upon the example and conduct of America?" The advertisement added:
"It is particularly hoped that Ladies will join in the debate."[27] In some
debating societies, such as "The Female Parliament," only women were
permitted to speak and questions for debate included, "What reason can
be assigned for precluding the Fair from the privileges of Civil Society, or
from a liberal participation in their discussions?" The Female Parliament
met in the Casino, a hall in Great Marlborough Street, as part of a commercial consortium entitled the "University of Rational Amusements."[28]

Ambiguities of the political public sphere

Although the short period of peace and economic recovery following the
end of the American war in 1783 temporarily dampened the movement
for constitutional reform, a resurgence of political radicalism came at the
end of the decade. The ratification of the US Constitution, the growing
strength of the abolitionist movement, popular celebrations commemorating the centenary of the Glorious Revolution, and of course, the
revolutionary drama unfolding in France, created a politicized climate
initially favorable to radical demands for reform. Although few radicals
apart from Thomas Paine proposed abolishing the monarchy outright
and creating a republic, the doctrines of universal rights being preached
across the Channel did help to unite radicals around the cause of universal
male suffrage. Associations like the London Corresponding Society and
provincial counterparts like the Sheffield Society for Constitutional Information revived the petitioning campaigns of the previous decade. Even
though the activist core of British radicalism remained largely middle

[27] Quoted in Donna T. Andrew, ed., *London Debating Societies 1776–1799* (London, 1994),
87.
[28] *Ibid.*, ix; Andrew, "Popular Culture and Public Debate: London 1780," *Historical Journal*
39 (1996), 413.

class, the poor harvests and depressed economic conditions of the 1790s helped broaden the movement's social base by attracting poorer artisans and journeymen. By 1792 the London Corresponding Society had around 5,000 members, the Sheffield Society around half that number.[29]

This radical revival proved short lived, however, and by the mid-1790s the movement was clearly on the wane. Scholars have usually attributed this decline to "Pitt's Reign of Terror," the campaign of systematic repression and harassment carried out by a government convinced that radicals were subversive agents of the French. As the French Revolution grew increasingly radical and war with France appeared ever more likely, the Pitt government responded at home by banning radical organizations and arresting or exiling their leaders.

Repression from above certainly helped stem the tide of British radicalism, but it was only part of the story. Although demands for political reform had been an important impetus behind the effervescence of extraparliamentary politics from the 1760s on, there was nothing intrinsically "progressive" about politics out-of-doors in eighteenth-century Britain. Although Habermas viewed the political public sphere of the eighteenth century as oppositional in tenor, it was in fact quite ambiguous in its manifestations. To be sure, the expansion of an extraparliamentary arena of politics was in some respects the child of reform. Yet it was also the offspring of patriotic, often xenophobic climates of opinion aroused by war and the colonial project it championed. The oppositional techniques honed by supporters of constitutional reform could also provide an extraparliamentary vehicle for religious bigotry and jingoism. A case in point was the popular anti-Semitism unleashed by the Jewish naturalization bill of 1753, when fifteen constituencies drafted petitions instructing their MPs to oppose the government's efforts to relax civil disabilities on selected Jewish subjects. Another was the anti-Catholic Gordon riots of 1780. The Protestant Association, which helped instigate the riots by enlisting thousands of members across Britain to oppose the Catholic Relief Act of 1778, was organizationally no less a creature of Britain's expanding public sphere than was Wyvill's Association movement. Or consider, finally, Wilkes himself, the consummate master of the new politics, who owed much of his support to the English xenophobia he so skillfully tapped with his violent attacks on the "foreign" (i.e., Scottish) Lord Bute.

The political public sphere of eighteenth-century Britain was protean in its manifestations, then, and nowhere were its ambiguities more evident than in the dramatic upsurge of popular loyalism during the 1790s.

[29] Dickinson, *Politics of the People*, 230–42.

Precedents for this mass expression of support for the British crown had been evident during the Jacobite rebellion of 1745, when more than 200 localities sent declarations of loyalty to George II, some 50 associations of armed citizens rose to the king's defense, and London tradesmen banded together to form organizations like the Laudable Association of Anti-Gallicans (the title being an expression of the anti-Jacobite conviction that the Stuart pretender was an agent of French interests). But such outpourings of loyalty to the Hanoverian regime were little compared to the range and depth of popular support garnered by the government in the 1790s, especially after the commencement of war with France in early 1793. Though provoked by fears of foreign invasion, this militant loyalism vented much of its wrath on domestic enemies. Already in 1792, John Reeves's Association for the Preservation of Liberty and Property against Republicans and Levellers was denouncing to the government printers and booksellers who circulated radical literature. Reeves himself claimed that his organization had inspired the formation of 4,000 similar societies, an estimate that at least one historian has found plausible.[30] The loyalist cause was also waged in the press, in London by newspapers like the *Star* and the *True Briton* and in provincial organs like the *Liverpool Phoenix* and the *Manchester Mercury*. Such papers easily exceeded their radical counterparts in number and circulation, though government subsidies certainly boosted their distribution. The 1790s were also the decade when Britain's masonic lodges, previously hotbeds of Wilkite radicalism, became staunchly loyalist and illustrated how loyalism was able to build a broad social base by appropriating associational networks once mobilized by radicals. Loyalists also employed the forms of street theater and crowd action that Wilkes's supporters had used so effectively several decades earlier. Loyalist crowds in hundreds of towns and villages burned effigies of Thomas Paine in the winter of 1792–93, for example, while others intimidated local radicals by threats and physical assaults.

The collapse of British radicalism in the 1790s owed much to this upsurge of popular loyalism and was not simply the result of government repression. It is true that loyalist agitation was not always spontaneous but was sponsored and manipulated by the government, the Anglican clergy, and local elites. Historians have long suspected, for example, that the loyalist Reeves was a government agent. But aside from the condescension implied in viewing popular loyalism as a mere puppet of the British establishment, interpreting the movement as the creation of elite manipulation misses the point. This manipulation would have been ineffective

[30] *Ibid.*, 280–81.

had there not existed at some level deep reserves of popular attachment to the crown and to British institutions of government. More to the point, even if one assumes that loyalism was a movement sponsored by elites for popular consumption, it could never have exercised such influence without the communications media, associational networks, techniques of extraparliamentary mobilization – in short, the new public sphere of politics – that had done so much to transform British political culture by the late eighteenth century. "The government of this country," wrote the industrialist and social reformer Robert Owen in 1817, "cannot now resist the influence of the public voice, whether it be right or wrong."[31]

Bibliographical note

Once dominated by Sir Lewis Namier and his school, scholarship on the political history of eighteenth-century England long minimized the significance of public opinion. In Namier's classic *Structure of Politics at the Accession of George III* (London, 1929; 2nd. ed. 1957), politics was a more or less closed world peopled by parliamentary elites scrambling for the spoils of office and patronage. For an example of J. C. D. Clark's revisionism, see his *English Society, 1688–1832* (Cambridge, 1985). The work of John Brewer does much to reestablish the importance of ideology, electoral conflict, and popular politics. See, for example, his *Party Ideology and Popular Politics at the Accession of George III* (Cambridge, 1976), and more recently, his beautifully written and handsomely illustrated work of synthesis, *The Pleasures of the Imagination: English Culture in the Eighteenth Century* (London, 1997). Brewer's *Sinews of Power: War, Money and the English State, 1688–1783* (Cambridge, Mass., 1988) focusses on state institutions but also explores their importance for the circulation of public information; my own discussion of lobbies draws on Brewer's insights. Engagingly written, Linda Colley's *Britons: Forging the Nation 1707–1837* (New Haven and London, 1992) is especially good on the development of popular patriotism. On the continued vitality of electoral politics, see Frank O'Gorman, *Voters, Patrons, and Parties: The Unreformed Electoral System of Hanoverian England 1734–1832* (Oxford, 1989); O'Gorman, *The Long Eighteenth Century: British Political and Social History 1688–1832* (London, 1997); Nicolas Rogers, *Whigs and Cities: Popular Politics in the Age of Walpole and Pitt* (Oxford, 1989); and Rogers, *Crowds, Culture, and Politics in Georgian Britain* (Oxford, 1998). H. T. Dickinson, *The Politics of the People in Eighteenth-Century Britain* (New York, 1995) is excellent on popular politics, as is Kathleen Wilson's *The Sense of the People: Politics, Culture, and Imperialism in England, 1715–1785* (Cambridge, 1995); I have profited especially from Wilson's stress on the significance of war and empire for the expansion of a political public sphere. J. A. W. Gunn's *Beyond Liberty and Property: The Process of Self-Recognition in Eighteenth-Century Political Thought* (Kingston and Montreal, 1983) discusses the growing importance of "public opinion" in British political thought. See also his "Court

---

[31] Quoted in Peter Fraser, "Public Petitioning and Parliament before 1832," *History* 46 (1961), 195.

Whiggery – Justifying Innovation," in Gordon J. Schochet, ed., *Politics, Politeness, and Patriotism*, Folger Institute Center for the History of Political Thought, 4 (Washington, DC, 1993).

Paul Monod's *Jacobitism and the English People, 1688–1788* (Cambridge, 1989) is good on the Jacobite movement as a fount of extraparliamentary activism. On the Tory party as a force in English electoral politics, see Linda Colley, *In Defiance of Oligarchy: The Tory Party 1714–60* (Cambridge, 1982). Bolingbroke's importance for the theory and practice of political opposition in early Hanoverian England is examined in Isaac Kramnick, *Bolingbroke and His Circle: The Politics of Nostalgia in the Age of Walpole* (Cambridge, Mass., 1968). On Wilkes, the most recent biography by P. D. G. Thomas, *John Wilkes: A Friend to Liberty* (Oxford, 1996) is rather pedestrian; still worth reading is the older study by George Rudé, *Wilkes and Liberty: A Social Study of 1763 to 1774* (Oxford, 1962). John Brewer, "Commercialization and Politics," in Neil McKendrick *et al.*, eds., *The Birth of a Consumer Society: The Commercialization of Eighteenth-Century England* (Bloomington, 1982) is good on the "selling" of Wilkes as a politician; on extraparliamentary movements for political reform after Wilkes, see Ian Christie, *Wilkes, Wyvill, and Reform: The Parliamentary Reform Movement in British Politics, 1760–1785* (London, 1962), and Eugene C. Black, *The Association: British Extraparliamentary Political Organization, 1769–1793* (Cambridge, Mass., 1963). Donna Andrew has drawn attention to the extensive network of debating societies that developed in late eighteenth-century London. See her "Popular Culture and Public Debate: London 1780," *Historical Journal* 39 (1996) as well as her edited volume, *London Debating Societies 1776–1799* (London, 1994). On women's involvement in electoral politics in late eighteenth-century England, see Elaine Chalus, "That Epidemical Madness: Women and Electoral Politics in the Late Eighteenth Century," in Hannah Barker and Elaine Chalus, eds., *Gender in Eighteenth-Century England* (New York, 1997). The origins of popular loyalism in the 1790s remains a contested issue. For differing views, see H. T. Dickinson, *British Radicalism and the French Revolution, 1789–1815* (Oxford, 1985), and the essays in Mark Philp, ed., *The French Revolution and British Popular Politics* (Cambridge, 1991).

Historians have devoted considerable attention to the development of the press in eighteenth-century England. Lois G. Schwoerer, "Liberty of the Press and Public Opinion: 1660–1695," in J. R. Jones, ed., *Liberty Secured? Britain Before and After 1688* (Stanford, 1992), and Paul Monod, "The Jacobite Press and English Censorship, 1689–95," in Eveline Cruickshanks and Edward Corp, eds., *The Stuart Court in Exile and the Jacobites* (London and Rio Grande, 1995), reevaluate the origins and impact of parliament's failure to renew the Licensing Act in 1694. On government policies toward the press, see Frederick Siebert, *Freedom of the Press in England 1476–1776* (Urbana, 1952); Laurence Hanson, *Government and the Press 1695–1763* (London, 1936); John Feather, "From Censorship to Copyright: Aspects of the Government's Role in the English Book Trade 1695–1775," in Kenneth Carpenter, ed., *Books and Society in History* (New York and London, 1983); and Eckhart Hellmuth, "The Palladium of All Other English Liberties: Reflections on the Liberty of the Press in England during the 1760s and 1770s," in Hellmuth, ed., *The Transformation of Political Culture: England and Germany in the Late Eighteenth Century* (Oxford, 1991). J. A. Downie, *Robert Harley and the*

Press: Propaganda and Public Opinion in the Age of Swift and Defoe (Cambridge, 1979), describes the government's extensive use of press subsidies to shape public opinion in the early eighteenth century. An excellent comparative survey of the rise of political journalism in Britain and France is Bob Harris, *Politics and the Rise of the Press: Britain and France, 1620–1800* (London and New York, 1996). On the press and public opinion, see Michael Harris, *London Newspapers in the Age of Walpole: A Study of the Origins of the Modern English Press* (London and Toronto, 1987); Robert Harris, *A Patriot Press: National Politics and the London Press in the 1740s* (Oxford, 1993); Manfred Schlenke, *England und das friderizianische Preussen 1740–1763: Ein Beitrag zum Verhältnis von Politik und öffentlicher Meinung in England des 18. Jahrhunderts* (Freiburg and Munich, 1963); and Marie Peters, *Pitt and Popularity: The Patriot Minister and London Opinion during the Seven Years War* (Oxford, 1980).

2 Opacity and transparency: French political culture in the eighteenth century

Ever since the mid-seventeenth century, an influential variant of British constitutional theory had defined Britain as a mixed monarchy in which king, Lords, and Commons respectively embodied the principles of monarchy, aristocracy, and democracy.[1] According to this view, which became a central presupposition of Country ideology, a proper balance among these three principles required the independence of each. Because each was obliged to resist encroachments by the others, contestation and conflict were implicit in this model. So after 1720, for example, as critics came to see the Commons as increasingly dominated or manipulated by the crown, Country politicians like Bolingbroke repeatedly invoked this model of mixed monarchy to legitimate their oppositional stance.

In France, the theories of divine-right absolutism that had held sway since the seventeenth century invested sovereignty in a single individual – the king – whose authority emanated from God. In contrast with British theories of mixed monarchy, royalist theory in France did not acknowledge any locus of public authority outside of the crown. The king was the sole public actor, and for that reason there could be no legitimate politics outside of the king and no legitimate effort to overturn his will.

Royalist theorists were nonetheless careful to emphasize that France was not a despotism. Indeed, French absolutism had developed within a social order that limited royal authority in principle as well as in practice. This order rested on older, medieval ideals that conceived of kingship in fundamentally passive and static terms. The king governed within a constitutional order instituted by God and therefore immutable. As God's earthly representative, the monarch was obligated to preserve this order in accordance with the principles of religion and justice. Louis XV expressed the idea of a fixed and immutable constitutional order when he declared in 1768 that the state he bequeathed to his successors should have the same constitution it possessed when he inherited it. Here the

---

[1] See J. G. A. Pocock, *Virtue, Commerce, and History: Essays on Political Thought and History, Chiefly in the Eighteenth Century* (Cambridge, 1985), 77–79.

sovereign's rule was defined in terms of conservation, not transformation, and the functions of kingship were fundamentally judicial rather than administrative. Hence in 1725 the jurist Mathieu Marais declared that "according to public law the king is a judge," and Bishop Bossuet, the renowned seventeenth-century theorist of the divine right of kings, observed in his *Politics Drawn from the Very Words of Holy Scripture* (published posthumously in 1709):

> The end of government is the good and the preservation of the state. To preserve it, first one must maintain therein a good constitution.... The good constitution of the body of the state consists in two things, namely religion and justice: these are the internal and constitutive principles of states. By the former, God is given his due, and by the latter, men are given that which is fitting and proper to them.[2]

Within this judicial discourse, "fitting and proper" meant among other things the rights of property and person attendant on one's birth and estate. The realm was understood as a diverse congerie of corporate bodies and estates – the clergy, nobility, municipalities, *parlements*, guilds, or universities, to name just a few – membership in which often overlapped, but each carrying its own juridically sanctioned privileges. A king governed his subjects justly, giving what was fitting and proper to them, when he honored those privileges. The magistrates of the *Parlement* of Paris expressed this concept of royal justice in a 1776 remonstrance to the crown: "Justice, sire, is the first duty of kings. The first rule of justice is to preserve for every man what belongs to him . . . a rule that consists not only in maintaining the rights of property, but also in preserving rights attached to the person and those which derive from the prerogatives of birth and estate."[3] The concept of the public sphere implied in this judicial model of kingship was highly restricted. By enjoining the king to honor the privileges of those he governed, it sharply delimited the areas in which the crown could legitimately intervene in the lives of its subjects.

Although from the reign of Louis XIV on, an increasingly activist and administrative style of government had undermined this older vision of kingship, privilege remained a cornerstone of French absolutism up to the end of the Old Regime. The very essence of privilege was particularity, since the privileges (literally "private laws") of a given estate or corporate

---

[2] Quotes taken from Michel Antoine, "La monarchie absolue," in Keith Baker, ed., *The French Revolution and the Creation of Modern Political Culture*, vol. I: *The Political Culture of the Old Regime* (Oxford and New York, 1987), 11, and Keith Baker, *Inventing the French Revolution: Essays on French Political Culture in the Eighteenth Century* (Cambridge, 1991), 113.

[3] Quoted in Baker, *Inventing the French Revolution*, 114.

body were shared by no other group and were thus unique. Because the privileges enjoyed by each corporate entity were particular, no individual or institution apart from the crown could speak or act for the political community as a whole. France did have something of a national representative assembly in the form of the Estates-General, which the crown had periodically summoned since the late Middle Ages in order to secure additional taxes or mobilize support in times of war. But aside from the fact that the crown had not convoked the Estates-General since 1614, its very structure reinforced the particularism and privilege upon which French society was based. Up until 1789 delegates from the three estates (clergy, nobility, and commoners) assembled and voted not in common but separately, drafting their grievances and petitions accordingly. Delegates to the Estates-General did not represent the nation in any abstract sense, but only the corporate bodies and regional jurisdictions that made up the respective estates. Each was related to the whole only through the person of the king, who was the sole public figure in whose person the nation was embodied.

Thus, as Keith Baker observed, within the traditional judicial model of absolute monarchy "there can be no useful discussion of political questions, since there is no public apart from the person of the king."[4] The king alone was deemed capable of perceiving the political community as a whole and of making decisions affecting the entire realm. Only the king was privy to the mysteries of the state, and the crown's repeated use of the formula "secret du roi" expressed a vision of the public sphere that restricted legitimate political action to the king and his counselors. The bitter legacy of the sixteenth-century wars of religion – confessional strife, the disintegration of the realm into competing aristocratic factions, the assassination of two kings in less than three decades – had seemed to confirm the royalist belief that the range of individuals and groups with claims on public political discourse must be narrowly circumscribed. During the second half of the seventeenth century this view was further strengthened by the rise of divine-right theories that elevated the king's person to the point of deification. These theories gave theological sanction to the notion of politics as a "secret" or "mystery" to which none but the king and his counselors could be privy. By portraying the secrecy of the king's counsels as analogous to the mystery and unfathomability of God's wisdom, theories of divine right gave religious sanction to royal claims that the sphere of political action and deliberation belonged to the king and his counselors alone.

Despite the absence of national representative bodies through which opposition to royal policies could be legitimately expressed and negotiated,

[4] *Ibid.*, 114.

a vehicle for institutionalized opposition did exist in the judicial institutions known as *parlements*. Technically the *parlements* were royal courts, having been created by the crown in the thirteenth century. These bodies exercised higher judicial authority both as courts of appeal and through their responsibility for verifying whether a royal edict was in accord with the existing laws of a province or region. Where inconsistencies or violations were found, the magistrates of a *parlement* submitted to the crown a remonstrance detailing their objections. Although French kings could and did disregard a remonstrance, the refusal of a *parlement* to register a royal edict seriously compromised its legitimacy and undermined its effective implementation. At a time when the expanding fiscal and administrative role of the crown increasingly clashed with its traditional role of safeguarding the property and privileges of its subjects, the *parlements'* responsibility for verifying the legality of royal legislation placed them at the center of opposition. Because of their frequent opposition to fiscal and agrarian reform, the *parlements* have sometimes been viewed as self-serving defenders of aristocratic privilege. Although there is some merit to this interpretation, it defines the significance of the *parlements* too narrowly. However self-interested or obstructionist it may have been on occasion, the opposition of the *parlement* provided an institutional wedge through which the crown's efforts to control public political debate were successfully contested – even if, as a consequence, the *parlements* fell victim to the very public they helped to create.

Jansenism and the emergence of an oppositional public sphere

A major limitation of Habermas's model of the public sphere is the lack of importance it assigns religion. Habermas viewed the new public sphere of the eighteenth century as a fundamentally secular phenomenon, philosophically rooted in the Enlightenment. Yet religious issues provoked intense controversy in the eighteenth century, and their role in expanding the public spheres of politics and print deserves more emphasis. Anti-Catholicism remained deeply entrenched in eighteenth-century English political culture, as evident in the relentless stream of anti-Jacobite pamphlets generated during the first half of the century, the effigy burnings of the pope that so often accompanied popular political celebrations and protests, and in London's anti-Catholic riots of 1780. In the territories of the Holy Roman Empire, similarly, polemical battles between and within the Protestant and Catholic confessions occasioned far more pamphlets than did secular controversies. The thousands of books and pamphlets growing out of the debates between German Pietists and their orthodox

Lutheran opponents in the late seventeenth and early eighteenth centuries, the outpouring of Protestant propaganda provoked by the archbishop of Salzburg's expulsion of 20,000 Protestants from his territory in 1731, and the flood of print unleashed by supporters and opponents of Joseph II's religious reforms in Habsburg lands during the 1780s, abundantly testify to this fact.[5]

The impact of religious controversy on the expansion of the public sphere was visible above all in France, as evidenced by the religious movement known as Jansenism. Originating in the seventeenth century out of Catholic debates over the relationship between grace and free will, Jansenism emphasized the sinful nature of human beings and their utter dependence on God's unmerited grace for salvation. The Jansenists were highly critical of those in the church, especially the Jesuits, who accorded greater efficacy to free will and were thus more optimistic about the ability of individuals to gain salvation through good works and the mediation of the church. Jansenism's strict views on penance held that individuals should seek absolution and participate in communion only after undergoing a process of inner conversion and contrition. The austerity and predestinarian tendencies of Jansenism bore a certain resemblance to Calvinism, and already in 1653 the papacy was sufficiently convinced of the movement's heterodoxy to condemn as heretical several positions attributed to Jansenist theology.

Although Jansenism found adherents throughout Catholic Europe, papal calls for the suppression of the movement aroused particular opposition in France owing to the kingdom's longstanding Gallican traditions. Gallicanism had emerged in the late Middle Ages as a reaction against papal assertions of universal sovereignty, and staunchly defended the autonomy of the French church *vis-à-vis* Rome. The crown had embraced Gallican arguments to justify its efforts to exert political and fiscal authority over the French church. The *parlements*, eager to defend their own jurisdictional authority against intrusion by the church, were even more aggressively Gallican in their views. So in 1713, when the papal Bull *Unigenitus* denounced as heretical 101 propositions found in a New Testament commentary published by the French Jansenist Pasquier Quesnel, his

---

[5] On Pietism's impact on the public sphere, see Martin Gierl, *Pietismus und Aufklärung: Theologische Polemik und die Kommunikationsreform der Wissenschaft am Ende des 17. Jahrhunderts* (Göttingen, 1997), and James Van Horn Melton, "Pietism and the Public Sphere in Eighteenth-Century Germany," in James Bradley and Dale Van Kley, eds., *Religion, Politics, and Enlightened Europe* (Notre Dame, 2001). Mack Walker, *The Salzburg Transaction: Expulsion and Redemption in Eighteenth-Century Germany* (Ithaca, 1992), discusses the publicistic response to the Salzburg expulsions. On the impact of Joseph's reforms on Viennese print culture, see Leslie Bodi, *Tauwetter in Wien: zur Prosa der österreichischen Aufklärung* (Frankfurt am Main, 1977).

defenders could draw on a well-stocked arsenal of Gallican polemic in protesting the Bull's publication in France.

The crown was unmoved by Jansenism's Gallican rhetoric, and indeed, Louis XIV had been hostile to the movement from the very start. Its anti-papal arguments held little appeal for the crown, which no longer viewed the papacy as a serious threat to royal sovereignty. The French crown was much more concerned with preserving doctrinal unity, and it associated Jansenist polemics with the confessional discord that had ravaged the kingdom during the sixteenth-century wars of religion. The pope in fact had promulgated *Unigenitus* not on his own initiative but under the persistent prodding of Louis XIV, who had ordered the razing of the Port-Royal convent (a Jansenist stronghold) in 1710. The crown remained opposed to the movement throughout the eighteenth century, having officially declared *Unigenitus* a "law of church and state" in 1730. The French ecclesiastical hierarchy shared this antagonism, and anti-Jansenist bishops repeatedly tried to suppress the movement by instructing priests to refuse the sacraments to those suspected of Jansenist sympathies.

But it was not simply fear of religious schism that inspired the crown's hostility to Jansenism. Louis XIV branded the Jansenists as "republicans," a charge that for all its hyperbole nonetheless pointed to the movement's potential for political opposition. Anti-absolutist tendencies in Jansenism can be traced back to its roots in late-medieval conciliarist theories, which viewed the authority of the church hierarchy as having been delegated by the body of believers who constituted the church as a whole. Over the course of the eighteenth century, Jansenist constitutional discourse transferred this idea of delegation to the political sphere, challenging the absolutist claims of the crown by defining royal authority as a delegation of the sovereign rights of the nation. Jansenism's proto-republican features were further reinforced by the role it assigned the lower clergy in church government, an emphasis on lay participation, and the disapproval of royal pomp and display implicit in its austere world view.

The popular appeal of Jansenism first became evident in 1727, when reports of miraculous cures performed at the tomb of a former Jansenist deacon began to draw crowds of pilgrims to the Parisian cemetery of Saint Médard. Over the next five years thousands made their way to Saint Médard, attracted by accounts of afflicted individuals who had visited the site and been cured of their maladies after experiencing violent spasms and convulsions.[6] When neither government harassment nor episcopal threats of excommunication succeeded in suppressing the

---

[6] On the convulsionary movement, see Robert Kreiser, *Miracles, Convulsions, and Ecclesiastical Politics in Early Eighteenth-Century Paris* (Princeton, 1978).

so-called *convulsionnaires*, Cardinal Fleury (Louis XV's chief minister at the time) condemned the gatherings as an occasion for "licentious discourse" and closed the cemetery in 1732. The government continued to persecute recalcitrant *convulsionnaires* who assembled elsewhere in Paris, and by 1735 the phenomenon had run its course.

Its effect, however, was to broaden Jansenism's popular base as an oppositional movement. This opposition gained institutional potency by the support it enjoyed in the *Parlement* of Paris, some of whose magistrates had Jansenist leanings or at least opposed the persecution of Jansenists on grounds of constitutional principle. David Bell has shown how Jansenist sympathies were especially widespread among the *avocats au parlements*, the barristers licensed to argue cases in the courts of the *parlements*. There are a number of possible reasons for why the milieu of the *parlement* proved so receptive to the Jansenist movement. Its puritanical side may have been appealing to parlementary magistrates and barristers, who had traditionally prided themselves on their austerity and moral probity. Other scholars have found affinities between constitutionalism *parlementaire*, with its belief that royal authority would always be subject to abuse unless restrained by the judicial authority of the courts, and Jansenism's Augustinian emphasis on the corruptibility of human nature. But what especially stiffened opposition of the *parlements* to *Unigenitus* was the conviction that efforts by ecclesiastical prelates to enforce the Bull subverted the jurisdictional authority of the *parlements*. Here spokesmen asserted the authority of *parlements* to hear appeals from accused Jansenists who had been denied the sacraments or had suffered other forms of persecution owing to their opposition to *Unigenitus*. Jansenist polemicists played on these jurisdictional concerns with consummate skill. Their attacks on papal "despotism" resonated in the staunchly Gallican milieu of the *Parlement* of Paris, and pleas for the right of persecuted Jansenists to seek redress in *parlement* courts found a willing ear in judicial bodies traditionally protective of their jurisdictional authority. The *Parlement* of Paris was not a political or ideological monolith: like other royal institutions it was ridden with factionalism, and only a small minority of magistrates was aggressively Jansenist in its beliefs. But the rhetorical ingenuity of Jansenist propaganda, its strategic blend of religious polemic with appeals to the Gallican traditions and jurisdictional claims of the *parlements*, enabled the movement at critical moments to elicit parlementary support in the campaign against *Unigenitus*.

By 1730, opposition by the *parlements* to *Unigenitus* had taken an active turn. The *Parlement* of Paris began hearing appeals from persecuted Jansenists, and in 1732 the crown exiled 139 magistrates from the capital for defying a royal declaration restricting parlementary remonstrances over the issue. During the next three decades *Unigenitus* remained an issue of bitter contention between crown, *parlement*, and church, the three most powerful institutions in the monarchy. Anti-Jansenist bishops continued to denounce opposition to *Unigenitus*, and persistent attempts to withhold the sacraments from accused Jansenists helped keep the controversy alive. The *Parlement* of Paris retaliated by prohibiting the distribution of various anti-Jansenist tracts, reaffirming its jurisdictional rights over the French church, and denying the status of *Unigenitus* as a law of state. The position of the crown was more ambiguous. Although it remained hostile to Jansenism, the crown was mainly concerned with containing the controversy by working behind the scenes with moderates on both sides or by periodically imposing "silence" on the contending parties.

Silence, however, proved difficult to enforce. The convulsionary phenomenon had served to popularize the Jansenist controversy, which had now begun to spread well beyond the institutions of crown, church, and *parlement*. Moreover, not since the anti-government pamphleteering of the Fronde (1648–52), the largest uprising in French history prior to the Revolution, had printed propaganda issued forth on such a scale. Already under the Regency (1715–23) Jansenist opponents of *Unigenitus* had published hundreds of pamphlets attacking the Bull, and in 1728 the *Nouvelles ecclésiastiques* began its remarkable career as a clandestine champion of the Jansenist cause. Published every three or four weeks, this broadsheet detailed the tribulations of simple parish priests and ordinary laypeople persecuted for their beliefs. The *Nouvelles ecclésiastiques* legitimized lay opposition to *Unigenitus* as a "public" of ordinary men and women possessing the capacity to venture reasonable opinions on theological matters. The journal portrayed itself as the spokesman for this public, a tribunal defending the persecuted victims of a hostile crown and corrupt ecclesiastical establishment. "The public is a judge they have been unable to corrupt," declared the journal in 1732.[7]

The depiction of the public as a tribunal, an independent, infallible, unitary organ judging the actions of those institutions that had traditionally wielded power, was to be a key element of the concept as it developed in eighteenth-century French political discourse. As the Jansenist controversy unfolded, appeals to "public opinion" figured prominently in the rhetorical arsenal employed by Jansenist barristers in the cases they argued before the *Parlement* of Paris. Owing to their oratorical training and experience, barristers were well equipped to assume the mantle of public

[7] Quoted in Peter R. Campbell, *Power and Politics in Old Regime France 1720–1745* (London, 1996), 303.

tribune. Their outspokenness also reflected the relative freedom of expression they enjoyed as members of the bar. Barristers customarily submitted their legal arguments in written form, and if they desired they also had the right to publish their briefs and circulate them among the public at large. These documents, commonly known as *mémoires judiciares*, often ran to hundreds of pages, and more than a hundred thousand appeared during the course of the eighteenth century. Most importantly, *mémoires judiciares* were not subject to preliminary censorship – an exemption, as Bell has noted, that made them virtually unique in the publishing world of the Old Regime. Although originally justified as a journalistic recourse for clients who were victims of legal improprieties, the *mémoires* became an important weapon of Jansenist opposition journalism. In published and often sensationalized appeals on behalf of clients persecuted by anti-Jansenist bishops, Jansenist barristers used their well-honed polemical skills to mobilize public opposition to *Unigenitus*. The crown understandably viewed these lawyers with distrust: the marquis d'Argenson, an adviser to Cardinal Fleury, likened the Parisian barristers to the radical Tory opposition and called them "a sort of absolutely independent little republic at the center of the state."[8] But the barristers were able to resist royal efforts to curb their independence with threats of judicial strikes, and in defending their autonomy they employed the language of parliamentary constitutionalism in ways that foreshadowed the later, more radical doctrines of popular sovereignty emerging after 1750. This radicalization of the Parisian bar continued right up to the Revolution: in 1789 almost half of the deputies to the Third Estate were barristers, and as the examples of Brissot, Danton, and Robespierre illustrate, lawyers would occupy central positions of leadership in the revolutionary regime.[9]

Hence barristers played a key role in the process whereby the religious and constitutional conflicts of the 1730s and 1740s moved out of the monarchy's traditional institutional framework and into a broader public arena. The decade of the 1750s, when conflicts over *Unigenitus* resumed with unprecedented acrimony, showed how far this process had progressed. The occasion for renewed conflict came in 1749, when the anti-Jansenist archbishop of Paris instructed the Parisian clergy to refuse the last rites to those suspected of Jansenist sympathies. The *Parlement* of Paris condemned the archbishop's action and ordered the clergy to disregard the instruction, employing traditional Gallican and conciliarist arguments in charging that the archbishop had exceeded his constitutional

---

[8] Quoted in David Bell, *Lawyers and Citizens: The Making of a Political Elite in Old Regime France* (New York and Oxford, 1994), 6.
[9] *Ibid.*

authority. During the next five years the tone of the debate grew increasingly violent as Jansenist barristers once again carried the controversy into the public arena via pamphlets, broadsheets, and *mémoires*. In 1754 the monarchy, in accordance with its traditional role of adjudicating religious debates in the interest of public tranquility, imposed a law of silence on the contending parties. Here the implication, again, was that the crown had the sole authority to make public pronouncements on vital matters of state.

Yet as Baker has argued, the intensity of the controversy made it impossible for the crown to enforce that claim – even after Louis XV attempted to quash the debate by exiling both the parlementary magistrates and the archbishop from the capital. Indeed, the crown's measures only served to broaden the debate when the *Parlement* of Paris took the unusual step of publishing its remonstrances, which circulated throughout the kingdom. Even more ominously for the king, defenders of the exiled magistrates now made the crown rather than papal or episcopal authority their central polemical target. In the process, traditional conciliarist arguments began to crystallize into secular, anti-absolutist notions of popular sovereignty.

France now "broke out of its absolutist mold" (Baker) not just because doctrines of popular sovereignty were being explicitly elaborated but because the rules of the political game had fundamentally changed. By the 1760s it had become difficult for the crown to sustain the pretense that political discourse was a royal preserve. The Jansenist controversy had unmasked the crown's inability to control public debate, a failure underscored by the unpopularity of other royal policies. Criticism of the crown mounted in the wake of France's poor military performance during the Seven Years War, the monarchy's unpopular attempt to liberalize the grain trade in 1763–64, and growing criticism of royal fiscal policy. During the tense decade of the 1750s, the *Parlement* of Paris had issued fifteen remonstrances protesting royal legislation; in the 1760s the number grew to twenty-five.[10]

Moreover, during the 1760s the *philosophes* became increasingly visible as self-appointed representatives of enlightened opinion. Under Diderot's editorship, the *Encyclopédie* (1751–75) served not only as a compendium of Enlightenment thought but also as a publishing enterprise around which the *philosophes* developed a cohesive identity. Parisian salons, which reached their peak of fashion during this time as centers of Enlightenment sociability, further fostered this cohesion. Voltaire's widely publicized campaign protesting the execution of Jean Calas, the Protestant who

[10] Dale Van Kley, *The Damiens Affair and the Unraveling of the "Ancien Régime," 1750–1770* (Princeton, 1984), 100.

in 1762 had been falsely charged with murdering his son to prevent his conversion to Catholicism, dramatized the emergence of the *philosophes* as arbiters of enlightened public opinion. When Voltaire wrote in 1764 that "opinion governs the world, but in the long run it is the wise who govern opinion,"[11] he expressed not only the growing importance of public opinion but also his confidence in the capacity of men of letters to shape it.

The politics of publicity

Paradoxically, mounting political disaffection in the 1760s coincided with the waning of Jansenism as a source of political contestation. Jansenist agitation reached its apogee in the early 1760s, when the movement helped orchestrate the successful campaign to expel the Jesuits. Thereafter, however, Jansenism no longer generated the kind of controversy it had sparked during the struggles of the 1750s. Roger Chartier has viewed Jansenist decline as symptomatic of the more general process of dechristianization that occurred over the course of the century (a development that Jansenism itself accelerated by undermining popular confidence in the authority of the church hierarchy), while David Bell points to the waning appeal of Jansenism among a younger, more secular-minded generation of barristers less interested in championing Jansenist *causes célèbres* than Enlightenment ones.

Whatever the reasons for its declining appeal, Jansenism had proven critical in fostering an oppositional milieu that continued to broaden even as the controversy over *Unigenitus* receded. By the 1760s the recasting and secularization of the conciliarist ecclesiastical model into a doctrine of popular sovereignty was well advanced in parlementary circles. This transmutation found expression in the tendency of the various *parlements* of the realm to view themselves not as provincial institutions whose judicial authority was confined to their respective jurisdictions, but as a single body representing the nation as a whole. The constitutional implications of this vision were not lost on the crown, which vigorously denied the right of the *parlements* to act in concert. In 1766 Louis XV scolded the *Parlement* of Paris for efforts to coordinate its opposition to royal policies with the *parlements* of Pau and Rennes: "What has happened in my *parlements* of Pau and Rennes is no concern of my other *parlements*; I have acted with regard to these two courts as my authority required, and I owe an explanation to nobody." The king lashed out at the claim that

---

[11] Quoted in J. A. W. Gunn, *Queen of the World: Opinion in the Public Life of France from the Renaissance to the Revolution, Studies on Voltaire and the Eighteenth Century*, 328 (Oxford, 1995), 175 (my translation from the French).

"all *parlements* together are but one and the same body," and that this body was "the seat, the tribunal, the spokesman of the nation." Louis instead reaffirmed the crown's traditional claim that it alone had the authority to act and to speak for the whole, insisting that "public order in its entirety emanates from me." "The rights and interests of the nation, which some dare to regard as a separate body from the monarchy, are necessarily united with my rights and interests, and repose only in my hands." The king especially condemned the *publicness* of the opposition, as expressed in the publication of remonstrances. He promised to treat the remonstrances of the *parlements* with due consideration, but only "when their secrecy keeps them decent and useful ... Let [the magistrates] keep their deliberations secret and let them consider how indecent it is and how unworthy of their character to broadcast invective against the members of my council to whom I have given my orders and who have shown themselves so worthy of my confidence."[12]

But the Maupeou crisis of 1771–74 further demonstrated the crown's inability to contain the new politics of publicity. In 1771 the royal chancellor, Maupeou, implemented a series of measures aimed at curbing the independence of the *parlements*. His reforms abolished the venality of their offices, thus ensuring that magistrates could now be appointed or removed according to the king's wishes. The measures also restricted the right of remonstrance, reorganized their jurisdictions, and attempted to pack the *parlements* with more pliant magistrates. Widely condemned as an expression of royal despotism, Maupeou's reforms unleashed a torrent of oppositional writing. In addition to the sober judicial remonstrances that circulated in print or manuscript throughout the kingdom, the reforms provoked an outpouring of vituperative and often crude placards, engravings, and doggerel. These were accompanied by more than 160 oppositional pamphlets of varying length, some published in runs of as many as 5,000 copies. The storm of opposition finally led Louis XVI to revoke most of the reforms upon his accession in 1774, further evidence of the extent to which public opinion had acquired political agency.

In fact, by this time, the crown had begun to belie its own absolutist premises by acknowledging the existence of a public to which the crown, no less than its critics, had to appeal. A few years before his accession to the throne Louis XVI had himself written that "I must always consult public opinion; it is never wrong"; Jakob-Nicolas Moreau, a royalist propagandist and historian, expressed this acquiescence when he wrote

---

[12] The speech is published in Keith Baker, ed., *The Old Regime and the French Revolution* (Chicago, 1986), 48–50; see also Baker's discussion in *Inventing the French Revolution*, 226–32.

in 1762: "In this century, when the people judge everything and has so much half-knowledge which it abuses, it is necessary to oppose false opinions with useful and proven ones. It seems to me that the art of dispensing these truths effectively, and the method of establishing them, deserve a part of the government's attention."[13] Efforts by the crown to mobilize public support for its policies were not in themselves new. During the Fronde, supporters as well as opponents of the government had produced thousands of pamphlets. Even Louis XIV had acknowledged the value of printed propaganda and did not hesitate to publish detailed justifications for his war policies, which were circulated among his subjects on a mass scale. Joseph Klaits has in fact suggested that the crown's unwillingness to summon an Estates-General, which the monarchy had relied upon extensively prior to the seventeenth century as a means of mobilizing popular support in times of war, had made it all the more necessary for the crown to employ print as a vehicle of propaganda.

What was significant about the crown's entry into the journalistic arena after 1750 was not its efforts to influence "public opinion," but the fact that they occurred at a time when public opinion itself was acquiring meaning and agency as a political category. Such had not been the case during the Fronde: however bitter their opposition to the Mazarin regime, anti-government pamphleteers had not demanded a fundamental redistribution of sovereign power or appealed to public opinion as the ultimate source of political legitimacy. They did not challenge the sovereignty of the royal will, but rather contended that dishonest and unscrupulous advisers had subverted it. By the accession of Louis XVI, however, a political culture had emerged in which public opinion was conceived as a sovereign tribunal whose judgments were binding on everyone, including the king. Once the crown entered this arena as an actor in its own right, it sanctioned a new definition of politics as open and transparent, not closed, arcane, and secret. Once the monarchy acknowledged the existence of a public to which the crown, no less than its critics, had to appeal, it undermined its own traditional claims to sovereignty.

Under Louis XVI, the new importance that the crown assigned to public opinion was evident in efforts by reform-minded ministers to harness it by giving it institutional expression. Anne-Robert-Jacques Turgot, minister of finances from 1774 to 1776, approved submission of a far-reaching plan that would have created a hierarchy of representative assemblies extending from the village to the national level. Turgot's assemblies were designed less to check royal authority than to rationalize its exercise by

---

[13] Quotes taken from John Hardman, *Louis XVI* (New Haven, 1993), 35, and Baker, *Inventing the French Revolution*, 71.

facilitating the flow of accurate social information from society to the state. Turgot's brief tenure ensured that his plan was never implemented, but Jacques Necker, the former banker who served as finance minister in 1777–81 and again in 1788–89, showed an even keener sensitivity to the importance of public opinion as a political force. Toward the end of his life Necker observed that under Louis XVI "there arose an authority which, though possessing no definite power, watched over the conduct of the government... it is the authority of public opinion of which I speak."[14] The weight Necker assigned to public opinion grew out of the fiscal imperatives of his first ministry, when he faced the daunting task of financing French participation in the War of American Independence. Convinced that additional taxation was neither economically desirable nor politically feasible, Necker relied heavily on credit to finance the war. He recognized, however, that the crown's ability to raise loans depended on the confidence of potential creditors in the fiscal integrity of the monarchy. Credit required credibility, and credibility resided in public confidence – in other words, public opinion.

In underscoring the relationship between public credit and public opinion, Necker echoed what had become conventional wisdom in eighteenth-century fiscal theory. English commentators often argued that public credit and absolute monarchy were incompatible because absolutist regimes were too powerful and capricious to sustain public financial confidence. They praised public credit as a barrier to despotism, since no government could risk losing public confidence by acting arbitrarily. John Law, the notorious Scottish financier to whom the French crown had entrusted the management of the newly created Bank of France in 1718, had insisted that absolutism could be reconciled with institutions of public credit by amalgamating the king's personal funds with those of the bank and thereby tying the private interests of the crown to the public interest of his subjects. The fate of the bank, which was merged with Law's commercial monopoly in Louisiana (the so-called Mississippi Scheme) and then closed following the collapse of the company in 1720, helped discredit the idea of a national bank in France for the remainder of the Old Regime and seemed to confirm the axiom that absolutism and public credit were incompatible.[15] But the financial costs of the Seven Years War, which forced the monarchy to rely heavily on loans as its primary fiscal expedient, further highlighted the issue of credit and its relationship to

---

[14] Jacques Necker, "Le credit," in *Dernières vues de politique et de finance, offertes à la Nation Française par M. Necker* (n.p., 1802), 269.

[15] See the insightful discussion in Thomas E. Kaiser, "Money, Despotism, and Public Opinion in Early Eighteenth-Century France: John Law and the Debate on Royal Credit," *Journal of Modern History* 63 (1991), 4–16.

public confidence. The crown's growing dependence on borrowing helps further explain why public opinion, owing to its presumed relationship to credit, became such a central category in French political discourse from the end of the Seven Years War to the collapse of the Old Regime.

The importance Necker assigned to public opinion found expression in his famous *Compte rendu* of 1781, when he took the unprecedented step of publishing the budget of the crown. Necker's *Compte rendu* quickly sold more than 20,000 copies and aroused a wave of controversy. Necker defended his published account of revenues and expenditures as a measure that would boost public confidence in the fiscal operations of the crown, but his actions appalled those in the government, such as the foreign minister Vergennes, who condemned Necker's actions for violating hallowed traditions of royal secrecy. The *Compte rendu*, which supposedly proved that Necker's policies had created a budgetary surplus, was no doubt a self-serving document and historians continue to debate its veracity. But it would be wrong to dismiss it as an opportunistic expedient. Necker's appeal to public opinion was fully consistent with another controversial feature of his ministry, namely his experimental plan to establish provincial institutions of self-government.

Necker's plan, which he implemented in 1778 and 1779 in the administrative districts of Berri and Haute-Guienne, shifted responsibility for broad areas of provincial administration from royal *intendants* to elected assemblies of property owners. In effect, Necker's experiment sought to create institutional organs of public opinion through which the fiscal system of the monarchy could be overhauled and reformed. A perennial weakness of French fiscal administration was the problem of assessment. Backed by the *parlements*, landed proprietors had bitterly resisted efforts by the crown to conduct land surveys as a means of verifying local tax rolls. Such resistance reflected the distrust of royal fiscal policy that pervaded all levels of French society, as well as the widely held belief that preserving the secrecy of family finances was a basic liberty of French subjects. Necker was himself convinced that the crown's efforts to coerce compliance with its taxation policies were self-defeating and merely provoked further evasion and resistance. He also believed that coercion played into the hands of the *parlements*, who in opposing royal fiscal policy could pose as defenders of the rights of the nation. Necker had little use for the *parlements*, which had opposed his initial efforts to institute a more equitable assessment of the *vingtième* (the property tax intermittently imposed by the crown since 1749). But although he viewed the constitutional rhetoric of the *parlements* as a mask for their own selfish corporate interests, he acknowledged that the strength of the *parlements* as an oppositional force had rested on their success in mobilizing the support of public opinion.

Therefore, as Necker declared in his 1778 proposal for the establishment of provincial assemblies, "it is necessary either to take that support [i.e., public opinion] from them or prepare for repeated battles which will disturb the peaceful reign of Your Majesty...."[16] By establishing provincial assemblies, Necker hoped to create organs of enlightened opinion that could provide an institutional counterweight to the opportunistic demagoguery of the parlements.

Necker envisioned the assemblies as a means of injecting publicity into the opaque fiscal system of the monarchy. The assemblies were themselves to assess and collect the direct taxes (the *taille*) levied by the crown, and were also to assume responsibility for poor relief and other public works. By exposing to public view the procedures through which taxes were assessed and collected, Necker believed the assemblies could dispel suspicions of corruption and arbitrariness that had long undermined the credibility of royal fiscal administration. As a minister of the crown, he did not intend for the assemblies to limit the king's ultimate fiscal authority. Although they could allocate taxes among the proprietors of their districts as each saw fit, the crown itself established the tax quota of each province. The idea was to build public confidence by entrusting the assessment and collection of direct taxes to the localities that paid them. To ensure that the assemblies did not become mere guardians of aristocratic privilege, Necker further insisted that half of the deputies come from the Third Estate.

Necker's prescription appears to have been followed in practice, but too little is known about the assemblies to gauge their effectiveness. They must have enjoyed some success, since the later finance minister, Charles Alexandre de Calonne, proposed creating more of them in the reform package he presented to the Assembly of Notables in 1787. Calonne's successor, Loménie de Brienne, also pushed for provincial assemblies in the hopes that their creation would forestall growing demands for the convocation of an Estates-General. Accordingly, seventeen additional assemblies had been created by the time Necker returned as finance minister in August of 1788. Brienne also devised a tier of municipal assemblies whose deputies were elected by a franchise based almost entirely on property rather than juridical estate. Although their proposed assemblies differed from each other organizationally, Necker, Calonne, and Brienne all saw them as repositories of enlightened opinion whose support would enable the crown to circumvent the entrenched opposition of the *parlements*. Calonne wrote to the king in November of 1786 that if the *parlements*

---

[16] Quoted in Robert D. Harris, *Necker, Reform Minister of the Old Regime* (Berkeley and Los Angeles, 1979), 93.

were to resist his proposals to establish a uniform land tax, "their voice will be drowned out by the *vox populi* which will necessarily prevail, especially since the establishment of... the provincial and district assemblies will give the government the help of that national interest which at present is null and which, if well directed, can smooth all difficulties."[17] Under Brienne's ministry the behavior of the assemblies, which generally supported royal measures that the *parlements* had stubbornly opposed, seemed to bear out such hopes. In fact, however, the provincial and municipal assemblies only hastened the process through which political initiative shifted from crown and *parlements* alike to the nation at large. As the assemblies began to circulate printed accounts of their deliberations, political and constitutional debate became increasingly national in scope. From the village to the provincial level, the assemblies had the effect of introducing ever wider circles of society into the administration of the realm. In the process, they expanded the political consciousness of many who later gained election to the National Assembly. By fostering at the municipal and provincial levels the creation of a political society that paralleled and ultimately rivaled the older administrative structures of the crown, the assemblies contributed to the general disarray of royal government that had become so evident by 1789. As such, they showed what a dangerous game the monarchy's appeal to public opinion had turned out to be. In relinquishing its monopoly on political debate and deliberation, the crown had effectively relinquished its sovereignty.

Secrecy and its discontents

In the spring of 1789, as political initiative rapidly devolved from a feckless crown to the assembled deputies of the Estates-General, the mood across the Channel was quite different. Throughout England, hundreds of popular demonstrations and addresses congratulated George III on his recovery from illness. Never, it seemed, had the Hanoverian dynasty enjoyed such popularity and support. The contrast is even more jarring if one then moves forward to the winter of 1792–93: as the Convention in Paris was preparing to execute its deposed king, loyalist crowds throughout England were burning effigies of the arch-republican Thomas Paine. How does one explain these contrasting scenes? Why, at a time when the French monarchy was spending its last reserves of credibility, did those of its British counterpart seem deeper than ever? Part of the answer can be found by looking more closely at "public opinion" and its contrasting configurations in Britain and France.

[17] Quoted in John Hardman, *French Politics 1774–1789: From the Accession of Louis XVI to the Fall of the Bastille* (London and New York, 1995), 237.

The term public opinion appears much more frequently in French journalistic writing of the eighteenth century than in British political discourse. This at first seems paradoxical, since France, at least prior to 1787, lacked the institutionalized conduits of public opinion that Britain possessed in its parliament. Yet it is precisely this absence that helps to explain why the term gained such currency in absolutist France. British writers and politicians might have disagreed on whether or not parliament adequately represented "the sense of the nation," but few disputed that parliament had at some level to be responsive to it, even if opposition voices might call for extraparliamentary action as a means of pressuring the Commons into fulfilling that duty. In theory at least, public opinion had an institutional locus, and for this reason the concept was less vexatious in British political discourse than it was in France. There the absence of representative bodies claiming to represent the views and interests of a national constituency meant that "public opinion" was simultaneously more frequently invoked and more difficult to define. Although the journalist Louis-Sebastièn Mercier observed in the 1780s that "public opinion [*l'opinion publique*] today has an overwhelming force that cannot be resisted," he also noted the difficulty of identifying it in a political culture that lacked institutions for expressing it: "Does the public exist? What is the public? Where is it? By which organs does it manifest its will?"[18] From the 1720s on the term appears repeatedly in police reports, and the crown's obsession with public opinion (Louis XV eagerly awaited the weekly reports of his police commissioners) in part reflected the difficulty of gauging it in a regime lacking vibrant institutions of representative government.[19]

At the same time, the absence of such organs gave the concept of public opinion an elusiveness and indeterminacy that enabled a range of voices to claim its mantle. As we have seen, by the 1770s appeals to public opinion had become standard among groups ranging from *parlementaires* and *philosophes* to government ministers. Although these circles sometimes overlapped (Malesherbes, for example, was at various times a government censor, patron of the philosophes, and spokesman for the *parlements*), their interests and positions often diverged. This heterogeneity extended to the government itself, where the notorious factionalism of the French court often generated pamphlets designed to mobilize opposition to a particular minister. Much of what passed for "public opinion" in eighteenth-century France was not the spontaneous expression of popular attitudes, but originated in pamphlets, café gossip, and street rumors

---

[18] Louis-Sébastien Mercier, *Tableau de Paris* (Amsterdam, 1782–83), III:282, IV:135.
[19] On this point see Gunn, *Queen of the World*, 282.

instigated by factions at court.[20] But if "public opinion" was in practice anything but a unitary phenomenon, the absence of institutions that could legitimately claim to represent it allowed divergent groups to invoke its authority. Lacking the legitimizing agency of representative government, each of them was all the more compelled to depict public opinion as unitary and indivisible. To some extent, as François Furet observed, this tendency proceeded logically out of an absolutist political culture in which a single individual, the king, had traditionally claimed the sole authority to speak for the nation as a whole. In Britain, where parliament accommodated a diverse range of economic and social interests, there was a greater tendency to conceive of public opinion in plural terms. In the 1730s, when the term first began to appear regularly in British political writing, supporters of the Walpole ministry countered the opposition's claims to speak for public opinion with a critique that rings almost postmodern in its nominalism. Typifying this stance was the pro-government writer in the London *Daily Courant*, who in 1731 attacked the opposition for basing its legitimacy on "a Rule wholly chimerical, the imaginary Opinion of a vague and indeterminate Publick, which can be no ways ascertained or collected."[21]

The existence of a relatively unfettered press is another reason why British usages were more inclined to define public opinion as plural in composition. Since the early eighteenth century, British readers had been accustomed to an array of newspapers and political journals expressing a wide spectrum of viewpoints. By comparison, the indigenous press in France was much more uniform in tone. At first glance the French periodical press seems to have experienced impressive growth, with the number of periodicals increasing more than fourfold between 1720 and 1800 (see below).[22]

1720–29	40
1740–49	90
1770–79	148
1790–99	167

But only a tiny fraction of these – never more than four or five – carried political news prior to the Revolution, and the overwhelming majority dealt with literary, philosophical, and scientific topics. This paucity of

[20] See Jeremy Popkin, "Pamphlet Journalism at the End of the Old Regime," *Eighteenth-Century Studies* 22 (1989), 358–59.
[21] Quoted in J. A. W. Gunn, "Court Whiggery – Justifying Innovation," in Gordon J. Schochet, ed., *Politics, Politeness, and Patriotism*, Folger Institute Center for the History of Political Thought, 4 (Washington, DC, 1993), 140.
[22] Harris, *Politics and the Rise of the Press*, 56.

printed political news is all the more striking when one considers that London alone boasted eighteen newspapers by 1746. Circulation figures are even more telling: while weekly sales of British newspapers averaged 340,000 in 1780, a generous estimate finds a corresponding figure in France of 80,000–90,000. This disparity is all the more glaring given that the total population of Great Britain was only one-third that of France and its urban population less than half.[23]

The relative scarcity of French newspapers was largely the result of a system of royal censorship dating back to Cardinal Richelieu. Richelieu imposed precensorship on most publications and made the printing trade more amenable to royal control through the creation of privileges and monopolies. This censorship regime temporarily collapsed during the civil wars of the Fronde, but Louis XIV subsequently imposed even stricter controls by establishing the Office of the Book Trade as the central organ of censorship. This bureau worked closely with the Paris Book Guild, the small group of licensed publishers who enjoyed a legal monopoly on the production and distribution of all material printed in Paris. Outside of the capital, provincial publishing guilds exercised an analogous monopoly in their respective towns and cities. The Paris guild as well as its provincial counterparts cooperated with the government by inspecting book cargoes and bookshops and seizing printed material that royal censors deemed harmful to the crown, the church, or public morals. On paper the penalties were harsh. In 1757 the crown decreed the death sentence for anyone who wrote, commissioned, published, or distributed "writings which tend to attack religion, excite spirits, injure royal authority, and trouble the order and tranquility of the state."[24] In practice the system was more flexible and porous. Between 1659 and 1789 only 941 individuals – on average fewer than 7 per year – actually suffered incarceration in the Bastille for offenses related to the book trade. Relatively few works were condemned outright and burned by the public hangman in the courtyard of Paris's Palais de justice, as prescribed by law. During the two decades preceding the Revolution, for example, the number of condemned books and pamphlets averaged less than five per year.[25] The system also rested heavily on the discretion of the censors themselves, who were sometimes men of enlightened views. The censorship regime of Malesherbes (1750–63),

---

[23] *Ibid.*, 59–60.
[24] Quoted in Raymond Birn, "Malesherbes and the Call for a Free Press," in Robert Darnton and Daniel Roche, eds., *Revolution in Print: The Press in France 1775–1800* (Berkeley and Los Angeles, 1989), 51.
[25] Daniel Roche, "Censorship and the Publishing Industry," in Darnton and Roche, eds., *Revolution in Print*, 23–24, and in the same volume, Robert Darnton, "Philosophy under the Cloak", 27.

under whose tacit protection the *Encyclopédie* was allowed to circulate and who eased restrictions on the importation of foreign newspapers and journals, was especially known for its liberality. Moreover, clandestine publishers and smugglers inside and outside France often showed remarkable ingenuity and persistence in evading detection and arrest. The illicit book trade played a crucial role in the diffusion of Enlightenment writings, and the *Nouvelles ecclésiastiques* (1728–1803), the leading organ of the Jansenist opposition, maintained a secret network of publication and distribution inside the kingdom that royal agents were never able to eradicate.

But if royal censorship was anything but omnipotent, the fact that no more than four or five political papers published in France ever circulated at any time in Paris prior to the Revolution is evidence of the monarchy's relatively successful containment of political journalism. Old Regime France had only one daily, the *Journal de Paris*, and its format tended in any case to be more cultural than political. Up until 1778, in fact, the official news organ of the monarchy, the *Gazette de France* (founded under Richelieu's direction in 1631), held a royal monopoly on the publication of political news. Although the *Gazette*'s coverage of foreign news was reasonably neutral and balanced, information on domestic affairs centered almost exclusively on the ceremonial life of the king and his court. Political conflict and controversy were absent from its pages, and its presentation of politics was fundamentally official and static.[26] In 1778 the *Gazette*'s monopoly was purchased by Charles Joseph Pankcoucke, the wealthy Parisian press baron who assumed editorial control of the newspaper in 1786. Pankcoucke also established two other papers, the *Journal de Genève* and the *Journal de Bruxelles* (despite their titles both were published in France), with identical political sections. *The Journal général de France*, which began publication in 1784, also carried political news.

Like the *Gazette*, all licensed Parisian papers – if they carried political news at all – presented an image of royal authority as absolute and uncontested. During the pre-revolutionary period (1787–89), pamphlets rather than newspapers served as the journalistic forum for debates leading up to the convocation of the Estates-General in 1789. The provincial press was no different. Up to 1759, the crown had placed tight restrictions on the publication of provincial newspapers. Nine emerged in the decade following Malesherbes's relaxation of these restrictions in 1759, ten more were established between 1772 and 1777, and by 1788 forty-four provincial

---

[26] Jeremy Popkin, "The Prerevolutionary Origins of Political Journalism," in Baker, ed., *Political Culture of the Old Regime*, 207.

papers were being published in the kingdom. Most tended to avoid political news, however, even on the eve of the Revolution, when they published mainly poetry, book reviews, and articles on science, medicine, and local history.[27]

By far the best source of published news on domestic politics lay outside the kingdom. Foreign papers like the *Gazette de Leyde* in Holland, the *Courier du Bas-Rhin* in Germany, and Simon-Nicolas-Henri Linguet's *Annales civiles, politiques, et littéraires* in Brussels helped compensate for the scarcity of domestic news presented in the indigenous French press. The initial impetus behind the growth of an extraterritorial French-language press had been Louis XIV's expulsion of French Protestants (Huguenots) in 1685, which fostered the formation of a Francophone journalistic diaspora just beyond the borders of the kingdom. Smuggled into the monarchy clandestinely or tacitly permitted entry under more lax royal censors, these newspapers were the closest thing to a genuine political press to be found in France. Prior to the 1750s the French government had allowed only five to circulate in the monarchy, and those at an expensive price. Malesherbes eased these restrictions and by 1780 nine foreign newspapers were legally circulating in France at more affordable prices.

Foreign papers like the *Gazette de Leyde* gave readers an image of the French monarchy very different from that presented in the licensed domestic press. During the Maupeou crisis of 1771–74, for example, the *Gazette* presented sympathetic accounts of parlementary resistance, and in 1787–88 they were a forum for attacks on Calonne (finance minister from 1783–87) by his domestic critics. Depicting a realm riven by political opposition and controversy, such reportage stood in stark contrast to the static and tranquil image of the monarchy presented in the *Gazette de France*.[28] The importance of the extraterritorial press as a source of political information inside France is a reminder of the extent to which the media that shaped literate opinion in Enlightenment Europe were often trans-national in origin. The public sphere of print was never exclusively national in character, especially in France, where a relatively centralized regime of censorship often forced writers and editors to publish their work abroad. Indeed, as Elizabeth Eisenstein has pointed out, almost every major work of the French Enlightenment first appeared outside of France.

Still, even these extraterritorial enclaves of press freedom were not immune to official interference and control. By relaxing restrictions on the circulation of foreign periodicals in 1759, the crown was able to exercise

[27] Harris, *Politics and the Rise of the Press*, 56–57.
[28] Popkin, "Prerevolutionary Origins of Political Journalism," 207–10.

considerable leverage on reportage from abroad. If a foreign newspaper published articles consistently critical of French foreign and domestic policies, the government could retaliate by banning its circulation and depriving the paper of a lucrative market. Conversely, the crown could influence coverage by giving a foreign gazette preferential treatment in the form of lower postal fares or the suppression of competitors. Ministers of the crown also shaped foreign reporting by feeding newspapers information that cast their policies in a more favorable light. That was of course a game that opponents could play, and on the eve of the Revolution oppositional factions at the French court regularly supplied information to foreign journalists in an effort to undermine the Calonne ministry.

Despite the availability of political news in foreign newspapers, there is little doubt that French subjects enjoyed considerably less access to printed political news than their British counterparts. France had fewer newspapers and substantially lower rates of circulation, and apart from brief periods of liberalization, the crown enjoyed substantial success in muting press criticism. If, then, British journalism acquired increasing autonomy over the course of the eighteenth century, the French periodical press was more tightly regulated on the eve of the Revolution than it had been half a century earlier.

French subjects, of course, had other sources of political information besides newspapers. The requirements of eighteenth-century state-building tended by their very nature to undermine the efforts of any government to shroud itself in a cloak of secrecy. As the scope of state activity widened, and as the fiscal and administrative exigencies of war necessitated an increasingly activist style of rulership, government was becoming less secret, less mysterious, and more visible. At the highest levels of government, the sheer growth of the court militated against absolutist secrecy. Louis XIV's Versailles may have employed as many as 20,000 people, for example, and so many eyes and ears made the French court anything but hermetically sealed. From high-ranking ministers down to the servants who drove their coaches or served them at table, the expansion of the court broadened the circle of individuals with access to its secrets and mysteries. The subaltern clerks who chatted indiscreetly in cafés and taverns, the liverymen who impressed their fellows by sharing kernels of information gleaned from the conversations of their masters, the gossip that ministerial rivals exchanged in private letters or in the corridors of Versailles, all made the walls of the court highly permeable.

Court factions were an especially important vehicle for the outflow of information and gossip. Although the crown may have presented its will as unitary and indivisible, factions were a structural component of court politics right up to the Revolution. The treacherous politics of court intrigue were an arcane and opaque affair, all the more so because a courtier's political survival depended on the ability to conceal his motives, opinions, and alliances. La Bruyère, the seventeenth-century moralist, observed that "a man who knows the court is master of his gestures, of his eyes and face; he is profound, smiles at his enemies, constrains his moods, disguises his passions, goes against his better feelings, speaks and acts against his sentiments. . . ."[29] Knowledge was power in a world where dissimulation was a cardinal principle of behavior, and the opacity of court society tended by its very logic to generate information that rendered its political workings more transparent. Spies, routinely employed by ministers, factions, and foreign courts, were one vehicle. For provincial officials and elites whose careers depended upon a knowledge of what went on at court, or for those who simply hungered for news and gossip, handwritten newsletters were also a coveted source of clandestine information. The authors of these sheets did a thriving business in eighteenth-century France, despite repeated efforts by the crown to suppress them. Parisian newshawkers often maintained extensive networks of informers, ranging from tavern-keepers and domestics in great households to agents abroad who forwarded news from foreign papers. They were sometimes assisted by the notorious corruption of the French postal service, whose clerks could be bribed to supply news and gossip intercepted in private and official correspondence. Other newshawkers were in the pay of the government, like the chevalier de Mouchy, who from the 1740s into the 1770s regularly supplied reports to the police. Mouchy was also a prominent source for Louis Petit de Bachaumont's *Mémoires secrets*, another newsletter and scandal sheet whose political and literary gossip remains a valuable source for historians of the period. Being handwritten and thus more resistant to royal censorship, manuscript newsletters circulated widely among prominent figures inside and outside the court. A 1708 inquiry, for example, found that recipients included the president of the Dijon *parlement*, the bishop of Montpellier, and the *intendant* of Burgundy.[30] Newsletters were notoriously unreliable in their accuracy, but even Louis XVI was known to read them and foreign rulers like Frederick II of Prussia subscribed to several on a regular basis.

But what of the common people, who had less access to printed or handwritten sources of political news? It is likely that even the most humble subjects of the crown were more informed about political affairs than might otherwise have been expected. Wars accelerated the flow of political

---

[29] Quoted in Campbell, *Power and Politics in Old Regime France*, 69.

[30] Joseph Klaits, *Printed Propaganda under Louis XIV: Absolute Monarchy and Public Opinion* (Princeton, 1976), 51–53.

information. The fiscal sacrifices and material hardships imposed by war led even the most zealous guardians of royal secrecy to acknowledge the obligation of kings to explain to their subjects their reasons for fighting. Jean de La Chapelle, a royalist propagandist under Louis XIV, declared that kings were obliged "to inform their subjects of major resolutions whose consequences will be felt throughout the world," while Joachim Legrand, another hired pen of the Sun King, likewise argued that rulers were morally bound to explain to their subjects the reasons for going to war: "It is not enough that the actions of kings be always accompanied by justice and reason. Their subjects must also be convinced of it, particularly when wars are undertaken which, although just and necessary, nearly always bring much misery in their wake."[31] In addition to published manifestoes, the crown also used the pulpit as a vehicle for disseminating information about military and diplomatic events. The *Te Deum* mass, for example, traditionally called to commemorate royal births and marriages, had by the eighteenth century become an occasion for announcing important military developments. Royal letters composed expressly for the occasion were sent out to bishops and archbishops, who then circulated copies among the parish clergy of their dioceses with instructions that the letters be read aloud to their assembled congregations. Sometimes the letters explained the king's reasons for declaring a war and called upon his subjects to pray for victory, while others provided detailed descriptions of military triumphs and enjoined their audience to give thanks. The *Te Deum* combined information and royal propaganda: letters written for the thirty-two *Te Deum* masses called by Louis XV during France's participation (1744–47) in the War of the Austrian Succession not only gave detailed accounts of the progress of the war; composed in the first person, the king's epistles repeatedly referred to "my state," "my armies," "my conquests," or "my efforts."[32] This use of the personal pronoun served to emphasize France's status as an absolute monarchy, and the religious setting in which the letters were read lent the king's words an aura of gravity and sanctity. The patriotic tone must also have served to cultivate in their audience a sense of participating in events on a broader political stage, as well as an awareness of membership in a larger political community.

But these "ceremonies of information" were royal monologues, *ad hoc* and intermittent. They could not compare with the regular and sustained debates on policy found in eighteenth-century Britain, where the relatively open discussion of public affairs both inside and outside parliament

---

[31] Quoted in *ibid.*, 200, 248.
[32] Michèle Fogel, *Les cérémonies de l'information dans la France de XVIe au XVIIIe siècle* (Paris, 1989), 329.

yielded a more fluid and transparent circulation of political information. To be sure, the polemics of opposition politicians like Bolingbroke or Wilkes bristled with allusions to sinister cabals and secret influence in government. But their rhetoric was powerful and compelling precisely because it articulated a vision of transparency and openness widely shared in British political culture, one to which even a court politician like Walpole felt bound at least to pay lip service. In France's absolutist regime, on the other hand, secrecy was not a political aberration but a normative principle of government. Although the assumptions on which this principle had been based increasingly unraveled amidst the bitter controversies over the religious and financial policies of the French crown, it affected public discourse at every level of society.

In a regime that elevated secrecy to the status of a political principle, restricted the circulation of political information in the press, and lacked the sustained dialogue between government and subject made possible through the institutionalized openness of representative government, rumor was an endemic feature of political culture. Rumor was the natural offshoot of a political culture rooted in secrecy, since the regime's efforts to preserve the opacity of its operations made it difficult to confirm or contradict any version of an event – all the more so because the slow pace of communication meant that considerable time was required before false or uncertain reports could be disproved or clarified. Rumors were the medium through which subjects discerned meaning in their political world, and they were interwoven into the discourse of daily life: rumors in August of 1721 that the boy-king Louis XV was being poisoned by his regent; a rumor in December of 1723 that a Great Dane had devoured the regent's heart as it was about to be interred; a rumor in September of 1729 that the poll tax would be suspended following the birth of the dauphin; a rumor in January of 1762 that the king had been assassinated; rumors in August of 1773 that a priest had impregnated the daughter of a parlementary magistrate. "Paris," wrote the Paris police commissioner Dubuisson, "is the place where one can learn more than anywhere else in the world, and where what one learns is less reliable than anywhere else in the world."[33]

Allegations of conspiracy were often involved, above all in the rumors that circulated in times of famine. In every major subsistence crisis of the eighteenth century, substantial numbers of French subjects believed that grain shortages resulted not from bad weather but from a sinister plot to

---

[33] Quoted in Arlette Farge, *Subversive Words: Public Opinion in Eighteenth-Century France*, trans. Rosemary Morris (University Park, Pa., 1995), 26.

starve the people.[34] The cast of villains varied, but they often involved a
royal minister or even the king. Rumors circulating during the famine of
1725–26 held that the ministry of the duc de Bourbon had taken over the
grain trade and then engineered a rise in prices in order to raise money for
the Treasury. During the subsistence crises of 1738–41, rumors of artificially induced dearth revolved around charges that Orry, the controller-
general of finances, had manipulated the market in collusion with grain
monopolists. Other rumors charged the king with involvement, either for
reasons of personal aggrandizement or to fill the coffers of the crown. In
1747 famine was blamed on the controller-general, Machault, who it was
alleged had bought up surplus grain in order to enrich speculators and
financiers close to the government. During the so-called "Flour War" of
1775, when riots erupted throughout the Paris region in the wake of the
shortages that followed the government's efforts to deregulate the grain
trade, the controller-general Turgot countered attacks on his policies with
a conspiracy theory of his own: the embattled minister blamed the riots
on a plot orchestrated by provisioning companies which, he claimed, his
policies of economic liberalization were putting out of business.

Hence rumor and allegations of conspiracy were structures of belief
pervading all levels of French society. As Kaplan has shown, not only the
common people subscribed to the famine plot persuasion but also magistrates, government ministers, even members of the royal family. It would
be a mistake to attribute the predisposition for conspiracy theories to simple credulity or paranoia. Rumors carried such force in the political culture of the Old Regime precisely because of their verisimilitude. Rumors
that a parish priest had deflowered the daughter of a saddlemaker may
have been false, but there *were* priests who seduced their female parish-
ioners. Suspicions that a famine had been artificially precipitated may
have been unfounded, but examples of corrupt officials and unscrupulous grain speculators were sufficiently abundant to render such rumors
plausible. The conviction that an official account of an event concealed
what actually occurred may have been groundless, but suspicions that
the government was withholding information were understandable in a
regime that had traditionally deemed secrecy an indispensable element
of rulership.

Here again, the differences between France and Britain are revealing.
Not that rumor or suspicions of conspiracy were absent from British political culture. Quite the contrary: in 1776 American colonists justified

---

[34] See Steven L. Kaplan, *The Famine Plot Persuasion in Eighteenth-Century France*, Transactions of the American Philosophical Society, 72 (Philadelphia, 1982).

their revolt as the legitimate response to a conspiracy by the king and his
ministers to destroy their liberties, and in England itself charges of government cabals and secret influence were part and parcel of oppositional
rhetoric in the 1760s and 1770s. As in France, furthermore, the innumerable crowd actions that accompanied periods of rising bread prices were
also fueled by the popular conviction that grain shortages were artificially
induced.[35] But these actions differed from their French counterparts in
one important respect: while in France almost every major famine in the
eighteenth century was accompanied by widespread suspicion of government complicity, in England popular suspicion appears to have been
directed exclusively at local or regional targets – grain dealers, millers,
exporters, or, occasionally, bakers. English crowds may have faulted the
crown for failing to fulfill its paternalistic duty of regulating prices and
provisioning in times of shortage, but one does not find accusations, so
common in eighteenth-century France, that the crown or its ministers
had deliberately created the shortages for personal enrichment or to fill
state coffers.

This difference is important, for it goes to the heart of how French
and British subjects viewed their respective governments. Issues of grain
supply and provisioning affected every aspect of eighteenth-century society. Most people in the eighteenth century obtained the bulk of their
calories from grain, and by far the largest percentage of their household
incomes went to obtain it. It was a source of employment and income
for vast numbers of people and a major source of revenue for the state.
Grain, then, was a political issue, and how people explained and reacted
to dearth was a key index of a regime's legitimacy. So why did the famine
plot persuasion lack the broader political dimension in Britain that it had
in France?

A chronic weakness of French absolutism, namely the low level of
public confidence in its fiscal operations, was partly responsible. During the major subsistence crises that afflicted France from the Regency

---

[35] See E. P. Thompson's classic essay, "The Moral Economy of the English Crowd in the
Eighteenth Century," recently republished in Thompson, *Customs in Common: Studies in
Traditional Popular Culture* (New York, 1993). On the preoccupation with conspiracy in
the eighteenth-century Anglo-American world, see Gordon S. Wood, "Conspiracy and
the Paranoid Style: Causality and Deceit in the Eighteenth Century," *William and Mary
Quarterly* 39 (1982). Timothy Tackett, "Conspiracy Obsession in a Time of Revolution:
French Elites and the Origins of the Terror, 1789–1792," *American Historical Review* 105
(2000), 711, goes so far as to argue that "the 'paranoid style' was probably much less in
evidence among the educated classes in France than in England and North America."
Here Tackett is at any rate careful to distinguish (p. 709) between the beliefs of France's
educated classes and those of "a [French] popular culture permeated with fears of plots
and conspiracies and less touched by the rational scepticism of the Enlightenment."

up to the end of the Old Regime, allegations of government conspiracy were inextricably linked to distrust of the crown's fiscal policies. In the dearth of 1725–26, for example, rumors flourished in Paris cafés that the crown had preferred to pay off one of its bankers through speculative ventures in the grain trade rather than to risk the unpopularity of additional tax levies. Similar allegations circulated during the shortage of 1738–41, when rumors blamed Cardinal Fleury for creating dearth in order to reduce a deficit of 40,000,000 livres incurred by military and naval expenses. Whether or not such allegations were true (and there are historians who have contended that famine plots did indeed exist in eighteenth-century France) is beside the point. What gave them such resonance and virulence was their plausibility. The indebtedness of the monarchy was notorious, and the crown did in fact resort to all manner of surreptitious maneuvering to meet the demands of its creditors. At the same time, rumors implicating the crown or its ministers were all the more virulent owing to their unverifiability. The opacity of the monarchy's fiscal operations accounts for why even royal officials, such as the royal police lieutenant D'Argenson in 1740, or Turgot in 1775, could suspect some degree of government complicity.

The lack of public confidence in the fiscal integrity of the French crown placed it at a serious disadvantage relative to its British rival. Already in the eighteenth century, observers (including Necker) were arguing that Britain's success in financing the costs of war and imperial expansion rested on the high level of public confidence in its financial operations. The relative transparency of the government's fiscal policies did much to create this trust. The collection of taxes in England was more centralized and hence more subject to oversight by the royal treasury, while the introduction of any tax measure was accompanied by extensive debate in the Commons as well as in the press. Governmental officials submitted detailed reports on why a tax was necessary, how it was be collected, and the revenues it would yield. Trade and manufacturing lobbies opposed to a tax likewise submitted data, either in the press or in parliamentary petitions, supporting their opposition to it. All of this meant that by the time a tax was imposed, it had been sufficiently discussed to defuse public suspicions about its legitimacy. The American colonies, where parliamentary authority to levy taxes was contested beginning in the 1760s, were an obvious exception. But overall the British government experienced little of the stubborn, sometimes violent, opposition to taxes that the French crown confronted. The relative transparency of the British fisc bolstered the financial credibility of the crown, and inspired confidence among the taxpayers and foreign and domestic investors on whom the state depended to finance its wars and the expansion of its empire.

In France, by contrast, taxation remained a perennial source of tension between the crown and its subjects. It was not that the French bore a higher fiscal burden relative to British subjects. On the contrary, by the 1780s per capita taxation was three times higher in England than in France.[36] The problem lay rather in the impenetrability of the French fiscal system. There was no conduit, either institutionally or in the press, through which fiscal information was made available or discussed in a public forum. The fact that the collection of taxes was entrusted to a private corporation, the Farmers-General, made any kind of public oversight over French finances even more difficult. It is noteworthy that at the end of the Seven Years War, when the crisis of confidence occasioned by France's defeat provoked an intense public debate on tax reform, agreement was lacking on even the most basic fiscal data. Estimates of the royal debt, for example, ranged from 1.2 to 2.4 billion livres. This absence of information was to be expected in a regime that considered the royal budget a *secret du roi*, and which in 1759 consigned an obscure Swiss writer to the Bastille for circulating a manuscript listing the purported income and expenditures of the monarchy. Appalled by Necker's publication of the royal budget in 1781, the foreign minister Vergennes expressed the traditional adherence to the principle of fiscal secrecy when he lamented that the *Compte rendu* followed "the example of England, which publishes its accounts – an example for which Your Majesty's ancestors have shown such considerable and well-justified aversion."[37] The bitter debates over the accuracy of the *Compte rendu*, the fact that fundamental budgetary data could be the source of profound disagreement at the highest levels of royal government, is potent testimony to what Necker called the "darkness and obscurity" of the French financial system. Not for nothing did the surname of a mid-eighteenth-century French finance minister, Étienne de Silhouette, come to designate figures with dark interiors, opaque within and discernible only in their bare outlines.[38]

In the Revolution, observed the late François Furet, "the idea of plot . . . served as a reference point for organising and interpreting action. It was the notion that mobilised men's convictions and beliefs, and made it possible at every point to elaborate an interpretation and justification of what had happened."[39] Lynn Hunt and Timothy Tackett have likewise

---

[36] John Brewer, *The Sinews of Power: War, Money and the English State, 1688–1783* (Cambridge, Mass., 1988), 89.

[37] Quoted in Hardman, *French Politics 1774–1789*, 239.

[38] Cf. James C. Riley, *The Seven Years War and the Old Regime in France: The Financial and Economic Toll* (Princeton, 1986), 154.

[39] François Furet, *Interpreting the French Revolution*, trans. Elborg Forster (Cambridge, 1978), 53.

emphasized the centrality of plot in the revolutionary imagination.[40] Indeed, from the "Great Fear" in the summer of 1789, when peasants throughout France took up arms against an imaginary conspiracy of brigands and aristocrats, to the conclusion of the Terror in July of 1794, when Robespierre ascended the guillotine for allegedly plotting against the Republic, the language of conspiracy incited and justified the rising spiral of revolutionary and counterrevolutionary violence. For Furet this obsession with plot and conspiracy was a new phenomenon, the bastard offspring of a revolutionary consciousness for which public and open opposition to the popular will was unimaginable. According to the logic of revolutionary ideology, argued Furet, the opponents of the Revolution were morally evil, their designs were never transparent but always hidden, secret, conspiratorial.

Furet was surely correct in pointing to the importance of plot and conspiracy in the revolutionary imagination. But he was certainly wrong in viewing the idea of the plot as a revolutionary invention. Though more violent in its consequences and intensified by the moral absolutism of Jacobin ideology, the revolutionary tendency to view events through the lenses of plot and conspiracy had its roots in patterns of belief originating out of the political culture of the Old Regime. A willingness to believe in hidden motives and surreptitious actions, a readiness to perceive duplicity, an inclination to suspect that the surface appearance of an event concealed deeper layers of meaning, were less the perverted offspring of revolutionary ideology than the inverted expression of absolutist secrecy. During the final decades of the Old Regime, as the new absolutist politics of publicity came to be juxtaposed with a traditional absolutist politics of secrecy, the resulting tensions proved too explosive for the monarchy to accommodate. The monarchy's misfortune was that its style of rulership was too public to evade scrutiny, but also too opaque to inspire confidence.

Bibliographical note

Keith Baker's *Inventing the French Revolution: Essays on French Political Culture in the Eighteenth Century* (Cambridge, 1991) is a brilliant analysis of the Old Regime's ideological underpinnings and their transmutation in the eighteenth century. Baker describes the rise of a political public sphere chiefly through the prism of political discourse; Roger Chartier's readable synthesis, *The Cultural Origins of the French Revolution*, trans. Lydia G. Cochrane (Durham, NC, 1991), is more concerned with modes of sociability and the ways in which ideas and texts were appropriated by their audience. On the differences in their approaches, see

---

[40] Lynn Hunt, *Politics, Culture, and Class in the French Revolution* (Berkeley, 1984), 13; Tackett, "Conspiracy Obsession in a Time of Revolution," 692.

the exchange between Baker and Chartier in "Dialogue sur l'espace public: Keith Michael Baker, Roger Chartier," *Politix: travaux de science politique* 26 (1994). On the concept of public opinion in eighteenth-century France, see J. A. W. Gunn, *Queen of the World: Opinion in the Public Life of France from the Renaissance to the Revolution*, Studies on Voltaire and the Eighteenth Century, 328 (Oxford, 1955); Gunn, "Public Opinion," in Terence Bell *et al.*, eds., *Political Innovation and Cultural Change* (Cambridge, 1989); and Mona Ozouf, "'Public Opinion' at the End of the Old Regime," *Journal of Modern History* 60 (1988). Also insightful on the problem of public opinion is Thomas E. Kaiser, "The Abbé de Saint-Pierre, Public Opinion, and the Reconstitution of the French Monarchy," and "Money, Despotism, and Public Opinion in Early Eighteenth-Century France: John Law and the Debate on Royal Credit," respectively in vols. 55 (1983) and 63 (1991) of the *Journal of Modern History*.

Baker emphasizes the importance of the 1750s, when disputes over the refusal of sacraments to Jansenist dissenters escalated into a more general "politics of contestation" in which various participants in the dispute (including the crown itself) sought to legitimate their claims through appeals to public opinion. Much of the scholarship on Jansenism, however, points to the 1720s and the 1730s as the crucial decades in this process. See Arlette Farge, *Subversive Words: Public Opinion in Eighteenth-Century France*, trans. Rosemary Morris (University Park, PA 1995), as well as the detailed discussion in Peter R. Campbell, *Power and Politics in Old Regime France 1720–1745* (London, 1996). On the convulsionary phenomenon, see Robert Kreiser, *Miracles, Convulsions, and Ecclesiastical Politics in Early Eighteenth-Century Paris* (Princeton, 1978). My analysis has above all relied on the pioneering work of Dale Van Kley on the political and constitutional significance of French Jansenism. A concise summary of his arguments can be found in his "Jansenist Constitutional Legacy in the French Prerevolution," in Keith Michael Baker, ed., *The French Revolution and the Creation of Modern Political Culture*, vol. I: *The Political Culture of the Old Regime* (Oxford and New York, 1987). See further, Van Kley, *Religious Origins of the French Revolution: From Calvin to the Civil Constitution, 1560–1791* (New Haven, 1996); Van Kley, *The Damiens Affair and the Unraveling of the "Ancien Régime," 1750–1770* (Princeton, 1984); and Van Kley, *The Jansenists and the Expulsion of the Jesuits from France, 1757–1765* (New Haven, 1975). David Bell's *Lawyers and Citizens: The Making of a Political Elite in Old Regime France* (New York and Oxford, 1994) is excellent on the legal profession as an agent of Jansenist oppositional ideology.

Jansenism had waned as a source of domestic conflict by the 1770s, but the issues of food provisioning, finances, and royal justice continued to galvanize popular opinion and opposition from the *parlements*. On the politics of bread, I have based my discussion on Steven L. Kaplan's *Bread, Politics, and Political Economy in the Reign of Louis XV*, 2 vols. (The Hague, 1976) and especially his *The Famine Plot Persuasion in Eighteenth-Century France*, Transactions of the American Philosophical Society, 72 (Philadelphia, 1982). James C. Riley's *The Seven Years War and the Old Regime in France: The Financial and Economic Toll* (Princeton, 1986) examines the fiscal problems facing the crown. On the parliamentary opposition see, most recently, Julian Swann, *Politics and the Parlement of Paris under Louis XV, 1754–1774* (Cambridge and New York, 1995), and the older study by Jean Egret,

Louis XV et l'opposition parlementaire, 1715–1774 (Paris, 1970). The Maupeou era is examined in Durand Echeverria, *The Maupeou Revolution: A Study in the History of Libertarianism. France, 1770–1774* (Baton Rouge and London, 1985).

Appealing to public opinion was not just an oppositional tactic, nor was the crown's use of propagandistic media anything new in the eighteenth century. Michèle Fogel's *Les cérémonies de l'information dans la France de XVIe au XVIIIe siècle* (Paris, 1989) provides interesting glimpses into how the early modern French crown publicized its policies. Peter Burke's *The Fabrication of Louis XIV* (New Haven, 1992) is a well-written and nicely illustrated study of public relations under Louis XIV, and Joseph Klaits, *Printed Propaganda under Louis XIV: Absolute Monarchy and Public Opinion* (Princeton, 1976) is good on the Sun King's use of print. By the 1770s, however, the fiscal crisis of the monarchy and the crucial importance that credit had assumed in royal finances gave public opinion unprecedented importance for the crown and its ministers. Robert D. Harris's *Necker, Reform Minister of the Old Regime* (Berkeley and Los Angeles, 1979) makes it clear how important public opinion had become to the crown by the 1770s. On attempts by Necker and his ministerial successors to revive provincial assemblies as a means of mobilizing public support for their policies, I have relied on Harris's study as well as P. M. Jones, *Reform and Revolution in France: The Politics of Transition, 1774–1791* (Cambridge, 1995) and Jean Egret, *The French Prerevolution 1787–1788*, trans. Wesley D. Camp (Chicago and London, 1977). The crown's relationship to public opinion at the end of the Old Regime is treated in John Hardman, *French Politics 1774–1789: From the Accession of Louis XVI to the Fall of the Bastille* (London and New York, 1995), ch. 12.

On politics and the French-language press, see the survey by Jack R. Censer, *The French Press in the Age of Enlightenment* (London, 1994). Jeremy Popkin has made important contributions to the subject: see, for example, his "Pamphlet Journalism at the End of the Old Regime," *Eighteenth-Century Studies* 22 (1989), and Popkin, *News and Politics in the Age of Revolution: Jean Luzac's Gazette de Leyde* (Ithaca, 1989). See also the anthology edited by Censer and Popkin, *Press and Politics in Pre-Revolutionary France* (Berkeley, 1987), as well as the essays in Claude Bellanger *et al.*, *Histoire générale de la presse française*, vol. I: *Des origines à 1814* (Paris, 1969). On royal censorship, see Robert Darnton, "Philosophy under the Cloak," and Daniel Roche, "Censorship and the Publishing Industry," both in Darnton and Roche, eds., *Revolution in Print: The Press in France 1775–1800* (Berkeley and Los Angeles, 1989). Elizabeth L. Eisenstein, *Grub Street Abroad: Aspects of the French Cosmopolitan Press from the Age of Louis XIV to the French Revolution* (Oxford, 1992), emphasizes the importance of the extraterritorial francophone press.

Part II

Readers, writers, and spectators

3   Reading publics: transformations of the literary public sphere

Reading publics had long existed as aggregates of readers. As a social and cultural act, however, reading underwent a fundamental transformation in the eighteenth century. Not only did the production of print rise significantly; what readers read also changed. Not only did more people read; people also read more. And as the quantitative and qualitative effects of these changes became increasingly evident to contemporaries, "the reading public" became an object of discussion, dissection, and debate. Even as Enlightenment writers and critics assigned this public unprecedented importance as an arbiter of taste, they also grappled with the intractable problem of how to shape, control, and even define it.

Literacy in the eighteenth century[1]

Literacy is notoriously difficult to measure or even define. Is it the ability to sign one's name? Read a newspaper? Understand a governmental regulation or comprehend a scholarly text? Part of the problem is that literacy is not one skill but a hierarchy of discrete ones. In early modern Europe these could include the capacity to read but not write, or conversely, the ability to sign one's name without knowing how to read a relatively simple text. In some cases reading was an extension of memory. Here individuals were able to "read" certain Biblical passages they had once memorized, but not others less familiar.

Compounding the problem are the limits of the sources. Historians have traditionally used the ability to sign one's name as an index of literacy. In France, where brides and grooms were required from 1686 on to sign the local parish register, efforts to estimate literacy rates on the basis of signatures date back to the late nineteenth century. Since then, historians of literacy have also tallied signatures on baptismal records, petitions, oaths, military conscription lists, or court depositions. Signatures are to

---

[1] For the sources from which I have derived the statistics cited in the section below, see the bibliographical essay at the end of this chapter, 119–20.

be sure a blunt instrument of measurement, for they tell us little about the spectrum of literacy skills possessed by any particular person. The ability to sign one's name did not always mean an individual could read, nor can illiteracy always be inferred from an inability to sign. Because women, for example, often learned to read without ever knowing how to write, counting signatures will necessarily yield a lower rate of female literacy. But for all their methodological shortcomings, signatures are the only universal standard of literacy historians have at their disposal. However rough an indicator, signatures provide a statistical constant through which scholars can make comparisons over time between different social groups and regions. Supplemented by other data, such as wills, household inventories, the availability of schooling, and the detailed if impressionistic observations of contemporaries, signatures shed at least some light on the expansion (or sometimes contraction) and distribution of literacy during the early modern period.

If, then, the ability to sign one's name is a reliable index of literacy, the aggregate data show a notable rise in the numbers of men and women able to read and write during the eighteenth century. In Scotland, literacy among adult males rose from approximately 25 percent in 1643 to 65 percent in the 1750s. Figures for England in the 1640s suggest a literacy rate for adult men of around 30 percent; by the mid-eighteenth century this percentage had grown to 60 percent, with a corresponding rate for adult females at around 35–40 percent. Statistics for France point to a similar rise. In 1686–90, only about 29 percent of men and 14 percent of women were able to sign their names in parish marriage registers; by 1786–90, the percentage had grown to 48 percent of men and 27 percent of women.

Although the figures for Germany are more scattered owing to the empire's political fragmentation, they too suggest expanding literacy. Indeed, despite conventional assumptions of Germany's "backwardness" in the eighteenth century, recent studies point to levels of literacy comparable to those in England and France. In Germany, as elsewhere, there was broad regional variation. In East Prussia, a heavily rural area of relatively low literacy, only 10 percent of peasant adult males could sign their names in 1750. This percentage grew to 25 percent in 1765 and by 1800 had reached around 40 percent. But in the Duchy of Oldenbourg in northwestern Germany, the signature rate ranged from around 80 percent (male) and 46 percent (female) in some districts to as high as 93 percent and 84 percent in others. Disputing Rudolf Schenda's contention that most Germans in the late eighteenth century were a "people without books," Hans Medick's analysis of inventories in the Swabian village of Laichingen between 1748 and 1820 shows that 550 out of

557 peasant households owned books. Moreover, the size of their libraries was surprisingly large, growing from a household average of approximately eleven books in 1748–51 to around fourteen in 1781–90. In urban areas, at least, literacy in Germany may actually have been higher than in France. In household inventories from Paris (*c.* 1750), Lyon (1750–1800), and Rouen (1785–89), the percentage that mention books are 22 percent, 35 percent, and 63 percent, respectively. Significantly higher were corresponding figures for the German towns of Frankfurt am Main, Speyer, and Tübingen, which around 1750 respectively totaled 77 percent, 88 percent, and 77 percent. As Étienne François has suggested in a study of Catholic schooling in the Rhineland, the Protestant–Catholic split may have encouraged a higher rate of literacy in the empire. Particularly in areas where Protestant and Catholic populations were mixed or adjoined each other, fears of losing adherents to the rival faith forced the competing confessions to establish schools and provide more extensive religious instruction. This cultural and confessional rivalry would help to explain why, for example, Catholic territories partly or wholly surrounded by Protestant ones, such as Trier or Würzburg, would have had higher literacy than confessionally more homogeneous regions like Brandenburg.

Still, the expansion of literacy in the eighteenth century was neither constant nor irreversible. In Provence, for example, literacy did not significantly rise between 1690 and 1740, and in some areas it even declined. Moreover, since the distribution of reading skills varied significantly according to region, national comparisons are not always meaningful. In France, literacy was higher in the more densely populated north than in the south, and in Germany the divide was between the more literate western half of the empire and the less literate eastern territories. Overall scholars have distinguished between a more literate northwest-European belt, consisting of northern France, western Germany, the Netherlands, and England, and a less literate zone that included southern France and eastern Germany.

To what extent was confession a determinant of literacy? Protestantism has often been associated with literacy because of its supposed stress on the importance of lay Bible-reading. Conversely, the distrust of lay Bible-reading often found in post-Tridentine Catholicism has likewise encouraged scholars to correlate literacy with Protestantism. As late as 1713, after all, the papal Bull *Unigenitus* had condemned the proposition that "the reading of scripture is for all." The relationship between confession and literacy is in fact more complex. Protestant reformers of the sixteenth century often expressed reservations about the indiscriminate promotion of Bible-reading among the laity. The spread of radical sects like the Anabaptists convinced some Protestant leaders of the need to restrict and control lay-Bible reading, and to rely instead on oral catechistic instruction as a safer tool of religious instruction. Lutheran school ordinances in Brandenburg-Prussia did not begin to emphasize reading until the late seventeenth century, and, throughout the Holy Roman Empire, exclusively oral forms of religious instruction remained common in Protestant as well as Catholic rural schools well into the eighteenth century.

The relationship between Protestantism and literacy is more direct in the case of the so-called "Second Reformation," which began with the rise of Puritanism in late sixteenth-century England. In the seventeenth century this second wave of reform spread to Protestant Germany in the form of Pietism, taking root especially in Prussia and Württemberg. Fueling the revival was the belief that the established Protestant churches had failed to fulfill the Reformation's spiritual promise. Exhibiting none of Protestantism's earlier ambivalence toward lay Bible-reading, proponents of a "Reformation in the Reformation" placed special emphasis on the reading of scripture. They sponsored schools and conventicles where scripture was discussed, and published devotional literature to be read in the household. In England the impact of Protestant dissenters on literacy is suggested by the Quakers. By the mid-eighteenth century the ability to sign marriage registers was universal among Quaker men and women, as compared with only 60 percent of the adult male population as a whole. In Germany the relationship between Pietism and the promotion of literacy is seen in the Canstein Bible House, a Pietist foundation in the Prussian town of Halle, which printed more than 400,000 cheap copies of the Bible and New Testament between 1712 and 1727. Pietist-inspired reformers were also behind state-sponsored efforts in Prussia (1763–65) and Austria (1774) on behalf of universal schooling.

But in Catholic Europe as well, attitudes toward lay literacy also changed. Confronted by the Protestant challenge, Catholic reformers increasingly came to view popular literacy as a necessary tool for propagating the faith. In France, the Brothers of the Christian Schools, a late Counter-Reformation order founded by Jean-Baptiste de la Salle at the end of the seventeenth century, established free schools teaching religion, reading, writing, and arithmetic to the urban poor. The spread of literacy in eighteenth-century France owed much to orders like the Brothers, and in areas passed over by the Counter Reformation (the Limousin plateaux of the Massif Central, for example) literacy remained decidedly lower. In eighteenth-century Austria, the heavily visual, theatrical, and non-literate orientation of Baroque piety came under increasing attack by Catholic reformers anxious to stem what they saw as the declining influence of the church at the popular level. Pleading that processions, pilgrimages, and cults of the saints or Virgin were no longer effective in guaranteeing the laity's adherence to the Catholic faith, these reformers called for a greater emphasis on literate media of religious instruction. In alliance with enlightened state officials, they proved a major force behind Maria Theresia's compulsory school edict of 1774. By 1781, when Joseph II decreed that "every common man should have a copy of the Bible," popular literacy had come to be accepted as a social good.

Hence the eighteenth century witnessed a convergence of Protestant and Catholic attitudes regarding the desirability of popular literacy. Whatever confessional constraints on literacy may have operated earlier, they progressively weakened after 1700. Rates of literacy could vary dramatically within both Catholic and Protestant regions, and the similarities between confessions are as striking as the differences. Aggregate literacy in Protestant England was roughly identical to that in northeastern France, for example, as was Protestant and Catholic literacy in western Germany along the Middle Rhine. The Catholic region of Haute-Vienne had one of the lowest literacy rates in eighteenth-century France, but so did the heavily Protestant Cévennes region to the southeast. Where significant differences in Catholic and Protestant literacy did exist, they were often the product of circumstances other than confession.

One determinant was the degree of urbanization. Literacy in towns and cities was generally more widespread than in the countryside. The rate of literacy among artisans in seventeenth-century London was two to three times higher than it was for their rural counterparts, while 69 percent of domestic servants in London could sign their names compared with only 24 percent in the countryside. Figures for France show a similar discrepancy: in the 1740s, 60 percent of urban men were literate as compared with only 35 percent of rural males (the respective figures for women were 40 percent and 13 percent). The superiority of town over country rested in part on the greater availability of schooling in urban areas. Also important was the higher concentration of professions and occupations requiring literacy, such as law, medicine, teaching, retail trade, and printing. In addition, urban inhabitants had more access to print culture through the presence of bookshops, libraries, and coffeehouses.

As we have seen, literacy also varied by sex. The discrepancy was widest when it came to writing ability, a skill considered less necessary for women. A higher percentage of women learned to read than to write, but there too men held a significant edge. In rural France during the 1740s only one out of eight women could read, as opposed to one out of three men. The gap between male and female literacy tended to narrow, however, the higher one advanced on the social scale. In the Rhineland town of Koblenz and the French city of Lyon, for example, upper-class women and men alike were almost universally literate by the end of the eighteenth century. The differences were more noticeable lower down on the social scale. Among day laborers in Koblenz, 47 percent of men and 28 percent of women could sign their names, while in Lyon the figures were 37 percent and 19 percent respectively.

Indeed, wealth and social position were probably the greatest determinants of literacy. Whether one was male or female, rural or town dweller, wealth lowered the obstacles to literacy posed by gender or geography. To be sure, the social spectrum of literacy had broadened since the sixteenth century, when literacy had generally been restricted to the noble, mercantile, and professional classes. During the following two centuries the ability to read and write percolated downward to include significant percentages of artisans and peasants. In early eighteenth-century Paris books were listed in only 13 percent of inventories compiled from the households of deceased journeymen, and by 1780 this figure had risen to 35 percent. Yet neither artisans nor peasants were undifferentiated strata, and literacy ranged widely within them. In seventeenth-century England, around 70 percent of highly skilled artisans such as goldsmiths and harness-makers were literate, but in most other trades the percentage dropped to about 50 percent and only around a quarter of building laborers, fishermen, and agricultural workers could sign their names. In rural Oldenbourg (Germany) around 1750, the gulf between prosperous peasants and their farm servants was deep: among adult males, 98 percent of the former were literate but only 53 percent of the latter. Virtually identical was the gap between large peasants and rural day laborers in the French village of Sailly-Labourse in Artois. There, during the period from 1761 to 1791, 95 percent of the former could sign the marriage register as opposed to 54 percent of the latter.

So while aggregate literacy rose in the eighteenth century, determinants such as region, urbanization, sex, and wealth shaped its distribution. Literacy was in general more common among men than women and more prevalent in towns than in the countryside, but property and wealth could neutralize those differences. Women as well as men made the "reading revolution," as will be seen later in this chapter.

The reading revolution

The spread of literacy in the eighteenth century both fueled and reflected an explosion of print culture. The sheer volume of published material increased dramatically, from books, newspapers, and periodicals down to broadsheets, handbills, and political cartoons. Much of what was produced differed little in format from what had been published during the previous century. Indeed, one effect of the eighteenth-century print revolution was to complete the work of the Protestant and Catholic Reformations by making Bibles and devotional manuals more available to broader segments of the population. The tendency among historians to view the Enlightenment as an era of secularization and "de-Christianization" has obscured this basic fact. The high-pitched polemical tracts spawned by the Jansenist controversy in France, the spiritual fervor of German Pietist literature, the rabid hostility to Catholicism that pervaded English journalism, attest to the enduring significance of religion in eighteenth-century print culture. The volume of religious works published in the eighteenth century did not shrink but grew, bringing to fruition earlier processes of confessionalization.

The weight of religious tradition was especially heavy in the countryside, where devotional works continued to make up the main part of peasant reading material. In the Württemberg village of Laichingen in southwestern Germany, 98.5 percent of the books listed in peasant inventories between 1748 and 1820 were religious in content. Devotional works predominated in urban households as well, although to a lesser degree. In Tübingen, 460 burgher inventories listed a total of 4,730 book titles in the decade between 1750 and 1760; of those, 3,891 (about 80 percent) dealt with religious subjects. Evidence from France yields a similar picture. An examination of 84 private libraries in western French towns between 1785 and 1789 showed that two-thirds consisted almost exclusively of religious literature.[2]

Traditional genres also made up much of the secular material published in the eighteenth century. Almanacs, which had flourished since the sixteenth century, were particularly popular in the countryside and offered readers everything from medical and agricultural advice to interest rates and astrological predictions. Some almanacs enjoyed sales that were enormous by eighteenth-century standards. In late eighteenth-century Germany, around 20,000 copies of the popular *Badische Landeskalender* were published each year. This print run was modest compared with the *Vox Stellarum*, a best-selling British almanac: 107,000 copies were printed

---

[2] Hans Medick, "Buchkultur und lutherischer Pietismus. Buchbesitz, erbauliche Lektüre und religiöse Mentalität in einer ländlichen Gemeinde Württembergs am Ende der frühen Neuzeit: Laichingen 1748–1820," in Rudolf Vierhaus *et al.*, eds., *Frühe Neuzeit – Frühe Moderne? Forschungen zur Vielschichtigkeit von Übergangsprozessen* (Göttingen, 1992), 301; Günther Erning, *Das Lesen und die Lesewut: Beiträge zur Fragen der Lesergeschichte* (Bad Heilbrunn, 1974), 38; Jean Quéniart, "Alphabetisierung und Leseverhalten der Unterschichten in Frankreich im 18. Jahrhundert," in Hans Ulrich Gumbrecht *et al.*, *Sozialgeschichte der Aufklärung in Frankreich*, vol. I (Munich and Vienna, 1981), 143–44.

in 1768, and by 1789 the number had risen to 220,000.[3] Also popular were small chapbooks containing traditional fables, romances, and adventure tales. In France these cheap pamphlets made up the so-called *bibliothèque bleue* (named after the blue paper in which they were bound), and were especially popular among peasants in the northeastern part of the kingdom. The content and format of the *bibliothèque bleue* changed little during the early modern period, and it has been estimated that 30–40 percent was religious in subject matter. The remainder was a hodge-podge of cooking and medicinal recipes, along with tales populated by heroes of popular legend like Fortunatus, Gargantua, and Till Eulenspiegel.[4]

But if traditional genres persisted, the print explosion of the eighteenth century was nonetheless marked by a fundamental transformation of reading tastes. Although an unprecedented number of Bibles, sermons, and other devotional works were published in the eighteenth century, they represented a declining percentage of the literary market as a whole. Catalogues of the Leipzig book fair, the largest book distribution center in eighteenth-century Germany, show a decline in the percentage of theological and devotional works from 38.5 percent in 1740 to 24.5 percent in 1770; by 1800, the percentage had further dropped to 13.5 percent. In France the decline occurred at a comparable rate. In the late seventeenth century religious titles had comprised around half of all books published in Paris. By the 1720s the percentage had dropped to one-third, by the 1750s to a fourth, and by the 1790s to one-tenth.[5]

Accompanying this falling proportion of religious works was a decline in the ratio of books published in Latin to those appearing in the vernacular. Early modern print culture had remained heavily Latinate up to the eighteenth century. Around 1600, for example, only 36 of 6,000 books in Oxford's Bodleian Library were in English. At the Leipzig and Frankfurt book fairs, the ratio of Latin to German books sold in 1650 was better than two to one. By 1700, however, Latin print culture was in visible retreat and would decline further over the next century. In Paris, the percentage of books published in Latin declined from 30 percent in 1600 to

---

[3] R. A. Houston, *Literacy in Early Modern Europe: Culture and Education 1500–1800* (London and New York, 1989), 185.

[4] Roger Chartier, "Livres bleus et lectures populaires," in Henri-Jean Martin and Roger Chartier, eds., *Histoire de l'édition française*, vol. II: *Le livre triomphant 1660–1830* (Paris, 1984), 498; Quéniart, "Alphabetisierung und Leseverhalten," 135–36; Houston, *Literacy in Early Modern Europe*, 199–200. For English counterparts, see Margaret Spufford, *Small Books and Pleasant Histories: Popular Fiction and its Readership in Seventeenth-Century England* (Athens, Georgia, 1981), 129–55.

[5] Rudolf Jentzsch, *Der deutsch-lateinische Büchermarkt nach den Leipziger Ostermesse-Katalogen von 1740, 1770, and 1800 in seiner Gliederung und Wandlung* (Leipzig, 1912), table 1; R. Chartier, *The Cultural Origins of the French Revolution*, trans. Lydia G. Cochrane (Durham, NC, 1991), 70–71.

Table 2 *Vernacular and Latin books in Germany, 1673–1800 (percentage)*

	1673	1690	1700	1740	1770	1800
German	42	63	62	72	86	96
Latin	58	37	38	28	14	4

Source: Jentzsch, *Der deutsch-lateinische Büchermarkt,* 333.

10 percent in 1700.[6] Table 2 above, based on the published catalogues of the Leipzig book fair, points to a slower but nonetheless constant decline in Germany.

But beyond these basic changes in the publishing market, there was also a transformation in how books were read. The social historian Rolf Engelsing characterized this change as a shift from "intensive" to "extensive" reading. At the beginning of the eighteenth century, the literary diet of most readers was limited to the repetitious consumption of a small number of texts. This practice of intensive reading partly reflected the relative inaccessibility of books for most households. Reading clubs and lending libraries did not yet exist, and books were simply not affordable for most households. A copy of Luther's German Bible of 1534 cost around a month's wages for an unskilled laborer. By the early eighteenth century he would have found the Bible somewhat less expensive, but it still would have consumed around a day and a half of a German artisan's earnings. In seventeenth- and eighteenth-century France, even a relatively cheap pamphlet from the *bibliothèque bleue* cost about 10 percent of a laborer's weekly income. Classics and "high" literature were prohibitively expensive for all but the wealthy. The price of Daniel Caspar von Lowenstein's baroque novel *Arminius and Thusnelda* (1689), for example, was roughly equal to the monthly salary of a German town clerk.[7]

Hence most literate households around 1700 owned at best only a few books, and these primarily religious in character. Here the predominance of intensive reading reflected its devotional setting. For most Christian households reading was neither a source of information about the outside world, nor an autonomous leisure activity, but rather a devotional aid. The act of reading served to confirm one's faith through the repetition of its precepts, which required only a limited number of texts. As a devotional

[6] Houston, *Literacy in Early Modern Europe,* 204; Alain Viala, *Naissance de l'écrivain: Sociologie de la littérature à l'âge classique* (Paris, 1985), 143.
[7] Richard Gawthrop and Gerald Strauss, "Protestantism and Literacy in Early Modern Germany," *Past and Present* 104 (1984), 40; Houston, *Literacy in Early Modern Europe,* 186; Reinhard Wittmann, *Geschichte des deutschen Buchhandels* (Munich, 1991), 106.

tool, moreover, reading was often a household and not a solitary activity. It might occur in the evenings or after church, when the head of the household read aloud to its members. The fact that reading was so often an oral and familial activity reinforced the practice of intensive reading, since reading aloud was slower than silent reading.

So in contrast with the more promiscuous modern reader, intensive readers tended to read the same book again and again. In 1690 the pious Madame Maintenon advised the staff of the convent school at Saint-Cyr: "Do not accustom them to a great diversity of readings; seven or eight books in use will suffice."[8] Perhaps taking heed of William Penn's advice to "keep but few books, well chosen and well read," Quakers who borrowed books from their meeting-house libraries in the late seventeenth century did so on an average of no more than once a year. An examination of household inventories in western French towns between 1725 and 1730 revealed that out of the 112 households which listed books, 36 had only one and 34 had from two to five.[9]

Intensive reading was not confined to the lower classes, but also prevailed among educated professionals. Laurentius Babst (d. 1672), a physician at the Dresden court, claimed to have read the Bible seventy-two times in thirty-seven years, while the Leipzig jurist Benedikt Carpzow (1565–1624) read it fifty-three times.[10] The intensive reading of a limited number of texts had been the rule at universities throughout the early modern period. Most students could afford a handful of books at best, and access to university libraries was often restricted to professors. As in medieval universities, professors in the early eighteenth century typically instructed their students by reading from or commenting on a text deemed authoritative on the subject. Their students then demonstrated proficiency by mastering the text and their professors' lectures on it. Not until the late eighteenth and early nineteenth centuries did this practice substantially change. By that time the principle behind the modern research university, namely, that academic study entails the extensive mastery of an ever-expanding body of scholarly literature, had begun to take root at German universities like Göttingen and Berlin.

[8] Quoted in Carolyn C. Lougee, *Le Paradis des Femmes: Women, Salons, and Social Stratification in Seventeenth-Century France* (Princeton, 1976), 192.

[9] Penn quoted in Roger Chartier, "The Practical Impact of Writing," in Chartier, ed., *A History of Private Life*, vol. III: *Passions of the Renaissance* (Cambridge, MA, and London, 1993), 133; statistics taken from Houston, *Literacy in Early Modern Europe*, 195, and Quéniart, "Alphabetisierung und Leseverhalten," 142.

[10] Rolf Engelsing, "Die Perioden der Lesergeschichte in der Neuzeit," *Archiv für Geschichte des Buchwesens*, 10 (1970), 966.

In the course of the eighteenth century, however, the act of reading became more mobile and variegated. The extensive reader moved among a greater variety of texts instead of returning repeatedly to the same ones. Intensive reading practices did not disappear – on the contrary, they probably remained the norm in the countryside well into the nineteenth century. Extensive reading did not replace intensive reading so much as supplement it, taking root among the traditionally literate strata of urban middle- and upper-class readers who had access to a greater variety of reading material. One index of the shift was a growth in the size of private libraries. In late seventeenth-century France, for example, the personal libraries of nobles and legal professionals ranged from 20 to 50 volumes. By the 1780s, a library of some 300 volumes was the norm for these groups. During the same period, the modal number of books owned by a member of the French clergy likewise grew from 20–50 volumes to between 100 and 300.[11]

James Boswell's classic biography of Samuel Johnson gives an intimate glimpse into the reading practices of a man who was probably the most extensive reader of his age (Adam Smith quipped that Johnson knew more books than any man alive). Boswell describes his rooms as a chaotic clutter of books and manuscripts, and Johnson's personal library totaled some 3,000 volumes.[12] But even though Johnson's world revolved around print, his attitude toward books themselves was remarkably casual and irreverent. Johnson did not so much read a book as gut it, skimming its contents impatiently until he found what he needed. Boswell relates a conversation that took place in 1773 between Johnson and a friend, James Elphinston, which illustrates the scholar's reading practices:

Mr. Elphinston talked of a new book that was much admired, and asked Dr. Johnson if he had read it. Johnson: I have looked into it. What (said Elphinston,) have you not read it through? Johnson, offended at being thus pressed, and so obliged to own his cursory mode of reading, answered tartly, No, Sir, do *you* read books *through*?[13]

Boswell also recalls that Johnson, in the presence of a large library, spent much of his time perusing the spines of the books rather than examining any one in particular. On one occasion Johnson's host noted this habit and observed that "it seems odd that one should have such a desire to look at the backs of books." Johnson rejoined that "when we enquire into any subject, the first thing we have to do is know what books have

---

[11] Chartier, *Cultural Origins of the French Revolution*, 69.
[12] Alvin Kernan, *Samuel Johnson and the Impact of Print* (Princeton, 1987), 213.
[13] James Boswell, *Life of Samuel Johnson, LL.D.* (Chicago, 1952), 213.

treated of it. This leads us to look at catalogues, and the backs of books in libraries."[14]

Johnson's insouciant attitude toward books as material objects highlights the broader transformation of print culture implied by the rise of extensive reading. As the practice of reading became ever more variegated and extensive, print itself was progressively demystified. Especially in the countryside, where print culture was less accessible and where reading occurred chiefly in a devotional context, books had traditionally had a sacred aura. Peasant households sometimes believed them to possess supernatural powers, and well into the nineteenth century some sought to avert evil or sickness by placing a Bible or devotional manual in the beds of newborn children, pregnant women, newlyweds, or the sick. The extensive reader, however, read more often in solitude, detached from a devotional milieu. Extensive reading thereby divorced print from its sacral context and profaned it. Hastening this process was an expanding literary market that was producing more and different kinds of books, periodicals, and newspapers. The resulting desacralization and commodification of books in turn fostered a more critical and less deferential attitude toward print.[15] Like consumers choosing from a variety of wares, extensive readers were more apt to make critical judgments and comparisons. In this respect, the kind of irreverence toward texts that Johnson expressed in his exchange with Elphinston helped foster the self-consciously critical spirit that characterized the public sphere of the Enlightenment. Extensive reading lowered the status of printed texts and transformed once venerable devotional objects into interchangeable units of cultural currency whose value was continually judged and compared.

Periodicals, novels, and the literary public sphere

Books *per se* were only one agent in the transition from intensive to extensive reading. Not until the second half of the eighteenth century, with the rise of lending libraries and reading clubs, did the extensive reading of *books* become conceivable for a broad reading public. Initially at least, newspapers and periodicals played a more decisive role in transforming reading practices. The reading of newspapers and journals was by definition extensive: readers moved from topic to topic, their attention continually shifting from one subject to the next. The topical diversity of journalistic media accustomed readers to a wider and more heterogeneous range of themes. News, as the word itself suggests, fostered a taste

---

[14] *Ibid.*, 258.
[15] See Chartier, *Cultural Origins of the French Revolution*, 89–91.

for novelty that could only be satisfied by reading more and different texts. Editors of newspapers and periodicals became conscious of how novelty and variety could attract readers. As the editors of the Stuttgart *Real-Zeitung*, a German newspaper, announced in 1765, "we have noticed for some time that most inhabitants of our blessed territory [Württemberg] have no particular inclination to read good and useful books...So we believed the easiest way to stimulate a taste for reading would be to publish a weekly that would cover diverse topics, *alluring the reader through the variety of material*" (my italics).[16]

At the same time, new formats like book reviews, abstracts, and notices stimulated the desire to read more and different texts. Book notices began to appear in English newspapers around 1646. These soon evolved into book abstracts, which in time developed into critical reviews. By the 1690s, journals like the *Athenian Mercury* and the *Compleat Library or News of the Ingenious* were devoting much of their space to book reviews and learned discoveries. By the 1730s and 1740s reviews had become an integral part of popular journals like the *Gentleman's Magazine* (1731) and the *Monthly Review* (1745). On the continent, book reviewing came of age in journals like the *Année littéraire* (founded 1754) in France and the *Allgemeine Deutsche Bibliothek* (1765) in Germany.

On one level the emergence of the book review epitomized the lofty moral and pedagogical ideals of the Enlightenment public sphere. From the perspective of enlightened editors and reviewers, book reviews and notices contributed to the formation of an informed and sophisticated reading public. They kept readers abreast of an ever-expanding body of print, and helped them discriminate between good and bad books. But these new formats were also a form of advertising designed to stimulate consumer demand, and were symptomatic of an increasingly commercialized literary market. This process of commercialization had set in earliest in England, which had a more elastic literary market less fettered by censorship than that of continental regimes. By the 1770s virtually all English newspapers and journals included advertisements, although in France, where journalism was more heavily subsidized by the crown, only about a fifth did.[17] Stimulating a demand for books, advertising also fostered a taste for novelty. Booksellers and publishers used advertising to market fashionable "new" works that every self-respecting reader needed to know. Novelty became an important criterion for what made a book

---

[16] Quoted in Erning, *Das Lesen und die Lesewut*, 56.
[17] S. Botein, J. R. Censer, and H. Ritvo, "The Periodical Press in Eighteenth-Century English and French Society: A Cross-Cultural Approach," *Comparative Studies in Society and History* 23 (1981), 473.

desirable and interesting, so much so that English publishers in the later eighteenth century sometimes post-dated works that had appeared a few years earlier in order to make them seem new. In 1761 a young woman from a provincial English town noted the obsession with literary novelty when she complained to the novelist Samuel Richardson that "in this foolish town, we are obliged to read every foolish book that fashion renders prevalent."[18]

From the mid-eighteenth century on, the "foolish book that fashion renders prevalent" was likely to be a novel. Literary scholars rightly view the rise of the novel as one of the most significant developments in eighteenth-century letters. What concerns us here is not the formal and aesthetic dimensions of the eighteenth-century novel but its historical significance as the single most important growth industry in the eighteenth-century literary market. Bare statistics tell part of the story. In England, the number of new novels appearing in any given year never exceeded twelve between 1700 and 1720. By contrast, in 1790 some eighty-five to ninety new titles were published.[19] In Germany, the production of novels grew from 2.6 percent of the works listed in Leipzig book catalogues in 1740, to 4 percent in 1770 and 11.7 percent in 1800.[20] By the end of the century, novels made up almost as large a percentage of the Leipzig catalogue as religious works, which represented 13.5 percent of the titles. The list below shows the spectacular rise of novel production in Germany during the second half of the eighteenth century:[21]

1750–60	73
1761–70	189
1771–80	413
1781–90	907
1791–1800	1,623

As for France, the list below tells a similar story. While the production of new French novels actually declined during the second and third decades of the century, it then surged in the 1730s and never fell to less than 285 in any subsequent decade; 2,663 new titles appeared between 1751 and 1800, as compared with only 939 in the previous half-century.[22]

---

[18] Quoted in James Raven, *Judging New Wealth: Popular Publishing and Responses to Commerce in England 1750–1800* (Oxford, 1992), 62–63.
[19] *Ibid.*, 34.
[20] Jentzsch, *Der deutsch-lateinische Büchermarkt*, table 2.
[21] Erich Schön, *Der Verlust der Sinnlichkeit oder Die Verwandlung des Lesens: Mentalitätswandel um 1800* (Stuttgart, 1987), 44.
[22] S. P. Jones, *A List of French Prose Fiction from 1700–1750* (New York, 1939), xiv; A. Martin, V. G. M. Mylne, and R. Frautschi, eds., *Bibliographie du genre romanesque français 1751–1800* (London and Paris, 1977), xxxvi–xxxix.

1701–10	136
1711–20	119
1721–30	99
1731–40	248
1741–50	318
1751–60	285
1761–70	512
1771–80	426
1781–90	662
1791–1800	735

But before the novel could acquire the broad popularity it would enjoy after the mid-eighteenth century, it had first to contend with an entrenched tradition of theological hostility to the reading of imaginative literature. Invoking the New Testament's admonition to "refuse profane and old wives' fables, and exercise thyself rather unto godliness," Catholic and Protestant authorities alike had long warned that the reading of secular poetry and fiction distracted individuals from their religious and devotional duties. Works of profane literature were at best fabricated tales and hence a waste of time; at worst, their stories of love and romance aroused unhealthy appetites. In 1703 the Jesuit *Journal de Trévoux* condemned novels on the grounds that "the corrupt morality that fills these books ... leaves an amorous impression, a penchant for gallantry, and a taste for intrigue, which stifle in the young all sense of piety and modesty." In France such criticism culminated in efforts (largely futile) by the monarchy in 1737–38 to ban novels altogether. Calvinists in England and Pietists in Germany launched similar attacks in the early eighteenth century. The Swiss Calvinist Gotthard Heidegger reasoned in 1698 that because our time on earth should be devoted "to the service of God and the edification of our neighbor and ourselves," "the time devoted to the reading of novels and other love stories" was "wasted and lost for eternity."[23]

Religious hostility to the novel never entirely abated, and throughout the century it repeatedly resurfaced as the genre's popularity grew. But the rise of moral weeklies in the early eighteenth century did much to disarm critics of the novel. The moral weekly originated in London with the tri-weekly *Tatler* (1709–11), edited by the dramatist Richard Steele, and the daily *Spectator* (1711–12), a collaborative effort launched by Steele and the poet Joseph Addison. Although the *Tatler* initially included foreign

---

[23] Quotes taken from Vivienne Mylne, *The Eighteenth-Century French Novel: Techniques of Illusion*, 2nd ed. (Cambridge, 1981), 12 (my translation), and Marianne Spiegel, *Der Roman und sein Publikum im früheren 18. Jahrhundert 1700–1767* (Bonn, 1967), 39.

and domestic news, politics gradually receded from view and the journal's primary focus became manners, morals, and letters. The *Spectator* renounced party politics altogether, and offered instead a kaleidoscopic commentary on everything from religion to marriage, child-raising, etiquette, dress, and commerce. It upheld religion and morality against unbelief and libertinism, attacked drunkenness and infidelity, and generally echoed the Puritan condemnation of Restoration morals. Yet the *Spectator*'s moralism shunned the dour jeremiads of conventional Puritanism, preferring a moderate and gentle tone that sought to instruct its readers with humor and wit. "To enliven morality with wit – to temper wit with morality," was how Addison summed up the moral agenda of his weeklies. In this regard the *Spectator* propagated what one recent scholar has called the "culture of politeness," the Whiggish balance between morality and civility, order and liberty, learning and conviviality, in which the post-1689 social and political order was ideologically embedded. The periodicals of Addison and Steele articulated an emerging vision of commercial society that defined virtue in terms of manners and sociability rather than the civic ideals of classical antiquity.[24]

The *Spectator*'s public was broad, ranging from the gentry to the middling ranks of merchants and professionals. Beginning with a print run of 3,000–4,000 copies, the *Spectator* soon reached daily sales of 20,000–30,000. But even these circulation figures, remarkable for their time, do not adequately express the journal's popularity. For the *Spectator* belonged to the culture of the coffeehouse, where it was read (often aloud) and discussed. It inspired countless spin-offs, first in England and later on the continent. Some 106 journals modeled on the *Spectator* (many albeit ephemeral) had appeared in England by 1750, and although the French monarchy's tighter censorship restrictions limited the spread of moral weeklies and periodicals in general, Addison and Steele had their imitators across the Channel as well. The dramatist and novelist Pierre de Marivaux (1688–1763) modeled his *Spectateur français* (1722) on Addison's journal, as did the novelist Antoine-François Prévost in his *Pour et Contre* (1733–40). The genre found more fertile soil in the Holy Roman Empire, where the first German weekly, the Hamburg *Vernunftler* (1713–14), consciously emulated the style of Addison and Steele. German moral weeklies attained the height of their popularity between 1720 and 1750, when at least fifty were published.

One can hardly exaggerate the importance of moral weeklies. They eased the transition to a more secular and diverse print culture by showing

[24] Lawrence E. Klein, *Shaftesbury and the Culture of Politeness: Moral Discourse and Cultural Politics in Early Eighteenth-Century England* (Cambridge, 1994).

that a non-religious genre, aimed at a broad readership, could simultaneously entertain and morally instruct its readers. Crafting a moral discourse that would inform the works of novelists like Richardson in England, Marivaux and Prévost in France, and Gellert in Germany, moral weeklies served to neutralize traditional attacks on the novel. Moral weeklies were also important for the themes they explored. These dealt almost exclusively with the realm of private experience, and moral weeklies consciously avoided explicitly political topics. Addison, though himself a Whig with considerable experience in party politics, announced in the first issue of the *Spectator* his intention "to observe an exact neutrality between Whigs and Tories." His goal was not, as he wrote in a later issue, "to encrease the Number either of Whigs or Tories, but of wise and good Men." The anonymous editor of the *Visiter* (1723–24), a London periodical aimed at women, promised in the first issue that "I never will touch upon any thing which in the least relates to Publick Affairs." In *Der Patriot* (Hamburg, 1724–26), one of the first and most popular German moral weeklies, the narrator's admission that "I don't get mixed up in public matters, for that I haven't any vocation," was typical of the genre.[25] Moral weeklies showed how individuals could be virtuous and happy outside of the political realm, in a privatized world of marriage, family, and friends.

This preoccupation with the private realm of social experience was significant. Demonstratively abstaining from politics, the moral weekly implicitly distinguished the social from the political, the private from the public, and thereby pointed toward modern notions of civil society as a sphere autonomous from the state. In the context of the eighteenth century, the moral weekly's validation of sociability as an autonomous and non-political arena implicitly contested the cultural dominion of the court. It is no accident that in England, the moral weekly's popularity came at a time when the cultural influence of the royal court was rapidly dwindling. The same was true in France, where the emergence of the moral weekly under the regency coincided with the decline of Versailles as an arbiter of cultural and aesthetic tastes. In German-speaking Europe, the moral weekly's distance from the court is indicated by the fact that the genre first flourished in cities without a princely residence, such as Hamburg, Zurich, and Leipzig.

Finally, the moral weekly's preoccupation with private experience served to attract a substantial female readership. By focussing on themes

[25] Quotes taken from *The Spectator*, ed. with an introduction and notes by Donald F. Bond (Oxford, 1965), I:5 (March 1, 1711), 4:501 (June 18, 1714); Kathyrn Shevelow, *Women and Print Culture: The Construction of Femininity in the Early Periodical* (London and New York, 1989), 158; Wolfgang Martens, *Die Botschaft der Tugend: die Aufklärung im Spiegel der deutschen Moralischen Wochenschriften* (Stuttgart, 1968), 334.

like marriage, child-raising, and fashion, moral weeklies were especially calculated to appeal to middle-class female readers. Given these women's lack of formal education and their exclusion from political and professional life, the moral weekly's non-political orientation spoke directly to their experience in a way that more scholarly or politically oriented works did not. The appeal to women was deliberate and calculated, so much so that Jonathan Swift snidely dismissed the *Spectator*'s pursuit of female readers as "fair-sexing it." Addison wrote in the tenth issue of the *Spectator* that "there are none to whom this paper will be more useful than to the female world," and in no. 205 he listed twenty-four issues devoted exclusively to women's concerns. Out of the 1,081 articles appearing in Addison and Steele's periodicals, 420 were specifically concerned with women.[26]

Moral weeklies were "feminist" in so far as they deemed women to be as capable of enlightenment as men. Most advocated reforms in female education and defended the right of women to participate in the literary culture of their day. But with a few exceptions, they did not believe women should make a profession of their intellectual interests. Reading was to improve them morally, not advance them professionally, by making them better daughters, wives and mothers. Women were encouraged to read only as long as it did not distract them from performing their household duties. In this regard, moral weeklies reinforced ideas of sexual difference that distinguished between a male public realm and a female domestic one. Paradoxically, the early English periodical fastened women more firmly to the sphere of household and family even while it enfranchised them within eighteenth-century print culture.[27]

Yet here moral weeklies helped prepare the foundations for the eighteenth-century novel and its audience. The eighteenth-century novel was a "feminized" genre for the same reason the moral weekly had been: it was preoccupied with the realm of domestic experience and validated the household – an arena that in the eighteenth century was increasingly associated with women – as a legitimate focus of literary concern. The novel, like the moral weekly, thereby not only acquired a substantial female readership, it also fostered a public/private disjunction that came to inform eighteenth-century notions of the public sphere.

This dimension of eighteenth-century fiction was particularly visible in the sentimental novels of Richardson and Sterne in England, Rousseau in France, and the young Goethe in Germany. Here Richardson's *Pamela*

---

[26] Shevelow, *Women and Print Culture*, 1; J. Heinrich, *Die Frauenfrage bei Steele und Addison* (Leipzig, 1930), 2.

[27] On this point, see Shevelow, *Women and Print Culture*, passim.

(1740–41) and *Clarissa* (1747–48) set the standard. These novels were "feminine" not merely by virtue of their heroines, but also in their careful attention to the minute details of domestic life. Richardson's preoccupation with female domesticity was precisely what put off some male readers of the day, and here, as with the early periodical, some have tended to identify Richardson's domestic focus with a broader cultural strategy that sanctioned women's confinement to the private sphere of the household. Yet there are two problems with such a view. First, it can easily obscure the extent to which the sentimental novel also legitimated the participation of women in the literary public sphere. By validating a realm of eighteenth-century female experience – namely, the domestic household – as a legitimate subject for the novelist, Richardson opened up a new literary world to women. And as will be seen in Chapter 4, women would populate this world not simply as readers but also as writers. Second, it is wrong to see the eighteenth-century middle-class household as a rigidly segregated "separate sphere" that sealed women off hermetically from the outside world. "The idea that the home was a refuge insulated from the social world is one that would have perplexed the well-established in this period," as Amanda Vickery has perceptively observed of the eighteenth-century English gentry.[28] The lives of middle-class women in the eighteenth century were at any rate much more public than is often assumed, as their patronage of theaters, salons, spas, and other public venues demonstrates. But even within the sphere of the household itself, as Vickery argues, women were integrated into a dense network of social and economic relationships connecting them with worlds that extended far beyond the domestic arena. The frequent entertainment of visitors dictated by longstanding traditions of hospitality, for example, ensured that the household was never a purely private realm. As a venue for the intermingling of the sexes, social visits were an occasion for sharing gossip or exchanging views on religious, literary, or political matters. Letters, books, and periodicals sustained and expanded the networks linking women to the world outside the household.

The eighteenth-century novel was linked to emerging notions of the public sphere in other ways. One of the most popular fictional genres in the eighteenth century was the epistolary novel, epitomized by works such as Montesquieu's *Persian Letters*, Richardson's *Clarissa*, Rousseau's *Nouvelle Héloïse*, Goethe's *Sorrows of Young Werther*, and Laclos's *Liaisons dangereuses*. In the seventeenth century, female novelists like Aphra Behn in England and Madeleine de Scudéry in France had helped establish the epistolary form; moral weeklies further popularized it through their

[28] Amanda Vickery, *Women's Lives in Georgian England* (New Haven and London, 1998), 9.

regular and innovative inclusion of real or fictitious letters to the editor. Epistolary novels reached their pinnacle of popularity between 1750 and 1790 – by 1760, for example, they made up one-third of new fictional titles published in England.[29]

As the term indicates, the epistolary novel took the form of letters the author claimed to have received or discovered. Epistolarity functioned in part to create an illusion of authenticity, a stratagem designed in response to traditional attacks on novelists as frauds and liars. But what linked the epistolary form to the communicative structure of the public sphere was its directness, transparency, and intimacy. In the moral weekly, the publication of letters reputedly written by actual readers fostered the impression of a direct and reciprocal dialogue between editor and public. Here letters served to construct a public arena where readers and writers were engaged in a real or imagined dialogue. The moral weekly's use of letters pretended to eliminate the boundaries between writers and readers, dissolving both into a public whose members engaged in a continual and reciprocal process of communication.[30]

The epistolary novel was dialogical, too, though in a different fashion. Its characters communicated with each other directly through the medium of writing, which encouraged a frankness and openness that enabled them to reveal to each other and to the reader the motives underlying their actions. Diderot perceived this aspect of the epistolary novel in his laudatory essay on Richardson: "It is he who carries the flame to the depths of the cavern, it is he who teaches how to discern the subtle and dishonest motives that are hidden and concealed. . . ."[31] Letters rendered the opaque transparent, making what had previously been private and secret now public and open. In Laclos's *Liaisons dangereuses*, they bring to light the unscrupulous sexual schemes of Valmont and the marquise de Merteuil. In *Clarissa*, they give proof of the heroine's innate if tragic virtue. Even when the author of a letter is false and duplicitous, like the seducer Valmont in his letters to the virtuous but unwitting Présidente de Tourvel, the reader acquires enough knowledge from other letters to see through the deception. By making the intimate sphere public and rendering hidden motives transparent, epistolarity achieved in the novel what the language of "public opinion" aspired to in the political realm. The discourse of public opinion acquired its political force by invidiously contrasting its own claims of openness and transparency with the secrecy and opacity of the absolutist court. The epistolary novel, for its part,

[29] Raven, *Judging New Wealth*, 46.
[30] See Shevelow, *Women and Print Culture*, 37, 104.
[31] Diderot, "Éloge de Richardson," in Diderot, *Oeuvres Esthétiques*, ed. Paul Vernière (Paris, 1963), in his *Oeuvres complètes*, vol. V (Paris, 1970), 32.

acquired literary force through its ability to unmask motives and secrets otherwise hidden from view.

The obsession with rendering the private public also characterized other genres of the period. One was eighteenth-century autobiography, whose self-revelatory, almost exhibitionist tone is epitomized in Rousseau's *Confessions*. Despite their apparent similarities, the autobiography differed from the memoir in its concern with the private and the intimate. The memoir was traditionally an aristocratic genre that focussed on the author's public life – most typically as a statesman, a figure at court, or a military officer. In general, a memoir neglected the more intimate details of the author's life, as if implying that the only achievements worthy of description were public ones. In eighteenth-century autobiography, on the other hand, the personality and private experiences of the author rather than his or her public actions took center stage. Here, autobiography functioned to bring to light an author's otherwise hidden motives, sentiments, and experiences.[32]

The so-called *mémoires judiciares*, a genre that the historian Sarah Maza has called "one of the most important, possibly the single most popular, form of ephemeral literature circulating in Paris in the two decades before the Revolution,"[33] also illustrates this preoccupation with exposing to public view what had previously been private and secret. The *mémoire* was a legal brief written on behalf of a party in a criminal or civil case. Traditionally it had been a handwritten document, intended solely for the court, in which a lawyer narrated the details of his party's case. But in the course of the eighteenth century *mémoires judiciares* were increasingly published and sold to a wider public. The more sensational ones in the 1770s were published in printings ranging from 3,000 to 6,000 copies. Those appearing in the 1780s commonly ran to 10,000 and one brief had a remarkable print run of 20,000.

Lawyers systematically employed the *mémoire* to transform often obscure lawsuits or criminal cases into *causes célèbres* that captured the imagination of the public. The authors often had literary ambitions of their own: one of the most popular *mémoires* of the 1770s was penned by the playwright Beaumarchais, whose best-selling account of his treatment at the hands of a venal Parisian magistrate did much to popularize the genre. Heavily emplotted in the sentimental and melodramatic style of the eighteenth-century stage and novel, briefs narrated the sufferings of their

---

[32] Jean Marie Goulemot, "Literary Practices: Publicizing the Private," in Chartier, ed., *History of Private Life*, III:382–92, and Madeleine Foisil, "The Literature of Intimacy," 329, in the same volume, 329, 382, 392.

[33] Sarah Maza, *Private Lives and Public Affairs: The Causes Célèbres of Prerevolutionary France* (Berkeley, 1993), 122. My discussion below is based on Maza's work.

protagonists in terms that a broader public could understand. The setting was often the domestic household, with their "characters" – virtuous villagers, grasping aristocrats, servant girls pursued and wronged by their masters – assuming Rousseauean or Richardsonian proportions. Beyond the literary qualities of the *mémoires*, however, Maza also underscores their political import. Their rising popularity during the 1770s coincided with the Maupeou crisis (1771–74), the bitter political struggle that followed the French chancellor's abolition of the parlements in 1771 (see Chapter 2). Just as the flood of anti-Maupeou pamphlets sought to expose the "despotism" of the crown to public view, so did the *mémoires* (themselves often written by lawyers active in the anti-Maupeou cause) expose to their public a system of justice traditionally shrouded in secrecy. Courtroom proceedings in the Old Regime took place in secret; published *mémoires* rendered them open and transparent. They did so, moreover, using language and social imagery that transposed abstract political issues onto a private and personal plane. A spouse's violation of the marriage contract was equated with a ruler's violation of the social contract; a venal judge became the synecdoche of a hopelessly corrupt judicial system. This conflation of the personal and the political helped render republican concepts like liberty, despotism, and the popular will intelligible to readers less versed in political abstractions. More ominously, this melodramatic politicization of the private realm also anticipated the political and rhetorical excesses of the Jacobin Republic of Virtue.

Finally, the enormous vogue of erotic literature – what we would today call pornography – also reveals the late eighteenth-century fascination with publicizing the private. It has been estimated that during the final two decades of the Old Regime, pornographic works made up more than 20 percent of French market demand for illicit books.[34] Graphic sexual description was of course no eighteenth-century invention, but as Robert Darnton observes, what made the erotic literature of the period so distinctive was its voyeurism. Sexual encounters took place in private or secret settings, with billowy female garments alternately concealing and revealing the act of intercourse. Ostensibly private trysts were often described through the eyes of a narrator hidden behind a door or drape. "Everywhere," writes Darnton, "characters observed one another through keyholes, from behind curtains, and between bushes, while the reader looked over their shoulders."[35] Popular if illicit works such as the *Histoire de Dom Bougre* (Gervaise de La Touche?, 1741), John Cleland's

---

[34] Robert Darnton, *The Forbidden Best-Sellers of Pre-Revolutionary France* (New York and London, 1995), 72.
[35] *Ibid.*, 72–73.

Memoirs of Fanny Hill (1745), or the Comte de Mirabeau's *Erotica Biblion* (1783), exposed the private sexual lives of their characters to public view. The reader entered the intimate world of the boudoir, and like a voyeur, became privy to its sexual secrets.

This dialectic of opacity and transparency, secrecy and openness, was yet another point at which literary and political practices intersected in the eighteenth century. In France the convergence of political and porno-graphic discourse was increasingly evident toward the end of Louis XV's reign, when the unpopularity of the monarchy found expression in scur-rilous pamphlets "exposing" the sexual licentiousness of the king and his mistresses. Under Louis XVI the trend culminated in slanderous as-saults on Marie-Antoinette, often in the form of pornographic exposés detailing her allegedly insatiable and unnatural sexual appetites. This libelous intermingling of sex and sedition had a long tradition – here the so-called *mazarinades* of the Fronde, with their scurrilous attacks on Cardinal Mazarin and Anne of Austria, are just one example. But the pornographic exposés of court life that became so common under Louis XV and Louis XVI contained new elements. They were longer, sometimes taking the form of multivolume narratives instead of the tra-ditional pamphlet, and the denser publishing and distribution networks of the eighteenth century allowed them to be more widely circulated. Moreover, while pornographic portrayals of Henry IV or Louis XIV had portrayed the king as a gallant if randy figure, libels such as *The Private Life of Louis XV* or *Anecdotes on the Countess du Barry* depicted him as a weak and near-impotent man wholly dominated by his mistresses. More to the point, these libels portrayed political corruption and despotism as systemic, the product not of a single individual but of the entire structure of royal government.[36]

With the political pornography of pre-revolutionary France we are clearly a long way from the moral weekly of the early eighteenth cen-tury. The moral weekly had sought to construct in its readers a social and moral identity distinct from the public power of the state. By the end of the eighteenth century, however, that boundary had begun to dissolve. Like the politically charged *mémoires judiciares*, libelous attacks on the sexual morality of the court were a symptom of how the political realm had come increasingly to be judged according to the moral standards of private life. Richard Sennett found a similar process at work in British political culture with the Wilkesite affair of the 1760s, when the issues of parliamentary reform and liberty were inextricably joined with the per-sonality of the controversial and rakish politician. The political theatrics

[36] *Ibid.*, 208–14.

of the Wilkesite movement, argues Sennett, were so effective because of their success in superimposing private imagery on public issues.[37] Whatever texts or events they choose to examine, those who seek insight into the prurient political culture of our own day might well begin with the latter half of the eighteenth century. For then, like today, the capacity of public figures to govern wisely and legitimately came to be linked to their private, often sexual behavior.

The rise of the lending library

Despite the growing size and diversity of the eighteenth-century literary market, a mass reading public did not yet exist. That would not come until the nineteenth century, when technological innovations in the printing industry made it possible to produce books cheap enough for a mass audience to afford. In the late eighteenth century, book-buying on a regular basis was still beyond the financial means of most readers. In Germany the price of books rose sharply between 1750 and 1785, largely owing to growing demand, the higher cost of paper, and rising wages in the publishing industry. In England around 1750, the price of a novel was roughly equivalent to that of a stone of beef or a pair of women's shoes. By this standard, the frequent purchase of novels – say, one a month – would have been feasible for well-to-do merchants and professionals but not for unskilled laborers or domestics.[38]

Compensating for the relatively high price of books was the rise of lending libraries and reading rooms. Libraries played a minimal role in the circulation of print prior to the mid-eighteenth century. The great princely and aristocratic libraries of the baroque era were preeminently representational in function, and served more to symbolize the power and wisdom of their owners than to provide access to books. Typical in this respect was the royal *Bibliothèque du Roi* in Paris, where those requesting permission to consult the library's collection were carefully screened. Visitors were admitted two days a week under careful supervision, largely to view its collection of precious medallions and engravings. Access to cloister libraries was similarly restricted, and usually required a letter of recommendation from someone connected with the monastery. University libraries were primarily designed to supplement the private libraries of professors, and their use was confined to a relatively small circle of

[37] Richard Sennett, *The Fall of Public Man: On the Social Psychology of Capitalism* (New York, 1974), 99–106.

[38] For a discussion of book prices and affordability, see James Raven, *British Fiction 1750–1770: A Chronological Check-List of Prose Fiction Printed in Britain and Ireland* (Newark, London, and Toronto, 1987), 25–32.

scholars. Ordinances for the Cambridge University library (1581–83) restricted entry to masters of arts, bachelors of law, or persons of high degree. The ordinances further stipulated that "at one tyme there be not above Ten in the sayde Librarie together." In 1742 Oxford's Bodleian Library received no more than 257 requests for books, a figure indicative of its small readership. At the University of Paris, visitors had to be accompanied by a fellow to enter the libraries of its colleges, while the splendid library at Heidelberg was still closed to non-university users at the end of the eighteenth century. In 1729 a visitor expressed surprise and gratitude that the library at the University of Leipzig was open to visitors for two hours on Wednesdays and Saturdays. Probably the closest one came to "public" libraries in the modern sense were the municipal libraries of England. Founded in the late sixteenth and seventeenth centuries in provincial towns like Manchester, Norwich, Newcastle, and Bristol, these libraries were closely associated with the Puritan cause. Their small holdings consisted primarily of theological and devotional works, and while municipal libraries were in principle open to the entire community, they were patronized chiefly by students and clergy.

Accessibility to traditional libraries did begin to broaden somewhat in the eighteenth century. Enlightenment writers criticized the heavily representational function of princely and aristocratic libraries, and urged that they be made more open to readers. Libraries, as the Berlin *Aufklärer* Friedrich Nicolai pleaded, should actually be used and not just seen. Although the libraries of provincial academies in France had earlier restricted entry to members, some began opening their collections to the outside public. In the 1730s and 1740s, for example, academies in Bordeaux, Pau, La Rochelle, and Nancy opened their libraries to the public two or three days a week. Funding for the British Museum Library (founded in 1753 under an Act of Parliament) was raised through a public lottery and the library was open to general readers every weekday between 9 a.m. and 3 p.m. By the 1780s, similarly, both the imperial library in Vienna and the royal library in Berlin had begun opening their doors to the public every morning from 9 a.m. until noon. The ducal library in Wolffenbüttel, where the dramatist and critic Gotthold Ephraim Lessing was director between 1770 and 1781, was especially renowned for its accessibility. Beyond being open to the public every weekday morning and afternoon, it also functioned as a lending library. Between 1714 and 1799 it loaned out 31,485 volumes to 1,648 borrowers, roughly half of them in the period between 1760 and 1780. The Wolfenbüttel library served a relatively broad clientele: 75 percent of borrowers were middle class, 61 percent non-academic, and around 12 percent were women. The literary tastes of these readers reflected the growing popularity of novels, which made up the single largest category of books borrowed.[39]

As a court library, however, Wolfenbüttel was atypical. Most remained closer to the baroque world of symbolic display than they were to the Enlightenment public sphere. Access remained relatively restricted, and if books were loaned out at all it was to a limited circle of court officials and academics. Moreover, the holdings of traditional libraries were usually dominated by older works, e.g., erudite legal treatises or rare editions of classical and Christian authors. Periodicals, so important for the diffusion of Enlightenment culture, were generally absent. Traditional libraries were repositories of *books*, with periodicals considered ephemeral and unworthy of collection.

Hence traditional libraries contributed little to the expanding readership of the eighteenth century. More important was the proliferation of reading clubs and booklending shops during the second half of the century. Reading clubs were of various types. Some, like the English book club or French *musée* of the 1780s, met regularly to discuss literary works and social or political issues of the day. Predominantly middle class, their members paid annual dues to purchase books and periodicals. These were circulated among the membership and then either sold or kept in the society's permanent library. Somewhat different were the so-called subscription societies popular in England. These were basically book-buying cooperatives, membership in which was open to anyone who could afford the annual dues (usually around a guinea a year). The members elected a committee to select books for purchase, which were then made available to readers in the society's reading room. Unlike book clubs, subscription societies had no explicitly social, political, or literary aim beyond that of supplying their subscribers with a steady supply of new books and periodicals. Fifty-eight of them have been identified in England for the period between 1758 and 1800. Some accumulated sizable collections: by 1782 the Bristol Library Society (1773) had 137 members and a library of 2,296 volumes. Between 1773 and 1798 members borrowed more than 35,000 books, a figure that suggests how important these societies could be for the circulation of print.[40]

---

[39] The above statistics are taken from Mechthild Raabe, *Leser und Lektüre im 18. Jahrhundert: die Ausleihbücher der Herzog August Bibliothek Wolfenbüttel 1714–1799*, vol. I: *Die Leser und ihre Lektüre* (Munich, 1989), l–liii.

[40] Paul Kaufman, "The Community Library: A Chapter in English Social History," *Transactions of the American Philosophical Society*, new series, 57/7 (1967), 26–33 and appendix B.

Unlike subscription societies, lending libraries were commercial enterprises and were usually run by booksellers. London newspaper advertisements from the early eighteenth century already attest to the practice of booksellers loaning out books for a fee, and by the 1720s commercial booklending had spread to provincial cities like Bath, Bristol, and Birmingham. These circulation libraries, as they were called, spread rapidly during the second half of the century. For this period, one scholar has identified 112 in London and 268 in the provinces, but this is probably a conservative figure; in 1801 the *Monthly Magazine* estimated the number to be around 1,000.[41] Some circulation libraries sent book-laden carriages into outlying villages, adding thousands to the ranks of library readers. Fashionable spas and resorts like Bath and Tunbridge Wells boasted spacious libraries where visitors could borrow books during their stay. These libraries also functioned as social centers where patrons exchanged the latest news and gossip, or engaged in political and literary discussions.

In France, Parisian and provincial booksellers from the 1760s on set up reading rooms (*cabinets de lecture*) where one could read or borrow books for an annual fee of 10–20 livres. Forty-nine *cabinets de lecture* (13 in Paris and 36 in the provinces) have been identified for the period between 1759 and 1789, but doubtless there were many more obscure or ephemeral ones for which no record survives. Their clientele appears to have consisted largely of individuals who were literate but could not afford to purchase books and periodicals on a regular basis – e.g., professionals, teachers, military officers, skilled artisans and small merchants.[42] Catering to a more plebeian clientele were *bouquinistes*, small shops or stalls where book lenders loaned out cheap or second-hand books and pamphlets by the day or even the hour. In the *bouquinistes*, wrote the journalist Louis-Sébastien Mercier, "there are works that excite such a ferment that the bookseller is obliged to cut the volume in three parts in order to satisfy the pressing demands of many readers; in this case you pay not by the day but by the hour."[43] For many lower-class readers lending shops were an important source for the latest novel, political pamphlet, or scandal sheet.

The "take-off" period for German lending libraries also began in the second half of the century. By 1800 almost every town had at least one, and cities could boast several. Frankfurt am Main had at least eight

[41] *Ibid.*, 10.
[42] Jean-Louis Pailhès, "En marge des bibliothèques: l'apparition des cabinets de lecture," in Jolly, ed., *Histoire des bibliothèques françaises*, 416–19. Two provincial *cabinets de lecture* are discussed in Robert Darnton, *Édition et sédition: l'univers de la littérature clandestine au XVIIIe siècle* (Paris, 1991), 80–86, and Darnton, "First Steps toward a History of Reading," *Australian Journal of French Studies* 23 (1986), 25–26.
[43] Quoted in Chartier, *Cultural Origins of the French Revolution*, 70.

between 1750 and 1790, while Leipzig, the center of the north German book trade, had nine in 1799. Dresden's first lending library opened in 1777, and by 1809 the Saxon capital had eleven. With their relatively literate populations, university towns were especially well supplied. Königsberg's first lending library was established in 1765, and by 1800 the town had ten. Göttingen booksellers began lending their wares in 1769, and by 1800 the town had at least three lending shops.[44] As in England, the lending-library business sometimes radiated out into the countryside. In the 1790s one finds references to booklenders who dispatched agents to loan books in outlying villages.

Lending shops varied widely in the size of their inventories. A circulation library catalogue published in 1778 by John Bell, a London bookseller, listed around 8,000 titles in areas ranging from history and biography to surgery and divinity. At the other extreme was James Sanders's circulating library in Derby, which in 1770 advertised no more than 207 titles, most of them fiction. The catalogue of Göttingen's first lending library listed 442 volumes in 1769, a humble enterprise compared with the 3,009 volumes carried by the bookseller J. C. Seiler in 1780.[45] Such a large inventory was not unusual for eighteenth-century lending libraries, which were at times major commercial enterprises.

But what sorts of books did they loan? Lending libraries were not as devoid of "serious" works as contemporary critics sometimes charged. Surviving catalogues routinely include rubrics for philosophy, theology, and history. But, on the whole, lending libraries catered to the rising demand for fiction. Between August 1770 and 1772, almost three-quarters of the titles loaned out by the Warwick bookseller Samuel Clay were novels. In a lending catalogue published in 1772 by the Lyon bookseller Claude Morley, by far the largest percentage of books (40 percent) advertised were *belles-lettres*. Novels made up over half of the titles listed in the 1766 lending catalogue of Jacques-François Quillau, owner of a Parisian *cabinet de lecture*, and the 1803 catalogue of H. B. Lüddecke, a Blankenburg bookseller. Overall, lending libraries were the single most important source of fiction for eighteenth-century readers. The British novelist Elizabeth Griffiths estimated in 1786 that lending shops purchased 40 percent of the novels sold and printed in England.[46] Confirming Griffiths's observation, a recent study of eighteenth-century English

---

[44] Alberto Martino, *Die deutsche Leihbibliothek: Geschichte einer literarischen Institution (1756–1914)* (Wiesbaden, 1990), 61–105.

[45] Kaufman, "The Community Library," 11–12; Martino, *Die deutsche Leihbibliothek*, 111, 113.

[46] Peter Borsay, *The English Urban Renaissance* (Oxford, 1989), 134; Pailhès, "En marge des bibliothèques," 418; Martino, *Die deutsche Leihbibliothek*, 123; Kaufman, "The Community Library," 14.

publishing concludes that "most readers of new fiction were not library owners, but library goers." As for Germany, it has been estimated that lending libraries provided the market for three-quarters of the works of *belles-lettres* published in the empire.[47]

Who patronized lending libraries? Because few detailed patron lists survive, the historian is left with the scattered observations of contemporaries. The German observer Friedrich Reinhard Rücklefs noted in 1796 that although members of reading clubs were cultivated and respectable men of good taste, lending libraries catered to uneducated artisans and laborers. English and German references to the lower-class clientele of lending libraries abound after 1789, when they were charged with spreading seditious revolutionary propaganda. But such observations cannot be taken at face value, for they often reveal more about the political anxieties of their authors then they do about library patrons. In principle, lending libraries did make print a more affordable commodity for less affluent readers. Most libraries offered a differentiated fee structure that included yearly, monthly, and daily rates. In some London bookshops readers could borrow up to two books a day for an annual fee of 16 shillings, a rate quite affordable for lower-middle and upper-working-class patrons. In 1796 the Frankfurt bookseller Johann Gottlob Pech loaned out books for 1 Kreuzer apiece, a fee well below the price of a pound of bread or a liter of milk.[48] Yet despite the affordability of lending libraries, major obstacles impeded the lower-class use of them. One obstacle was of course illiteracy, which generally rose the lower one's position on the social scale. But even for the literate peasant or laborer, the long working day left little time or daylight for reading. Moreover, living quarters were cramped in a period when the home was often one's place of work, and the absence of domestic quiet and privacy would also have inhibited reading. Finally, despite the incipient efforts of booksellers to branch out into the countryside, the lending library was an urban institution that touched the lives of relatively few peasants. As we have seen, the reading tastes of literate peasant households changed little over the course of the century. In general, then, one should not overstate the extent to which lending libraries "democratized" reading. While they undoubtably accelerated the circulation of books, especially fiction, they were probably less important for creating new readers than for enabling those who already read to read more. Here the role of lending libraries was significant indeed, for they fundamentally fueled the rise of extensive reading.

[47] Raven, *Judging New Wealth*, 54; Schön, *Verlust der Sinnlichkeit*, 45.
[48] Cheryl Turner, *Living by the Pen: Women Writers in the Eighteenth Century* (London, 1992), 135; Martino, *Die deutsche Leihbibliothek*, 67.

The public and its problems

By the end of the century the transformation of reading practices had become an object of discussion by contemporaries. Some viewed the change negatively, as symptomatic of a reading public that increasingly preferred novelty and entertainment to edification and enlightenment. Bemoaning the short attention span that he attributed to the reading public of his day, the German publicist J. G. Pahl wrote in 1792:

> Germans today are no longer accustomed . . . to read as our fathers did. Our fathers studied the writers they took up, reading them several times through, pondering their maxims and arguments, becoming thoroughly familiar with them, and setting them aside only after they had become a part of their flesh and blood. We, however, have grown used to a hasty kind of reading. We rush fleetingly through an author, never penetrating below the surface, perhaps reading only isolated passages that the table of contents suggests might be entertaining; we then begin to yawn and yet again reach for another book, for novelty amuses us.[49]

In Samuel Jackson Pratt's *Family Secrets*, a popular English novel published in 1797, Mr. Clare exclaims in response to an old-fashioned friend who insists on the importance of reading a book from cover to cover: "'Read books to the end, hey!' said Mr. Clare, having now filled and lighted his pipe: 'I wish you could see the circulators at my friend Page's shop . . . They begin with the end, return to the title, skip preface, jump to middle, dash again to end, and away for another vol!'"[50]

Growing references to "reading mania" pointed to the transformation of reading practices. In Germany, where late eighteenth-century discussions of reading mania (*Lesewut*) have been studied in detail, traditionalists and enlightened publicists alike voiced concern over the effects of excessive reading. Some pointed to its destructive effects on daily work routines. Observing in 1785 that "the reading of books has become a more frequent and general activity than it was before," an anonymous Silesian correspondent acknowledged that the spread of reading had contributed to popular enlightenment. The author nonetheless warned that "the merchant, artisan, peasant, etc., spend hours reading that would be better devoted to their work and business." Another diagnosis of reading mania dwelled on the medical consequences. According to Johann Georg Heinzmann, a Bern journalist writing in 1795, these included "oversensitivity, susceptibility to colds, headaches, poor eyesight, heat rash, gout, arthritis, hemorrhoids, asthma, apoplexy, lung disease, poor digestion,

---

[49] Quoted in Martino, *Die deutsche Leihbibliothek*, 10.
[50] Cited in Kaufman, "Community Library," 18.

constipation, nervous disorders, migraines, epilepsy, hypochondria, and melancholy."[51]

Diagnoses of reading mania usually blamed novels. This charge was a secularized variant of an older theological discourse, which had condemned novels as a sinful distraction from spiritual concerns. As seen earlier, the moral didacticism of the Enlightenment novel had done much to neutralize this critique, with defenders of the novel emphasizing its morally edifying potential. But during the last quarter of the century, as novels flooded the market and became increasingly available through lending libraries, novels again became a target of criticism. Women, who made up much of the novel-reading public, were a particular target of concern. Critics feared that middle-class women had become so addicted to novel-reading that many ignored their domestic duties. In 1785 the Silesian author cited above warned of dire domestic consequences "if a woman devotes all her time to reading...and neglects her obligations as wife, mother, and household manager."[52]

The common belief that novels whetted female sexual appetites also spurred fears regarding the effects of excessive reading on women. Concerns about the sentimental novel's alleged eroticism accounts for part of the backlash against the genre that set in toward the end of the century. Critics charged that for all their moralism, sentimental novels inflamed the senses through their celebration of love and passion. At best they made women unfit for the often harsh realities of marriage by creating a fantasy world of romantic love, at worst they encouraged sexual licence. The sentimental novels of Richardson sparked these criticisms from the very outset. The subtitle of *Pamela Censured* (London, 1741), an anonymous attack on Richardson's novel, read as follows: "Shewing That under the Specious Pretence of Cultivating the Principles of Virtue in the Minds of the Youth of both Sexes, the MOST ARTFUL and ALLURING AMOROUS IDEAS are convey'd." Elsewhere, the Bern editor Heinzmann asserted that women who read too many novels "lose all inhibitions to their sexual drives" and that "men who marry such women become cuckolds."[53]

Finally, political fears also underlay concerns about the effects of excessive reading. Traditionalist defenders of social hierarchy warned that

---

[51] Quotes taken from the *Neue Bunzlauische Monatsschrift zum Nützen und Vergnügen*, vol. II (1785), 267, and Martino, *Die deutsche Leihbibliothek*, 15–16.

[52] *Neue Bunzlauische Monatsschrift*, II:267.

[53] Quotes taken from Janet Todd, *Sensibility* (London and New York, 1986), 72–73, and Helmut Kreuzer, "Gefährliche Lesesucht? Bemerkungen zu politischer Lektürekritik im ausgehenden 18. Jahrhundert," in *Leser und Lesen im 18. Jahrhundert*, Colloquium der Arbeitsstelle 18. Jh. Gesamthochschule Wuppertal. Schloss Lüntenbeck, 24–26 October, 1975 (Heidelberg, 1977), 64.

indiscriminate reading undermined habits of deference and obedience by exposing readers to seditious ideas. To these critics, even the seemingly a-political romance or adventure novels that were so popular in the late eighteenth century were suspect. Particularly after the French Revolution, conservatives charged that novels, by creating a world of fantasy and illusion, left readers dissatisfied with the world as it was and hence susceptible to utopian schemes for political improvement. Yet the attack on popular reading tastes at the end of the century was not confined to supporters of the old order. In revolutionary France, for example, it found expression in the cultural policies of the Jacobin regime and early Directory. The condition of the French book market during the 1790s was somewhat anomalous. There, in contrast with Britain and Germany, the publication of prose fiction plummeted. The number of new titles dropped from more than 100 in 1789 to 16 in 1794, reviving only slowly under the Directory. The decline reflected the collapse of the book trade as a whole: deregulation of the publishing industry after 1789 ruined many publishing firms that had earlier enjoyed royal protection, while foreign and domestic markets contracted under the impact of war and emigration. By early 1794, conditions in the book trade had become so dire that the National Convention finally intervened with subsidies. Here the motives of the revolutionary government were political as well as economic. Jean-Baptiste Lefebvre de Villebrune, director of the Bibliothèque Nationale, argued that if left on its own the commercial market would pander to the pre-revolutionary taste for escapist fiction. He expressed the views of most revolutionary leaders in condemning popular novels for corrupting republican virtue by encouraging an immoral taste for pleasure and leisure. Athough he opposed suppressing these works as a violation of press liberty, he argued that generous subsidies to writers and publishers could neutralize the undesirable effects of the commercial market by encouraging the publication of works more conducive to the public good. This policy was in fact adopted between 1794 and 1796, when millions of livres went to subsidize works in the natural and applied sciences as well as revolutionary plays, poems, ballads and pamphlets. The canonization of the *philosophes* also began during these years, with subsidies going to support editions of Rousseau, Mably, Condorcet, and Diderot. Popular novels, however, were rarely subsidized, although novel production resumed its rapid rise as a result of the revival of the French book trade that set in toward the end of the Directory. In the meantime, republican critics continued to complain that novels fostered a preference for private pleasure over civic virtue. Their concerns, as Carla Hesse has observed, were symptomatic of the cultural contradictions arising from the clash of market capitalism and republican ideology.

In Germany, the "progressive" critique of popular reading tastes came from Kantians worried that indiscriminate reading and the lure of novelty undermined the emancipatory promise of the Enlightenment. In 1806, Johann Gottlieb Fichte, Kant's successor as the most influential philosopher in Germany, observed that for much of the public reading had become a means of escape rather than instruction. "Like other narcotic remedies," wrote Fichte, "it places those who use it in the pleasant condition between sleeping and waking, and lulls them into sweet self-forgetfulness without calling for the slightest exertion on their part."[54] Johann Adam Bergk, a radical disciple of Kant who like Fichte had once been an avid supporter of the French Revolution, took a similar position in his *Art of Reading* (Jena, 1799): "Reading should be a pedagogical path to autonomy, but for most it is a sleeping potion. Reading should emancipate us, but for how many is it nothing more than a source of entertainment that keeps us in a state of perpetual dependence?" Bergk bemoaned the low literary standards that prevailed among the majority of readers, who now preferred second-rate novels of romance and adventure to the works of Wieland or Goethe. These novels of escape were literary opiates that only rendered the bonds of despotism more tolerable:

They [readers of popular novels] will put up with anything as long as their torpor is not disturbed, and they are open to anything that promises pleasure. They will patiently endure the most shameful bonds of slavery if only they are given their food and drink, and they witness the destruction of press freedom and freedom of thought without the slightest murmur or resistance. They stupefy themselves with mindless and tasteless novels and cannot grasp how someone could have any desire higher than physical sustenance and pleasure.... The worst books are precisely the ones most widely read and distributed, and because they go through the most editions, some of our booksellers seek to outdo each other in the low quality of their wares if only their colors are lurid and their characters grotesque.[55]

Invoking Kantian ideals of moral autonomy and freedom – norms central to the ideology of the Enlightened public sphere – Bergk saw these very principles being undermined by an increasingly commercialized and trivialized literary marketplace. Confronted by a widening gap between their own normative premises and popular reading tastes, critics like Bergk had begun to question the viability of an enlightened public sphere.

Such doubts pointed to the extent to which a commercialized literary market had deepened the gulf between popular and educated tastes. Novels of entertainment abounded – ghost stories, adventure tales, comic or

---

[54] Johann Gottlieb Fichte, *Characteristics of the Present Age*, trans. William Smith (London, 1889), 97.
[55] Johann Adam Bergk, *Die Kunst, Bücher zu lesen* (Jena, 1799), 410, 414–15.

ʳdy fiction, light romances, many of them hastily written in accordance ...ᵤ proven formulas. Some were dashed off so quickly and shoddily that their authors inadvertently changed a character's name, occupation, or nationality in the course of the narrative. Novels had become an industry, its new products crowding the shelves of bookshops and lending libraries. As London's *Monthly Review* observed in 1790: "Novels spring into existence like insects on the banks of the Nile; and if we may be indulged in another comparison, cover the shelves of our circulation libraries, as locusts crowd the fields of Asia." In 1800 the poet Wordsworth lamented that "the invaluable works of our elder writers, I had almost said of Shakespeare and Milton, are driven into neglect by frantic novels, sickly and stupid German Tragedies, and deluges of idle and extravagant stories in verse." Here he echoed what a German visitor to London had noted a few years earlier:

The romances of a Richardson, a Fielding, and others, which were formerly in high repute, begin to be laid aside, as books which make the reader soon sleepy; and the rather, since almost every week new romances, in two or more little pocket volumes, are published in London, which are written with so much ease, and are so entertaining...

In 1785 a visitor to the Prussian city of Magdeburg found its lending library "heaped full with miserable novels, lamentable plays, and sappy poetry...A good book sits alone on the shelf like a poor orphan, while bad books spread like an epidemic through the entire town and its surrounding area." In 1796 Friedrich Reinhard Rücklefs found the quality of books supplied by lending libraries so low that he pleaded for the appointment of enlightened censors to purge them. "Seldom," wrote Rücklefs of lending libraries, "does one find the masterpieces of Goethe, Wieland, Herder, Schiller, Engel, Garve, and others; but novels of the supernatural, ghost stories, knights' adventures, fairy tales, erotic stories, monster tales, prophecies, and similarly wretched works can be found in abundance."[56]

Such observations anticipated what in fact was to become a central dilemma of nineteenth-century criticism: how was it possible to impose standards of taste on an expanding and increasingly heterogeneous print culture? Which texts and authors were to be ranked over others? In some ways the so-called quarrel between the Ancients and Moderns (or what Jonathan Swift called the "battle of the books") had already raised these

---

[56] Quotes taken, respectively, from Raven, *Judging New Wealth*, 68; Wordsworth, preface to the *Lyrical Ballads* (1800), in *The Prose Works of William Wordsworth*, ed. W. J. B. Owen and Jane Worthington Smyser (Oxford, 1974), I:128; Frederick August Wendeborn, *A View of England Towards the Close of the Eighteenth Century*, 2 vols. (Dublin, 1791), II:61; F. Schulz, "Kleine Wanderungen durch Teutschland in Briefen an den Doktor K.," *Teutsche Merkur*, Heft 1 (1785), 51; Martino, *Die deutsche Leihbibliothek*, 29.

questions earlier in the century. This scholarly and literary controversy, which raged in England as well as on the Continent from around 1690 to 1730, was fundamentally a debate over what we would today call the canon. In fields ranging from history and philosophy to science and literature, protagonists in the controversy argued over which authors were to serve as authoritative models in the world of learning and letters. Defenders of the Ancients, including Swift and Pope, invoked the classical authors of Greece and Rome. Partisans of the Moderns, such as the academician and man of letters Fontenelle, asserted that modern authors like Descartes, Shakespeare, and Milton had equaled and sometimes even surpassed their ancient forebears.

No clear victor emerged from the quarrel, which was not so much resolved (variants of the debate persist into our own day) as submerged by subsequent changes in the eighteenth-century literary market. During the second half of the eighteenth century, the proliferation of books and concomitant transformation of reading practices and tastes dissolved the authority of ancient and modern classics alike. The literary institutions of the Enlightenment public sphere were products of as well as reactions to this process. The organs of Enlightenment criticism – salons, journals, encyclopedias, literary lexicons, reading clubs – were generated by the eighteenth-century print explosion, but also were an attempt to impose order on it. Samuel Johnson's influential *Lives of the English Poets* was nothing if not an exercise in canon construction, a literary yardstick with which an ever-growing body of print was to be measured. In like fashion the intellectual luminaries who gathered weekly in Johnson's Literary Club, men like Edmund Burke, Edward Gibbon, and Joshua Reynolds functioned as a kind of synod for establishing standards of literary and artistic canonicity. In France, Diderot and his *philosophe* collaborators on the *Encyclopédie* were engaged in a similar enterprise. A sense of urgency pervaded Diderot's vision of the project: the printing press, he argued, had filled entire buildings with books, and soon the information they contained would be so vast as to render it unmanageable. The *Encyclopédie* was a means of ordering that knowledge. In Germany, Enlightenment journalism was driven by similar aims. As editor of the *Allgemeine Deutsche Bibliothek* (1765–1806), the Berlin journalist Friedrich Nicolai deemed it his mission to review annually every single book published in Germany. In doing so he hoped to foster an educated, homogeneous reading public that could distinguish between works of genuine quality and the dross he saw being produced by the literary marketplace. When the periodical ceased publication in 1806, it had reviewed some 80,000 books in 264 volumes.

Yet by the 1780s it was already clear that the Enlightenment's institutions of criticism could not control popular reading tastes and habits.

Their ability to do so foundered on a basic contradiction. On the one hand, the existence of the Enlightenment public sphere rested on a capitalized literary market that made books more accessible. Enlightenment critics welcomed this market – indeed, their works of popularization helped enlarge it – in so far as it conformed to their own project of diffusing useful knowledge. On the other hand, the very quantity and diversity of literary output was destined to elude their control. They watched with alarm and dismay as a commercialized literary market, like the sorcerer's apprentice, assumed an autonomous existence resistant to their tutelage.

Another problem was the inherent instability of the public enshrined in Enlightenment criticism. The concept of the public entered Enlightenment aesthetics in the early eighteenth century, with the work of influential critics like Joseph Addison in England and the Abbé Jean-Baptiste Dubos in France. Addison and Dubos attacked the formalistic, rule-based criteria of seventeenth-century classicism. What validated a work of art, they argued, was not simply its conformity to preestablished rules but also its public reception. A work of art was to be judged by how it moved its audience, not just its "objective," internal structure. By subordinating the formal properties of a work to the subjective response of its audience, Addison, Dubos, and subsequent eighteenth-century critics legitimized the role of the public as an aesthetic tribunal. Public judgment (or what Addison called the taste of the "town" and Dubos the "parterre"), not the metaphysical maxims of classicist poetics, determined whether or not a work of art was beautiful and pleasing.

But for Enlightenment critics, the public did not include just any reader or spectator. To be valid, the aesthetic judgments of a public had to be informed by taste, a concept that was to dominate the history of aesthetics from Shaftesbury through Kant. The possession of taste, or what Kant defined as the "capacity to judge the beautiful," determined whether a particular judgment was valid and universal. Most Enlightenment critics believed that everyone was in principle capable of acquiring taste and thereby rendering valid public judgments. Accordingly, they often wrote of the public as if it were a homogeneous entity, united by a general consensus regarding the value of any particular work. Conceiving of the public in this way had a certain tactical value, for by claiming to speak on behalf of the public these critics bestowed an aura of universality on their own judgments. But the myth of a homogeneous public also expressed their enlightened faith in the power of reason to produce agreement and consensus.

As in the sphere of politics, however, the literary public conceived by these critics was relatively narrow. In general, they held that only those with a sufficient level of culture and education could make reliable aesthetic judgments. To participate in the literary public, one had to be able to understand its products, and this in turn required a substanti degree of literacy and education. This criterion obviously disqualified the illiterate, i.e., the bulk of the rural and urban lower classes. It also excluded those who could read but whose lack of education or wealth impeded their material and intellectual access to the organs and institutions of the literary public sphere. Hence the public invoked by Enlightenment critics was in the end a relatively restricted stratum of educated, propertied, principally bourgeois and noble readers.

But by the late eighteenth century these critics could no longer ignore the fact that a broader, more inchoate public now threatened to dwarf the literary public they had once championed. To them the readers of Gothic novels, romances, and adventure tales were less interested in moral and aesthetic instruction than they were in entertainment and escape, and publishers were only too happy to meet the demand. While some writers and critics clung to the ideal of a homogeneous reading public, others responded with disillusionment. Friedrich Schiller, who earlier in his career had announced that "the public is everything to me, my school, my sovereign, my trusted friend," declared toward the end of his life that "the only relationship with the public that one cannot regret is war."[57] Disdain for "the public" was to be a common theme in Romantic criticism. Aware of the chasm separating themselves from popular reading tastes, haunted by a growing sense of alienation from the public of their day, Romantic critics like Coleridge in England or August Wilhelm Schlegel in Germany became all the more inclined to find refuge in a transcendent and autonomous realm of art. They upheld this realm not in the name of the public, but in conscious opposition to it.

A more constructive response to the disintegration of the literary public sphere was pedagogical. Neo-humanist in conception, it looked to the construction of a new literary canon to bridge the gulf between popular and elite tastes. In Germany, the pedagogical theorist Friedrich Immanuel Niethammer prescribed such a solution in an 1808 plan submitted to the Bavarian ministry of education. Niethammer's proposal began by pointing to the cultural and aesthetic consequences of the reading revolution:

The rage to read, which has become a German national vice, invariably seizes only upon what is new, mixing the bad with the good, ignoring or forgetting both in like fashion. In light of this condition, how can one form a standard for aesthetic judgment and feeling? Out of this deluge of books, which indiscriminately carries

[57] Friedrich Schiller, *Sämtliche Werke*, ed. G. Fricke and H. Göpfert (Munich, 1959), V:856; Schiller, *Briefe*, ed. G. Fricke (Munich, 1955), 266.

away in its current the best as well as the most vulgar, how is it possible to create anything enduring, anything that can awaken and confirm true aesthetic sensibility and taste?[58]

Niethammer's remedy was to propose the creation of a "national book" (*Nationalbuch*), an anthology of German literature that could be introduced into German secondary schools and universities. In Reformation Germany, argued Niethammer, Martin Luther's Bible had provided a uniform standard of literary expression that had joined together all social classes in a common culture. For more than two centuries Luther's translation had served as "a rallying point for the culture (*Bildung*) of every estate, whether refined or vulgar, high or low; to each [the translation] was equally important, equally well-known, equally familiar."[59] But now, Niethammer argued, the secularization and diversity of reading tastes had dissolved that common cultural denominator. He envisioned his anthology as a project of recanonization, an attempt to create a new cultural consensus that could reconnect high and low, elite and popular culture.

In Victorian Britain, the critical essays of Matthew Arnold marked a similar attempt to salvage the legacy of the public sphere of letters. Arnold advanced what remains a compelling diagnosis of the public sphere and its collapse. His *Culture and Anarchy* (1869) described a fragmented, class-ridden culture where disparities in wealth and education had all but destroyed any common standard of literary taste. In phrases redolent of public-sphere ideology, Arnold declared elsewhere that no coherent public existed because there was no "literary tribunal," no "supreme court of literature," no "sovereign organ of opinion" that "sets standards in a number of directions, and creates, in all those directions, a force of educated opinion, checking and rebuking those who fall below those standards, or who set them at nought." His proposed remedy, like that of Niethammer's, was to reconstitute the reading public through the state and its educational institutions. Like Niethammer, Arnold spent much of his career as a school official, serving more than two decades as a government inspector. Both men believed that the state alone, in league with an educated elite, was capable of fashioning a common literary culture informed by high standards of taste. For them the state functioned as a socially transcendent institution that could restore unity to a public shattered by social and cultural divisions. It would delegate this task to a cultured elite driven by

[58] Friedrich Immanuel Niethammer, "Das Bedürfnis eines Nationalbuches als Grundlage der allgemeinen Bildung der Nation," in Johann Wolfgang von Goethe, *Werke*, Abt. 2, Bd. 42 (Weimar, 1907), 401.

[59] *Ibid.*, 405.

a passion for diffusing, for making prevail, for carrying from one end of society to the other, the best knowledge, the best ideas of their time; who have laboured to divest knowledge of all that was harsh, uncouth, difficult, abstract, professional, exclusive; to humanize it, to make it efficient outside the clique of the cultivated and learned, yet still remaining the *best* knowledge and thought of the time, and a true source, therefore, of sweetness and light.[60]

Arnold's diagnosis seems remarkably prescient in light of our current preoccupation with issues of multiculturalism and the canon. Clearly he was better at posing questions than answering them. Today we are too aware of the state's complicity with social interests, too hip to the "hegemonic" claims of high culture, to consider his prescriptions much more than a Victorian profession of faith. Arnold's now classic definition of criticism – "a disinterested endeavor to learn and propagate the best that is known and thought in the world" – rings quaintly in postmodernist ears, if mellifluously to cultural conservatives still reeling from revisionist assaults on the traditional canon.

They ought to console themselves with the thought that the canon has always been subject to debate in one form or another, whether one speaks of the church fathers in the fourth century who debated which texts to include in the Bible, or the fifteenth-century humanists who by challenging the scholastic canonization of Aristotle gave birth to what we today call the humanities. One might in fact argue that the most yeasty movements in Western cultural history, such as the Scientific Revolution and the Enlightenment, have always been driven by attacks on prevailing conceptions of the canon. Efforts to revise or expand the canon need not, then, be lamented as a distressing symptom of cultural decline, but hailed as an auspicious sign that books and ideas still somehow matter in our culture. After all, to argue about what should not be included in the canon is still to affirm its existence. It presupposes, in other words, that a distinction can be made between excellence and mediocrity, good and bad literature. So while Arnold's elitism might discomfort those who press for a radical revision of the canon, in doing so they reaffirm his view that the role of the critic is to judge and discriminate. It is a conception of criticism that may not be as fashionable as it once was, but it is a major legacy of the Enlightenment public sphere.

Bibliographical note
R. A. Houston, *Literacy in Early Modern Europe: Culture and Education 1500–1800* (London and New York, 1988) and Roger Chartier, "The Practical Impact

---

[60] Matthew Arnold, "The Literary Influence of Academies," in *The Complete Prose Works of Matthew Arnold*, vol. III: *Lectures and Essays in Criticism*, ed. R. H. Super (Ann Arbor, 1962), 241; Arnold, *Culture and Anarchy*, ed. Samuel Lipman (New Haven and London, 1994), 48.

of Writing," in Chartier, ed., *A History of Private Life*, vol. III: *Passions of the Renaissance* (Cambridge, Mass., and London, 1993), provide excellent general discussions of the literacy question in early modern Europe. These works and a variety of other secondary sources provide the statistics on literacy I have cited in the first part of this chapter. These include Roger Chartier, *The Cultural Origins of the French Revolution*, trans. Lydia G. Cochrane (Durham, NC, and London, 1991); David Cressy, "Literacy in Context: Meaning and Measurement in Early Modern England," in John Brewer and Roy Porter, eds., *Consumption and the World of Goods* (London and New York, 1993); Rolf Engelsing, *Analphabetentum und Lektüre: Zur Sozialgeschichte des Lesens in Deutschland zwischen feudaler und industrieller Gesellschaft* (Stuttgart, 1973); Étienne François, "Alphabetisierung und Lesefähigkeit in Frankreich und Deutschland um 1800," in Helmut Berding, Étienne François, and Hans-Peter Ullmann, eds., *Deutschland und Frankreich im Zeitalter der französischen Revolution* (Frankfurt am Main, 1989); François, "Die Volksbildung am Mittelrhein im ausgehenden 18. Jahrhundert. Eine Untersuchung über die vermeintlichen 'Bildungsrückstand' der katholischen Bevölkerung Deutschlands im Ancien Régime," *Jahrbuch für westdeutsche Landesgeschichte* II (1977); François Furet and Jacques Ozouf, *Reading and Writing: Literacy in France from Calvin to Jules Ferry* (Cambridge, 1982); Richard Gawthrop and Gerald Strauss, "Protestantism and Literacy in Early Modern Germany," *Past and Present* 104 (1984); François Lebrun *et al.*, eds., *Histoire générale de l'enseignement et de l'education en France*, vol. V (Paris, 1981); R. A. Houston, *Scottish Literacy and the Scottish Identity* (Cambridge, 1985); Hans Medick, "Buchkultur und lutherischer Pietismus. Buchbesitz, erbauliche Lektüre und religiöse Mentalität in einer ländlichen Gemeinde Württembergs am Ende der frühen Neuzeit: Laichingen 1748–1820," in Rudolf Vierhaus *et al.*, *Frühe Neuzeit – Frühe Moderne? Forschungen zur Vielschichtigkeit von Übergangsprozessen* (Göttingen, 1992); James Van Horn Melton, *Absolutism and the Eighteenth-Century Origins of Compulsory Schooling in Prussia and Austria* (Cambridge, 1988); Rudolf Schenda, *Volk ohne Buch: Studien zur Sozialgeschichte der populären Lesestoffe* (Frankfurt am Main, 1970); David Vincent, *Literacy and Popular Culture: England 1750–1914* (Cambridge, 1989).

For popular reading habits, the English and French contexts are explored in Margaret Spufford, *Small Books and Pleasant Histories: Popular Fiction and its Readership in Seventeenth-Century England* (Athens, Georgia, 1981); Roger Chartier, *The Cultural Uses of Print in Early Modern France*, trans. Lydia G. Cochrane (Princeton, 1987), chs. 6–8; and Jean Quéniart, "Alphabetisierung und Leseverhalten der Unterschichten in Frankreich im 18. Jahrhundert," in Hans Ulrich Gumbrecht *et al.*, *Sozialgeschichte der Aufklärung in Frankreich*, vol. I (Munich and Vienna, 1981). For Germany, see Rolf Engelsing's *Analphabetentum und Lektüre* (cited above). It was Engelsing who first developed the "reading revolution" thesis, in his "Die Perioden der Lesergeschichte in der Neuzeit," *Archiv für Geschichte des Buchwesens* 10 (1970). Engelsing's argument is reassessed in Reinhard Wittmann, "Was There a Reading Revolution at the End of the Eighteenth Century?," in Guglielmo Cavallo and Roger Chartier, eds., *A History of Reading in the West*, trans. Lydia G. Cochrane (Amherst, 1999); see also the criticisms or modifications in John Brewer, "Cultural Consumption in Eighteenth-Century England: The View of the Reader," in Vierhaus *et al.*, eds., *Frühe Neuzeit – Frühe*

Moderne? (cited above), and Robert Darnton, "Readers Respond to Rousseau: The Fabrication of Romantic Sensitivity," in *The Great Cat Massacre and Other Episodes in French Cultural History* (New York, 1984). On the transformation of reading tastes in the eighteenth century, see also Darnton's "First Steps toward a History of Reading," *Australian Journal of French Studies* 23 (1986), and Erich Schön, *Der Verlust der Sinnlichkeit oder die Verwandlungen des Lesens. Mentalitätswandel um 1800* (Stuttgart, 1987).

Moral weeklies have been the subject of several fine studies. Lawrence E. Klein, *Shaftesbury and the Culture of Politeness: Moral Discourse and Cultural Politics in Early Eighteenth-Century England* (Cambridge, 1994), is excellent on the cultural and intellectual background of Addison and Steele's journalism. Kathyrn Shevelow, *Women and Print Culture: The Construction of Femininity in the Early Periodical* (London and New York, 1989), reexamines women's relationship to moral weeklies; see also the older study by J. Heinrich, *Die Frauenfrage bei Steele und Addison* (Leipzig, 1930). On German moral weeklies, Wolfgang Martens, *Die Botschaft der Tugend. Die Aufklärung im Spiegel der deutschen Moralischen Wochenschriften* (Stuttgart, 1968) is indispensible. French studies have focussed on Marivaux: see M. Gilot, *Les journaux de Marivaux: itinéraire moral et accomplissement esthétique,* 2 vols. (Lille and Paris, 1974), and Peter France, "The Sociable Essayist: Addison and Marivaux," in France, *Politeness and Its Discontents: Problems in French Classical Culture* (Cambridge, 1992).

On novels and their reading public in eighteenth-century England, Ian Watt, *The Rise of the Novel* (London, 1957) remains essential. On the development of the novel in eighteenth-century France and Germany, see Georges May, *Le dilemme du Roman au XVIIIe siècle* (New Haven and Paris, 1963); Vivienne Mylne, *The Eighteenth-Century French Novel: Techniques of Illusion,* 2nd ed. (Cambridge, 1981); and Marianne Spiegel, *Der Roman und sein Publikum im früheren 18. Jahrhundert 1700–1767* (Bonn, 1967). There is now a considerable body of scholarship on women as readers of novels. Joan DeJean, *Tender Geographies: Women and the Origins of the Novel in France* (New York, 1991) focusses on the seventeenth century. The relationship of women to the cult of sensibility in eighteenth-century English fiction is explored in Nancy Armstrong, *Desire and Domestic Fiction: A Political History of the Novel* (New York, 1987); Terry Eagleton, *The Rape of Clarissa: Writing, Sexuality and Class Struggle in Samuel Richardson* (Minneapolis, 1982); and Janet Todd, *Sensibility* (London and New York, 1986). The popularity of pornographic novels is examined in Robert Darnton's engaging *Forbidden Best-Sellers of Pre-Revolutionary France* (New York and London, 1995), which is also good on the politics of the genre. On political pornography see also the essays by Lynn Hunt, "The Many Bodies of Marie Antoinette: Political Pornography and the Problem of the Feminine in the French Revolution," and Sarah Maza, "The Diamond Necklace Affair Revisited (1785–86): The Case of the Missing Queen," in Lynn Hunt, ed., *Eroticism and the Body Politic* (Baltimore and London, 1991). On pornography in the eighteenth century, see in addition Lynn Hunt's introduction to *The Invention of Pornography: Obscenity and the Origins of Modernity* (New York, 1993), as well as Jean-Marie Goulemot, *Ces livres qu'on ne lit que d'une main: lecture et lecteurs de livres pornographiques au XVIIIe siècle* (Aix-en-Provence, 1991), and Goulemot, "Literary Practices: Publicizing the Private," in Chartier, ed., *History of Private Life,* vol. III (cited above).

On libraries and their publics, *Histoire des bibliothèques sous l'Ancien Régime*, ed. Claude Jolly (Paris, 1988) has useful essays on early modern France. For England, see Thomas Kelly, *Early Public Libraries: A History of Public Libraries in Great Britain before 1850* (London, 1966), and for Germany the exhaustive study by Alberto Martino, *Die deutsche Leihbibliothek: Geschichte einer literarischen Institution (1756–1914)* (Wiesbaden, 1990). Paul Kaufman, "The Community Library: A Chapter in English Social History," *Transactions of the American Philosophical Society*, n.s. 57/7 (1967), is good on eighteenth-century English circulation libraries; for their French counterparts, see Jean-Louis Pailhès, "En marge des bibliothèques: l'apparation des cabinets de lecture," in Jolly, ed., *Les bibliothèques sous l'Ancien Régime* (cited above); On the growing importance of the "public" in Enlightenment aesthetics, I have profited from Thomas E. Kaiser, "Rhetoric in the Service of the King: The Abbé Dubos and the Concept of Public Judgement," *Eighteenth-Century Studies* 23 (1989–90). See also Klaus L. Berghahn, "From Classicist to Classical Literary Criticism, 1730–1806," in Peter Uwe Hohendahl, ed., *A History of German Literary Criticism, 1730–1780* (Lincoln, Neb., and London, 1988), 40–42.

The impact of commercialization on reading tastes is discussed in James Raven, *Judging New Wealth: Popular Publishing and Responses to Commerce in England 1750–1800* (Oxford, 1992), and Carla Hesse, *Publishing and Cultural Politics in Revolutionary Paris, 1789–1810* (Berkeley, 1991), chs. 4–5. The challenges this posed to enlightened literary critics are explored in Terry Eagleton, *The Function of Criticism: From the Spectator to Post-Structuralism* (London, 1984). German scholars have dealt most extensively with the phenomenon of "reading mania" and the cultural anxieties it aroused. See Günther Erning, *Das Lesen und die Lesewut. Beiträge zur Fragen der Lesergeschichte* (Bad Heilbrunn, 1974), and Helmut Kreuzer, "Gefährliche Lesesucht? Bemerkungen zu politischer Lektürekritik im ausgehenden 18. Jahrhundert," in *Leser und Lesen im 18. Jahrhundert*, Colloquium der Arbeitstelle 18. Jh. Gesamthochschule Wuppertal. Schloss Lüntenbeck, 24–26 October, 1975 (Heidelberg, 1977).

4   Writing publics: eighteenth-century authorship

Samuel Johnson declared that he lived in *"The Age of Authors."* Dr. Johnson, who may well have read more authors than anyone else in the eighteenth century, was referring to his native Britain. Yet he might just as easily have been speaking of the Continent, for there, as in Britain, the dramatic increase in the production and consumption of the printed word gave a new importance to authors. For one thing, there were considerably more of them. In 1761 a German observer remarked of his native land that "we live generally in an age when ... almost everyone is afflicted by a passion to be an author. From the throne down to the shepherd's hut, anyone who knows how to hold a pen writes books."[1] Hyperbole to be sure, but more dispassionate commentators also noted the proliferation of authors. In the late eighteenth century the lexicographer Johann Georg Meusel estimated the number of German authors to have totaled between 2,000–3,000 during the 1760s, rising to 4,300 in 1776, 5,200 in 1784, and 7,000 in 1791. French lexicons attested to a similar increase in France. *La France litteraire*, a guide to French writers and their books published during the second half of the eighteenth century, listed 1,187 authors in 1757, 2,367 in 1769, and 2,819 in 1784. Citing these statistics, Robert Darnton concludes that by 1789 France had at least 3,000 authors, well over twice the number for 1750.[2]

But it was not just the *quantity* of literary producers that made the eighteenth century, relative to previous periods, the age of the author. The modern idea of the author was itself an eighteenth-century creation. Only then did writers come to view their craft as a full-time profession, even

---

[1] Rochus Friedrich Graf zu Lynar, cited in Reinhard Wittmann, *Geschichte des deutschen Buchhandels* (Munich, 1991), 147.

[2] J. G. Meusel, *Das Gelehrte Teutschland*, 5th ed. (Lemgo, 1796–1806), Preface, as cited in Hans J. Haferkorn, "Zur Entstehung der bürgerlich-literarischen Intelligenz und des Schriftstellers in Deutschland zwischen 1750 und 1800," in Bernd Lutz, ed., *Deutsches Bürgertum und literarische Intelligenz 1750–1800* (Stuttgart, 1974), 202; Robert Darnton, "The Facts of Literary Life in Eighteenth-Century France," in Keith Michael Baker, ed., *The French Revolution and the Creation of Modern Political Culture*, vol. I: *The Political Culture of the Old Regime* (Oxford and New York, 1987), I:267–68.

if relatively few could subsist at it. Only then did a burgeoning literary market encourage large numbers of authors, including an unprecedented number of women, to seek a living from their pens independently of private patrons. And only in the eighteenth century did there emerge the idea of authorship as *ownership*, or what we today call copyright, with authors considered the proprietors of work that could not be published or sold without their consent. An expanding publishing market and reading public, the rise of periodicals and newspapers, the rapidly growing demand for belletristic works, innovative techniques for selling and marketing books, all expanded the range of possibilities open to writers. For one, writing for money lost the stigma once attached to it; for another, authors could expect to be paid more for what they wrote than in the previous century. Authors at the same time acquired a new cultural and political identity. To the extent that the ideal of the public sphere rested on the assumption that print was the medium best suited for the effective and rational articulation of public opinion, the function of authors became central. They were simultaneously teachers and tribunes, seeking to educate the public while also representing its interests *vis-à-vis* those who exercised formal power over it. In the process authorship acquired an autonomous function in Enlightenment culture that seemed to mirror its new marketability.

The status of the author in England, France, and Germany

Prior to the eighteenth century, the ideal of the author had been that of the gentleman amateur. The older humanist prototype of the accomplished courtier viewed writing as one of several courtly talents one cultivated along with dancing, fencing, horsemanship, music, and so forth. Outwardly at least, the gentleman-poet disdained the idea of writing for money or even for an audience larger than a small circle of cultivated connoisseurs and patrons. Those few writers who were able to profit handsomely from the sale of their works were often criticized for their vulgarity or cupidity. Even the act of publishing one's work, especially poetry, bore a certain stigma. Many seventeenth-century poets, such as John Donne or Andrew Marvell in England, rarely printed their verse. They wrote chiefly in manuscripts that were circulated among a select group of friends and patrons who then disseminated copies to a wider readership. The preference for scribal over printed publication partly reflected the higher prestige that a handwritten text enjoyed over a printed one. More practical considerations, like the desire to evade censorship or imprisonment, also came into play. Sir Robert Filmer's *Patriarcha*, the notorious defense of absolutism that provoked Locke's *Two Treatises of Government*, originally circulated only in manuscript and was not printed until almost three decades after the author's death. Moreover, in an age of literary patronage, scribal rather than printed publication could also be in an author's financial interest. An author who presented a manuscript to a patron received as much as one who dedicated a printed book, and the work could then in turn be presented to other patrons as well. Scribal publication also eliminated the bookseller/publisher as middleman, for once an author had paid the scribe(s) who copied his manuscript, he profited directly from all sales.

All of this helps to explain why so many writers in the early eighteenth century still preferred to publish their works anonymously or pseudonymously. Most major German poets of the early eighteenth century wrote under pseudonyms, and even so prolific a writer as Jonathan Swift insisted on omitting his name from the title pages of his books. Not until the posthumous publication of Swift's collected works in 1735 did his name appear as author. The poet Thomas Gray also illustrates the persistence of traditional attitudes toward publication. Gray had never intended to publish his "Elegy Written in a Country Churchyard," a poem destined to become one of the most widely read works of eighteenth-century British poetry, but instead preferred to circulate it in manuscript among a small circle of friends and patrons. Only in 1751, after learning that a pirated edition was about to appear, did he ask his friend Horace Walpole to arrange its publication with the London bookseller Thomas Dodsley. Even then Gray accepted no money for the work, and sought to distance himself from the enterprise by asking if the publisher "would add a Line or two to say it came into his Hands by Accident."[3] A similar disregard for authorial identity characterized the stage. The playwright William Congreve (1670–1729) was the first British playwright to have his name featured on playbills, and in Paris it was not until the eighteenth century that the author's name routinely appeared on theater placards. Likewise, the audience's practice of summoning an author to appear on stage at the conclusion of a successful premier only became common around the mid-eighteenth century. In Paris, Voltaire was the first to merit this honor following the 1743 premier of his *Mérope*.

The tendency to conceal authorial identity was symptomatic of the extent to which writing for publication had yet to gain acceptance as a professional activity. Inhibiting the professionalization of writing was not only the persistence of traditional attitudes toward authorship, but also the absence of a literary market sufficiently large to enable authors to

[3] Quoted in Alvin Kernan, *Samuel Johnson and the Impact of Print* (Princeton, 1987), 64.

support themselves from the sale of their works. An author's financial remuneration usually took the form of a flat sum (or "honorarium") paid by the publisher, who in return acquired full rights to the sale of the work. Honoraria were generally low and writers sometimes contented themselves with free copies of their work, which they then sold surreptitiously or presented to friends, fellow authors, or prospective patrons. John Milton sold the rights to his *Paradise Lost* for a paltry £20 and appeared more interested in the free copies promised him by his publisher. Descartes received no honorarium from his Leyden publisher for the rights to his *Discourse on Method*, being satisfied instead with the complimentary copies he was given.

The new opportunities posed by the expanding literary market of the eighteenth century were first visible in England. The English market enjoyed important advantages *vis-à-vis* the Continent, not the least being the relatively mild censorship regime that developed after the Glorious Revolution of 1688. Moreover, the business and political culture of Augustan England also offered new prospects for writers, and it was no coincidence that the term journalist first gained currency at this time. As we have seen, the financial and commercial revolutions of the early eighteenth century created a ravenous public appetite for information relevant to foreign and domestic markets – wars, political events at home and abroad, natural disasters – and newspapers and commercial sheets multiplied accordingly. The emergence of a party system also provided work for writers willing to enlist in the cause of government, opposition, or in some cases both. Under William III (1689–1702) and Anne (1702–14) the recruitment of pamphleteers by government and opposition created new sources of support for writers. Walpole's government (1726–42) subsidized journalists to the tune of thousands of pounds each year, although the more talented writers of the age (e.g., Pope, Swift, and Gay) tended to line up behind the opposition. To those authors the Walpole regime had little interest in rewarding literary merit and preferred instead to subsidize mediocre writers willing to sell their pens to the highest bidder.

The legend of the Grub Street hack, the shabby writer willing to prostitute whatever talents he possessed to eke out a miserable living, had its origins during this period. The stereotype owed much to Pope and his circle, for whom Grub Street was less a place than a metaphor. It represented a publishing market spun out of control, one in which standards of literary quality were submerged in a sea of mendacity and mediocrity. It also served as an image of urban squalor and disorder: the street itself lay in a district of London long associated with disease, crime, and civil discord. A center of plague, prostitution, and Puritan pamphleteering in the seventeenth century, Grub Street symbolized the ills of an increasingly urban and commercial society.

Yet the herd of penurious pamphleteers and talentless hacks whom Pope satirized in his *Dunciad* (1728–43) was symptomatic of the literary success to which growing numbers of authors, however modest their abilities, could at least aspire. Often acknowledged as one of the first authors of the century to achieve financial self-sufficiency solely through the sale of his works, Pope was himself a beneficiary of the print explosion he viewed with such disdain. He began his career as poorly paid as any aspiring writer, receiving in 1712 a mere £7 for his *Rape of the Lock*. But in the coming years he was able to amass a sizable fortune through the clever and calculated management of his literary career. He achieved much of his financial success through the skillful use of subscription campaigns. Under this marketing technique an author announced his or her intention to publish a particular work, and invited prospective readers to purchase tickets entitling them to receive the work upon completion. Tickets were advertised in periodicals and newspapers, or given to friends and supporters to sell at coffeehouses, salons, or other gatherings. The subscription system represented a transitional phase in the development of the eighteenth-century literary market, a shift from private patronage to that of a public willing and able to invest in literary culture.

Pope's first successful use of subscription patronage came with his translation of the *Iliad* (1720). Having lined up 575 subscribers at 6 guineas each, Pope was able to earn approximately £5,320 for the six-volume work. He followed up his success with a translation of *The Odyssey*, which attracted 600 subscribers and earned Pope some £4,500.[4] Using as a financial yardstick what another man of letters, Samuel Johnson, estimated it cost him to live for a year in mid-eighteenth-century London (£30), one can appreciate just how sizable a sum this was.

Subscription campaigns subsequently spread to France, where the *philosophes* and their supporters used them for a variety of enterprises. The *Encyclopédie*, one of the most successful publishing enterprises of the eighteenth century, was marketed partly through subscriptions. Voltaire raised money for the Calas family by selling subscriptions of engravings depicting their misery, and he himself became the object of a subscription campaign organized by the Parisian salon of Suzanne Necker to raise funds for a statue of him in 1770. For the *philosophes*, subscription served as a vehicle for the mobilization and articulation of an enlightened public opinion. For those who wanted to belong to that public, subscription was a way of gaining membership.[5]

---

[4] See Pat Rogers's introduction to his edition of Pope's writings in *The Oxford Authors* series (Oxford, 1993), xv.

[5] Dena Goodman, *The Republic of Letters: A Cultural History of the French Enlightenment* (Ithaca and London, 1994), 179–81.

Overall, however, subscription never acquired the importance in France and Germany that it enjoyed in Britain. In France the cumbersome machinery of royal, ecclesiastical, and parlementary censorship inhibited its use, while in Germany the territorial fragmentation of the Holy Roman Empire limited the scale and feasibility of subscription campaigns. Fear of identifying publicly with a controversial work or author may also have posed an obstacle. Here it is revealing that while English books published through subscription prominently displayed the list of subscribers, French books seldom did so.[6]

At any rate, most successful British writers of the period published their work through subscription at one time or another, including women authors who used it to target and mobilize a female audience. The novelist Frances Burney, for example, earned £3,000 from subscriptions to *Camilla*.[7] Subscription publishing enabled authors and publishers alike to build and expand a public, beginning with relatively small circles of friends and supporters and, if a work was successful, reaching a broader audience.

As publishers perceived the profits gleaned from this audience, they became willing to pay authors more for works they believed had commercial potential. The typical copyright payment to authors rose from £50 at the end of Queen Anne's reign to £100 in 1750, and then to £150 by 1770. Already in the 1720s, the playwright and poet John Gay received £400 for the copyright to his *Beggar's Opera*, £1,200 for its sequel, *Polly*, and £1,000 for his *Poems*. Defoe earned enough from his novels to purchase estates for himself and for his daughter alike. Oliver Goldsmith was paid £500 for each of his plays and 800 guineas for his *Natural History*. Fielding earned £600 for the copyright to *Tom Jones* and 1000 guineas for his fourth novel, *Amelia* (1751). And it has been calculated that during the last two decades of his life, Samuel Johnson earned from his writings alone an average of £300–400 per year – more than ten times what he calculated he needed for his annual living expenses. Authors of popular histories and works of travel could also command large sums, especially those with established reputations. William Robertson received £4,000 for his *History of Charles V*, while John Hawkesworth's best-selling account of Cook's South Sea Expedition brought him £6,000.[8]

---

[6] *Ibid.*, 177.

[7] Cheryl Turner, *Living by the Pen: Women Writers in the Eighteenth Century* (London, 1992), 112–13.

[8] A. S. Collins, *The Profession of Letters: A Study of the Relation of Author to Patron, Publisher, and Public 1780–1832* (New York, 1929), 85; J. W. Saunders, *The Profession of English Letters* (London and Toronto, 1964), 122; Kernan, *Samuel Johnson and the Impact of Print*, 103.

Such sums help explain the envy often felt by French writers toward their British counterparts. "In England," wrote the *philosophe* Friedrich Melchior Grimm following the publication of the final ten volumes of the *Encyclopédie* in 1766, "the *Encyclopédie* would have made the fortune of authors." When Charles George Fenouillot de Falbaire, an observer of the Parisian literary scene, learned in 1770 of the £4,000 Robertson had received for his *Charles V*, he wrote that "if a Parisian publisher had paid an eighth of this sum, he would believe himself to have treated an author very generously."[9] But even though French authors on the whole commanded less for their work than comparably successful writers across the Channel, in France, too, an expanding literary market increased what writers could expect to earn from their works. Diderot, renowned like Pope for his ability to subsist off his writing, estimated that over a twenty-year period his published works had earned him around 40,000 écus – approximately £240 a year, a comfortable income for the time. Rousseau received from his publisher over 13,000 francs (£520) for his *Dictionary of Music*, Marmontel earned 10,000 francs for his collected works, while Mercier was paid 6,000 francs for the last four volumes of his *Tableau de Paris*. As in Britain, the rise of journalism offered new sources of income. The *philosophe* Jean-François de La Harpe received an annual salary of 6,000 francs when he assumed the editorship of the semi-official *Mercure de France* in 1778, and the anti-*philosophe* Élie Fréron sometimes earned as much as 20,000 francs a year as editor of the *Année littéraire* from 1754 to 1775. Simon-Nicolas-Henri Linguet, commissioned in 1774 by the Parisian publishing czar Charles-Joseph Panckoucke to assume the editorship of the *Journal de politique et de la littérature*, received an annual salary of 10,000 livres. When in 1785 the journalist and critic Jean-Baptiste Suard became editor of the *Journal de Paris*, Paris's first daily newspaper, he pocketed 20,000 francs a year in salary and profits.[10]

Yet the French monarchy, with its stricter regime of censorship and relatively inelastic book market, placed greater constraints on the profession of letters than its British counterpart. As we have seen, there were limits to the range of royal censorship and countless authors were able to publish their works illicitly or abroad. Still, the delays often suffered in securing a royal *privilège*, the legal risks of illegal publication, and the forfeiture of copyright protection entailed by publishing abroad, all made authorship a more difficult enterprise in France than it was in England.

[9] Quotes taken from John Lough, *Writer and Public in France: From the Middle Ages to the Present Day* (Oxford, 1978), 200.

[10] *Ibid.*, 210–14, 234. David Pottinger, *The French Book Trade in the Ancien Régime* (Cambridge, MA, 1958), 98–99; Darlene Gay Levy, *The Ideas and Careers of Simon-Nicolas-Henri Linguet: A Study in Eighteenth-Century French Politics* (Urbana, 1980), 172.

These conditions doubtless help explain why royal and ecclesiastical patronage played a larger role in French letters than it did across the Channel. Once viewed as social and political outsiders driven by rage and resentment against aristocratic wealth and privilege, the *philosophes* were far more integrated into the prevailing social and political structures of the Old Regime than previously believed. The *philosophes* who congregated in the Parisian salon of Baron D'Holbach, notorious in his day for his philosophical radicalism, were anything but outsiders. D'Holbach's inherited wealth had enabled him in 1756 to purchase a royal office that gave him a substantial income as well as noble rank. The historian and pamphleteer François-Jean, chevalier de Chastellux, was descended from an ancient aristocratic family long distinguished for its military service to the crown. Charles-Georges Le Roy, the *Encyclopédiste* and zoologist, was a noble who inherited from his father a court position overseeing the royal hunting grounds and parks of Versailles. The poet and essayist Jean-François de Saint-Lambert, the scion of an old if impecunious noble family, had served with distinction as an officer in the French army. The chemist Jean Darcet, who was of petty-noble origins, wound up director of research at the royal porcelain works in Sèvres as well as inspector-general of the royal mint. Melchior Grimm, the son of a Lutheran church official in the upper Palatinate, was later in life elevated to an imperial baronage. Diderot, whose father was a master-cutler as well as a landowner, justly prided himself on his independence from patrons but ultimately accepted an annual pension of 1,000 *livres* from Catherine the Great. Claude-Adrian Helvétius, the son of a physician to Louis XIV, grew up at Versailles and later purchased the right to be a tax farmer. The uproar caused by the publication of his materialist tract, *De l'esprit*, did not prevent him from amassing an estate valued at almost 4 million *livres* (approximately £160,000) at his death.[11]

These were not free-floating intellectuals who attacked the Old Regime from its margins. They were, to use Darnton's words, "respectable, domesticated, and assimilated."[12] Once regarded as the product of a rising middle class spawned by a nascent capitalist order, French men of letters as a whole now appear considerably less "bourgeois" than they once seemed. On the eve of the Revolution, the first and second Estates (i.e., the clergy and nobility, who comprised less than 5 percent of the population) made up around one-third of all authors whose social position can be identified. The percentage was even higher in the provincial academies, the main seat of Enlightenment culture outside of Paris, where nobles

---

[11] Alan Charles Kors, *D'Holbach's Coterie: An Enlightenment in Paris* (Princeton, 1976), passim.

[12] Robert Darnton, "The High Enlightenment and the Low-Life of Literature," in Darnton, *The Literary Underground of the Old Regime* (Cambridge, MA, 1982), 5.

and clergy respectively comprised 37 percent and 20 percent of academy membership. Although the largest percentage of writers in eighteenth-century France came from middle-class backgrounds, these were not the economically dynamic bourgeoisie of liberal and Marxist lore but a more traditional, Old Regime bourgeoisie. The great majority had backgrounds in the professions as lawyers, doctors, teachers, or clergy, not in manufacturing and commerce. Those with wealth tended to draw it from traditional sources, most notably offices and annuities sold or granted by the crown.[13]

Robert Darnton's now classic thesis holds that the revolutionary challenge to the Old Regime came not from the *philosophes* and their epigones but from a literary underground of frustrated, aspiring writers unable to gain entry into this privileged literary world. These young men, drawn to Paris in the hopes of becoming the next Voltaire or Diderot, found a world closed to those lacking the patronage and connections so necessary for a successful literary career. They joined the ranks of a burgeoning literary underworld, eking out a precarious existence as copyists, composers of pornographic and libelous pamphlets, or in the case of the future revolutionary, Brissot, police spies. This literary proletariat seethed with resentment toward an Old Regime they deemed hopelessly corrupt and a cultural elite from which they felt unjustly excluded. Their Grub Street-like garrets, concluded Darnton, not the comfortable salons of the *philosophes*, were the literary and intellectual incubators of the Revolution.

Recent scholarship challenges one of Darnton's basic assumptions, namely that opportunities for men of letters were shrinking on the eve of the Revolution. Against the desperate poverty and the stymied careers that Darnton viewed as the lot of Paris's literary Grub Street, Elizabeth Eisenstein has painted a more sanguine if less romantic portrait. She suggests that on the whole these writers were not proto-revolutionary "hacks" but quasi-professionals, many of whom succeeded in making a modest living popularizing Enlightenment science and philosophy. Even if, as Darnton claims, the book trade in France was depressed during the 1780s, French writers continued to profit from the brisk demand for their works outside of France. Owing to the thriving market for francophone books in England, Holland, and Switzerland, French writers did not have to depend on Paris for their literary sustenance. Hence Brissot and Marat, who for Darnton typified the evolution from Grub Street hack to revolutionary, both spent a considerable part of their prerevolutionary careers abroad. Marat subsisted in London for more than a decade, where he observed

---

[13] The statistics above are cited in Hans Ulrich Gumbrecht, Rolf Reichardt, and Thomas Schleich, "Für eine Sozialgeschichte der französischen Aufklärung," in Hans Ulrich Gumbrecht *et al.*, eds., *Sozialgeschichte der Aufklärung in Frankreich* (Munich, 1981), 12–14, and Darnton, "The Facts of Literary Life in Eighteenth-Century France," 275.

the meteoric rise of John Wilkes. The travels of the well-heeled Brissot included a voyage to America (1788), where he toured the world's youngest republic. At any rate, Eisenstein observes, neither was exactly a literary proletarian stifling in the fetid air of a Parisian garret. In their case it may have been rising expectations acquired abroad, not declining opportunities at home, that nourished their radicalism.

Relative to the French scene, writers in eighteenth-century Germany faced both advantages and drawbacks. On the positive side was the diversity of political and confessional cultures. Censorship in the Holy Roman Empire varied from territory to territory, and what could not be published for political or religious reasons in one might well be tolerated in another. The empire's territorial fragmentation had also encouraged a more extensive and varied network of newspapers and periodicals than existed in France. Germany's lack of a metropolitan capital comparable to Paris or London was sometimes considered a sign of cultural "backwardness," but it undoubtably helped foster a thriving and diverse journalistic culture. Here it is indicative that Christoph Martin Wieland, the only German author of the Enlightenment who consistently supported himself through his literary endeavors, largely did so not through his poetry or translations but in his capacity as editor and publisher of a periodical.

On the negative side, the political structure of the empire rendered it difficult for authors to reap much commercial profit from their work. Germany's fragmentation made it almost impossible to prevent a book published in one territory from being pirated in another. Literary piracy was a problem everywhere in Europe, but in the Holy Roman Empire the existence of more than 300 semi-autonomous principalities militated against the promulgation of copyright legislation valid for Germany as a whole. Piracy was rampant, compounding the risks publishers had to assume and making them less willing to pay adequate honoraria to their authors. Hence German authors on the whole earned less than their English or French counterparts, and for that reason both the idea and reality of professional authorship emerged more slowly. Traditional attitudes toward authorship persisted long after they had faded in Britain and France. As Goethe later wrote in his autobiography, up to the mid-eighteenth century "the production of poetical works was looked upon as something sacred, and in this case the acceptance or increase of any remuneration would have been regarded almost as simony."[14]

But as Goethe hastened to add, by mid-century the substantial returns that major publishing houses had begun to realize from an expanding

---

[14] *The Autobiography of Johann Wolfgang von Goethe*, trans. John Oxenford, II vols. (Chicago, 1974), II:139.

book market made authors conscious of the gap between their own small earnings and the profits of their publishers. The vicissitudes of Christian Fürchtegott Gellert, who in the 1750s was the most popular poet and playwright in Germany, were a particularly glaring example. The first edition of Gellert's *Didactic Poems and Stories* (1754) sold 6,000 copies, a phenomenal publishing success, and in the next two years subsequent editions yielded sales of 100,000. But although his works made his Leipzig publisher a wealthy man, Gellert himself earned no more than his original honorarium of 45 Reichsthaler – just over £6.[15] The contrast between his publisher's windfall and Gellert's trifling recompense had a galvanizing effect on many of his fellow writers, as Goethe later observed. Beginning in the 1760s, a desire for more financial independence led to efforts at establishing author-run publishing houses (*Selbstverlage*). These literary cooperatives sought to circumvent commercial publishers, establishing a direct relationship between author and public and in the process increasing what writers earned. In 1767, for example, Lessing and the translator Johann Joachim Christoph Bode founded a non-profit publishing house where authors of the day could publish their works. The most ambitious and publicized of these schemes was conceived in 1773 by Friedrich Gottlieb Klopstock, the most celebrated German poet of his day and the literary godfather of the pre-Romantic Storm and Stress movement. Outlined in a subscription campaign for his forthcoming *German Republic of Letters* (*Deutsche Gelehrtenrepublik*), Klopstock's plan entailed the creation of a dense consumer network of German authors and readers that would liberate the literary marketplace from the dominion of niggardly publishers. Any author desiring to publish a work could publicize it among the network's members, who in turn were to advertise it throughout their communities and collect subscriptions from anyone wanting to buy it. Given sufficient interest, the author could then publish the work privately and send the copies to selected distribution points (Klopstock proposed the creation of sixty-eight). From those towns and cities, members of the network would send the books and collect the subscription fees. Klopstock anticipated that most members of the network would perform this service gratis, out of altruism, but proposed that others be given a book discount of 15–20 percent as an added incentive.

Klopstock's proposal caught the attention of German readers, and the following year his *German Republic of Letters* appeared with an unprecedented 3,678 signatures from more than 263 locales. As the largest subscription campaign in the history of German letters to date, it was a

---

[15] Albert Ward, *Book Production, Fiction, and the German Reading Public 1740–1800* (Oxford, 1974), 89.

cultural phenomenon in its own right. Throughout Germany a largely middle-class public of students, professors, pastors, officials, and merchants voluntarily collected subscriptions and distributed books. Patriotic sentiment played some role, since Klopstock had become to educated Germans of the time a symbol of Germany's literary and cultural revival. More importantly, the enthusiastic response to Klopstock's campaign symbolized educated readers' growing consciousness of themselves as a public, membership in which was a source of cultural status and identity.

But although subsequent authors tried to replicate Klopstock's success, subscription publishing did not prove to be the panacea the German poet had prophesied. Part of the reason was that Klopstock's *German Republic of Letters*, with its bombastic style and arcane allusions to Germanic myth, ultimately flopped with critics and readers alike. As Goethe later recalled, it so disappointed subscribers that German readers became less willing to support subsequent subscription campaigns. Subscription publishing was at any rate difficult to carry out effectively in a country where the reading public was so dispersed and lacked the concentrated literary market of a metropolitan capital like London. In the ensuing years a few works, such as Gottfried August Bürger's poems, Johann Heinrich Voss's translation of *The Odyssey*, and Lessing's *Nathan the Wise*, were successfully marketed through subscription. But, on the whole, subscription publishing in eighteenth-century Germany never proved the boon for authors that it did in Britain.

Nor did author-run publishing houses live up to the hopes of their founders. Their failure resulted largely from the machinations of the established commercial publishers in Leipzig, the center of the German book trade. In the case of Lessing's author-run house in Hamburg, Leipzig publishers deliberately pirated its books and then sold them at half price to drive the interloper out of business. This cut-throat capitalism was highly effective, and author-run publishing enterprises proved invariably short lived.

As in England and France, however, German authors did ultimately if belatedly succeed in exacting higher payments from their publishers. From the 1770s on, successful authors like Klopstock, Wieland, and Lessing saw their honoraria increase as much as five-fold from the previous decade. Yet of these three, only Wieland was able to support himself without outside patronage or employment. During most of his career Klopstock received support from his patron, the king of Denmark; Lessing, after struggling more than a decade to subsist off his literary work, finally gave up in 1770 and accepted a position as court librarian in Wolfenbüttel. With exhausted resignation, Lessing wrote to his brother: "Take my brotherly advice and give up your plan to live by the pen ... See that you become a secretary or get on the faculty somewhere. It's the only way to avoid starving sooner or later." Friedrich Schiller, who began his literary career with the intention of living solely off his writing, ultimately found it an elusive goal. As he wrote in 1791: "To satisfy the strict demands of art while at the same time subsisting on the basis of one's literary exertions is not possible in our German world of letters. I struggled for ten years to do both, only barely succeeding at the cost of my health." Even Goethe, already a literary legend by the end of the century, is estimated to have earned about 152,000 Taler during his entire literary career – roughly what Sir Walter Scott averaged in three years.[16]

To a greater degree even than in France, then, German writers and intellectuals depended on support from extra-literary sources. Their ties to the state were more direct than in England or France, reflecting the post-Reformation role of German universities as a training ground for territorial officials and a state clergy. Most writers and intellectuals of note held what were, in effect, civil service positions as university professors, Lutheran pastors, and princely officials. Hence the two leading philosophers of the early German Enlightenment, Christian Thomasius and Christian Wolff, were professors at the University of Halle in Prussia; their literary counterparts, Gellert and Gottsched, occupied chairs at the University of Leipzig. The statist tinge of German letters did not substantially fade during the second half of the century. Goethe spent much of his early career in the employ of the duke of Saxony-Weimar, Herder was a Lutheran pastor, Schiller became a professor at Jena, and August Ludwig Schlözer, the leading political journalist of the 1770s and 1780s, was a Göttingen professor. Kant, a professor in Königsberg, evoked the German symbiosis of Enlightenment and territorial state in his distinction between the citizen's public use of reason (which was to be free) and the civil servant's private use of reason (which could be legitimately curbed because of his official status). There was no German Grub Street, at least not of the politically subversive sort that Darnton described for France. Closely tied to the territorial states that employed them as pastors, professors, or officials, German men of letters overall favored reform from above rather than revolution from below.

However varied its manifestations, the expanding literary market of the eighteenth century helped foster a greater sense of authorial identity and autonomy. Print technology itself drove home the concept of authorship

---

[16] Quotes taken from Martha Woodmansee, "The Genius and the Copyright: Economic and Legal Conditions of the Emergence of the 'Author,'" *Eighteenth-Century Studies* 17 (1984), 431, and Haferkorn, "Zur Entstehung der bürgerlich-literarischen Intelligenz," 170. The comparison between Scott and Goethe is found in Hans-Ulrich Wehler, *Deutsche Gesellschaftsgeschichte. Bd. I: Vom Feudalismus des Alten Reiches bis zur defensiven Modernisierung der Reformära 1700–1815* (Munich, 1987), 315.

through its capacity to reproduce a work in thousands of copies, each bearing the author's name on its title page. Moreover, in the eighteenth century the author began to acquire an individual identity through the genre of literary biography, popularized in works like Johnson's *Lives of the Poets*. And most important of all, the expansion of the publishing market was accompanied by a corresponding decline in the significance of individual patronage. The view of patronage as a state of dependence that compromised the author's integrity became more and more common. Pope boasted of his independence not only from private patrons but from political ones as well. "I take myself to be the only Scribbler of my Time," he wrote in 1723, "who never received any Places from the Establishment, any Pension from a Court, or any Presents from a Ministry. I intend to preserve this Honor untainted to my Grave." Samuel Johnson expressed his disdain for private patrons in 1754, when he bitterly defined a patron as "one who looks with unconcern on a man struggling for life in the water, and, when he has reached ground, encumbers him with help."[17]

Thus the ideal of independence and autonomy became increasingly central to authorial identity in the eighteenth century. Paradoxically, the close relationship between men of letters and the state that developed in France and Germany in the seventeenth and eighteenth centuries ultimately enhanced that sense of autonomy. In France, this relationship found expression in the Parisian and provincial academies chartered by the crown under Richelieu and Louis XIV. In Germany, it was evident in the princely bureaucracies and universities where writers so often found employment. These ties to the state helped foster in authors a transcendent vision of themselves as servants of the public good. From there it was a relatively small step for them to view themselves as independent representatives of "public opinion," especially after an expanding publishing market had served to multiply organs of literary and political expression. The *philosophe* Jean le Rond D'Alembert described this evolution from servants of absolutism to autonomous intellectuals in a 1753 essay celebrating the important social role men of letters had acquired in the Old Regime.[18] He traced this role back to the centralized system of cultural patronage established under Louis XIV, which had elevated the status of men of letters through the royal pensions and academies created for them. As a result, men of letters were not as sycophantic as they once had been, a change evident from the fact that it was no longer fashionable for

---

[17] Pope is quoted in Collins, *Authorship in the Days of Johnson*, 125; James Boswell, *Life of Samuel Johnson, LL.D.* (Chicago, 1952), 72.

[18] D'Alembert, *Essai sur la société des gens de lettres et des grands, sur la réputation, sur les Mécènes, et sur les récompenses littéraires* (1753).

them to preface their works with fawning dedications to patrons: "such baseness," observed D'Alembert, "inspires ridicule that very few men of letters have the courage to brave." Having become servants of the public good through their intimate relationship to the state, their task was now to "legislate for the rest of the nation in matters of philosophy and taste." But fulfilling this task demanded that they be independent *vis-à-vis* both the state and the Old Regime's hierarchy of rank and privilege. The former required freedom of the press and the ability to pursue truth without undue outside interference; the latter entailed equality within the Republic of Letters, with merit the only criterion for esteem and advancement.

Authorship as property: the rise of copyright

Also contributing to the rise of the author was an emerging definition of literary property. The notion that authors were owners of their work was relatively new. Renaissance and neoclassicist theories tended to view authors as artisans who crafted their work according to a body of rules inherited from classical rhetoric and poetics. Here the author was less the creator of an original work than a craftsman who manipulated preexisting forms in a manner pleasing to a cultivated and often courtly audience. To be sure, some authors were acknowledged to be more skilled than others. In cases where authors displayed extraordinary gifts, their talents were explained by reference to some external cause – the muses were often invoked, at other times divine inspiration. In both instances the writer, whether as workmanlike artisan or inspired poet, was conceived more as a vessel than as an original creator. As artisans, authors were simply the vehicle of received aesthetic rules; if inspired and gifted, they were the passive instruments of superhuman or divine forces. But in neither case were they really considered the creators of their work, nor, by extension, its owners.[19]

Prior to the eighteenth century, legal provisions did exist in most territories that sought to protect the rights to a published work. But their chief goal was not to defend authors against literary piracy, but to shore up the trade monopoly of a relatively small group of licensed publishers. Laws against book piracy were also part of a machinery of governmental censorship established in the sixteenth and seventeenth centuries, which had attempted to regulate the sale and distribution of works deemed morally, spiritually, or politically harmful. In Restoration England the unauthorized publication and distribution of printed material had fallen under the

[19] See Woodmansee, "Genius and the Copyright," 426–27.

Licensing Act of 1662, which restricted the ownership of most copyrights of any value to a small group of bookseller-publishers in London. The Licensing Act had at the same time created the censorship apparatus that operated throughout the Restoration. This same blend of censorship and protectionism characterized the French book trade, where royal permission to publish a work included prohibitions against the sale of pirated editions. Here too, such provisions were designed to protect not authors but the monopoly of a small number of publishers, almost exclusively Parisian. In Germany, rights of censorship and protection of the book trade likewise went hand in hand, although for the most part they were exercised by territorial governments rather than the emperor.

The eighteenth-century debate over copyright originated in England, where it was precipitated by Parliament's refusal in 1694 to renew the Licensing Act. As mentioned earlier, the lapse of the Licensing Act not only dismantled the cumbersome machinery of Restoration censorship but also deregulated the publishing trade. In the process, however, deregulation opened the door to pirated editions of Shakespeare, Milton, Dryden, and other works to which a relatively small number of London publishers had previously held the rights. In an effort to stem the tide of cheap reprints, London publishers petitioned Parliament for protection against book piracy. Their efforts led to the Statute of Anne (1709), the first copyright act in Europe. For books published after 1709 the statute limited copyright to a term of fourteen years, which could then be renewed as long as the author was still alive. For books already in print the copyright term was set at twenty-one years. While the statute ostensibly sought to curb piracy, its establishment of limited rather than perpetual copyright in effect broke the monopoly that the leading London publishers still exercised over much of the book trade. In response, these publishers now lobbied to amend the statute in favor of a perpetual rather than a limited grant of copyright. Perpetual copyright was of course in their interest, since they already held most copyrights of value. London publishers continued to press their case in Parliament, and the next half-century saw a struggle between proponents of limited and perpetual copyright. For Parliament the issue became unavoidable in 1735, when the twenty-one-year term protecting copyrights for pre-1709 imprints expired. London publishers now sought injunctions against other firms (many of them in Scotland and Ireland) that had begun to reprint works printed before 1709; those firms in turn invoked the Statute of Anne in their defense. At issue was whether booksellers who possessed the exclusive rights to Shakespeare and Milton, Newton and Locke, would continue to hold them, or whether all works published prior to the statute would now enter the public domain.

More fundamentally, the debate revolved around whether printed ideas, in this case much of Britain's literary legacy, could be "owned." London publishers insisted that without perpetual copyright, the world of letters and scholarship would collapse. Why, they asked, would authors toil over their work without the assurance that they and their heirs would reap the rewards from it? How could a publisher be expected to publish costly works of scholarship, with their more narrow market appeal, as long as competitors could issue cheap reprints with virtually no capital outlay? The latter question troubled not just publishers but those who feared that the elimination of perpetual copyright would lower cultural standards. These critics warned that without perpetual copyright authors would have no incentive to produce works of enduring value. The literary critic Catherine Macaulay made this point in her *Modest Plea for the Property of Copyright* (1774), which warned that the abolition of perpetual copyright would reduce letters to the production of "trifling, wretched compositions as please the vulgar; compositions which disgrace the press, yet are at best calculated for general sale."[20]

Opponents of perpetual copyright seized a different moral high ground. They insisted that perpetual copyright amounted to a monopoly that kept the price of books high and hence stifled the social diffusion of Énlightenment. The rights of the public, as Samuel Johnson argued, had to supersede the property claims of authors and publishers. Other opponents of perpetual copyright dismissed the London booksellers' avowed concern with the rights of authors as a disingenuous mask for their own greed. Here they could point to the fate of the Society for the Encouragement of Learning, formed in 1736 by a group of some hundred writers, poets, and patrons. The aim of the Society, like that of the German author-run publishing houses discussed earlier, was to enable authors to reap greater financial rewards from their work by circumventing commercial publishers. The Society paid the costs of printing a work, with authors reimbursing the Society from their profits but retaining the copyright. As later happened with its German counterpart, the plan failed owing to the collusion of the London book trade. Since the major London publishers were also booksellers, they used their control over distribution to keep Society-sponsored books off the market.

The debate culminated in the court case of Donaldson vs. Becket (1774). The case originated as a lawsuit against Alexander Donaldson, a Scottish bookseller who specialized in selling inexpensive reprints of the classics. One such edition was the poet James Thomson's *The Seasons*, copyright to which had been held by the London publisher Thomas

[20] Quoted in Turner, *Living by the Pen*, 41.

Becket. When Becket sued for piracy, Donaldson countered that the twenty-eight-year maximum term of copyright had expired. The case went all the way to the House of Lords. Convinced by the anti-monopoly rhetoric of the opponents of perpetual copyright, the House voted narrowly in favor of Donaldson. In effect, Donaldson vs. Becket upheld the principle of limited copyright originally formulated in the statute of 1709.

What is significant here is less the outcome of the debate than how it helped to fashion a new conception of authors as the ultimate originators and proprietors of their work. This notion arose in part from ideas of property articulated by natural-rights theorists, most notably John Locke. Locke derived property rights from the premise that individuals were owners of themselves. They then transformed the goods of nature into property by investing their labor and hence themselves into it. Transferred to the realm of intellectual activity, Locke's argument made authors the proprietors of their work by virtue of the labor they had invested in it. The concept of original genius was another idea that informed emerging notions of proprietary authorship. Renaissance and neoclassical models of authorship, as we have seen, had viewed the writer more as an instrument than an independent creator; what made a work inspired were elements external to the author. The eighteenth-century concept of genius, on the other hand, shifted the locus of creative inspiration from outside to inside the author. If authors produced works of inspiration, they did so because of special gifts unique to their talent, not through some external agency. Implicit in this idea of genius was a notion of originality around which a concept of authorial property could cohere. For to say that certain authors had produced original works was to say that they had written something unique, and to that extent they "owned" it.

Donaldson vs. Becket was at heart a compromise between the interests of authors, publishers, and public. It did not entirely eliminate book piracy, for the potential profits to be earned from an expanding book market were too tempting to discourage unauthorized reprints altogether. Especially in Ireland, where British copyright law did not apply until the Act of Union in 1801, publishers continued to deluge the market with pirated editions. But in England itself, the ruling did curb piracy by providing authors and publishers with legal recourse against copyright infringement. Donaldson vs. Becket also benefited consumers, since it placed much of Britain's literary legacy in the public domain. Because publishers could now legitimately reprint any book published before 1709, the British book market was opened up for new and cheaper reprints of Shakespeare, Milton, Chaucer, and other now classic authors. The expansion of the public domain of letters encouraged competition in the book trade by breaking the stranglehold that London publishers had traditionally held on copyrights. As a result, the number of bookseller-publishers in

London nearly tripled between 1772 and 1802, from 111 to 308.[21] Authors benefited in turn, since the proliferation of publishers heightened the competition for manuscripts and thereby increased what authors on the whole received for their work.

In France as in Britain, book piracy escalated in the eighteenth century in response to the monopolistic control of the market by a small group of licensed publishers. The legal book trade was dominated by Parisian publishers, whom the crown had incorporated as the Paris Book Guild in the seventeenth century. This relatively small group enjoyed a legal monopoly on the production and distribution of all material printed in Paris. Outside of Paris, provincial publishing guilds exercised an analogous monopoly in their respective towns and cities.

Since the era of Richelieu, these licensed guilds had functioned both as organs of censorship and as objects of protectionist economic policy. The Paris guild cooperated with the Office of the Book Trade (the royal bureau in charge of censorship), and helped inspect book cargoes and bookshops to root out printed material that royal censors had deemed harmful to the crown, the church, or public morals. At the same time, a royal *privilège* granted to a licensed publisher sanctioned the publication of a work, and provided the publisher exclusive rights to it for a period from ten to twenty years. In practice, licensed publishers often held these rights in perpetuity, much as in England prior to 1709.

Culturally, the licit publishing market of the Old Regime was for the most part conservative and stagnant. The privileged booksellers who dominated the trade tended to publish traditional works of theology, piety, and jurisprudence, along with the now standard neoclassical works of seventeenth-century poetry and drama. Up to the final decades of the eighteenth century, the legal publishing world remained fundamentally closed to Enlightenment culture. Far more important for circulating the works of the *philosophes* was the illicit book trade of clandestine publishers and smugglers operating either underground or abroad, usually in Holland or Switzerland. The journalist Louis-Sébastien Mercier defined book smugglers as "those who traffic in the only good books that one can still read in France," while the enlightened censor, C.-G. de Lamoignon de Malesherbes, declared that "a man who had read only books that originally appeared with the formal approval of the government would be behind his contemporaries by nearly a century."[22] Such observations

---

[21] Kernan, *Samuel Johnson and the Impact of Print*, 59.
[22] Louis-Sébastien Mercier, *Tableau de Paris*, 8 vols. (Amsterdam, 1782–3), I:135. Malesherbes is quoted in Robert Darnton, *The Forbidden Best-Sellers of Pre-Revolutionary France* (New York and London, 1995), xix.

highlighted the split that characterized the French book trade in the eighteenth century, a division that was not only legal but cultural.

During the final decades of the Old Regime, however, the monopoly of the publishing guilds began to unravel. Here the major catalyst was a series of reforms carried out by the Administration of the Book Trade in 1777, which followed in the spirit of the attack on commercial monopolies waged a year earlier by the reformist minister of finance, Anne-Robert-Jacques Turgot. The reforms sought to liberalize the Paris book trade by abolishing perpetual copyright and limiting a publisher's rights to the lifetime of its author. Thereafter, texts belonged to the public domain and could be published by any licensed bookseller with the permission of the crown. In one fell swoop the reforms legalized all pirated editions published prior to 1777. Moreover, for the first time in French publishing history authors were legally recognized as the proprietors of their works. They and their heirs acquired exclusive and perpetual rights to their work unless they chose to sell them to another party.

The immediate effect of the decrees was to abolish the Paris guild's exclusive rights to thousands of titles, which could now be published by provincial booksellers. The privileged Parisian publishers naturally condemned the reforms. Much like the London publishers in Donaldson vs. Becket, the guild invoked Lockean principles of natural rights to argue that the decrees violated contractual agreements freely concluded between authors and publishers. The guild charged that the crown, by despotically revoking those agreements, had violated the right of authors to dispose freely of their property. As in England, this professed concern for the rights of authors was disingenuous, since in 1700 the Parisian guild had itself supported a royal decree prohibiting authors from selling their own works.

At any rate, the Paris Book Guild took its case to the highest judicial court in France, the Parlement of Paris. The parlement, recently emboldened by its success in forcing the crown to revoke the anti-parliamentary measures of Chancellor Maupeou, once again defied the crown and ruled in favor of the Paris guild. As the conflict escalated, the crown sought to compromise by allowing the guild to prohibit the sale in Paris of those pirated editions recently legalized by the decrees. But the guild remained adamant, and refused to recognize royal authorizations to publish works over which Parisian publishers had previously held a privilege. Indeed, the guild openly defied the crown by seizing shipments of the newly authorized editions.

As in Britain, conflicts over copyright raised broader issues. As Carla Hesse has shown, two opposing positions with fundamentally different epistemological premises underlay the French debate. The first was elaborated in 1764 by Diderot, who defended the idea of perpetual copyright and hence supported the position of the Paris guild. Diderot contended that the ideas in a book could be considered as individual property because they originated in the author's mind. For this reason authors, or publishers if they had purchased the literary rights, enjoyed a perpetual property right over their work. The counter position was outlined in 1776 by Condorcet, Diderot's fellow *philosophe*. Condorcet attacked the claims of the Paris Book Guild on the basis of a sensationalist epistemology derived from Locke. The ideas that comprised a book, he argued, were not property. For unlike, say, a landed estate, an idea did not originate out of the mind or labor of any particular individual. Ideas arose from sense experience, which everyone shared. An idea could not therefore be claimed or owned by any single individual, but belonged by right to all of society. Hence Condorcet rejected the principle of proprietary authorship and opposed any form of copyright as an impediment to the free circulation of knowledge.

The positions of Diderot and Condorcet illustrate the uneasy tension between the Enlightenment notions of property rights on the one hand, and the norms of openness and accessibility that marked the Enlightenment public sphere on the other. Diderot justified proprietary authorship in the name of property rights, but in so doing he also upheld the very system of guild privilege that had helped stifle the diffusion of Enlightenment culture. In wanting to remove all obstacles to the free circulation of knowledge, Condorcet advanced a concept of the public sphere seemingly more open and accessible than that of Diderot. But by denying authors any proprietary claim to their work, Condorcet's "authorless world" (Hesse) would have effectively eliminated the literary marketplace through which that public sphere had functioned.

In France as in England, the question of intellectual property was ultimately resolved through a compromise that balanced the proprietary claims of authors and publishers with the interests of readers. The need for a clear definition of literary property became urgent after 1789, when a deregulated publishing market was now deluged with pirated editions, anonymous works, and libelous or seditious pamphlets. The resulting collapse of the book trade seemed to threaten not only the economic survival of publishers but also the stability of the new regime. For the revolutionary government, then, literary property became crucial as both an economic and a political issue.

The provisions enacted by the Jacobin government in July of 1793 were to form the basis of modern copyright law in France. Like Donaldson vs. Becket in Britain, they represented a compromise. Authors received exclusive rights to their works (unless they had ceded them to others), which could then be passed on to their heirs for a term of ten years. But the law did not apply to copyrights granted under the Old Regime, which were abolished. This provision was important, for it brought the entire literary, philosophical, and scientific legacy of prerevolutionary France into the public domain. Works published prior to 1789 could now be legally reprinted in relatively inexpensive editions and made available to a larger reading public. The revolutionary government couched its policy in civic rather than commercial terms, viewing the right of authors to reap economic benefits from their work as not so much a property right as a reward for their contribution to public enlightenment. But the aim of the law was identical to that of Donaldson vs. Becket: to achieve a compromise between the demands of the market on the one hand, and the norms of the public sphere on the other.

Reinhard Wittmann has examined the problem of literary piracy in the Holy Roman Empire, where hundreds of principalities exercised more or less autonomous jurisdiction over trade in their respective domains. Principalities did promulgate protectionist measures on behalf of licensed publishers within their territories. But while such legislation could protect publishers against piracy *inside* a territory, it obviously had no effect *outside* it. Governments themselves encouraged the pirating of editions published in other principalities. This state-sanctioned piracy stemmed the flow of money outside the territory, and was justified on mercantilist grounds as a way to promote native manufacturing. The Viennese publisher, Johann Thomas Edler von Trattner, made a fortune publishing pirated editions of North German works – all with the tacit encouragement of his sovereigns, Maria Theresia and Joseph II, who were apparently persuaded by Trattner's argument that his piracy impeded the flow of money outside the monarchy.

Piracy was further encouraged by shifts within the German book trade. Since the late sixteenth century, the imperial book trade had been concentrated in Leipzig and Frankfurt. Leipzig's annual book fair served as the primary point of exchange and distribution for Protestant North German publishers and booksellers, while Frankfurt's book fair was the Catholic, south-German counterpart. Up to the 1760s, business at both fairs had been conducted on the basis of the so-called exchange system. Instead of buying or selling individual titles for cash, publishers and booksellers exchanged unbound works they had transported to the fair in large barrels. Manuscripts were normally exchanged according to bulk, sheet for sheet, although exceptionally fine or illustrated editions might command a higher rate of exchange. Here the exchange system points to the relatively undeveloped concept of authorship in early modern Germany, where the exchange value of a manuscript was determined as much by quantity as by the identity of the author.

Around mid-century, however, the exchange system began to break down. The underlying cause was a deepening of the cultural split separating the mostly Protestant territories in the north, where the Enlightenment had taken firm root by the 1740s, from the Catholic territories to the south, where Enlightenment culture developed more slowly. Leipzig publishers, who catered to a reading public increasingly oriented toward the Protestant culture of the Enlightenment, now became less interested in exchanging their wares with the primarily Catholic firms of South Germany. The exchange system had become unprofitable for Protestant publishers and booksellers, who had difficulty marketing the books they obtained through exchanges with their Catholic counterparts. In 1764 this commercial asymmetry finally led Leipzig publishers like Philipp Erasmus Reich to abandon the exchange system. Reich closed down his branch operations at the Frankfurt book fair, and in Leipzig he began requiring payments in cash from visiting booksellers and publishers. This shift from book barter to cash payments was a severe blow to south German and Austrian publishers. Already burdened with transportation costs and unfavorable exchange rates, they simply did not have the cash reserves to do business on the Leipzig market.

No longer able to afford north German editions on the Leipzig market, south German publishers now pirated them. During the next two decades book piracy in the empire rose to unprecedented heights, as pirate publishers like Trattner in Vienna and Schmieder in Karlsruhe flooded the market with unauthorized reprints of north German editions. Reich and other Leipzig publishers protested this piracy, although their own actions had precipitated it. Their laments were echoed by writers like Lessing and Wieland, and scholars have tended to accept these condemnations of piracy at face value. The effects of piracy could indeed be egregious, both on writers and publishers. Like modern publishing firms, legitimate publishers depended on the profits they earned from more popular titles to finance serious scholarly works with a limited market appeal. Piracy cut into those profits, making publishers more reluctant to invest in authors whose work could not promise an immediate financial gain. Moreover, pirate publishers often showed a blatant disregard for the integrity of the texts they reprinted. To make a book more marketable they sometimes altered or domesticated the text. A notorious example was the pirating of Rudolph Zacharias Becker's *Handbook of Aid in Times of Need* (1st ed. 1788), a manual aimed at improving the moral and economic condition of the peasantry. A huge commercial success, Becker's work was quickly pirated throughout the empire. To make the book more palatable to a Catholic audience, Viennese editions deleted its overtly Protestant passages along with positive references to Frederick the Great of Prussia. Another edition from southwest Germany customized the language of the text in accordance with the local Swabian idiom. The original author, exasperated by the appearance of twelve pirated editions of the first part of his handbook, threatened to withhold publication of a second installment until the unauthorized reprints ceased. Undeterred, pirate publishers published a concocted edition of what purported to be the second part of the work.

But piracy in the empire also had a beneficial impact, at least for consumers. It expanded the literary public sphere by making available relatively inexpensive reprints of contemporary German works as well as translations of English and French texts. The resulting boost in the circulation of print was especially important in the Catholic south, where the collapse of the exchange system had made north German editions prohibitively expensive. Through the efforts of pirate publishers, countless works of the German and European Enlightenment found their way into south Germany and Austria. In this respect pirate publishers were not predators but cultural mediators whose efforts helped narrow the gulf between Protestant north and Catholic south. They also developed new marketing techniques that stimulated a demand for books. Excluded from the legitimate book trade, pirate publishers created distribution networks and markets in areas that had previously lacked access to print culture. Trattner's Vienna-based firm proved especially innovative, establishing distribution branches in the smaller or more remote towns of the Habsburg monarchy. In regions where the book market had once been weak or nonexistent, Trattner developed a commercial network of peddlars, bookbinders, schoolmasters, and even priests to advertise or sell his books. A sympathetic contemporary noted of Trattner and other pirate publishers: "Thousands of people from the most hidden corners of Germany, who would have found it impossible to think of buying books because of the high price, have now gradually assembled a small library of reprints."[23] Book piracy helped dissolve territorial and confessional boundaries, and thereby contributed to the cultural integration of an otherwise fragmented Holy Roman Empire.

To defenders of pirate publishers, then, the claim that literary piracy deprived authors and publishers of their just rewards had to be balanced against its stimulation of market demand. The Hamburg native, Johann Albrecht Heinrich Reimarus, an enlightened advocate of free trade, insisted in 1791 that "through their industriousness these publishers have encouraged a desire to read and to educate oneself. They have thereby created a larger market for other books in the publishing trade, and thus

---

[23] Quoted in Reinhard Wittmann, "Der gerechtfertigte Nachdrucker? Nachdruck und literarisches Leben im 18. Jahrhundert," in Giles Barber and Bernhard Fabian, eds., *Buch und Buchhandel in Europa im 18. Jahrhundert* (Hamburg, 1981), 313.

fully compensated for whatever damage they may have caused."[24] By stimulating a market for books, argued Reimarus, pirate publishers encouraged many to become authors who would not otherwise have done so. In other words, Reimarus and other apologists viewed pirate publishers as agents of enlightenment. For these writers, the Leipzig publishers who demanded the eradication of piracy were not merely conspiring to monopolize the book trade; they were abetting censorship by stifling the free circulation of ideas.

The idea of proprietary authorship nonetheless emerged, although the political structure of the empire prevented the effective implementation of copyright legislation until well into the nineteenth century. As Martha Woodmansee has shown, late eighteenth-century writers like Goethe, Herder, and Fichte elaborated a concept of proprietary authorship grounded aesthetically in pre-romantic conceptions of genius and originality. Goethe defined the act of writing as "the reproduction of the world around me by means of the internal world which takes hold of, combines, creates anew, kneads everything and puts it down again in its own form."[25] Here writers, like an organism ingesting alien matter, processed ideas and made them a part of themselves. In that way authors became the creators and hence proprietors of their work. Fichte's justification of proprietary authorship rested on a distinction between the various properties of a book. Those who acquired a book owned it as a material object and were free to employ its ideas however they pleased. But authors were the owners of the *form* in which those ideas were expressed, and to that aspect of their texts they held a valid property claim.

If the eighteenth-century "invention of copyright" brought benefits to authors, it also illustrated some of the ambiguities and contradictions inherent in their relationship to the market and the public sphere. On the one hand, eighteenth-century copyright helped establish the principle that authors were the owners of their work. This proposition assumed the existence of a relatively open market where authors, like any other producer of a commodity, could sell their work. On the other hand, the concept of proprietary authorship coexisted uneasily with prevailing notions of authors as agents of enlightenment whose moral legitimacy rested on their service to the public good. The tension between these two conceptions of the author – as proprietor and as public servant – manifested itself at various points in the eighteenth-century debate over copyright. Critics of copyright, as we have seen, attacked it as incompatible with the author's responsibility to the public. If authors were agents of the public

[24] J. A. H. Reimarus, "Nachtrag zu der Erwägung des Bücherverlags und dessen Rechte," *Deutsches Magazin* 1 (1791), 323.
[25] Quoted in Woodmansee, "Genius and the Copyright," 447.

good, it was argued, how could they justify the restrictions that copyright placed on the free circulation of ideas?

As seen in the previous chapter, the very same market that helped to define the author as a creator and producer was also transforming literary tastes and standards in a direction that many enlightened observers could only condemn. The commercialization of literature, the emergence of a mass-market producing literary works for their entertainment value rather than their moral utility, threatened to undermine the moral identity of authorship even as it made writing more lucrative. In a sense, enlightened proponents of proprietary authorship wanted it both ways: although applauding the prospects of financial independence that the market seemed to offer, they were less prepared to accept the cultural costs.

Women and authorship

Most published writers in the eighteenth century were men, and the obstacles to female authorship were formidable. Higher education was generally closed to women, as were the professions (law, medicine, university teaching, bureaucratic service) that supported so many male writers of the century. Even affluent bourgeois or aristocratic women who received a relatively extensive education from family tutors risked social disapproval by becoming published authors. The same attitudes that inspired concern about women readers extended to female authors: if married, a woman who aspired to enter the world of letters was bound to neglect her domestic duties; if unmarried, she violated conventional notions of feminine modesty. By exposing herself in print she became a "public woman" accessible to everyone, just as eighteenth-century streetwalkers were commonly known as "public girls."

Yet women in the eighteenth century did write, and in ever-increasing numbers. Already in the late seventeenth century women were a visible presence in the literary marketplace. In London's 1695–96 theater season, for example, one-third of all the new plays were written by women. The prolific author of one of those plays, Aphra Behn, is sometimes credited with writing the first true English novel, *Love Letters between a Nobleman and His Sister* (1684–87). One of the most successful authors of the Restoration and the first female British writer to earn a comfortable living from the pen, Behn blithely acknowledged that she was "forced to write for Bread and not ashamed to owne it."[26]

---

[26] Figures on the London theater are taken from Paula R. Backscheider, *Spectacular Politics: Theatrical Power and Mass Culture in Early Modern England* (Baltimore, 1993), xiii. Behn is quoted in Catherine Gallagher, *Nobody's Story: The Vanishing Acts of Women Writers in the Marketplace 1670–1820* (Oxford, 1994), 16.

Moreover, any discussion of female authorship must distinguish between writing and publishing. Literate women who did not necessarily enter the publishing world often found avenues of literary expression in private diaries and letters. Female diaries had become relatively common in seventeenth-century England, where they were an expression of the spiritual introspection and self-examination central to Puritan devotional culture. In France and Germany, Jansenism and Lutheran Pietism similarly encouraged female diaries. Letter-writing likewise came into vogue among upper-middle-class and aristocratic women. In France the new interest in the art of letter-writing was tied to the intimate, conversational style of Parisian salon culture (see Chapter 6). Like the salon, epistolary writing offered a communicative medium that was more intimate and direct than traditional models of courtly interaction. Letters fostered a personal and conversational tone, which in turn helped their female authors to develop the intimate style characteristic of the eighteenth-century novel. In this respect the vogue of epistolarity was an important prelude to the flowering of female authorship in the eighteenth century. As a "private" medium, furthermore, letters did not mark their female authors with the stigma of publicity. Private correspondence enabled literate and educated women to cultivate their literary capacities without endangering the modesty that might be compromised in print. In the course of the eighteenth century epistolary writing came to be viewed as a quintessentially female genre. As Tilney tells Catherine Morland in Jane Austen's *Northanger Abbey* (written 1798 or 1799), "everybody allows that the talent of writing agreeable letters is peculiarly female."

Other developments in the world of eighteenth-century letters encouraged women to "go public" with their writing. As we have seen, women made up a substantial part of the eighteenth-century reading public. Given their prominence as readers, it was natural that many would become authors as well. Moral weeklies were one vehicle. These periodicals, whose appeal to female readers was discussed in the previous chapter, often employed women as editors or contributors. Delarivière Manley, herself a successful dramatist, capitalized on the success of Steele's *Tatler* by launching *The Female Tatler* (1709–10), and the prolific novelist Eliza Haywood later followed suit by editing *The Female Spectator* (1744–46). The German moral weekly of the early eighteenth century is often associated with Johann Gottfried Gottsched, but his wife, Louise Adelgunde Gottsched (née Kulmus) played an equally important role as coeditor, reviewer, and contributor. The first German moral weekly edited solely by a woman was Ernestine Hoffman's *For Hamburg's Daughters* (*Für Hamburgs Töchter*), which appeared in 1779. It was followed by others, including Charlotte Hetzel's *Weekly for the Fair Sex* (*Wochenblatt für's schöne Geschlecht*).

Women were less visible in French journalism, partly because royal censorship placed tighter restrictions on periodical publishing in general. Between 1700 and 1789, approximately twenty-five French periodicals (of which fourteen were published outside of France) were aimed specifically at women, as opposed to eighty-five in Germany during the same period and eighty in England between 1690 and 1760.[27] A female version of the *Spectator* (*La spectatrice*), edited by Mlle Barbier, appeared between 1726 and 1730, but it ran afoul of the government owing to its anti-clerical tone and was shut down. The most successful periodical for women was the *Journal des Dames*, founded in 1759. From 1761 to 1775 the journal was owned and edited by three women. The first female editor, Mme de Beumer, was a staunch feminist with republican leanings who advocated a more active public role for women. Her social and political radicalism embroiled the journal in censorship battles, and in 1763 Beumer turned it over to a less controversial editor, Catherine Michelle de Maisonneuve, who was then succeeded in 1769 by Mme de Montanclos, a disciple of Rousseau and probably a freemason. Although Montanclos followed Rousseau in celebrating the civic importance of motherhood, she also defended the right of women to enter the professions. In 1775 she handed over the editorship to Louis-Sébastien Mercier, and three years later the journal was shut down by government censors.

Targeting a female readership, then, moral weeklies and other periodicals also provided a new forum for women writers. The rise of the novel expanded this arena. The affinity between women's writing and eighteenth-century fiction is particularly evident in the epistolary novel, which reached the height of its popularity between 1750 and 1780. Because educated women in the eighteenth century were often practiced in the art of letter-writing, epistolary novels were a genre especially calculated to appeal to female readers. At the same time, the central characters – e.g., Richardson's Pamela, Rousseau's Heloïse, Goethe's Lotte – projected an image of women as literate, stylistically adept, and in short – as *writers*. "I cannot live without a pen in my hand," declared Pamela.

Women novelists during the second half of the eighteenth century enjoyed an unprecedented degree of literary and financial success. They did especially well in the relatively lucrative British literary market, where

---

[27] Suzanna Van Dijk, *Traces de femmes: présence féminine dans le journalisme français du XVIIe siècle* (Amsterdam and Maarssen, 1988), 6–7, appendices I–II; Alison Adburgham, *Women in Print: Writing Women and Women's magazines from the Restoration to the Accession of Victoria* (London, 1972), 26, 273; S. Schumann, "Das 'lesende Frauenzimmer': Frauenzeitschriften im 18. Jahrhundert," in Barbara Becker-Cantarino, ed., *Die Frau von der Reformation zur Romantik* (Bonn, 1980), 142.

the rate of women who published for the first time increased by roughly 50 percent every decade between 1760 and 1800. Their number rose from four in the 1730s to seventeen in the 1760s and sixty-three in the 1790s.[28] In 1753 Samuel Johnson observed that the woman writer was no longer a rare, "eccentric being," and the Gothic novelist Clara Reeve noted in 1769 that "I see many female writers favourably received, admitted into the rank of authors, and amply rewarded by the public; I have been encouraged by their success, to offer myself as a candidate for the same advantages."[29]

In Germany, the first female author to earn a significant income from her writing was Anna Luise Karsch (1722–91). Born in humble circumstances, Karsch turned to writing after her first husband, a weaver, abandoned her with three children, and her second husband, a drunken tailor, left her with four more when he was conscripted into the Prussian army. Her first published poetry, patriotic verse in honor of Frederick the Great, won the acclaim of the Berlin critics Johann Georg Sulzer and Karl Wilhelm Ramler. In 1764 they helped Karsch publish her first book of poems, which earned the author the substantial sum of 2,000 *Taler* (around £285). Sophie LaRoche (1730–1807), the first female novelist in Germany, was the daughter of an Augsburg scholar and physician. Inspired by the epistolary novels of Richardson and Rousseau, her *History of Lady Sophia Sternheim* (*Geschichte des Fräuleins von Sternheim*, 1771) targeted a female audience and went through numerous editions. As the first sentimental novel in Germany and the first full-fledged German epistolary novel, it was a pioneering work that prepared the ground for the Storm and Stress movement of the 1770s. This movement gave added impetus to the now fashionable cult of literary sensibility, which further spurred the development of women's writing. Goethe's phenomenally successful *Sorrows of Young Werther* (1774), with its pre-romantic celebration of emotion, sentiment, and other qualities generally deemed female in the eighteenth century, had the same galvanizing effect on German female authors that Richardson's *Pamela* had had on British ones. Helene Unger, daughter of a noble Prussian family, achieved literary success with her novel *Julchen Grünthal*. Caroline de la Motte Fouqué was a prolific novelist who wrote from her rural estate outside Berlin. Dorothea Caroline Michaelis and Therese Marie Heyne, both daughters of prominent Göttingen professors, achieved literary prominence for their novels and essays.

[28] Judith Phillips Stanton, "Statistical Profile of Women Writing in English from 1660 to 1800," in Frederick M. Keener and Susan E. Lorsch, eds., *Eighteenth-Century Women and the Arts* (New York, 1988), 248–51.
[29] Quoted in Backscheider, *Spectacular Politics*, 81.

In light of the formidable social and cultural obstacles that women writers faced, what drove a growing number of them to enter the literary marketplace? As we have seen, the rise of genres enjoying a large female readership played a decisive role. Also important was the relative prosperity that the eighteenth century brought to the middling ranks of society, especially in England, which allowed middle-class women more leisure to pursue their literary and cultural interests. Yet economic hardship as much as affluence could induce women to become authors. Sometimes the death of a husband or father, or a reversal of family fortunes, were behind a woman's decision to embark on a literary career. Despite the social disapproval she might risk by publishing her work, writing could provide a middle-class woman suddenly bereft of financial support with an income that imperiled her respectability far less than, say, stage-acting or a manual trade. Becoming a professional writer also required little capital outlay, unlike opening a school or a business.[30]

Other women were encouraged to write by male mentors, friends, or husbands. Samuel Richardson was especially known for nurturing female literary talent. One of his protégés, the novelist Hester Mulso Chapone, wrote to him that "I never was a writing lady until you made me one."[31] Male mentorship also played a role in the careers of so-called "bluestocking" writers like Hester Lynch Salisbury, Frances Burney, and Hannah More. Although the term bluestocking came to refer to a woman, it was in fact originally used by Elizabeth Montagu and her circle to refer to male supporters like Samuel Johnson, Horace Walpole, Joshua Reynolds, and David Garrick, with whom they corresponded and socialized. The instruction and encouragement a father provided his daughter at home could also lay the foundation for a writing career. Elizabeth Carter learned Greek from her father, a skill that later enabled her to publish a celebrated translation of Epictetus. The father of Catherine Macaulay taught her history, and Hannah More was able to earn her living as a teacher through the tutoring provided by her father (although he discontinued her lessons in Latin and mathematics when she showed too much promise in such male subjects). In Germany, one encounters similar cases of male mentorship. Sophie LaRoche launched her literary career with the warm support of Wieland, her mentor and one-time fiancé. The critic and theologian Friedrich Schleiermacher interceded with publishers on behalf of the Berlin *salonière* Henriette Herz, while Friedrich Schiller arranged to have works by the dramatist and novelist Friederike Sophie Caroline von Beulwitz-Walzogen published in various literary journals.

[30] Turner, *Living by the Pen*, 79.
[31] Quoted in *ibid.*, 107.

It would be wrong, then, to assume that aspiring female writers confronted male obstruction and hostility at every turn. The emerging ideal of companionate marriage, with its notion that husbands and wives should be bound together by friendship as well as by property and procreation, did much to sanction a woman's literary pursuits. To the degree that intellectual partnership might constitute one dimension of a marital friendship, it could enjoin male writers to tolerate if not encourage the literary efforts of their wives. Accompanying such shifts in attitude were new public spaces where women with literary aspirations could establish useful contacts with prominent men of letters. One was the salon (see Chapter 6), where a woman might find an audience for her unpublished work or strike up friendships or love affairs with influential male writers. The Viennese writer Caroline Pichler first found encouragement for her poetry in the circle of *Aufklärer* who gathered weekly during the 1770s in the salon of her parents, Freiherr and Charlotte von Greiner. In Berlin salons of the 1780s and 1790s, aspiring authors like Helene Unger and Henriette Herz similarly profited from contacts with established writers like Karl Philipp Moritz, Moses Mendelssohn, the Humboldt brothers, and Friedrich Schleiermacher. The rise of commercialized leisure in the forms of spas and resort towns also played an important role. Arising in the early eighteenth century and originally catering to a chiefly aristocratic clientele, spas increasingly attracted bourgeois guests able and willing to pay for the accommodations and amenities they offered there. As places deemed acceptable for a woman to visit alone or in the company of a female friend, spas were often the place where women with intellectual and literary ambitions made contacts with more established men of letters at daily teas, dinners, or balls. In the empire, spas such as Karlsbad or Bad Pyrmont provided such a venue, as did the rise of English resort towns. With their assembly rooms, promenades, cafés, theaters, and bookshops, resorts like Bath or Tunbridge Wells were sexually mixed public spaces where men and women of letters could socialize. The British bluestockings, for example, established and cultivated many of their male literary friendships while taking the waters at Tunbridge Wells.

Still, female authors had to struggle with residual aversions to women who took up the pen. Even letter-writing continued to inspire a certain distrust, with traditionalists warning that private letters were a dangerous vehicle for surreptitious romances and infidelity. Traces of this attitude can even be found in Richardson's *Clarissa* and Laclos's *Dangerous Liaisons*, two epistolary novels otherwise known for their sympathetic portrayal of women. In both novels, after all, it is women's secret correspondence with dissolute rakes that in the end precipitates their downfall. A more stubborn and widespread prejudice was simply the belief that a woman with literary aspirations jeopardized her femininity, marriage, and family by entering the domain of letters. Typical of this attitude was a 1784 letter to the *Berlin Monthly* (*Berlinische Monatschrift*), the house organ of the Berlin Enlightenment, in which the anonymous author related how his wife's pursuit of literary fame had destroyed their marriage and household: "My fortune, our household, our child, our neighbors, the church, the poor – now nothing interested her. Gone was all shyness, modesty, and femininity, all transformed into the most impudent stubbornness, arrogance, and pedantry." Women writers themselves struggled with their authorial identities, seeking to reconcile gender and profession, femininity and writing. Frances Burney described her early desire to write as "an inclination at which I blushed... [and] had always kept secret." At one point the novelist Sarah Fielding had to assure her readers that she had not sacrificed her domestic responsibilities to her literary pursuits, "nor was the leisure she found for such acquirements produced by neglecting anything necessary or useful for the family."[32]

Some women writers chose consciously not to publish their work. Suzanne Necker (1739–94), who hosted one of the most renowned *salons* in eighteenth-century Paris, left at her death reams of unpublished essays and other writings (they were later published posthumously in five volumes by her husband, the noted finance minister of Louis XVI, in 1798). Although the sheer volume of her work suggests literary ambition if not ability, in the end she shunned the publicity that publication would have entailed. To have published her work, as Dena Goodman has argued, would have violated the qualities of selflessness and feminine virtue that she viewed as essential to her identity as a woman. Necker believed that a woman maintained her reputation not by seeking publicity, as did men, but by avoiding it. Women, she wrote, were like glow worms: "as long as they remain in darkness people are struck by their *éclat*; as soon as they wish to appear in the light of day they are scorned and people only see their faults."[33]

Other female authors sought to reconcile their identities as writers and women by publishing anonymously or under a pseudonym. The novelists Elizabeth Bonhote and Sarah Harriet Burney published at least their first novels anonymously, and all of Sarah Scott's works were written

---

[32] Quotes are from "Briefe an die Herausgeber, von dem Ehemann einer Sappho," *Berlinische Monatschrift*, vol. III (1784), 169; Backscheider, *Spectacular Politics*, 102; Janet Todd, *The Sign of Angelica: Women, Writing, and Fiction 660–1800* (London, 1989), 126.

[33] Quoted in Dena Goodman, "Suzanne Necker's *Melanges*: Gender, Writing, and Publicity," in Elizabeth C. Goldsmith and Dena Goodman, eds., *Going Public: Women and Publishing in Early Modern France* (Ithaca and London, 1995), 217.

anonymously or pseudonymously. The German writers Helene Unger and Caroline de la Motte Fouqué published their first works anonymously, while others wrote under the name of a husband or male friend. For Dorothea Veit, who published under the name of her lover (the critic Friedrich Schlegel), pseudonymity offered economic advantages. Driven to write out of dire financial need, Veit found it easier to publish and sell her work by writing under the name of an author who was both male and more established than she. For others, publishing under the name of a man avoided the stigma still attached to female writers. Therese Heyne, widowed by the death of her husband Georg Forster, remarried and published her first novel under the name of her second husband, Ludwig Ferdinand Huber. After the success of her novel she began writing under her own name, but a letter from 1807 described the psychological costs:

As a woman I find the whole business of writing a hateful one. As long as my husband enabled me to maintain my respectability by remaining unknown, it was *he* and not I who appeared before the public. My womanliness (*Weiblichkeit*) did not therefore suffer. Although I do not at all scorn women writers, it makes me unhappy to appear as one. It is the cause of much discord in my soul.[34]

The semi-autobiographical *Series of Genuine Letters between Henry and Frances* (1757–70), published by the dramatist and novelist Elizabeth Griffith in collaboration with her husband Richard, expressed a similar ambivalence toward publication. Frances, the central female character and a writer, takes pains to justify her literary activity in purely financial terms: "For Praise alone was never any ambition of mine; I was first dragged into Print, without my Consent, and continue still so averse to the unfeminine Vanity of a literary Name, that nothing, but the vulgar Consideration of Pounds, Shillings, and Pence, shall ever bribe me to enter the Lists again."[35]

The desire to become a writer without having "to appear as one" helps to explain why translating was such a common literary activity among women writers of the period. Translating allowed a woman to write in a voice not ostensibly her own. As a seemingly passive and neutral literary mediator, the female translator could appear more modest and self-effacing than she would have as an author in her own right. The eighteenth century is full of female translators: in England, Elizabeth

---

[34] Quoted in Eva Walter, *Schrieb oft, von Mägde Arbeit müde: Lebenszusammenhänge deutscher Schriftstellerinnen um 1800* (Dusseldorf, 1985), 50.

[35] Quoted in Susan David Bernstein, "Ambivalence and Writing: Elizabeth and Richard Griffith's *A Series of Genuine Letters between Henry and Frances*," in Keener and Lorsch, eds., *Eighteenth-Century Women and the Arts*, 270.

Carter achieved renown (and earned almost £1,000) for her translation of Epictetus, Sarah Fielding won equal fame for her rendering of Xenophon, and Mary Wollstonecraft published various translations of German works. In Germany, most of Luise Adelgunde Gottsched's works from the 1730s and 1740s were translations of Voltaire, Molière, Pope, and Addison.

Other female authors legitimated their entry into the literary marketplace through the moral didacticism of their writings. Of course most writing of the period, male or female, was didactic in tone, and the conviction that literature should encourage virtue and expose vice was a common theme of Enlightenment criticism. But women writers seem at times to have bent over backwards in their moralism, as if going public with their writing compelled them to dispel any suspicions about their private virtue. In their lives as well as in their work, they felt driven to temper their talent and learning with a display of modesty and delicacy. Not for nothing would "bluestocking" become a synonym for prudery. The eighteenth-century Englishwomen who inspired this sense of the term scrupulously avoided anything in their writing or behavior that might raise questions about their feminine virtue. A German counterpart was Sophie LaRoche, whose novels about virtuous women were intended to provide role models for upper-middle-class daughters, wives, and mothers. In his preface to LaRoche's *History of Fräulein von Sternheim*, her mentor Wieland felt compelled to emphasize the author's modesty along side the novel's moral utility. LaRoche, wrote Wieland in his preface to the first edition, "had never presumed to write for the world or to produce a work of art."[36]

Hence the position of female authors in the literary public sphere was paradoxical. To the degree that they endeavored to safeguard their respectability by upholding conventional views of women, their entry into the literary public sphere did more to reinscribe prevailing ideals of femininity than to challenge them. Many, like Elizabeth Rowe and Penelope Aubin in England or Madame de Tencin in France, preached obedience to parents, chastity before marriage, and submissiveness to husbands. Many, like Helene Unger and Caroline de la Motte Fouqué in Germany, did not believe women should assume an active role in public life. For these female authors, participating in print culture without endangering their respectability and femininity required that they not just conform to existing conventions of womanliness, but propagate them with a special intensity. To the extent that the literary public sphere of the eighteenth

---

[36] Quoted in Barbara Becker-Cantarino, *Der lange Weg zur Mündigkeit: Frau und Literatur (1500–1800)* (Berlin, 1987), 287.

century bolstered those conventions, it did so by fostering female authorship rather than suppressing it. In the short run, women's entry into the
literary public sphere of the eighteenth century may have come at the cost
of a cultural construct that consigned them to the parlor and bedroom.
But in the long run, the literary visibility women thereby acquired also
gave them the means of challenging that construct. The literary public
sphere of the eighteenth century was intrinsically neither misogynist nor
feminist. If it produced female writers who reaffirmed conventional views
of women, it would create others – witness Mary Wollstonecraft – who
defied them.

Bibliographical note
On the status of the author in eighteenth-century England, Alvin Kernan's *Samuel
Johnson and the Impact of Print* (Princeton, 1987) provides a stimulating discus-
sion. Useful overviews can be found in the older studies by A.S. Collins, *The
Profession of Letters: A Study of the Relation of Author to Patron, Publisher, and Public
1780–1832* (New York, 1929); Collins, *Authorship in the Days of Johnson* (London,
1928); and J.W. Saunders, *The Profession of English Letters* (London and Toronto,
1964). My discussion of scribal publication is based on Harold Love, *Scribal
Publication in Seventeenth-Century England* (Oxford, 1993). For London's Grub
Street I consulted Pat Rogers, *Grub Street: Studies in a Subculture* (London, 1972).

For France, Alain Viala's *Naissance de l'écrivain: sociologie de la littérature à l'âge
classique* (Paris, 1985) examines the social backgrounds and milieu of seventeenth-
century authors. For the eighteenth century, Robert Darnton's important work
substantially revised how scholars understood the relationship of French men of
letters to the Enlightenment and Revolution. See above all, the essays in his *Literary Underground of the Old Regime* (Cambridge, Mass., 1982). See also his *Business
of Enlightenment: A Publishing History of the* Encyclopédie *1775–1800* (Cambridge,
Mass., and London, 1979), which shed new light on the publishing world of the
French Enlightenment. For a concise analysis of the conditions of authorship in
eighteenth-century France, Darnton's "The Facts of Literary Life in Eighteenth-
Century France," in Keith Baker, ed., *The French Revolution and the Creation of
Modern Political Culture*, vol. I: *The Political Culture of the Old Regime* (Oxford and
New York, 1987), is also useful. For a recent critique of Darnton's views, see
especially, Elizabeth L. Eisenstein, *Grub Street Abroad: Aspects of the French Cosmopolitan Press from the Age of Louis XIV to the French Revolution* (Oxford, 1992).
On Darnton and his critics, see also the essays in Haydn T. Mason, ed., *The Darnton Debate: Books and Revolution in the Eighteenth Century*, Studies on Voltaire and
the Eighteenth Century, 359 (Oxford, 1998). Dena Goodman's *Republic of Letters:
A Cultural History of the French Enlightenment* (Ithaca and London, 1994) highlights the importance of the salon for French men of letters; I have treated her
argument in more detail in Chapter 6. Other works I have consulted on the social
position of French men of letters include Alan Charles Kors, *D'Holbach's Coterie:
An Enlightenment in Paris* (Princeton, 1976); John Lough, *Writer and Public in
France: From the Middle Ages to the Present Day* (Oxford, 1978); Haydn Mason,
French Writers and Their Society 1715–1800 (London, 1982); David Pottinger, *The*

French Book Trade in the Ancien Régime (Cambridge, Mass., 1958); Hans Ulrich Gumbrecht, Rolf Reichardt, and Thomas Schleich, "Für eine Sozialgeschichte der französischen Aufklärung," in Hans Ulrich Gumbrecht *et al.*, eds., *Sozialgeschichte der Aufklärung in Frankreich*, vol. I (Munich and Vienna, 1981).

For authorship in Germany, I am indebted to Hans Erich Bödecker for allowing me to read his unpublished essay, "Autoren, literarischer Markt, und Publikum im 18. Jahrhundert in Deutschland." See also Hans Haferkorn, "Zur Entstehung der bürgerlich-literarischen Intelligenz und des Schriftstellers in Deutschland zwischen 1750 und 1800," in Bernd Lutz, ed., *Deutsches Bürgertum und literarische Intelligenz 1750–1800* (Stuttgart, 1974). In English, the older studies by W.H. Bruford are still useful. See his *Germany in the Eighteeenth Century: The Social Background of the Literary Revival* (Cambridge, 1968) and *Culture and Society in Classical Weimar, 1775–1806* (London, 1962). On the conditions of literary production in the empire, see also Albert Ward, *Book Production, Fiction, and the German Reading Public 1740–1800* (Oxford, 1974). Henri Brunschwig's *Enlightenment and Romanticism in Eighteenth-Century Prussia*, trans. Frank Jellinek (Chicago and London, 1974) is a lively but not very convincing attempt to attribute the decline of the Enlightenment among German men of letters to shrinking career prospects. A more subtle treatment of the relationship between intellectuals and the *Aufklärung* is Anthony J. La Vopa, *Grace, Talent, and Merit: Poor Students, Clerical Careers, and Professional Ideology in Eighteenth-Century Germany* (Cambridge, 1988). La Vopa's "Herder's Publikum: Language, Print, and Sociability in Eighteenth-Century Germany," *Eighteenth-Century Studies* 29 (1995) explores the ambiguous relationship of German men of letters to their public. This is also a focus of Benjamin W. Redekop, *Enlightenment and Community: Lessing, Abbt, Herder, and the Quest for a German Public* (Montreal and Kingston, 2000), which appeared too late for me to consult.

On the emerging concept of proprietary authorship, I have drawn on several recent works. For the French case my discussion is based on the fine study by Carla Hesse, *Publishing and Cultural Politics in Revolutionary Paris, 1789–1810* (Berkeley, 1991); for Germany I found Martha Woodmansee's "The Genius and the Copyright: Economic and Legal Conditions of the Emergence of the 'Author'," *Eighteenth-Century Studies* 17 (1984) to be indispensible. See also Reinhard Wittmann, *Geschichte des deutschen Buchhandels* (Munich, 1991), and Wittmann, "Der gerechtfertigte Nachdrucker? Nachdruck und literarisches Leben im 18. Jahrhundert," in Giles Barber and Bernhard Fabian, eds., *Buch und Buchhandel in Europa im 18. Jahrhundert* (Hamburg, 1981). On the origins of copyright in England, I have relied on Mark Rose, "The Author as Proprietor: Donaldson *v.* Becket and the Genealogy of Modern Authorship," *Representations* 23 (1988). Reinhart Siegert's *Aufklärung und Volkslektüre* (Frankfurt am Main, 1978) traces the publishing vicissitudes of Rudolf Zacharias Becker's popular manual.

There is now a substantial body of scholarship on eighteenth-century women writers. For England, see the surveys by Janet Todd, *The Sign of Angelica: Women, Writing, and Fiction 1660–1800* (London, 1989), and Cheryl Turner, *Living by the Pen: Women Writers in the Eighteenth Century* (London, 1992). Catherine Gallagher, *Nobody's Story: The Vanishing Acts of Women Writers in the Marketplace 1670–1820* (Oxford, 1994), and Kathryn Shevelow, *Women and Print Culture: The*

Construction of Femininity in the Early Periodical (London and New York, 1989), emphasize the ambiguous relationship of English female writers to the literary market. On the extensive involvement of women in all levels of literary production and distribution, see the interesting study by Paula McDowell, *The Women of Grub Street: Press, Politics, and Gender in the London Literary Marketplace* (Oxford, 1998). The role of women in London journalism is also examined in Alison Adburgham, *Women in Print: Writing Women and Women's Magazines from the Restoration to the Accession of Victoria* (London, 1972).

On women writers in eighteenth-century France, the essays in Elizabeth C. Goldsmith and Dena Goodman, eds., *Going Public: Women and Publishing in Early Modern France* (Ithaca and London, 1995) are wide-ranging and insightful. My account of the *Journal des Dames* is based on Nina Rattner Gelbart, *Feminine and Opposition Journalism in Old Regime France* (Berkeley, 1987). I have also consulted Suzanna Van Dijk, *Traces de femmes: présence féminine dans le journalisme français du XVIIIe siècle* (Amsterdam and Maarsen, 1988).

A brief survey of women writers in eighteenth-century Germany can be found in Leslie Sharpe, "The Enlightenment," in Jo Catling, ed., *A History of Women's Writing in Germany, Austria, and Switzerland* (Cambridge, 2000). I have profited especially from Barbara Becker-Cantarino, *Der lange Weg zur Mündigkeit: Frau und Literatur (1500–1800)* (Berlin, 1987), and Eva Walter, *Schrieb oft, von Mägde Arbeit müde: Lebenszusammenhänge deutscher Schriftstellerinnen um 1800* (Dusseldorf, 1985). On Sophie La Roche, see Monika Nenon, *Autorschaft und Frauenbildung: das Beispiel Sophie von la Roche* (Würzburg, 1988), and Christa Baguss Britt's introduction to her English edition of LaRoche's *History of Lady Sophia Sternheim* (New York, 1991). The role of women in eighteenth-century German journalism is examined in Edith Krull, *Das Wirken der Frau im frühen deutschen Zeitschriftenwesen* (Berlin, 1939).

5   From courts to consumers: theater publics

In the theater, as in other areas of Enlightenment culture, the public assumed a new significance. For one, many theaters expanded their seating capacity. Drury Lane, London's most renowned theater, held around a thousand people in 1732. An expansion in 1762 enabled it to house around 2,360 patrons, and further renovations in 1792 boosted Drury Lane's capacity to more than 3,600. Its archrival, Covent Garden, experienced a similar expansion. Renovations in 1782 increased its capacity from 1,335 to 2,170 spectators, and another expansion in 1792 brought it to 3,013. Attendance at the Comédie Française, the leading stage in Paris, averaged 117,000 spectators annually between 1715 and 1750. Between 1750 and 1770 annual attendance reached 165,000 and it continued to grow into the Revolution.[1]

It was not just larger audiences that made theater publics more visible. Just as "public opinion" came to be seen as the ultimate arbiter in the political realm, so did writers on the theater come to view the audience as the ultimate arbiter of taste. A critic in London's *Daily Journal* (1737) accepted the public's dominion over the stage as a matter of course: "I believe we shall find the town [here the theater public – JVHM] in general to be justly and actually the governor of the stage, as it now stands: for tho' it be in the power of a manager to produce what actors and what pieces he pleases, yet the town, if they differ from him in opinion, will immediately bring him over to theirs."[2] The metaphor of the public as supreme tribunal, so prevalent in eighteenth-century political discourse, was commonly employed in reference to the theater as well. London's *Theatrical Guardian* proclaimed in 1791 that "the public is the

---

[1] Figures are taken from Harry William Pedicord, *The Theatrical Public in the Time of Garrick* (New York, 1954), 6; Joseph Donohue, "The London Theater at the End of the Eighteenth Century," in Robert D. Hume, ed., *The London Theater World, 1660–1800* (Carbondale and Edwardsville, Ill., 1980), 366; John Lough, *Paris Theatre Audiences in the Seventeenth and Eighteenth Centuries* (London, 1959), 173–74.

[2] Quoted in Leo Hughes, The *Drama's Patrons: A Study of the Eighteenth-Century London Audience* (Austin and London, 1971), 11.

160

only jury before whom the merits of an actor or an actress are to be tried, and when the endeavors of a performer are stampt by them with the seal of sanction and applause, from that there should be no appeal."[3]

At performances, the use of prologues and epilogues epitomized the recognition of the public's power in the theater. These direct appeals to the audience, which were especially common on the London stage, were popular and were often demanded by spectators at the beginning or close of a performance. Actors often employed them to flatter their audience, implicitly acknowledging the public's capacity for judgment. In a famous prologue written by Samuel Johnson for the opening of the 1747 theater season at Drury Lane, the renowned actor David Garrick affirmed the sovereignty of his public:

> Ah! let not Censure term our Fate our Choice,
> The Stage but echoes back the public Voice,
> The Drama's Laws the Drama's Patrons give,
> For we that Live to please, must please to live.

Samuel Johnson's epilogue to Oliver Goldsmith's "Good-Natured Man" (1768) compared the relationship between playwright and public to that between a politician and voters:

> Distrest alike, the statesman and the wit,
> When one a borough courts, and one the pit,
> The busy candidates for pow'r and fame,
> Have hopes and fears and wishes just the same.[4]

Yet opinions about the consequences of the public's dominion over the theater were mixed, much as they were in the political and literary arenas. Some spoke of theater audiences in the same tone used by enlightened journalists when they wrote about the reading public, or by statesmen in praising "public opinion." The *philosophe* Grimm observed of French theater audiences that no political assembly possessed judgment "more just, more final, and more prompt than our parterre." For others, however, recognition of the public's sovereignty over the stage was mixed with unease over the consequences of that power. Such critics portrayed theater audiences as unstable, arbitrary, and capricious. Despite his enormous success as a playwright, Voltaire viewed his public with cynicism: "Who? The public? This inconstant phantom, this monster with a hundred voices, this devouring Cerberus. . . ." Alexander Pope evoked similar

[3] Quoted *ibid.*, 5.

[4] Quotes taken from Benjamin Victor, *A History of the Theatres of London and Dublin, from the Year 1730 to the Present Time*, 2 vols. (London, 1761), I:86, and Hughes, *The Drama's Patrons*, 5.

imagery in referring to theater audiences as "the many-headed Monster of the Pit," and later on the dramatist Elizabeth Inchbald lamented the despotic power wielded by a theater public more interested in vulgar spectacle than in moral improvement. The playwright, Inchbald wrote in 1807, "is the very slave of the audience . . . He must have their tastes and prejudices in view, not to correct, but to humour them . . ."[5]

Such criticisms point to a basic fact: a theater's public was not unitary but multiple in character. In Pope's words it was a "many-headed Monster" whose social complexion varied according to where one sat (or stood), and whose composition shifted from day to day and often from hour to hour. The amorphous, unstable quality of audiences was the natural result of the early modern theater's evolution into a public and commercial stage, access to which depended not on social rank but on the price of a ticket. Most Enlightenment critics favored a public stage, convinced as they were that theaters had the power to instruct and improve people. But the accessibility of commercial theaters created audiences whose tastes, in disregarding or even dissolving the boundaries between a "high" and a "low" stage, threatened to undermine the didactic function critics assigned the theater.

This chapter begins by looking at how the theater, earlier an object of distrust and hostility, acquired a positive public role through the Enlightenment's moral rehabilitation of the institution. I then trace the development of the early modern stage as an institution initially linked to the absolutist court but increasingly beholden to the commercial public theaters came to serve. Turning then to the development of the public stage in eighteenth-century London, Paris, and Vienna, the remainder of the chapter looks at the dilemmas posed by this commercial public and the ways in which critics and reformers tried to come to terms with them.

The stage legitimated

Whether viewed as beneficent or corrupt, the power attributed to eighteenth-century theater audiences was symptomatic of the cultural importance the theater had acquired during the early modern period. The rise of theaters as centers of entertainment and sociability was part of a broader commercialization of leisure that had set in by the early eighteenth century. As with other centers of entertainment and sociability that were a product of this process – spas like Bath in England or Bad

---

5 Above quotes taken from Henri Lagrave, *Le théâtre et le public à Paris de 1715 à 1750* (Paris, 1972), 552 (Grimm), 546 (Voltaire); Hughes, *The Drama's Patrons*, 86 (Pope); Ellen Donkin, *Getting into the Act: Women Playwrights in London 1776–1829* (London and New York, 1995), 5 (Inchbald).

Pyrmont in Germany, the pleasure gardens of London's Vauxhall and Vienna's Prater, the cafés and music halls that lined the Palais-Royale in Paris – the commercially run public theaters of the eighteenth century accommodated a diverse clientele whose patronage rested not on birth or rank but on the ability to pay.

Various changes in the urban environment encouraged the growth of commercialized centers of entertainment and sociability. One was the disappearance of the plague, which had been endemic in much of Europe from its initial outbreak in the mid-fourteenth century up to the eighteenth century. London experienced its last outbreak in 1665–66, Paris in 1668 and Vienna in 1713–14. Municipal governments had traditionally responded to the outbreak of plague by banning public entertainments, and actors, a highly mobile group, were especially suspect as carriers. But as outbreaks of plague became more and more intermittent and finally ceased altogether, theaters and public entertainments in general no longer represented the dangers they had once posed. The impact was to encourage the proliferation of public spaces and institutions where people socialized and sought entertainment.

Even more important for the commercialization of entertainment in the eighteenth century were improvements in street illumination.[6] Before governments began systematically to introduce street lighting in the latter half of the seventeenth century, fear of crime and the hazards of negotiating dark and winding streets tended to keep people indoors or at least close to their neighborhoods after dark. In larger cities like London or Paris, those who could afford it hired torchbearers to accompany them when they had to venture out into the city after dark. But torchbearers offered only minimal protection, especially since they themselves were notorious for their links to the criminal underworld. In the sixteenth century some cities began requiring building owners to mount lanterns under the second-story windows of their dwellings, but when Louis XIV decreed in 1667 that lanterns be hung at regular intervals along Parisian streets, the French capital became the first European city with a centralized system of street lights. Some 2,700 lanterns were installed, a figure that had almost doubled by 1700. By 1750 around 8,000 candlelit lanterns illuminated the streets of Paris, and the use of lenses and reflectors added to the quality of street lighting. In the 1760s the invention of the so-called *réverbère*, oil lamps with reflectors placed over and around the flame, brought further improvements. Oil-burning lamps were already being used in English towns by the late seventeenth century, although London,

---

[6] For what follows, see Wolfgang Schivelbusch, *Disenchanted Night: the Industrialization of Light in the Nineteenth Century*, trans. Angela Davies (Berkeley, 1988), passim.

owing to its relatively decentralized municipal government, did not have a standardized system of street lighting until the 1730s.

Improvements in street illumination multiplied the sites and occasions of urban sociability, now less constrained by darkness and night. The throngs of people who after dark patronized the vaudevilles of the Parisian boulevards, the cafés and shops of the Palais-Royale, or the pleasure gardens of London's Vauxhall and Ranelagh, would have been unimaginable without illuminated streets and parks. The role of street lighting in creating what we now call night life is attested to by the progressively later performance times of eighteenth-century theaters. While theater performances in Restoration London had usually begun around three in the afternoon, the curtain times of London theaters in the late eighteenth century were generally around 6.30. Similarly, while in late sixteenth-century Paris a royal decree had ordered that plays end by 4.30 in the afternoon, late eighteenth-century performances usually closed by around ten in the evening. The fact that theaters opened progressively later during the course of the eighteenth century made it easier for those otherwise constrained by their work schedules, above all artisans and laborers, to attend.

But the prominence of the theater in eighteenth-century urban culture also reflected the moral rehabilitation of an institution that had contended with centuries-old traditions of religious hostility. Christian animosity toward the stage had its roots in late antiquity, when Church fathers like Tertullian, Augustine, and John Chrysostom associated the theater with paganism and condemned the Roman stage as licentious and idolatrous. The patron of the Roman theater had after all been Bacchus, the god of wine whose altar customarily stood to the right of the stage, and during the fourth and fifth centuries a series of church councils had threatened Christians who attended or acted in performances with excommunication. Hostility eased during the Middle Ages, when the church began to sponsor mystery plays and religious dramas, but the antagonism that had marked early Christian attitudes never entirely disappeared and in fact revived in the seventeenth century. Pangs of religious conscience led both Calderón and Racine, two of the most renowned dramatists of the period, temporarily to abandon their stage careers – evidence of how much the theater continued to be associated with the sinful and the profane.

Much of the impetus behind the renewed campaign against the theater came from reform movements within Protestantism and Catholicism. Puritans in England, Pietists in Prussia, and Jansenists in France all condemned the stage for some of the same reasons many denounced the novel: both genres stirred the passions, rested on sham and illusion, and distracted the faithful from the task of salvation. These attacks often bore fruit, the Puritan-sponsored closing of London theaters between 1642 and 1658 being only one example. Pietist theologians at the Prussian University of Halle were able to suppress stage performances in the city between 1700 and 1745, and Catholic priests in eighteenth-century France routinely denied actors the sacraments. Molière was denied them on his deathbed in 1673, and only the intervention of the crown ensured him a proper Christian burial. Antagonism to the theater was not restricted to religious zealots. Even at the University of Göttingen, a beacon of the German Enlightenment, fears that the presence of actors in the town would jeopardize student morals led professors to suppress the staging of comedies between 1746 and 1784. Rousseau's famous letter to D'Alembert in 1758, which denounced plans to establish a public theater in Geneva, also shows that hostility to the stage did not disappear with the Enlightenment. Even though Rousseau did little more than recapitulate traditional arguments against the theater, his attack does illustrate their tenacity.

Yet Rousseau's polemic stirred attention in large part because it was so perversely contrarian, penned at a time when theaters had become integral to the urban cultural landscape. However persistent the undercurrents of hostility, countervailing tendencies had served to rehabilitate the stage. One was the important role that theater had come to play in the confessional struggles of the sixteenth and seventeenth centuries, especially in Catholic Europe, where the Jesuits were avid proponents of the stage as an instrument of religious propaganda. Particularly in Bavaria and in the territories of the Austrian Habsburgs, where the campaign against Protestantism was waged with special intensity, Jesuit dramatists wrote and produced plays designed for performance at court or in schools and universities. Here, of course, a vast distance separated the Jesuit school drama from the Enlightenment stage, but the important pedagogical function that the Jesuits assigned to theater helped sanction it as legitimate entertainment. The flowering of the theater in eighteenth-century Vienna, for example, rested to a considerable extent on the traditions of the Jesuit stage.

From a more secular perspective, Enlightenment defenders of the stage rehabilitated the theater by investing it with a heavily moral function. In England the tone was set by Addison and Steele, who condemned the amoral cynicism of the Restoration stage but favored reforming rather than abolishing the theater. David Garrick devoted his career as an actor and theater director to making the stage morally respectable. As manager of Drury Lane (1747–76) he routinely altered or deleted morally questionable passages from older plays, including those of Shakespeare, whom he tirelessly championed. Richard Cumberland, whose sentimental dramas and comedies were popular on the London stage from the 1760s up to the end of the century, believed the playwright was morally bound "to give no false attractions to vice and immorality, but to endeavor ... to turn the fairer side of human nature to the public. ..." For French theorists of the stage, the theater had the same moral and didactic value. As Voltaire declared in 1733, "I view tragedy and comedy as lessons in virtue, reason, and propriety." For Diderot the object of all dramatic composition must be "to inspire a love of virtue and a horror of vice," and Mercier insisted similarly: "all comedy that does not correct vice is bad comedy." In Germany, this moral discourse was colored by an incipient patriotism that viewed the theater as a means of fostering a common language and culture. Lessing's declaration in 1767 that "the theater should be the school of the moral world" came amidst his efforts to establish a German "national" theater in Hamburg, while Schiller's famous 1784 address, "What Can a Well-Established Stage Actually Achieve?", saw the stage as a moral agent capable of fostering a German national spirit.[7]

The theater and the court

In the early modern period, standing theaters designed exclusively for staging plays first arose during the sixteenth century. In London the earliest commercial theaters coincided with the flowering of the Elizabethan stage. The first English playhouse, the Red Lion, was built in the London suburb of Whitechapel in 1567. It subsequently moved to the suburb of Shoreditch in 1576, where it was renamed the Theatre, only to close again in 1598 and reopen as the Globe – home, of course, to Shakespeare's plays. A competitor to the Globe, the Fortune Theater, opened in 1600, and in the meantime other playhouses like Blackfriars (1576), the Rose (1587), and the Swan (1595) were also hosting performances. In France the first standing theater was the Hôtel de Bourgogne, which opened in Paris in 1548. It was owned by the Confrérie de la passion, a religious confraternity organized in the Middle Ages to produce religious dramas. The Confrérie ran the Hôtel de Bourgogne purely as a commercial venture, however, leasing it to visiting French and Italian troupes. A French company took it over in 1629, and by the 1640s subventions from

---

[7] Above quotes are from L. W. Conolly, *The Censorship of English Drama 1737–1824* (San Marino, Cal., 1976), 138; Voltaire, *Lettres choisies* ed. Raymond Naves (Paris, 1963), 50; Diderot, "Entretiens sur le fils naturel," in *Oeuvres Esthétiques*, ed. Paul Vernière (Paris, 1963), 152; Eleanor F. Jourdain, "Die Theaterkritik im 18. Jahrhundert," in Dietmar Rieger, ed., *Das französische Theater des 18. Jahrhunderts* (Darmstadt, 1984), 84; Gottfried Ephraim Lessing, *Hamburgische Dramaturgie* [1767], in *Werke*, ed. Gerhard Stenzel (Stuttgart, n.d.), 683.

the crown had enabled it to become the main venue for the performance of French tragedy. Standing theaters developed more slowly in the Holy Roman Empire owing to the disruptive impact of the Thirty Years War on urban life, the relatively late emergence of German as a literary language, and the absence of a capital like Paris or London that could have otherwise sustained a major commercial stage. Courts like Vienna, Munich, and Dresden began adding lavish theaters to their residences in the seventeenth century, but these staged performances for an exclusive clientele and were not open to the public.

Prior to the establishment of standing theaters, performances were staged by troupes of players who moved from place to place providing entertainment. Theatrical performances for the public at large tended to take place in makeshift huts or in ballrooms, Ratskeller, and fencing halls. Market fairs were a common venue and remained so throughout the eighteenth century. In eighteenth-century London a visitor to St. Bartholomew's fair in late summer might encounter as many as six troupes on any particular day, while the fair theaters (*théâtres de la foire*) of Saint-Germain in Paris staged performances between February 3 and Easter week. Fair troupes performed on an elevated platform or in rented booths, some no more than 8 feet in width, flanked by the rope dancers, jugglers, and marionettists typically found on market squares. An especially talented or popular troupe was occasionally fortunate enough to receive an invitation to perform at court. Molière spent his theatrical career on the road until Louis XIV invited his troupe to perform at the Louvre in 1658, while the German company of Michael Daniel Treu (1634–1708) was a perennial favorite at the Wittelsbach court in Munich.

Crucial to the transition from wandering stage to standing theater was the rise of the absolutist court. The court and the theater shared a natural affinity: literally as well as figuratively, the stage was a central medium through which early modern rulers displayed their power and prestige. The political culture of the absolutist court was highly theatrical, its deeply encoded rituals providing a stage for the expression of authority relations and status differences. Fittingly, early modern descriptions of court life frequently employed the theater as a metaphor. The French author of an early seventeenth-century courtesy manual wrote that "the *Court* is an eminent and conspicuous *Theatre*, exposed to the sight and eyes of the world,"[8] while critics sometimes invoked the metaphor to highlight the artificiality and duplicity of court society. More directly expressing the centrality of the theater at court was the role it played in the education

---

[8] Eustache du Refuge, quoted in Jonas Barish, *The Antitheatrical Prejudice* (Berkeley, 1981), 176.

of rulers and aristocrats. Learning to perform on stage was an important preparation for participating in the requisite ceremonies of court life, and at a young age princes and princesses were given roles in plays performed at court. As a boy, Louis XIV appeared regularly in plays and ballets, as did Joseph II almost a century later. Theater taught a future sovereign the art of spectacle, the value of entrances and exits, the importance of comporting oneself with dignity and grace.

Theater was thus a prized form of entertainment for rulers, many of whom were intimately involved in the creation and patronage of theaters inside and outside the court. The Tudors and early Stuarts were active patrons of the London stage, a tradition Charles II resumed following the Puritan chill of the 1640s and 1650s. Charles granted two of his courtiers, William Davenant and Thomas Killigrew, the right to stage performances in the city, and Drury Lane dates back to his reign. Beyond being an avid theatergoer, Charles II promoted the stage as a political vehicle for glorifying his court and celebrating the ideals of kingship he associated with it. He commissioned the composition of new plays, solicited the translation of foreign ones, and occasionally designed scenery for performances. The bonds between theater and court were equally strong in seventeenth-century France. Henry IV of France and his wife Marie de Medici often visited the stage of the Hôtel Bourgogne, and Henry's successor, Louis XIII, attended twenty-three performances of a visiting Italian troupe in January and February of 1622.[9] Cardinal Richelieu, who as Corneille's patron worked to shape French drama in accordance with his royalist cultural program, himself commissioned the architect Jacques Le Mercier to build a theater for his residence in the Palais-Royale. The most important milestone in the French court's promotion of the theater was Louis XIV's establishment of the Comédie Française in 1680. Chartered in 1680 through the merger of three existing Parisian companies, the Comédie Française received from the crown an annual subsidy of 12,000 francs and the exclusive right to perform plays in French. The theater, which is today the oldest repertory company still in existence, became home to the tragedies of Corneille and Racine as well as to the comedies of Molière. It acquired unrivaled prestige throughout Europe and came to symbolize the preeminence of the French stage.

Unlike the Comédie Française or the licensed theaters of Restoration London, the court theaters of the Holy Roman Empire remained closed to the public well into the eighteenth century and staged performances exclusively for the court and its guests. In the beginning there was no regular theater season, and performances commemorated dynastic occasions like birthdays and marriages or celebrated the conclusion of peace treaties.

[9] Virginia Scott, *The Commedia dell'Arte in Paris, 1644–1697* (Charlottesville, 1990), 17.

Baroque opera, with its opulent sets and often enormous casts, had a special appeal as princes competed with one another to stage visually lavish spectacles. A Dresden performance of Johann Adolf Hasse's *Ezio* in 1755 employed 400 performers and 8 camels, while Nicola Jomelli's *Fetonte* (1768) at the Württemberg court opera in Stuttgart used 86 mounted hussars and 254 footsoldiers.[10]

But if standing theaters had evolved in close proximity to the absolutist court, the relationship between the two progressively weakened in the course of the eighteenth century. The tendency of the stage increasingly to emancipate itself from the institutional aegis of the court typified how absolutist culture by its very nature generated more inclusive forms of public space. Although Habermas portrayed the more open and accessible public sphere of the eighteenth century as antithetical to the socially exclusive, "representational publicness" of the court, the two forms of publicness were in fact related. Absolutist spectacle was not simply inner directed, nor was its public simply the court. It was designed to impress a larger audience, and the very scale and visibility of absolutist spectacle lent themselves to appropriation by a public larger than the court itself.

The theater is only one example of how the relatively exclusive sphere of the court could generate more inclusive arenas of sociability and entertainment. Pleasure gardens such as the Tuilleries and the Palais-Royal in Paris, or the Prater in Vienna, had originated in the sixteenth and seventeenth centuries as extensions of the court. During the eighteenth century, however, these and other pleasure gardens developed into centers of mass entertainment and sociability attracting a large and heterogeneous public. The Tuilleries palace and its surrounding gardens were originally built in 1563 by Catherine de Medici for use as a pleasure ground by the royal family. In the seventeenth century the gardens were opened to the aristocracy and upper bourgeoisie of Paris, and by the eighteenth century they had evolved into a place where people of all ranks congregated to socialize and promenade. Already in the late seventeenth century, the Duc de Saint-Simon lamented the resulting erosion of social distinctions: "the three estates are but one; the commoner proceeds the gentleman, and you have great trouble distinguishing the ladies from their attendants."[11] The Palais-Royal, bequeathed to the crown by Richelieu, had by the eve of the Revolution evolved into a veritable shopping and entertainment mall drawing throngs of people from every social milieu.

---

[10] Manfred Brauneck, *Die Welt als Bühne: Geschichte des europäischen Theaters*, 3 vols. (Stuttgart, 1993–99), I:722; Heinz Kindermann, *Theatergeschichte Europas*, 10 vols. (Salzburg, 1957–74), IV:590.

[11] Quoted in Carolyn C. Lougee, *Le Paradis des Femmes: Women, Salons, and Social Stratification in Seventeenth-Century France* (Princeton, 1976), 71.

Spas, which first began to flourish in the eighteenth century as centers of entertainment and leisure, offer a similar example of how space previously dominated by the court could become public and commercial. In the early eighteenth century, Bath had served chiefly as a summer refuge for the royal family and aristocratic guests, but subsequent commercial development quickly transformed the spa into a thriving resort where playhouses, promenades, bookshops and cafés catered to a broad clientele. German spas had also developed in close proximity to the court before evolving into centers of commercialized leisure. In Bad Pyrmont, located in the dwarfish principality of Waldeck in central Germany, the number of annual visitors grew from around 250 in the early eighteenth century to almost 1,200 in 1788.[12] The Waldeck counts who ruled the principality had originally developed the spa as a summer residence, but in the early eighteenth century they came to recognize its commercial potential and successfully marketed its waters as an antidote to rheumatism, nervous disorders, and gout. In the process, the counts transformed the spa into a mercantilist enterprise and their main source of revenue. By the mid-eighteenth century the spa had evolved from an appendage of the court into a resort renowned throughout Europe for its social and cultural amenities. The spa's social center was no longer the palace and gardens of the princely residence but the town itself, whose tree-lined promenade was lined with bookshops, cafés, a ballroom, a theater, and even a masonic lodge. There were definite limits to the inclusiveness of Pyrmont society: many of the balls, breakfasts, and picnics were by invitation only, and considerable care was taken to keep the main promenade free of plebeian intruders. Still, the Waldeck counts found it in their commercial interest to woo as broad a clientele as possible, and they went out of their way to encourage a relatively relaxed social atmosphere. Heinrich Matthias Marcard, a spa physician at Pyrmont, observed that "in general relations are easygoing and casual in Pyrmont, and there is a certain candor that is otherwise rare in this northern latitude."[13]

The logic of commercialization likewise accelerated the growing autonomy of the theater from the court. Fiscal necessity helped drive this process, for theaters like the Comédie Française or Drury Lane could never have survived on court subsidies alone. As we will see, even the court theaters of the Holy Roman Empire ultimately bowed to financial pressures and opened themselves to paying customers. However much rulers

---

[12] Reinhart P. Kuhnert, *Urbanität auf dem Lande: Badereisen nach Pyrmont im 18. Jahrhundert* (Göttingen, 1984).

[13] Quoted in Burkhard Fuchs, *Mondäne Orte einer vornehmen Gesellschaft: Kultur und Geschichte der Kurstädte 1700–1900* (Hildesheim, 1992), 140.

might have wanted the stage to mirror the values of the court, commercial theaters were by their very nature beholden to the public who paid to attend their performances. Arthur Murphy, a popular London playwright in the 1760s and 1770s, aptly employed the language of the marketplace when he enjoined theater managers in 1776 to "consider themselves at the head of a great warehouse; procure the best assortment of goods, get proper hands to display them; open their doors, be civil to the customers, and, Apollo foretells that the generosity of the public will reward their endeavors."[14]

London

The bond between theater and court that had marked the Restoration stage began to unravel soon after the death of Charles II. Although Charles II had established a small stage in Whitehall Palace, no British sovereign built anything comparable to the court theaters of Versailles, Vienna, or Dresden. Neither William and Mary nor Queen Anne were patrons of the stage, and they in fact shared the suspicions of critics who believed the theater to be immoral. George I, patron of Handel, did found the Royal Academy of Music in 1719 in an ill-fated attempt to create a court opera along French lines – Handel was to be for the Hanoverians what Lully had been for Louis XIV. But opera confronted stiff opposition in early Hanoverian England, including the hostility of Addison and Steele who attacked the sensual, contrived quality of the operatic stage as immoral and unnatural. English xenophobia also played a role, with critics condemning opera as a foreign import from France and Italy. In the end George I's enterprise failed because it proved too expensive for either the court or its limited public to afford, and by the 1740s Handel had largely abandoned opera in favor of oratorio composition.

The episode was symptomatic of the court's inability to impose its theatrical tastes on those of the capital. Residues of the older link between theater and court persisted: theater managers in eighteenth-century London were technically employees of the crown, and theatrical companies continued to refer to themselves as "Their Majesty's Servants." But London theaters received no royal subsidies, and unlike the Comédie Française, they did not include separate entrances for the royal family – a telling sign of the tenuous link between theater and court.[15] On those occasions when the king did put in an appearance at Drury Lane or Covent

---

[14] Quoted in Pedigord, *Theatrical Public in the Time of Garrick*, 155.

[15] Hans Lange, *Vom Tribunal zum Tempel: zur Geschichte und Architektur deutscher Hoftheater zwischen Vormärz und Restauration* (Marburg, 1985), 17–18; James L. Lynch, *Box, Pit, and Gallery: Stage and Society in Johnson's London* (Berkeley, 1953), 201.

Garden, his presence does not appear to have inspired particular deference in the audience. Christian Mylius, a German visitor to London who
was present at a performance attended by George II and Princess Amalia
in 1753, was shocked by how oblivious the audience seemed toward the
royal pair. J. H. Mayer, another German visitor to the city, noted with surprise how boisterously the audience behaved at a performance attended
by George III.[16]

Not that the London stage was unregulated; the 1737 Licensing Act
restricted dramatic performances to the so-called "patent" (or licensed)
theaters of Drury Lane and Covent Garden. Its provisions also required
theater managers to submit at least two weeks in advance the text of
any new production to the Lord Chamberlain, who was empowered to
censor part or all of the performance. Implemented by the Walpole government in response to Henry Fielding's political satires at the Little
Theater in the Haymarket, the Licensing Act sanctioned procedures for
precensorship as stringent as any existing on the continent. The measure
seems anomalous in light of the government's relatively liberal regime
of print censorship. The playwright Elizabeth Inchbald later highlighted
the disparity when she wrote in 1807 that the English novelist "lives in
a land of liberty, whilst the Dramatic Writer exists but under a despotic
government."[17] The government's unwillingness to accord theaters the
same latitude it granted publishers may partly have been a legacy of Puritan hostility to the stage. William Law's *Absolute Unlawfulness of the Stage
fully Demonstrated* appeared only a year before the passage of the Licensing Act, and though Law was himself no Puritan, his polemic drew on a
Puritan-inspired tradition of hostility to the stage that helped legitimate
its tighter regulation. Censorship of the theater also reflected widespread
agreement, in England and elsewhere, that the immediacy and publicness of the stage made it potentially more dangerous than the relatively
individualized act of reading. The London actor and playwright Colley
Cibber wrote in his autobiography (1740) that lies and calumny were
less dangerous in print than on the stage, since "the Poison has a much
slower Operation, upon the Body of a People, when it is so retail'd out,
than when sold to a full Audience by wholesale."[18] Joseph Heinrich von
Engelschall, a disciple of the theater reformer Gottsched and a professor of rhetoric in Vienna, observed in 1760 that "an actor can spread
more immorality in half a day than can be found in ten scurrilous books."
Those like Gottsched in Germany, who wanted to eliminate improvised

---

[16] John A. Kelly, *German Visitors to English Theaters in the Eighteenth Century* (Princeton, 1936), 27, 56.
[17] Quoted in Conolly, *Censorship of English Drama,* 11.
[18] *Ibid.*, 180.

performances and replace them with a repertory that adhered strictly to dramatic texts, or Oliver Goldsmith in England, who wrote that "it would be more for the interests of virtue if stage performances were read and not acted," were in effect hoping to safeguard the moral function of the stage by subordinating it to a print medium they considered less dangerous and more controllable.[19]

On the whole, the Licensing Act did succeed in eliminating overt political criticism from the London stage, although the effectiveness of the measure lay as much in the theater genres it encouraged as in the opinions it suppressed. The popularity of Richardson's novels helped inspire the sentimental dramas and comedies so in vogue on the London stage, but to the theater managers who staged them they also had the virtue of lacking any overtly political message. Even the canonization of Shakespeare, arguably the most lasting contribution of England's otherwise modest eighteenth-century theatrical legacy, was encouraged by the political vicissitudes of the London theater after 1737. Shakespeare's plays, of course, abound in moral and political ambiguity, but Garrick's Drury Lane productions purged potentially offensive passages and transformed the Bard into a respectable national symbol. Censorship of the London stage conformed not only to the interests of government ministers keen to silence criticism, but also to the ideals of an Enlightenment cultural agenda that considered the stage a vehicle of moral and social improvement. If, as most Enlightenment critics believed, a moral stage could improve people, an immoral one could corrupt them. Censorship was therefore needed to ensure that the theater exercised its influence for the good.

But here Garrick and others who invested the stage with a moral and didactic purpose were to be disappointed. Like the eighteenth-century publicists who believed the spread of print could create an enlightened public opinion, proponents of the stage as a moral and educational institution presupposed an audience relatively homogeneous in taste. But commercial theater publics, like eighteenth-century readers, were anything but homogeneous. London's patent theaters were sufficiently affordable to attract a socially diverse audience. Although an upper-class clientele of aristocrats, government ministers, and visiting dignitaries dominated the more expensive boxes, a less elite middle-class audience populated the parterre (or "pit") and even footmen and common laborers could afford to stand in the upper galleries. Especially affordable were the afterpieces, the one-act musicals, farces, and circus-like spectacles that followed the featured performance and admitted patrons for half-price.

---

[19] Joseph Heinrich von Engelschall, *Zufällige Gedanken über die deutsche Schaubühne* (Vienna, 1760), 46; Goldsmith quoted in John Brewer, *The Pleasures of the Imagination: English Culture in the Eighteenth Century* (London, 1997), 339.

As elsewhere in Europe, London theater audiences were also sexually mixed. Nowhere outside the salon did eighteenth-century women have more of a public presence than in the theater. Symbolizing their visibility was the presence of women on stage, a relatively recent phenomenon in London theaters, and the profession of actress achieved unprecedented respectability throughout Europe in the eighteenth century. In Greek and Roman antiquity, female roles had been performed by males, and medieval mystery plays continued this practice out of fears by the church that the presence of women on stage aroused the passions of the audience. In the mid-sixteenth century women began to appear in the Commedia del'arte performances of Italian troupes, and by the seventeenth century the use of women in female roles had become relatively common in French and Italian theaters. Perhaps owing to Puritan opposition, actresses did not appear on the London stage until considerably later. The first known occasion was in December of 1660, when Thomas Killigrew's King's Company cast an actress in the role of Desdemona for a performance of *Othello*. Two years later, Charles II decreed that henceforth all female roles were to be played by women, which did not, however, prevent women from playing men: eighteenth-century actresses like Madame Alt in Germany or Peg Woffington and Charlotte Clarke in England were famous for their "breeches roles" (Clarke and Alt especially for their portrayals of Hamlet).

As patrons, women moved with considerable freedom in London's commercialized theater world, where it was socially acceptable to attend in the company of a female friend or party without a male escort. Already in the late seventeenth century, Elizabeth Pepys (wife of the diarist Samuel) thought nothing of attending the sexually charged performances of the Restoration stage without her husband. Eighteenth-century theaters sought to attract female playgoers just as publishers wooed women readers. The disappearance after 1700 of much of the explicit sexuality that had marked the Restoration stage has been attributed to pressures from female patrons, and women, the target audience for Richardson's novels, were an important constituency for the sentimental comedies and dramas popular on the eighteenth-century London stage. In the late 1730s, the "Shakespeare Ladies Club" successfully lobbied Covent Garden's management to stage more plays by the dramatist and thereby helped pave the way for his subsequent revival by Garrick. These campaigns were waged by an educated if not upper-class clientele, but the social composition of female theatergoers was as varied as that of their male counterparts. Prostitutes were a common sight. High-priced whores at Drury Lane and Covent Garden gravitated toward the less expensive upper tier of side loges, where they conveniently met the gaze of wealthy patrons seated in the boxes opposite.

But the London theater public was heterogeneous in taste as well as social composition, and there was no simple correspondence between the two. The division between the "high" minority of playgoers who sought moral and aesthetic uplift, and the "low" majority primarily interested in entertainment, reflected class differences only insofar as the former tended to be literate and educated. The latter, those who went to the theater primarily to see the farces, musical comedies, and special effects that London's licensed theaters offered later in the evening, cut across class lines and ranged from aristocrats to their servants. As much as Garrick hoped to cultivate in London's theater public a taste for high comedy and tragedy, the financial survival of theater managers required them to satisfy an amorphous audience – hence the pantomimes and rope-dancers who followed performances of *Richard III*, or the slapstick musicals staged on the heels of Addison's *Cato*. The boundaries between high and low were not always so stark. John Gay's *Beggar's Opera*, first performed in 1728 at Lincoln's Inn Fields Theater and thereafter a perennial favorite of London audiences, succeeded partly through its brilliant blend of both genres. But the general trend was in the direction of a theatrical culture dominated more by spectacle and vaudeville than by a spoken stage. Reinforcing this tendency was the ability of smaller theaters to survive the government's restrictive licensing procedures, which had confined spoken dialogue to the two patent theaters, by staging musical comedies and one-man shows. From the 1760s on, vaudeville "burlettas" and light opera flourished in smaller theaters like Sadler's Wells and in pleasure gardens like Marylebone or Ranelagh, eventually leading patent theaters to adjust their repertoires accordingly. By the end of the century, the result was what one scholar has characterized as "an emphasis on the visual at the cost of the spoken word," or in the words of another, "a small island of legitimate spoken theater ... surrounded by a mass of popular entertainment."[20]

This proliferation of spectacle reflected an insatiable demand for novelty, a feature of theater audiences that had become a standard complaint of actors, playwrights, and managers throughout Europe by the late eighteenth century. As an anonymous German observer noted in 1789, "it is a universal complaint of theater directors from one end of Germany to another that the public (*Publikum*) lusts for more and more novelty."[21] A hunger for novelty was in some ways intrinsic to the theater's institutional development. The evolution of theaters into sedentary institutions with standard repertoires and performance times created publics

---

[20] Donohoe, "London Theater at the End of the Eighteenth Century," 356; Brewer, *Pleasures of the Imagination*, 388.

[21] "Übersicht des heutigen Zustandes des Theaters in Deutschland," *Journal des Luxus* 1 (1789), 72.

that were more demanding and conscious of their influence. Because a wandering troupe generally performed no more than a few weeks in any particular place, its audience was geographically dispersed and a handful of plays sufficed for its repertoire. By contrast, the theater season of a standing repertory company lasted for months and hence required a much more extensive inventory of plays. So while an itinerant troupe in sixteenth-century England needed no more than three or four plays in its repertoire, the resident troupe at London's Fortune Theater was staging as many as thirty-five a year by the early seventeenth century.[22] The audience of a standing theater demanded more variety, and commercial success depended on the ability of theater managers to satisfy an appetite for ever newer fare.

The behavior of eighteenth-century theater audiences also encouraged a stage that subordinated the spoken word to visual and musical spectacle. The unruliness of London theaters was legendary and even a source of pride for those who considered it a hallmark of English liberty. Colley Cibber found the Parisian stage far more heavily policed than London theaters, where, he claimed, he and his fellow actors had to contend with more rowdy audiences as a consequence. But such was the price of English liberty, shrugged Cibber: "let us rather bear this insult than buy its remedy at too dear a rate."[23] It must in any case have been difficult to hear an actor's speech amidst the chatter of the boxes or the catcalls that issued forth from the audience at the slightest occasion. Like taste, inattentive or disruptive behavior was no index of social rank. Seated in the privacy and intimacy of their loges, aristocratic theatergoers more often than not viewed the theater as an extension of the drawing room. Conversing freely with companions or casting coquettish glances at an object of amorous attention in an opposite box, one considered the play to be of secondary importance and it was a mark of poor taste to listen too closely to a performance. An epilogue to Henry Crisp's *Virginia* (1754) at Drury Lane satirized such behavior:

> May I approach into the boxes pray,
> And there search out a judgment on the play?
> In vain alas! I should attempt to find it!
> Fine ladies see a play, but never mind it:
> 'Tis vulgar to be mov'd by acted passion,
> Or form opinions till they're fixed by Fashion.[24]

For aristocratic patrons the theater was a stage within a stage, an arena for exhibiting the signs and prerogatives of rank. Aristocratic etiquette

---

[22] Andrew Gurr, *Playgoing in Shakespeare's London*, 2nd ed. (Cambridge, 1996), 122–23.
[23] Quoted in Hughes, *The Drama's Patrons*, 31.
[24] Quoted in Lynch, *Box, Pit, and Gallery*, 290.

dictated that one arrive after the performance had begun and depart before it ended, allowing for an ostentatious entrance and exit. Further indicative of the theater's significance as an arena of noble self-representation was the practice of allowing aristocratic spectators to pay for the privilege of sitting on the stage. Also common in French theaters, this practice was attacked by theater reformers for distracting the audience and disrupting performances. These critics could cite instances like a performance of *Romeo and Juliet* where the London actress Susannah Cibber had to push her way through the spectators on stage in order to enter the tomb of the Capulets. Voltaire's campaign succeeded in removing spectators from the stage of the Comédie Française in 1759, as did Garrick in 1762 as manager of Drury Lane. One reason the practice proved so persistent was the financial self-interest of the theaters themselves, where stage seats were usually the most expensive and lucrative in the house. Garrick was able to compensate financially for his elimination of stage seats only by increasing the number of regular seats when the theater was expanded the same year.

But the very size of London's patent theaters was a problem, at least as far as the performance of spoken drama was concerned. The commercial imperatives that fueled the architectural expansion of Drury Lane or Covent Garden in turn encouraged visual effect over the spoken word. Except for those who stood toward the front of the parterre, it was often impossible to hear an actor's speech. The English dramatist Richard Cumberland noted the effect of size on the repertoires of the two theaters when he complained that "there can be nothing very gratifying in watching the movement of an actor's lips when we cannot hear the words that proceed from them, but when the animating march strikes up, and the stage lays open its recesses to the depth of a hundred feet for the procession to advance, even the most distant spectator can enjoy his shilling's worth of show."[25] The simultaneous expansion of the theater and contraction of spoken drama symbolized the dilemma faced by proponents of an enlightened stage. They wanted to expand their public while continuing to guide it, goals that were not always compatible.

Paris

The presence of the crown was in some respects more visible in the theater life of the French capital than was the case in London. Paris's three royal theaters, the Comédie Française, the Comédie Italienne, and the Académie Royale de Musique (the official name of the Paris opera), were privileged by the crown and unlike the patent theaters of London,

---

[25] Quoted in Brewer, *Pleasures of the Imagination*, 385.

received subsidies. The presence of the crown was most palpable at the more socially exclusive opera, the royal spectacle *par excellence*, where Lully had established the tradition in Louis XIV's time of composing artful prologues praising the wisdom and justice of the king. But even at the more affordable and accessible Comédie Française and Comédie Italienne, the large contingent of soldiers who stood guard to keep out gate-jumpers (a common problem in eighteenth-century theaters) or quell unruly behavior embodied the authority of the crown over the stage. Paris's royal theaters had the reputation of being among the most heavily guarded in Europe. The systematic policing of Parisian theaters dated back to Louis XIV's reign, and was given additional muscle in 1751 when the Parisian police who had traditionally patrolled the two theaters were replaced by guards from the royal garrison. This measure increased the military presence of the crown, and by the eve of the Revolution no fewer than forty-six soldiers patrolled performances at the Comédie Française.[26]

But military supervision did not make Parisian audiences quiet and docile. Cibber's invidious contrast between the raucous liberty of London audiences and the enforced passivity of French playgoers (see above) says more about English francophobia than it does about Paris theaters. Drury Lane audiences may have expressed dissatisfaction with a performance by pelting the stage with oranges, but patrons at the Comédie Française voiced their disdain just as demonstratively with the shrill whistles they produced by blowing into the hollowed ends of their housekeys. The parterre, where spectators stood cheek by jowl amid concessionaires selling lemonade, was notoriously rowdy, and differences in opinion routinely ended in brawls during the performance. Like the patent theaters of London, the royal theaters of Paris were commercial enterprises dependent on and ultimately subject to their public. At the Comédie Française the crown's annual subsidy of 12,000 livres sufficed to pay the actors, but costumes, repairs, and other operating expenses had to be covered by ticket and subscription sales. The financial status of the Comédie Française was always precarious – by 1757 its debts had mounted to 487,000 livres – and its survival rested on the paying customers who patronized it.[27]

Competition among the theaters of the capital was often fierce and reinforced this dependence on the public. Despite its royal status, the

[26] Jeffrey Ravel, *The Contested Parterre: Public Theater and French Political Culture, 1680–1791* (Ithaca and London, 1999), 133–60, 161–90.

[27] On royal subsidies, see Claude Alasseur, *La Comédie Française au 18e siècle: étude économique* (Paris and the Hague, 1967), 37.

Comédie Française was never able to maintain the monopoly over spoken drama to which its privileges formally entitled it. From its creation in 1680 it had had to contend with stiff competition from the Comédie Italienne, which increasingly incorporated French rather than Italian dialogue into its *commedia dell'arte* performances.[28] The Comédie Française scored a temporary victory in 1697 when Louis XIV expelled the Italians for allegedly performing a piece that mocked his mistress, Madame de Maintenon. But the Regent, who found the staid neoclassical repertoire of the Comédie Française tedious, allowed them to return in 1716 and accorded them the same royal status as their jealous rival. The comic farces and musicals performed in the newly privileged theater retained elements of the *commedia dell'arte* tradition. But aside from the period from 1769 to 1779, when the theater was prohibited from performing in French, the Comédie Italienne was also home to French comedy. Most of Marivaux's comedies of the 1720s and 1730s, for example, premiered there.

Both theaters in turn confronted increasing competition from the fair troupes that had begun to take up more permanent residence along the newly constructed boulevards of the city. These broad arteries were rapidly becoming centers of commercial entertainment in the city, with theaters offering farces and bawdy skits to audiences that cut across the social spectrum. Although the royal theaters repeatedly lobbied the crown to close them, the government found the boulevard theaters harmless enough and preferred a policy of tacit toleration. The boulevard stage thrived as a consequence. On the eve of the Revolution the Boulevard du Temple alone had six theaters, some of which could accommodate as many as 1,300 spectators. By 1785, when the crown began granting long-term permits to boulevard theaters, the legal boundaries between the official and non-official stage had virtually dissolved. As in the printing industry, the Revolution hastened the process of deregulation and theaters sprouted accordingly: between 1785 and 1789 no more than eleven theaters had existed at any one time in Paris, but by the end of 1791 the city boasted thirty-five.[29]

Hence in Paris, as in London, an officially sanctioned stage had by the end of the Old Regime become submerged in a sea of mass theatrical

---

[28] The *commedia dell'arte* originated in sixteenth-century Italy and remained popular throughout Europe during the early modern period. Its chief characteristics were improvisation, stock characters (Arlequin, Colombine, Pantalon were the most common), the wearing of masks, and the use of sometimes elaborate special effects and stage machinery.

[29] Michèle Root-Bernstein, *Boulevard Theater and Revolution in Eighteenth-Century Paris* (Ann Arbor, 1984), 201. On the boulevard theaters see also Robert Isherwood, *Farce and Fantasy: Popular Entertainments in Eighteenth-Century Paris* (New York and Oxford, 1995), 167–191.

entertainment. Unlike in London, however, where strict enforcement of the Licensing Act preserved the patent theaters' monopoly on spoken drama, the government's willingness to tolerate the boulevard stage prevented royal theaters from upholding a similar monopoly. The boundaries between royal theaters and those of the boulevard became in fact quite porous, and the last two decades of the Old Regime witnessed a distinct convergence of the two. While the broad comedy and farce performed on the boulevard stage hearkened back to the fair tradition, its repertory also included parodies or adaptations of Corneille, Racine, Voltaire and others performed at the Comédie Française. Such poaching infuriated Voltaire, whose plays were often travestied on the boulevard despite his efforts to have the Parisian police suppress the practice. Yet plagiarism of this kind also enhanced the respectability of the boulevard stage, whose repertory was further gentrified in the 1770s and 1780s under the influence of the sentimental moralism of Diderot and other Enlightenment dramatists.

The lines of appropriation also ran in the other direction. The Comédie Française of the first half of the century had been a conservative institution devoted to nurturing its great seventeenth-century legacy of Corneille, Racine, and Molière. The tragedies of Corneille and Racine, where courtly heroes wrestled with the competing claims of love, honor, and duty to the sovereign, had enjoyed particular prestige and remained a standard feature of the theater's repertory. By the mid-eighteenth century, however, audiences had clearly begun to grow bored with the great tragedians. Productions of Corneille and Racine had accounted for 30 percent of the theater's audience in 1715–20, but by 1745–50 the percentage had dwindled to 11 percent.[30] Tragedies could still attract an audience, as Voltaire's popularity during the middle decades of the century proved. But by 1750 the court-inspired tragedy of the past was a genre in eclipse, overtaken in part by the "bourgeois" drama of writers like Diderot and Beaumarchais but also by competition from the fair and boulevard theaters. Already in the Regency, the Comédie Française had sought to boost lagging attendance by tagging slapstick farces and musicals onto its featured performance. Similar to the afterpieces London theaters began staging around the same time, these one-act entertainments (known as *petites pièces*) came straight out of the fair tradition. Voltaire deplored them and sometimes succeeded in blocking their use at performances of his own plays, but theater managers generally feared that audiences would shun the theater without them. Afterpieces were appended to roughly three-quarters of the theater's performances in 1720–25, and by 1745–50

---

[30] Lagrave, *Théâtre et le public*, 330–31.

the percentage had risen to 98 percent.[31] Even more indicative of the convergence of the official and unofficial stage was a perceptible overlap of repertory and personnel. By the 1770s the pressures of competition were forcing the Comédie Française to employ plays and artists from the boulevard stage, and actors routinely migrated back and forth between both theatrical milieus.

On the face of it this blurring of boundaries should have seemed a promising development for enlightened critics hostile to the traditionally bawdy antics of the boulevard stage. The theaters of the boulevard had, after all, become more refined under the influence of the nation's great theatrical tradition. To most critics, however, the glass was half empty rather than half full. The *philosophe* La Harpe found the boulevard adaptations of classical pieces to be of low quality, and bemoaned what he viewed as the plebeian debasement of the Comédie Française.[32] Contemporaries in the 1770s and 1780s often noted that audiences at the Comédie Française had become more plebeian, a development most enlightened critics viewed with regret. Such observations need not be taken in a strictly sociological sense. Although audiences at the Comédie Française had always been socially mixed, attendance was never as affordable as it was at Drury Lane or Covent Garden. Since a *parterre* ticket cost the equivalent of a whole day's wages for a middling artisan and his wife,[33] it is hard to imagine a Comédie Française bustling with *sans-culottes*. Working-class patrons would have found it feasible to attend on those rare occasions when the theater staged free performances or an actor friend passed along free tickets, but in general its public was dominated by aristocratic loges and a middle-class parterre and gallery. The oft-invoked spectre of a plebeianized Comédie Française thus rested more on aesthetic criteria than on strictly social ones. It is likely that the popularity of the boulevard stage had fostered a habit of theater-going among a mass audience previously unaccustomed to attending the theater on a regular basis. In that case, what contemporaries viewed as a process of social leveling was in fact the influx of a new public – propertied as well as plebeian – whose tastes had been shaped by the boulevard.

A central object of the anxieties aroused by the erosion of cultural and aesthetic boundaries was the parterre. During the seventeenth century the term parterre had come to refer both to the area directly in front of the stage and to the public who occupied it. More affordable than the aristocratic loges, the parterres of Paris's royal theaters were socially

---

[31] *Ibid.*, 351–59.
[32] Root-Bernstein, *Boulevard Theater*, 213.
[33] Lagrave, *Théâtre et le public*, 235.

more mixed and in numbers accounted for half to three-quarters of the audience.[34] Given its size and relative heterogeneity, the parterre became for enlightened critics a metaphor for the cultural promise as well as the pitfalls of a mass theater public. In the late seventeenth century it became a convention to praise the parterre as a stern but just and discerning tribunal. Often these praises came from dramatists eager to incur the favor of the largest (and loudest) segment of the audience, but the parterre was also considered the preserve of more educated and discriminating theatergoers – those who genuinely paid attention to the action on stage and willingly endured the discomforts of standing for the sake of a performance. Yet to its critics, the parterre also embodied the less desirable features of a commercial theater. Alongside the image of the parterre as a just and impartial tribunal was that of the noisy, disorderly crowd whose raucous behavior undermined its capacity for rational judgment. Even worse, it was corruptible, vulnerable to manipulation by the organized claques that playwrights often hired to cheer their own plays or jeer those of a rival. Claques, a notorious feature of eighteenth-century audiences, first appeared in Parisian theaters under the Regency. None other than Voltaire used them to orchestrate a successful premiere, and enemies accused him (probably falsely) of having purchased and distributed to supporters every parterre ticket for the 1748 opening of his *Sémiramis*. In the 1760s a certain Chevalier de la Morlière ran a professional claque from his table at the Café Procope, where he collected payment in exchange for hiring up to 150 spectators to applaud or disrupt a performance at the nearby Comédie Française.[35]

Beginning in the 1770s, debates over proposals to install seats in the parterre of the Comédie Française reflected the ambivalence of enlightened critics toward the theater public of their day. On one side was the *philosophe* La Harpe, who argued that replacing the standing parterre with benches would create a more orderly and refined public. Seating the parterre would have entailed raising ticket prices to compensate for the reduced number of spectators, which led opponents like Mercier to condemn the proposal as elitist. But for La Harpe, appalled by a theater public whose tastes he viewed as increasingly vulgar, filling the parterre with a better class of people was precisely the virtue of installing seats and raising ticket prices. Audiences would be better behaved, more reflective, and more receptive to an enlightened stage. The debate also had a gendered dimension. The likelihood of being mauled or otherwise accosted

[34] Lough, *Paris Theatre Audiences*, 99–100. On the parterre, my analysis follows that of Ravel, *The Contested Parterre*.
[35] Lagrave, *Le théâtre et le public*, 484–85.

had traditionally kept women out of the parterre, and the introduction of seating would have integrated women into a previously masculine area of the theater.

Le Harpe's position won the day in any case, for when the Comédie Française was rebuilt in 1782, the parterre of its new home included benches. The innovation proved unpopular, no doubt in part because the price of parterre tickets rose from 20 to 48 sous. But some also bemoaned the effects of the change on the psychology of the audience. Mercier declared that seating the parterre, far from making spectators more rational and discriminating, rendered them passive and lethargic. Others praised the standing parterre for having encouraged a process of collective consultation and debate among the spectators. Seating the parterre, they argued, effectively atomized it and thus deprived it of its critical function. Seats transformed active spectators into passive consumers and thereby undermined their sovereignty over the stage, which was now invested more in the hands of the actors and playwrights. At this point the debate foreshadowed the political issues raised in 1789. The issue of passive *versus* active spectators, sovereignty of the parterre *versus* sovereignty of the stage, went to the heart of revolutionary debates over the proper relationship between government and the popular will. The Rousseau disciple, Restif de la Bretonne, used a revealing metaphor when he wrote in 1788 that seating the parterre "deprived theatrical republicanism of its last refuge."[36] His lament was premature, however, and during the Revolution the theaters of the capital became a prime venue for the staging of republican festivals. The *salles de machines,* the theater in the Tuilleries originally commissioned by Mazarin to stage lavish spectacles for king and aristocracy, was remodeled to become the meeting place of the Convention in the spring of 1793. "Previously palaces were for kings," declared one revolutionary who endorsed the architectural project, "It is time the people had one of their own."[37] Theatrical space, once dominated by the crown, became a republican refuge.

Vienna

Court dominion over the theater proved more enduring in the Holy Roman Empire than in Britain or France. Having a theater in or attached to one's residence had been a mark of prestige for territorial rulers ever since

---

[36] Quoted in Jeffrey Ravel, "The Police and the Parterre: Cultural Politics in the Paris Public Theater, 1680–1789" (Ph.D. diss., University of California at Berkeley, 1991), 374.

[37] Quoted in James A. Leith, *Space and Revolution: Projects for Monuments, Squares, and Public Buildings in France 1789–1799* (Montreal and Kingston, 1991), 134.

the seventeenth century. Major courts like Vienna, Dresden, and Munich led the way, but even rulers of minor principalities like Saxony-Gotha or Ansbach-Bayreuth achieved renown throughout Europe for their court theaters. For lesser princes, lavish theaters provided a kind of "cultural capital" that helped compensate for a lack of political and military clout. Court theaters gave visual preeminence to the ruler. The opera that the architect Giovanni Burnacini built in 1652 for the Vienna court seated Ferdinand III and his wife under a canopy directly in front of the stage. In the opulent theater commissioned by August the Strong for his Dresden residence in 1717, and in the Berlin opera house built for Frederick II by his court architect Georg Wenzeslas von Knobelsdorf, the ruler also sat directly in front of the stage. The spatial articulation of the audience into loges demarcated further distinctions in rank. The first tier of boxes in Dresden's court theater was reserved for the upper nobility and foreign ambassadors, the second tier accommodated high officials and military officers, and lesser court personnel sat in the third. In Knobelsdorf's Berlin opera, the first two tiers of loges were reserved exclusively for ministers, other high officials, and guests of the court.

But as elsewhere in Europe, below the level of established court theaters there also existed a popular stage. Although strongly influenced by the Italian *commedia dell'arte*, a German-language *Volkskomödie* had by the eighteenth century developed its own indigenous comic traditions and characters. The best known figure of the German-language popular stage was the servant Hanswurst, a stock character in wandering troupes throughout the empire who found a theatrical home above all in Vienna. There the Hanswurst routines of Joseph Stranitzky, a footman's son from Graz who supplemented his acting income by pulling teeth, were so popular that in 1710 the city of Vienna opened the Kärtnertor Theater to house his performances. Stranitzky and his successors, Gottfried Prehauser and Joseph Felix Kurz, helped establish the Kärtnertor as the most commercially successful popular stage in the empire.

Like the boulevard theaters of Paris, the Kärtnertor often adapted or parodied pieces originally designed for a more courtly audience. Stranitzky and Kurz, for example, both employed themes and stage techniques borrowed from Jesuit theater. With its synthesis of classical humanism and baroque Catholicism, Jesuit drama depicted pagan as well as Christian subjects. Its use of Greek and Roman history and mythology were often thinly disguised paeans to the Habsburg emperor, and as such were highly popular at the Vienna court during the later seventeenth and early eighteenth centuries. In appropriating such themes, however, the Kärtnertor broke with Jesuit drama in one important respect: interwoven with the actions of the kings and aristocratic heroes who dominated the stage of

the Vienna court theater was the servant Hanswurst. Ridden with scato-
logical and sexual humor, the improvised antics of Hanswurst acquired
within the plot a significance that overshadowed the heroic actions of his
masters. Unlike his aristocratic lords who strove endlessly for fame and
glory, Stranitzky's Hanswurst was driven purely by the satisfaction of his
physical appetites. Thus when Hanswurst's master tells him that "it is
better to die than to soil one's honor through cowardice," the servant
replies: "You can have your honor but I'll keep my head... As soon as
my courage faces death, it falls straight down into my pants... I would
rather sit down with a jug of wine and be happy."[38] By the time Kurz and
Prehauser began performing at the Kärtnertor in the 1730s and 1740s,
their plebeian characters had appropriated the world of the baroque stage
in its entirety. Although the gods, heroes, and allegorical figures who had
dominated Jesuit drama still appeared, their roles had receded in comparison with the servants, common soldiers, and peasants who now occupied
center stage. The juxtaposition of aristocrats and plebs that characterized the Viennese popular stage in the early eighteenth century mirrored
the city's rapid growth following its repulsion of the Turks in 1683, when
the capital lured not only a growing segment of the Habsburg aristocracy
but also its entourage of servants. The Kärtnertor in fact drew both, as
Lady Mary Wortley Montague observed at a performance in 1716.[39]

In the 1720s, the Leipzig critic and theater reformer Johann Christoph
Gottsched launched a campaign to expel Hanswurst from the German-
language stage. Gottsched condemned the vulgarity and obscenity of
Hanswurst as unworthy of an enlightened German stage, and called for
the creation of a German dramatic repertoire based on French neoclassical models. The belated development of German as a literary language
had militated against the emergence of a literate (as opposed to improvised) German stage, and Gottsched's program entailed the creation of
a fixed repertoire performed in strict accordance with prescribed texts.
The "bourgeois" German stage envisioned by Gottsched and his followers was at heart an attempt to create a new theater public – one broader
than the socially exclusive audience of the court theater, with its primarily
French, Italian, and Latin repertoires, but more enlightened and refined
than the public of an improvised popular stage he considered coarse and
obscene. Gottsched's efforts centered on Leipzig, where he was a professor. There he developed a repertoire, performed by the theatrical troupe

---

[38] From "The Magnanimous Conflict between Friendship, Love, and Honor, or Scipio in
Spain with Hanswurst the Generous Slave," published in Rudolf Payer von Thurn, ed.,
Wiener Haupt- und Staatsaktionen, 2 vols. (Vienna, 1908), II:166–72.

[39] R. Halsband, ed., *The Complete Letters of Lady Mary Wortley Montague*, 2 vols. (Oxford,
1965), I:264.

of Caroline and Johann Neuber in a converted slaughterhouse, consisting largely of German translations of Racine and Molière as well as of pieces written by Gottsched himself. Gottsched and the Neubers inaugurated their reform program at a performance where the figure of Hanswurst was physically banished from the stage. Hanswurst's exile proved brief, however, for Gottsched's campaign was a spectacular failure. The austere staging and Alexandrine monotone of Gottsched's neoclassical productions had little appeal to an audience accustomed to the bawdy farces of Hanswurst, which – to Gottsched's disgust – the Neuber troupe was soon compelled to revive for commercial reasons.

By the 1750s the rather pedantic Gottsched had become an object of ridicule among the new generation of critics and dramatists associated with Germany's incipient literary revival. Looking to England rather than France for inspiration, dramatists like Gellert and Lessing found in the moral sensibility of Richardson's novels a model that promised both to entertain and improve their audience. Their hopes seemed confirmed by the successful premiere of Lessing's *Miss Sara Sampson* (1755), the Richardson-inspired drama that is generally regarded as Germany's first middle-class tragedy. An observer at the premiere (performed, of all places, in a Prussian drill hall in Frankfurt an der Oder) wrote that "the spectators listened for three and a half hours, still as statues, and wept."[40] Lessing and other proponents of a literary German stage now began to call for the establishment of a "national" theater, open to the public and independent of the court but also morally and aesthetically more refined than the popular stage of their day.

The Hamburg National Theater, founded in 1765 by local investors as an attempt to give the emerging German stage a permanent home, expressed these aspirations. Lessing accepted a position as dramaturgical advisor to the new theater, and devoted his energies as much toward building a public as he did to matters internal to the theater itself. His *Hamburgische Dramaturgie* (1767–69), a collection of essays and reviews that established the genre of German theater criticism, was intended to create an educated and discriminating audience for the theater's performances. Lessing attacked from one side the French neoclassical stage for its artificiality and subservience to the court. From the other side he condemned the harlequinades of Hanswurst as mindless entertainment catering to the lowest tastes of its audience. Lessing did not go as far as Gottsched in calling for Hanswurst's complete expulsion from the stage, but he did believe the comic figure needed to be reformed in accordance with enlightened moral and aesthetic standards.

[40] Ramler to Gleim, July 25, 1755, in Lessing, *Werke*, 163.

Lessing, however, proved no more able than Gottsched to build a public that conformed to his ideal of the stage. From the beginning the Hamburg National Theater was beset with financial problems and closed after only two years. The reasons for its commercial failure lay partly in a paucity of German dramatic texts – the literary German stage was still in its infancy – but above all in the lack of a sufficiently large public to sustain the kind of stage envisioned by Lessing and the theater's founders. Hamburg was no London or Paris, nor were Berlin or Vienna for that matter. In the empire, the difficulty of creating a self-sustaining theater independent of the court was exacerbated by a territorially dispersed public. The effects of this fragmentation were less critical in the case of print culture, whose virtue as a medium was precisely its ability to constitute a public abstractly, independent of place. But theater publics were not abstract but embodied entities, constituted through the physical presence of an audience. The educated public was too scattered in eighteenth-century Germany to support on its own the kind of theater proposed by Lessing and other supporters of a German national stage. It is telling that the Hamburg theater quickly found itself staging pantomimes and acrobatic acts in order to attract an audience. In the end no one was pleased: more serious patrons were put off by the theater's concessions to popular taste, while those accustomed to improvised farces were bored by the aesthetically more ambitious fare offered by the theater. Lessing left Hamburg in 1769, disillusioned by a theater public that in his eyes seemed uneducable.

In the end, ironically, it was the court theaters of the empire that proved most receptive to a reformed German stage. In the 1740s and continuing into the 1780s, territorial rulers throughout the empire began reorganizing their court theaters on a commercial footing. Previously closed to all but the court and invited guests, the court theaters of residences like Vienna, Dresden, Mannheim, Stuttgart, Gotha, and Weimar began opening their doors to the public at large. Financial considerations played a major role. The crippling expenses occasioned by the War of the Austrian Succession (1740–48) and the Seven Years War (1756–63) made it hard for rulers to maintain a court theater as a strictly exclusive and noncommercial enterprise. Their need to economize at court also encouraged the promotion of a German rather than foreign stage. It was not simply the commercial benefits of attracting a broader, German-speaking audience; the French acting troupes and Italian operatic companies traditionally favored at court brought prestige to a ruler, but they were also expensive. Not only did German troupes perform in a language a more socially mixed audience could understand, they also had the virtue of being cheaper to employ. Fiscal exigencies thus help to explain why courts like

Munich (1758), Bayreuth (1763), Dresden (1769), and Vienna (1772) dismissed their foreign companies and employed more affordable German ones. Even so notorious a francophile as Frederick II of Prussia curtailed the use of French and Italian troupes at his court theater after the Seven Years War.

These tendencies dovetailed with the agenda of theater reformers, some of whom were themselves court officials and favored the promotion of a reformed German stage on moral and patriotic grounds. Typifying the evolution from court to "national" stage was the development of the Vienna Burgtheater under Maria Theresia (1740–80) and Joseph II (1780–90). The Viennese court first opened its theater to the public in 1741 when Maria Theresia, amidst the desperate military and financial crisis occasioned by war with Prussia, gave the theater entrepreneur Joseph Carl Selliers permission to stage commercial performances of operas and plays in a ballroom of the Habsburg residence at the Hofburg. Selliers, who was then director of the Kärntnertor Theater, received this concession in exchange for assuming the cost of producing opera premieres for the court. This arrangement marked the beginnings of Vienna's Burgtheater, which by the 1820s would be one of the leading stages of Europe.

The theater's early years were financially shaky. The French-language plays that dominated its theatrical repertoire up to the 1770s tended to limit its commercial appeal, although Jean Georges Noverre's popular and elaborately choreographed ballets helped boost attendance. The theater nonetheless faced stiff competition from the popular Hanswurst farces performed by Kurz and Prehauser at the Kärntnertor. Maria Theresia, who detested Hanswurst as vulgar and obscene, banned the performances of Kurz and Prehauser in 1752. When the public shunned the French neo-classical pieces staged in their stead, however, Hanswurst returned to the Kärntnertor two years later. The campaign against the Vienna harlequin resumed in the 1760s, waged by Austrian followers of Gottsched who condemned the comic figure as immoral. "The more depraved the characters," wrote one critic of the Kärntnertor stage, "the more applause they win, and by the end of the play one has viewed neither the praise of virtue nor the reproval of vice."[41] Attacks on Hanswurst intensified when Joseph Sonnenfels, a leading figure of the Austrian Enlightenment, became theater censor in 1770 and promptly fired Kurz as director of the Kärntnertor. He then banned all stage improvisation and required that scripts be submitted to the censor at least a month in advance. The new censorship regime succeeded in domesticating Hanswurst, whose routines were shorn of their extemporaneity and whose character was increasingly

[41] Engelschall, *Zufällige Gedanken*, 16.

moralized in the sentimental comedies of Hafner and Heufeld. Only later did the improvised traditions of the Viennese popular stage return in the bitterly satirical performances of Johannes Nestroy during the 1830s and 1840s.

For the time being, however, proponents of a reformed German stage had scored a major victory in purging the Kärntnertor of extemporized comedy. The Burgtheater, for its part, continued its evolution into a commercial theater with a predominantly German repertoire. In 1772 its French troupe was dismissed for financial reasons, and Joseph II, son of Maria Theresia and coregent since 1765, began to take an active interest in promoting the theater as a German stage. An enlightened absolutist who shared with theater reformers a belief in the value of the stage as a means of creating a moral and virtuous citizenry, Joseph set out to make the Burgtheater a showpiece for German-language drama in the empire and a counterpart to the Comédie Française. In 1776 he announced that the crown would now administer the theater directly instead of leasing it out to impresarios, as it had in the past. The theater received a substantial annual subvention of 100,000 Gulden and Joseph took an active part in decisions concerning repertoire and personnel. Initially the theater was to stage no operas, ballets or frivolous afterpieces. Joseph wanted a literary stage and considered spoken drama the best medium for conveying moral and patriotic sentiments. (He later relented in the case of opera, especially the German *Singspiel* – several of Mozart's operas would be performed at the Burgtheater.) The theater's focus on spoken drama also reduced its expenses and allowed for an aggregate reduction of 20 percent in ticket prices. The least expensive tickets in the house, those for the fourth floor gallery, actually fell from a pricey 20 Kreutzer – enough in those days to buy 8 kilograms of bread – to a more affordable 7 Kreutzer. At the same time, the number of loges reserved for special guests of the court fell from seven in 1774 to two in 1789, a decline symbolic of the theater's evolution from court to public stage.[42]

Although Joseph is popularly depicted as a dilettantish martinet in artistic matters (witness his unsympathetic portrayal in the stage and film versions of "Amadeus"), his reform of the Burgtheater was an unquestionable success. In the first year of Joseph's administration the average number of spectators per performance increased by 470, with theater receipts rising 75 percent.[43] The audience remained predominantly aristocratic and middle class, and cheaper tickets seem not so much to have

---

[42] Otto G. Schindler, "Das Publikum des Burgtheaters in der josephinischen Ära: Versuch einer Strukturbestimmung," in Margret Dietrich, ed., *Das Burgtheater und sein Publikum*, vol. I (Vienna, 1976), 40, 81.
[43] *Ibid.*, 43.

democratized the theater's public as make it feasible for middle-class patrons to attend on a regular basis. More plebeian theatergoers gravitated to suburban stages like the Leopoldstadt Theater (founded 1781) or the Theater an der Wien (1787), located in outlying working-class districts.

If it is true, as some contemporaries noted, that theatergoing became habitual for increasing numbers of Viennese during the 1770s and 1780s, much of the credit goes to Joseph and the attention he lavished on the Burgtheater. The theater remained tightly censored, and the moral didacticism of the Josephinian stage could doubtless be tedious and hectoring at times. But if Gottlieb Stephanie der Jüngere's relentlessly highminded plays about patriotic soldiers and virtuous burghers occasionally wore thin, Friedrich Ludwig Schröder and his troupe earned considerable acclaim for their German-language performances of Shakespeare. It was also under Joseph that the Burgtheater developed into a major venue for Weimar classicism. Goethe and Schiller were regularly performed there from the 1780s on, and in the Biedermeier period (1815–48) Schiller's plays in fact became the theater's biggest box-office draw. One reason for the Burgtheater's success as a venue for spoken drama may have been its relatively modest size, which made for excellent acoustics. Its maximal seating capacity was 1,350, as opposed to 2,360 at Drury Lane (3,600 after 1792) and 2,000 at the Comédie Française.[44] Joseph's personal interest in the theater, symbolized by his presence in the royal loge night after night, may also have encouraged a more sedate atmosphere conducive to a spoken stage.

The Burgtheater, then, came closer than any of its counterparts in London or Paris to embodying the ideal of a literate stage held by enlightened dramatists and critics. The Burgtheater was a public institution, accessible to a relatively broad spectrum of patrons, but court supervision and subsidies enabled the court and its enlightened officials to shape its repertoire in accordance with the Enlightenment's moral vision of the stage. The success of Joseph's model spawned imitators like the Elector Karl Theodor of the Palatinate, who established the Mannheim Nationaltheater in 1779. Smaller than the Burgtheater but similar in repertoire, the Mannheim theater quickly won renown for its performances of Lessing, Goethe, and especially Schiller, whose *Robbers* premiered there in 1782. In the principality of Saxony-Weimar, Goethe himself served from 1791 to 1817 as superintendant of the Weimar court theater.

These theaters are rightfully viewed as having marked the origins of a "bourgeois" German stage, filling the longstanding gap between the

---

[44] *Ibid.*, 34.

traditionally exclusive court stage and a nonliterate popular one. But they owed their establishment not to a middle class seeking to free itself from the dominion of the territorial prince, but to the court itself. The success of the court theater in implementing the Enlightenment's vision of the stage rested on its ability to resolve the eighteenth-century tension between the stage as a moral enterprise on the one hand, and a commercial undertaking on the other. This was a tension, as we have seen, that also pervaded eighteenth-century print culture. The court theaters of the later eighteenth century were hybrid creatures, commercial but also more constrained than their London or Parisian counterparts by the aims and agenda of the court. As commercial institutions they conformed to enlightened ideals of accessibility, but as court creations they could be guarded against the unwanted incursions of a preliterate popular stage. Here again, it is clear that the institutions of the Enlightenment public sphere were not intrinsically subversive or oppositional. As the case of the theater suggests, they were as likely to affirm authority as they were to subvert it.

Bibliographical note

Jonas Barish, *The Antitheatrical Prejudice* (Berkeley, 1981) is good on the long tradition of hostility to the stage. On the ambivalence toward the stage in early modern England, see Jean-Christoph Agnew's imaginative *Worlds Apart: The Market and the Theater in Anglo-American Thought, 1550–1750* (Cambridge, 1986). The French debate is surveyed in Henry Phillips, *The Theater and its Critics in Seventeenth-Century France* (Oxford, 1980) and Moses Barras, *The Stage Controversy in France from Corneille to Rousseau* (New York, 1933); Rousseau's polemic can be found in his *Letter to M. D'Alembert on the Theater*, trans. with notes and an introduction by Allan Bloom (Glencoe, Ill., 1960). On Pietist opposition to the stage in Germany, see Wolfgang Martens, "Officina Diaboli: Das Theater im Visier des halleschen Pietismus," in Norbert Hinske, ed., *Zentren der Aufklärung I: Halle, Aufklärung, und Pietismus* (Heidelberg, 1989). For the Jesuit stage, see Willi Flemming, *Geschichte der Jesuitentheaters in den Ländern deutscher Zunge* (Berlin, 1923) and Kurt Adel, *Das Wiener Jesuitentheater und die europäische Barockdramatik* (Vienna, 1960).

On the tradition of fair theaters, Robert M. Isherwood's excellent *Farce and Fantasy: Popular Entertainments in Eighteenth-Century Paris* (New York and Oxford, 1995) is indispensable. Fair theaters in England and Germany are covered respectively in Sybil Rosenfeld, *The Theater of the London Fairs in the Eighteenth Century* (Cambridge, 1960) and Willi Flemming, *Das Schauspiel der Wanderbühne* (Leipzig, 1931). On the theatricality of court ceremony and ritual, Norbert Elias, *The Court Society*, trans. Edmund Jephcott (New York, 1983) is a classic study. See also Jean-Marie Apostolidès, *Le prince sacrifié: théâtre et politique au temps de Louis XIV* (Paris, 1985), and for the German courts, Volker Bauer, *Die höfische Gesellschaft in Deutschland* (Tübingen, 1993).

For the London stage, John Brewer's *Pleasures of the Imagination: English Culture in the Eighteenth Century* (London, 1997) has excellent chapters on the commercialization of London theaters and its cultural consequences. Useful analyses of London theater audiences can be found in Joseph Donohoe, "The London Theater at the End of the Eighteenth Century," in Robert D. Hume, ed., *The London Theater World, 1660–1800* (Carbondale and Edwardsville, Ill., 1980); Leo Hughes, *The Drama's Patrons: A Study of the Eighteenth-Century London Audience* (Austin and London, 1971); James L. Lynch, *Box, Pit, and Gallery: Stage and Society in Johnson's London* (Berkeley, 1953); and Harry William Pedicord, *The Theatrical Public in the Time of Garrick* (New York, 1954). On censorship of the London stage, see L. W. Conolly, *The Censorship of English Drama 1737–1824* (San Marino, Cal., 1976) and John Loftis, *The Politics of Drama in Augustan England* (Oxford, 1963).

On Parisian theater audiences, two recent studies deserve special mention. James H. Johnson, *Listening in Paris: A Cultural History* (Berkeley, 1995) brilliantly analyzes the changing behavior of Parisian opera audiences in the eighteenth and early nineteenth centuries, while Jeffrey Ravel, *The Contested Parterre: Public Theater and French Political Culture, 1680–1791* (Ithaca and London, 1999) ingeniously connects the behavior and perceptions of Parisian theater publics to broader political issues. Also excellent is the highly detailed study by Henri Lagrave, *Le théâtre et le public à Paris de 1715 à 1750* (Paris, 1972), and John Lough, *Paris Theatre Audiences in the Seventeenth and Eighteenth Centuries* (London, 1959). For individual theaters, see Claude Alasseur, *La Comédie Française au 18e siècle: étude économique* (Paris and the Hague, 1967); Virginia Scott, *The Commedia dell'Arte in Paris, 1644–1697* (Charlottesville, 1990); and Clarence D. Brenner, *The Théâtre Italien: Its Repertory, 1716–1793* (Berkeley and Los Angeles, 1961). On Paris's boulevard theaters, I have drawn extensively from Isherwood, *Farce and Fantasy* (cited above) and Michèle Root-Bernstein, *Boulevard Theater and Revolution in Eighteenth-Century Paris* (Ann Arbor, 1984). Barbara Mittman, *Spectators on the Paris Stage in the Seventeenth and Eighteenth Centuries* (Ann Arbor, 1984), examines the practice of seating spectators on the stage.

Useful surveys of the theater in the eighteenth-century German-speaking lands include W.H. Bruford, *Theater, Drama and Audience in Goethe's Germany* (London, 1950); Manfred Brauneck, *Die Welt also Bühne: Geschichte des europäischen Theaters* (Stuttgart, 1993–99), vols. II–III; and Heinz Kindermann, *Theatergeschichte Europas* (Salzburg, 1957–74), vols. IV–VI. On the commercialization of court theaters in the empire, I have consulted Ute Daniel, *Hoftheater: Zur Geschichte des Theaters und der Höfe im 18. und 19. Jahrhundert* (Stuttgart, 1995). Efforts by Lessing and others to create a German "national" stage is the subject of Roland Krebs, *L'Idée de "Théâtre National" dans l'Allemagne des Lumières* (Wiesbaden, 1985). I discuss attempts to reform the Viennese popular stage in "From Image to Word: Cultural Reform and the Rise of Literate Culture in Eighteenth-Century Austria," *Journal of Modern History* 58 (1986). On Gottsched and his disciples, see also Ruedi Graf, *Das Theater im Literaturstaat* (Tübingen, 1992) and Hilde Haider-Pregler, *Des sittlichen Bürgers Abendschule: Bildungsanspruch und Bildungsauftrag des Berufstheaters im 18. Jahrhundert* (Vienna, 1980). On the Vienna Burgtheater and its public, see Otto G. Schindler, "Das Publikum des

Burgtheaters in der josephinischen Ära. Versuch einer Strukturbestimmung," and Johann Hüttner, "Das Burgtheaterpublikum in der ersten Hälfte des 19. Jahrhunderts," in Margret Dietrich, ed., *Das Burgtheater und sein Publikum*, vol. I (Vienna, 1976): Dorothea Link's *The National Court Theater in Mozart's Vienna, Sources and Documents* (Oxford, 1998) provides a performance calendar of the Burgtheater for the years 1783–92.

The place of women in eighteenth-century theater publics deserves further investigation. Women and Restoration audiences are examined in David Roberts, *The Ladies: Female Patronage of Restoration Drama, 1660–1700* (Oxford and New York, 1989), and the influence of female patrons on the repertoire of the eighteenth-century London stage is documented in the older studies by John Harrington Smith, "Shadwell, the Ladies, and the Change in Comedy," *Modern Philology* 46 (1948) and Emmett L. Avery, "The Shakespeare Ladies Club," *Shakespeare Quarterly* 7 (1956). On female dramatists, see Paula R. Backscheider, *Spectacular Politics: Theatrical Power and Mass Culture in Early Modern England* (Baltimore, 1993), and Ellen Donkin, *Getting into the Act: Women Playwrights in London, 1776–1829* (London and New York, 1995). The appearance of women in female roles, rare prior to the seventeenth century, is examined in Elizabeth Howe, *The First English Actresses: Women and Drama, 1660–1700* (Cambridge and New York, 1992); for France and Germany see Renate Baader, "Sklavin – Sirene – Königin: Die unzeitgemässe Moderne im vorrevolutionären Frankreich," and Barbara Becker-Cantarino, "Von der Prinzipalin zur Kunstlerin und Mäitresse: die Schauspielerin im 18. Jahrhundert im Deutschland," in Renate Möhrmann, ed., *Die Schauspielerin. Zur Kulturgeschichte der weiblichen Bühnenkunst* (Frankfurt am Main, 1981).

Part III

Being sociable

6   Women in public: enlightenment salons

The salon occupied a distinctive place in Enlightenment culture. In contrast to other institutions of the Enlightenment public sphere, it revolved around a woman. True, the salons of Paris, London, Vienna, or Berlin owed much of their renown to the men of letters who frequented them, and the desire to participate in a male-dominated world of letters was precisely what led many women to host a salon in the first place. But no matter how luminous the men in her salon, the hostess was its social and communicative center. In this respect the salon was exceptional in according women such a degree of influence and leadership.

In other ways, however, the salon embodied essential features of the Enlightenment public sphere. First, the development of the salon was marked by a growing autonomy from the courtly world that had given birth to it. Although the salon had developed out of the Renaissance court as a place where men and women gathered to enjoy the pleasures of music, poetry, and polite conversation, in the eighteenth century it evolved into an institution independent from the court. Although court and salon circles might overlap, they became culturally and spatially distinct from each other. Second, the salon, like other institutions of the Enlightenment public sphere, enjoyed a close relationship to eighteenth-century print culture. Despite the centrality of conversation in the salon, its culture was not exclusively oral. Dominated by writers, it was a place where the written word was generated and circulated. Finally, the salon provided the occasion for individuals from different social and professional backgrounds to mingle on relatively equal terms. By eighteenth-century standards salon etiquette was fairly informal. Although salons usually met on appointed days (generally once or twice a week), no special invitations were issued. Conversation inside the salon reflected a reciprocal, egalitarian model of communicative exchange that assumed a willingness to suspend whatever criteria of social distinction may have existed outside it. This suspension of existing hierarchies was already evident in the more aristocratic salons of seventeenth-century Paris, which served to integrate an affluent, upwardly mobile bourgeoisie into the ranks of the nobility. In the late eighteenth century, the salons of Berlin and Vienna brought together not only noble and bourgeois but also Jew and gentile. The porous boundaries of the eighteenth-century salon are suggested by the social backgrounds of their hostesses. Two of the most prominent Parisian *salonnières* of the French Enlightenment were Suzanne Necker, the daughter of a Swiss pastor, and Julie Lespinasse, the bastard offspring of a French countess. The leading Viennese salon hostess of the 1770s and 1780s was Charlotte von Greiner, a soldier's daughter orphaned at the age of four. Rahel Levin and Henriette Herz, who dominated Berlin salon life in the late eighteenth and early nineteenth centuries, were from affluent Jewish families.

Not until after the French Revolution did the term salon come to refer to social gatherings of the sort discussed in this chapter. Earlier usages, however, did anticipate the social heterogeneity associated with salon sociability. Up to the mid-eighteenth century, the word most often referred to the spacious and lavish reception halls found in royal and aristocratic households. But around 1750 middle-class households began appropriating the term, which increasingly referred to what in English came to be known as the parlor. Designating a more modest room where individuals socialized on a relatively intimate basis, this newer usage reflected the salon's development into a more egalitarian arena of sociability. During the remainder of the century the term retained both its aristocratic and bourgeois overtones, testimony to the hybrid character of the salon as an arena where both classes met and interacted.

Another usage of salon was laden with literary and aesthetic connotations. Beginning in 1737, salon was used to refer to the biennial exhibitions of art sponsored by the French Academy of Painting and Sculpture held in the Louvre. These exhibitions represented a new kind of public space in eighteenth-century Paris. Not only were their audiences socially diverse – the journalist Pidansat de Mairobert described them as a "mixing, men and women together, of all the orders and all the ranks of the state" – salon exhibitions also symbolized a growing recognition that the value of a work of art had somehow to be validated through public judgment.[1] The idea of the salon as an arena of judgment and criticism found further expression in Diderot's *Salons* (1759–81), critical essays on art occasioned by the paintings the author observed at the Louvre exhibitions. Diderot's essays, along with the public exhibitions that inspired them, added two more layers of meaning to the term *salon*. The first was that of "publicness," implied in the heterogeneous audience who

[1] See Thomas E. Crow, *Painters and Public Life in Eighteenth-Century Paris* (New Haven and London, 1985), 1–7.

attended the exhibitions. The second was that of debate, discussion, and public judgment, as indicated by the critical texts they occasioned. These various connotations – spatial, social, and critical – all helped to define the place of the salon in Enlightenment public life.

The rise of the salon

The origins of the salon lay in the sixteenth-century Renaissance court. In Tudor England the literary circle around Catherine Parr, the sixth wife of Henry VIII, was a prototype, as were the courtly gatherings hosted by Isabella d'Este in Mantua and Elisabetta Gonzaga in Urbino. During the seventeenth century the salon came increasingly to be identified as a distinctively French institution, partly because the century was in general a period of French cultural ascendancy. The French salon, like French drama, letters, and indeed the French language, set the standard for the rest of Europe. But the heavily French imprint acquired by the salon also grew out of dynastic developments in France between 1560 and 1660, the period when the French salon came into its own. A striking feature of French political history during this period was the power exercised by women at court. On the one hand, French constitutional tradition (the so-called Salic law) barred women from succession to the throne. Hence in the early modern period, an age with a remarkable array of female rulers – Isabella of Castile, Mary and Elizabeth Tudor, Christina of Sweden, Maria Theresia of Austria – France had no female sovereigns. On the other hand, dynastic instability and biological accident yielded a string of female regents, including Catherine de'Medici, Marie de'Medici, and Anne of Austria, who administered the kingdom during the minorities of their male children. Instituted during critical periods of political transition – the outbreak of the wars of religion (1562), the assassination of Henry IV (1610), and the uprising known as the Fronde (1648–52) – these regents gave women unparalleled power and visibility at the French court.

Paralleling the political prominence of women during this period was their growing visibility in the world of letters. The first half of the seventeenth century was a heyday of French feminist writing. Some literary scholars have located the origins of the French novel in this period, while others have described the various ways in which the spread of Cartesian thought at this time helped legitimate the intellectual aspirations of educated Frenchwomen.

Hence the rise of the salon in seventeenth-century France must be understood in the context of a political, literary, and philosophical culture in which women, or at least those of the upper classes, enjoyed unprecedented prominence. The salon, an expression of this visibility, had arisen

during the second half of the sixteenth century as an institution closely
linked to the Valois court. Symbolic ties to the court could still be found
in the salon of the marquise de Rambouillet, established in 1610 and
generally acknowledged as the prototype for the seventeenth-century salon. The mansion (*hôtel*) that she commissioned to house her salon was
strategically located near the Louvre, the Parisian residence of the crown,
while the tapestries that adorned her reception rooms were a gift of Louis
XIII. Yet other features of the Rambouillet salon expressed its independence from the court. The social and architectural center of her salon was
the "blue room," the bedroom and library where the marquise received
guests while reclining on her daybed. Here the intimacy of her salon
stood in sharp contrast to the more formal atmosphere of the court, and
Madame de Rambouillet was herself known for her aversion to court life
and ceremonial. Envisioned as a haven from court politics and intrigue,
the Rambouillet salon pointed toward the institution's emergence as a
private space independent of the court.

During the next three decades the French salon developed into a center of literary discussion and production. Here again the Rambouillet
salon, attended by prominent male writers like the poet François de
Malherbe and the dramatist Pierre Corneille, set the tone. Out of the
559 published male authors whose identities can be established during
the period between 1643 and 1665, 162 frequented a salon.[2] Quite apart
from the men of letters who attended them, however, salons were also
arenas for female participation in literary culture. Because colleges, universities, and academies remained exclusively male preserves throughout
the Old Regime, the salon was distinctive as an institution where intellectually ambitious women could develop their cultural interests and talents.
Seventeenth-century novelists like Madeleine de Scudéry and Madame
de Lafayette honed their literary skills in the salon, and other *salonnières*
developed the distinctive literary style characterized by contemporaries
as "preciosity." The writings of the *precieuses* (a derisive term used by
seventeenth-century critics of the salon), with their artfully contrived
euphemisms and mannered witticisms, reflected the intimate, conversational tone of the salon. Their deeply encoded and private style also
expressed a detachment from the outside world, above all the crown,
and were thereby symptomatic of the salon's growing autonomy from the
world of the court.

As Erica Harth's study of "Cartesian women" has shown, the early salon also became important as a center of philosophical discussion. During
the 1630s and 1640s, when René Descartes published his chief philosophical works, the French salon was a major conduit for the discussion

---

[2] Alain Viala, *La naissance de l'écrivain* (Paris, 1985), 132–37, 306–16.

and popularization of Cartesian philosophy. Here again, the salon gave its female members access to a world of ideas otherwise closed to them in French academic institutions. The argument that women were intellectually inferior to men had traditionally been justified in terms of the physical differences between the sexes: weak female minds were the product of weak female bodies. But in divorcing the mind from the body, Descartes's philosophy undercut misogynist notions of female intellectual inferiority based on physical difference. If the mind was distinct from the body it was also distinct from sex, which in principle made women the intellectual equals of men. The Cartesian path to philosophical truth was therefore open to everyone, regardless of sex. For female disciples of Descartes (who included not only French *salonnières* but also Queen Christina of Sweden and Princess Elizabeth of Bohemia), Cartesian philosophy sanctioned their participation in the life of the mind.

Finally, the salon acquired importance in fostering social and cultural cohesion among the propertied elites of seventeenth-century France. During this period, the crown's increasingly common practice of selling offices and titles to obtain revenue made it easier for wealthy and ambitious bourgeois families to acquire noble status. Yet this practice also threatened to create divisions within France's ruling elites by breeding tensions between old and new noble families. Carolyn Lougee has shown how the salon's intermingling of aristocracy, lower nobility, and wealthy bourgeoisie helped to dissolve these tensions. For older but impecunious noble families, the salon was an arena where economically advantageous marriage alliances could be forged with wealthy bourgeois or recently ennobled families. These *parvenu* families for their part made important contacts and learned the manners and behavior requisite for their social ascent. The seventeenth-century salon was an aristocratic institution in that its model of sociability derived from courtly notions of polite discourse. Unlike the scholarly culture of the universities, which emphasized erudition over the social graces, salon culture sought to temper learning with refinement. Yet the salon also undermined traditional conceptions of nobility based on birth by encouraging a more elastic behavioral definition. Eminence in the salon depended not on blood-lines but on the refinement and *esprit* one exhibited in conversation with others. Politeness and cultivation thereby became qualities to which noble and bourgeois alike could aspire.

The heart of salon sociability was conversation, the rules of which differed fundamentally from those prevailing in the more hierarchical milieu of the court. Illustrative of the latter was Antoine de Courtin's *Nouveau traité de la civilité qui se pratique en France parmi les honnêtes gens* (New Treatise on the Civility Practiced in France among Well-Bred People). Written by a diplomat in the service of Louis XIV, this influential courtesy manual went through at least twenty-one editions between 1671 and the early eighteenth century. Courtin's conversational model was asymmetrical: how, and indeed whether, one conversed with others depended on rank. In the company of social betters, an individual was not to speak unless a member of the circle "bids us to confirm what he says as a witness or wishes us to say something that is to his advantage and that he would be embarrassed to say himself."[3] When beckoned to speak one should address those of highest rank, whose opinions should under no circumstances be contradicted.

The communicative structure of the salon, on the other hand, was more dialogical and egalitarian. Courtesy manuals emanating from salon circles criticized the rigidity and empty formality of court sociability. They viewed conversation not as an occasion for displaying or deferring to power and status, but as a form of reciprocal exchange in which differences in rank were temporarily suspended. The aim of conversation was to give pleasure to all participants by enabling each to contribute. Good conversation was the art of pleasing others through wit and refinement, which required ease of comportment and spontaneity of expression.

The feminist and egalitarian features of salon culture were not lost on contemporaries. Beginning in the 1660s, the social and sexual mingling fostered by the salon sparked a debate in which the issue of women's cultural role was linked to the question of how nobility was to be defined. Critics of the salon bemoaned the influence exercised by women, which they condemned as a feminizing force antithetical to the masculine and martial virtues on which nobility had once rested. Upholding older notions of nobility based on birth and military achievement, they at the same time denounced the salon for subverting differences in rank and undermining the veneration once accorded nobles of ancient lineage. Conversely, defenders of the salon praised the institution on both feminist and social grounds. Not only did it give women access to the literary and philosophical culture of the day, but the preeminent position of women in the salon served as a benign and civilizing influence, for it softened and domesticated the violent behavior that the military role of the nobility had sanctioned.

Women and sociability in Enlightenment thought

This defense of the salon was important, for it foreshadowed a central theme in eighteenth-century debates on women. The idea that women

---

[3] Quoted in Daniel Gordon, *Citizens without Sovereignty: Equality and Sociability in French Thought, 1670–1789* (Princeton, 1994), 86; for what follows see also Gordon, 95–100.

were civilizing agents, the notion that they somehow tamed the destructive impulses of men, helped to revise the older identification of women with "nature" and men with "culture." From classical antiquity onwards, the equation of women with the violent, uncontrollable forces of nature had been used to justify their subjection to men. This view implied that men alone possessed the reason and self-control needed to govern wisely and prudently. But during the Enlightenment the terms of this equation were reversed: women came to be seen as a civilizing force that tempered the violent and destructive behavior of men.

This view of women as civilizing agents grew to some degree out of a defense of commercial society. The argument accompanied a more general attempt to confer moral legitimacy on societies where the spread of commerce, wealth, and luxury were rendering older conceptions of social and political order obsolete. The defense of commercial society found its earliest and most systematic expression in Great Britain, where an expanding colonial market, burgeoning stock exchange, and national banking system were creating new sources of wealth. As J. G. A. Pocock has shown, the ideological defense of the new commercial order arose in response to those who condemned the corrupting effects of new wealth and luxury. Their critique of commercial society belonged to an older political discourse, that of civic humanism, which predicated English liberties on a virtuous citizenry of landed property-owners whose economic independence safeguarded their incorruptibility. With its emphasis on real property as a precondition for civic virtue, the ideology of civic humanism appealed particularly to the interests of landed gentry who felt threatened by the financial and commercial revolutions of early eighteenth-century England. In the 1720s and 1730s it found expression in the anti-Walpole coalition of Tories and dissident Whigs centered around Bolingbroke. For these critics, new forms of commercial and financial wealth had transformed England's governing elite into corrupt place-seekers and opportunistic stock-jobbers. The financing of a national debt through public credit had corrupted rulers and ruled with indiscriminate abandon, turning citizens into creditors and politics into patronage.[4]

In a world where this older language of civic virtue seemed increasingly remote from the realities of social and economic change, apologists for commercial society struggled to find a realm of ethical value outside the sphere of politics. They discovered it in the nonpolitical realm of manners and sociability that for them was the essence of modern civil society. These writers were chiefly Scots, most notably Adam Ferguson, William

---

[4] J. G. A. Pocock, *Virtue, Commerce, and History: Essays on Political Thought and History, Chiefly in the Eighteenth Century* (Cambridge, 1985), esp. 48–49, 67–69.

Robertson, Adam Smith, and John Millar. They saw commercial society as the culmination of a historical process through which relations between human beings had become progressively more complex and interdependent. The development of agriculture, manufacturing, commerce, and an increasingly complex division of labor had produced ever-expanding networks of communication, exchange, and sociability. For as wealth and leisure grew, individuals were able to devote more and more of their time to interactions with others. In the process, manners and politeness developed as a means of rendering human intercourse and sociability more pleasant and agreeable.

This process of civilization occurred chiefly in the private sphere of social relations, not in the realm of politics. In the older discourse of civic virtue, politics had been the primary arena of ethical action. Apologists for commercial society, however, discarded this vision in favor of a language of sociability that viewed the moral development of human beings as the product of their social rather than political interactions. Hence the very phenomena that the politically focussed discourse of civic humanism had condemned as corrupting – commerce, luxury, refinement – were here rehabilitated as the fruits of human progress.

This shift had profound implications for Enlightenment views on women. To the extent that the civic-humanist tradition had made politics, traditionally a male arena, its central concern, it had implicitly accorded women a lower moral status. To be politically virtuous required independence, and women, who gave up their legal autonomy when they married, were dependent and thus incapable of virtue. But apologists for commercial society restored women to history by making the private realm the locus of moral and historical progress. They thereby accorded a crucial role to women in the process of civilization. As sociability grew, they argued, so did social and romantic intercourse between the sexes. Men came to view women as objects of love rather than of brute desire. To obtain those objects men had to make themselves more lovable, more pleasing, more agreeable – in short, more civilized. Women were thus agents of civilization in so far as they forced men to become more sociable and refined. This idea was expressed later in the century by the Scottish physician William Alexander, who wrote in his two-volume history of women: "It is to the social intercourse with women, that the men are indebted for all the efforts they make to please and be agreeable; and it is to the ambition of pleasing them that they owe all their elegance of manners and perhaps all their acquisitions of mind."[5]

---

[5] William Alexander, *The History of Women from the Earliest Antiquity, to the Present Time*, 3rd ed. (London, 1782), I:iv–v, as quoted in Sylvana Tomaselli, "The Enlightenment Debate on Women," *History Workshop Journal* 20 (1985), 121.

Inspired in part by their reading of Scottish moral philosophy, the *philosophes* were similarly preoccupied with the sphere of human sociability. The term *sociabilité* came into usage in the early eighteenth century, and became a key category in the work of writers like Voltaire, Diderot, Holbach, and Suard.[6] Without explicitly challenging the absolutist structure of the French monarchy, this language of sociability articulated an apolitical sphere of human relations in which individuals were nonetheless free and unconstrained. Even as French absolutism sought to deny its subjects agency in the political realm, the discourse of sociability posited a nonpolitical sphere of human relations where individuals acted freely and without constraint. Within this depoliticized realm they became "citizens without sovereignty," to use Daniel Gordon's formulation.

Like the Scottish moral philosophers, moreover, the *philosophes* emphasized the civilizing role of women. Voltaire considered France the most sociable nation in Europe, a quality he attributed to the mingling of the sexes in polite society: "The continued commerce between the sexes, so lively and polite, has introduced a politeness quite unknown elsewhere. Society depends on women. All the peoples that have the misfortune to keep them locked up are unsociable."[7] Diderot and Montesquieu, though ambivalent about the benefits of civilization, believed the status of women to be a barometer of historical progress. The more barbarous or despotic a nation or a people, they argued, the more tyrannized and oppressed were their women.

Salon culture in eighteenth-century Paris

The preeminent salon of the Regency (1715–23) was that of the marquise de Lambert, which met twice weekly between 1710 and 1733. Frequented by aristocrats as well as by noted men of letters like Marivaux and Fontenelle, the Lambert salon became a center of the early French Enlightenment. Much of the so-called quarrel between the Ancients and Moderns (see Chapter 3), for example, was waged there. The marquise and her salon became a key player in the cultural politics of the capital, where she lobbied successfully to elect protegés like Montesquieu to the French Academy.

The high point of Parisian salon culture came in the decades between 1740 and 1780. Under the sponsorship of *salonnières* like Marie-Thérèse Rodet Geoffrin, Julie de Lespinasse, and Suzanne Necker, salons evolved into what Dena Goodman has called "the civil working spaces of the project of Enlightenment." While the seventeenth-century salon had

---

[6] See Gordon, *Citizens without Sovereignty*, 6.
[7] Quoted in Daniel Gordon, "Philosophy, Sociology, and Gender in the Enlightenment Conception of Public Opinion," *French Historical Studies* 17 (1992), 902.

functioned socially to assimilate an upwardly mobile bourgeoisie into the nobility, its Enlightenment successor served primarily as a means of entering and participating in the Republic of Letters. In Enlightenment salons the *philosophes* fashioned a collective identity through debate and the exchange of ideas and news. Aspiring writers found a forum for their work, and, if they were fortunate, financial patronage and literary fame. The salon was also a place where foreign visitors like David Hume, Edward Gibbon, or Benjamin Franklin won entry into Parisian intellectual circles.

Enlightenment salons generally met once or twice a week, usually for dinner followed by discussion. At one level salon society was exclusive: although members were allowed to bring guests, outsiders needed a letter of introduction from someone known and trusted by the salon. Inside the salon itself, however, distinctions of rank, class, and nationality were temporarily suspended. In the Geoffrin salon, wrote the *philosophe* Friedrich-Melchior Grimm, "all ranks are mixed: the noble, the official, the financier, the writer, the artist, all are treated the same, so that...no rank remains except that of good society."[8] The conversational style of the Enlightenment salon was antithetical to that of the court. The communicative structure of absolutism was monological and hierarchical: the crown passed judgment, which the passive subject was to obey; that of the salon, by contrast, was dialogical and reciprocal: its members were to communicate with each other on the basis of mutual friendship and equality. The Enlightenment salon was noticeably less aristocratic than its seventeenth-century predecessor. Julie de Lespinasse, for example, was of illegitimate birth, and with her modest means she could not afford to provide the dinners customarily served in the salon. Yet the relatively Spartan provisions were no affront to her guests, who, as Grimm wrote, "could dispense with beauty and wealth if only her superior qualities and *esprit* were proffered."[9]

Conversation was an indispensable part of salon sociability, but the orality of salon discourse was closely tied to the written word. Poems, essays, and letters were circulated or read aloud, a practice that provided authors with a kind of pre-publication review. If their work was favorably received, younger writers could expect support from more established and well-connected authors in the salon. Salons were also centers for the collection and dissemination of news. The Geoffrin salon was an important source of information for the *philosophe* Jean François Marmontel, editor of the semi-official monthly *Mercure de France*, who attended the

---

[8] Quoted in Peter Seibert, *Der literarische Salon: Literatur und Geselligkeit zwischen Aufklärung und Vormärz* (Stuttgart and Weimar, 1993), 63.
[9] *Ibid.*, 76.

salon and in fact resided in the Geoffrin household. The Parisian salon of Marie Anne Legendre Doublet, which met every Saturday from 1731 until 1771, actually produced and distributed a news and gossip sheet. On arriving at the Doublet salon, guests recorded in a special register any news and gossip they might have collected since the previous meeting. The entries were read aloud, along with letters from the salon's corresponding members (e.g., Voltaire). This material was then compiled in a newsletter, which was copied and sold or otherwise disseminated to friends and correspondents throughout Paris and the provinces. Goodman has observed that the Enlightenment salon's function as a news bureau distinguished it from the more isolated and self-referential world of its seventeenth-century predecessor. No longer a hermetic refuge from the world of the court, the Enlightenment salon actively sought to shape a rapidly expanding network of print and public opinion.

Within the salon, the position of the hostess was crucial. She of course supplied space and refreshments, but if she were wealthy she also dispensed patronage to struggling writers and artists. Yet the salon hostess was more than a social ornament or pliant patroness. As Goodman has shown, she served to regulate salon discourse through the sociability she fostered and the conversational boundaries she set. Hosting a salon was not a pastime but a career, one requiring a lengthy apprenticeship under an older and more experienced *salonnière*. The rewards were both intellectual and social: by attending and later hosting a salon, a woman was able to obtain the kind of education otherwise denied her in academies and colleges. The salon was her ticket into the Republic of Letters, so to speak, a place where she could play an active role in an expanding public sphere. Accordingly, to plan a salon meant more than just attending to one's toilette or supervising the servants; the hostess prepared much like a student or teacher prepares for a class. On the eve of her weekly salon, for example, Suzanne Necker spent the day reading or writing in her journal in order to focus her thinking.

When the salon assembled it was the hostess who set the agenda for discussion. Madame Geoffrin split her weekly salon into Monday and Wednesday meetings, the former attended by artists and the latter by writers. In her Wednesday salon she decreed that only literature and philosophy, not politics, could be discussed – a strategy designed to avoid dissension and factionalism. The point is not that salon conversation was a-political – political debate figured prominently in the salons of Julie de Lespinasse and Suzanne Necker – but rather that the salon mistress considered it her duty to enforce rules of politeness and civility. These helped to temper the combative and often personalized style of debate that otherwise came naturally to French men of letters. In their youth they had internalized this style in schools and colleges, often Jesuit, which sought to inculcate the disputational methods of neoscholastic pedagogy. André Morellet, a *philosophe* notorious for his combative temperament, recalled that as a student at the Sorbonne "I was, and never ceased to be, violent in dispute...Sometimes I would spit blood after an argument."[10] Enlightenment ideals of criticism reinforced this militant and polemical style, which subjected all to critical scrutiny. In the highly charged world of Enlightenment debate, the dilemma for the *philosophes* was how to maintain their critical and polemical edge without jeopardizing the solidarity they needed to survive in a sometimes hostile social and political environment.

Here the salon hostess played a crucial role in harmonizing the often strident and discordant voices in her circle. Marmontel wrote that in the presence of Julie de Lespinasse, men of divergent backgrounds and views nonetheless behaved sociably: "they find themselves in harmony, like the chords of an instrument played with a skilled hand."[11] Following the death of Lespinasse in 1767, D'Alembert gamely tried to keep her salon going. But the bickering and quarrels that soon divided the group led some to conclude that without the hostess the salon was ungovernable. "Everyone in these assemblies," wrote Suzanne Necker," is [now] convinced that women fill the intervals of conversation and of life, like the padding that one inserts in cases of china; they are valued at nothing, and [yet] everything breaks without them."[12]

By the 1780s, however, Parisian salons had begun to lose their importance as centers of debate and discussion. Goodman argued that as the public sphere of the Enlightenment expanded to include ever-widening circles of cultural consumers and producers, it spilled out of the relatively elite world of the salon to a more diffuse array of public spaces. One was the café, which by the 1780s had assumed the kind of political and literary importance it earlier enjoyed in London. Another was Masonic lodges and *musées*, both of which proliferated during the 1780s. (Freemasonry, which in France dated back to the 1720s, will be treated in Chapter 8.) *Musées*, the first of which was formed in Paris in 1778, were educational and debating societies where dues-paying members could meet for conversation and also take courses in languages, letters, the arts, and natural sciences. Forerunners of the political clubs that sprouted during the Revolution, lodges and *musées* were less elite than salons in their membership. In this respect, they illustrated the extent to which the social foundations of

---

[10] Quoted in Gordon, *Citizens Without Sovereignty*, 180.
[11] Quoted in Seibert, *Der literarische Salon*, 21.
[12] Quoted in Dena Goodman, "Governing the Republic of Letters: The Politics of Culture in the French Enlightenment," *History of European Ideas* 13 (1991), 185.

Enlightenment culture had expanded by the 1780s. As the public sphere of the Enlightenment moved from a relatively small coterie of *philosophes* and their supporters to include broader circles of society, salons became less important in defining public debate.

The decline of the salon has been attributed to the waning influence of women in late-Enlightenment culture. Joan Landes finds evidence for a growing masculinization of the public sphere in the work of Rousseau, whose attacks on the decadence and effeminacy of the French court and aristocracy implicitly condemned the visibility elite women had acquired in the Old Regime.[13] This critique was central to Rousseau's discourse of classical republicanism, with its invidious contrasts between the civic virtue of the ancients and the decadence of French society. Ancient citizens were manly and virtuous, the French court and aristocracy effeminate and corrupt. Women in antiquity were chaste and modest, French aristocratic women promiscuous and dissolute. Ancient women remained in their natural domain, the household, where they taught their sons civic and martial virtues. French aristocratic mothers abandoned their children to wet-nurses and governesses while devoting themselves to frivolous amusements and sexual intrigue. The French Revolution, Landes concludes, marked the triumph of Rousseau's masculinist vision of republican virtue. This vision rested on a public/private dichotomy that distinguished between a (male) public-political world and a private (female) domestic sphere where women fulfilled their natural roles as wives and mothers. Accordingly, from 1790 on the Revolution systematically disenfranchised women by restricting their rights of assembly, disbanding the Society of Republican Revolutionary Women, and executing politically prominent women from the queen to the feminist Olympe de Gouges.

Dena Goodman's more nuanced account gives much more agency to women in Enlightenment culture and thus rejects Landes's view of the public sphere as intrinsically masculinist. She instead attributes the decline of Parisian salon culture to the growing sense of autonomy that men of letters had acquired by the end of the Old Regime.[14] Having internalized an Enlightenment faith in the capacity of men to rule themselves, she argues, men of letters no longer felt the need to be "governed" in salons. Thus they cast off the authority of the *salonnière*, under whose bridle they had sometimes chafed, in favor of the more democratic if male-centered forms of association they found in lodges and museés. For Goodman, then, the decline of the salon was a symptom not of the waning power

---

[13] Joan Landes, *Women and the Public Sphere in the Age of the French Revolution* (Ithaca and London, 1988), especially chapters 2 and 3.

[14] Goodman, *Republic of Letters*, ch. 6.

of Enlightenment ideals, but of their fruition among men of letters who now shunned the tutelage of the salon just as they would soon reject that of their king.

So although Landes and Goodman deeply disagree about the status of women in the public sphere of the French Enlightenment, they concur in seeing this public sphere as having grown increasingly masculinist on the eve of the Revolution. They suggest, paradoxically, that this masculinization was spurred by a process of ideological and cultural democratization. In advocating popular sovereignty, argues Landes, Rousseau's republicanism also reaffirmed an older discourse of civic humanism that accorded women a subordinate political role. And as Enlightenment culture expanded beyond salon parlors and academies into broader circles of society, contends Goodman, it flourished in new spaces of sociability that were more broadly based socially but more exclusive sexually.

Yet, the institutions of Enlightenment sociability that Goodman sees displacing the salon on the eve of the Revolution were not as sexually exclusive as she makes them appear. A distinctive feature of French masonic lodges after 1740 was in fact their frequent admission of women, although Goodman rightly warns against exaggerating their presence and influence. Other examples point to a public sphere that was becoming sexually integrated, not segregated. Parisian cafés, especially those in bustling, commercialized centers of leisure and entertainment clustered along major boulevards or the Palais-Royal, were sexually mixed, and, changes in theater audiences also raise doubts about a masculinized public sphere. As seen in Chapter 5, it was precisely in the 1780s that the Comédie Française introduced seating in its parterre and thus fostered a more sexually integrated audience in what had been a traditionally male preserve. As for Landes, one must be skeptical of her treatment of Rousseau as somehow representative of Enlightenment views of women – or of anything else, for that matter. Quite aside from the fact that Rousseau can just as well be seen as a preromantic apostle of the counter-Enlightenment, his admittedly masculinist language of classical republicanism represented only one current in Enlightenment thought. It differed radically from, say, the assumptions of the *philosophe* Condorcet, who was fully capable of envisioning a society in which women exercised the same political rights as men, or the Prussian bureaucrat Theodor Gottlieb von Hippel, whose *On Improving the Status of Women* (1792) sharply criticized the French Revolution for failing to confer rights of active citizenship on women. It may well be that Jacobin ideology, inspired as it was by a revival of civic-humanist discourse, momentarily revived its masculinist assumptions. It is something else, however, to see the Jacobin moment as the defining legacy of Enlightenment views of women. That succeeding feminists from the nineteenth century up to our own day continued to draw on egalitarian assumptions developed in the Enlightenment is enough to shed doubt on the notion that its public sphere was intrinsically masculinist.

The salon in eighteenth-century England

If the rise of the French salon was fostered by the political visibility of women at court, then the salon should have flourished all the more in England. Early modern England boasted more female sovereigns than any other monarchy of the period, and English constitutional tradition, in contrast to the Salic law in France, did not bar women from the royal succession. Hence four women reigned in England between 1553 and 1714: Mary Tudor (1553–58), Elizabeth I (1558–1603), Mary II (co-ruler with William III, 1689–1702), and Anne (1702–14).

Paradoxically, however, the salon never acquired the importance in eighteenth-century English culture that it did across the Channel. To be sure, England appeared to be well on its way to developing a vibrant salon culture during the Tudor and early Stuart periods. The humanist circle around Catherine Parr, Henry VIII's sixth wife, was a prototype, as was that surrounding the countess of Pembroke, a leading patroness of the Elizabethan period. Salons became a fixture of courtly and aristocratic culture during the Stuart reigns of James I, when Jacobean poets like Ben Jonson and John Donne gathered regularly at the countess of Bedford's residence in Twickenham Park, and Charles I, when the countess of Carlisle, favorite of the queen-consort Henrietta Maria, presided over a salon modeled after that of Madame Rambouillet in Paris.

Yet the French model of the salon never fully took root in England. The disruptive impact of the English Civil War stymied the development of salon culture at a time when the institution was reaching its first great apogee in France. The Restoration did little to revive the salon, perhaps owing to the singular importance of the coffeehouse (see Chapter 7). By 1700, when cafés were not yet fashionable on the continent, London alone had some 2,000 of them. The coffeehouse, not the salon, was the center of literary sociability in Restoration and early Augustan England.

English coffeehouses were predominantly male in their clientele, and women, whatever their literary aspirations, generally shunned them. Yet there were other public spaces in eighteenth-century England accessible to intellectually ambitious women. Spas and resorts were one such venue. Symptoms of the precocious commercialization of leisure in eighteenth-century England, watering places and recreational towns originally served an exclusive aristocratic clientele. But, in the course of the century, resorts like Bath and Tunbridge Wells catered increasingly to affluent members of the middle class as well. Visitors were drawn to them not only for the medicinal benefits attributed to their waters, but also for their social and cultural amenities. Initially their social life revolved around balls, concerts, plays, and gaming; later in the century, visitors could also patronize an assortment of bookstores, lending libraries, and fashionable cafés. In the spa, as in the salon, individuals of different rank and nationality intermingled. A visitor to Tunbridge Wells in the 1760s observed that "in the great assembly rooms all ranks are mingled together without any distinction," while in Smollet's *Humphry Clinker* a visitor to Bath disapprovingly noted "the general mixture of all degrees... without distinction of rank and fortune." Although their social flavor was hardly plebeian, these spas did provide a cultural bridge between the aristocracy and the middle classes. Like salons, furthermore, spas and resorts offered women with literary and intellectual interests a place to meet like-minded men and women. Bluestocking writers such as Elizabeth Montagu and Elizabeth Carter (see below), for example, developed long-lasting intellectual friendships at English spas.

Overall, learned women in eighteenth-century England enjoyed more independence than their counterparts in France. Their intellectual lives were on the whole more variegated and less cloistered than those of Parisian *salonnières*, who depended so heavily on the salon for access to the world of letters. Differences in education may have played a role as well. It was common for upper-class French girls to be educated in convents, as was the case with the Parisian *salonnières* Madame d'Epinay and Madame de Deffand. By contrast, most girls of propertied English families were tutored at home (Protestant England of course had no convents), and hence their education tended to be less regimented and secluded.[15] By the time they reached maturity, then, they had a more varied experience of the world than their French counterparts.

Salons did exist in eighteenth-century England, most notably those of the Bluestockings. But here the example of the Bluestockings is instructive, for it highlights some of the fundamental differences between French and English women of letters. Among literary historians, the term bluestocking has come to refer to the circle of learned English women who met regularly from the 1750s into the 1780s. The group originated in the 1750s as gatherings hosted by Elizabeth Montagu and Elizabeth Vesey during their summers at Tunbridge Wells. Soon the two were holding salons during the winter in the drawing rooms of their London residences, and their circle of female friends would include Hester Chapone, Elizabeth Carter, and more peripherally, Fanny Burney and Hannah

[15] Evelyn Gordon Bodek, "Salonnières and Bluestockings: Educated Obsolescence and Germinating Feminism," *Feminist Studies* 3 (1976), 188–89.

More. The term bluestocking originally referred to a man: according to James Boswell, it was coined in 1781 when the naturalist Benjamin Stillingfleet, a friend of Elizabeth Montagu, visited her circle dressed in blue stockings. But as in Parisian salons, the soul of the Bluestocking salon was a woman. Elizabeth Montagu (née Robinson) was of gentry birth and well off financially, having married the wealthy grandson of the first earl of Sandwich at the age of twenty-two. She knew the salons of Paris well: she befriended Suzanne Necker in 1775–76 during a visit to Paris, where she also met Geoffrin and Deffand. Like those *salonnières*, Montagu recruited her male guests from among the most distinguished writers of her day, including Samuel Johnson, Edward Gibbon, Laurence Sterne, Oliver Goldsmith, and Edmund Burke. Like Geoffrin or Lespinasse, furthermore, Mrs. Montagu "governed" her salon by suggesting conversational topics, soliciting opinions, and enforcing standards of politeness and taste. Samuel Johnson called her the "Queen of the Blues"; others affectionately referred to her as "El Presidente." Montagu also played the role of patroness, organizing subscription campaigns or securing pensions for aspiring writers.

In other respects, however, the Bluestockings were quite different from their Parisian counterparts. The identity of a *salonnière* was inextricably tied to that of her male guests. Although they submitted to her authority and governance, her position ultimately rested on their approval. Bluestocking women were much less dependent on male approbation, and they enjoyed more autonomy *vis-à-vis* the men in their circle. The Bluestockings were first and foremost a women's circle (Horace Walpole called them "the first female club ever known") and although they valued the friendship of Johnson, Gibbon, and other men who attended their gatherings, a male presence was not essential to the functioning of the group. Describing a Bluestocking dinner party where no men were present, the writer Hannah More wrote: "Everything was very elegant, but we were as merry as if there had been no magnificence; and we all agreed that men were by no means so necessary as we had all been foolish enough to fancy."[16]

Yet the Bluestockings were no feminists, even by eighteenth-century standards. They neither demanded political rights for women nor did they challenge their subordinate role in marriage. Hester Chapone's *Matrimonial Creed* declared that "a husband has a divine right to the absolute obedience of his wife . . . [A]s her appointed ruler and head, he is undoubtedly her superior."[17] She did temper her call to obedience in arguing that

---

[16] *Bluestocking Letters*, ed. Reginald Brimley Johnson (London, 1926), 4.
[17] Reprinted in *ibid*. 195–202; here p. 197.

a woman should only marry a man "whom she can heartily and willingly acknowledge her superior." In accordance with the Bluestockings' ideal of companionate marriage, she enjoined the husband to exalt his wife "to the rank of his *first* and *dearest* friend, and to endow her, by his own free gift, with all the privileges, rights, and freedoms of the most perfect friendship."

But given their ready acceptance of women's subordinate position, how does one explain the relative autonomy of the Bluestockings? Much of the answer lies in the fact that most of the Bluestockings, unlike the *salonnières* of Paris, established literary identities in their own right. With the exception of the novelist Madame de Tencin (better known today as the mother of D'Alembert), who during the 1730s and 1740s succeeded the marquise de Lambert as the leading salon hostess of Paris, few *salonnières* of the eighteenth century sought literary fame and they rarely published their work. Suzanne Necker wrote voluminously but never published her work, and publication came posthumously on the initiative of her husband. *Salonnières* commonly engaged in literary production either privately in the form of unpublished letters, diaries, and essays, or vicariously through the male *philosophes* who attended their salons.

The Bluestockings present a quite different picture. Elizabeth Montagu won considerable renown as a literary critic, a reputation she owed to a celebrated essay defending Shakespeare against Voltaire's dismissive critique. Elizabeth Carter's translation of Epictetus continued to be reprinted in the nineteenth century, and Carter was also a successful poet whose collected verse went through four editions in her lifetime. Hester Chapone's *Letters on the Improvement of the Mind*, a pedagogical work written for young women, was one of the most popular conduct books of its day. Fanny Burney and Hannah More, both of whom had close ties to the Bluestockings, also enjoyed notable commercial success. Burney's first two novels, *Evelina* and *Cecilia*, were literary sensations, while More published numerous poems, dramas, and essays. Her greatest success came in 1777 with *Percy*, a romantic tragedy that earned her almost £600 on the London stage (it was later translated into German and performed in Vienna). More was also active in the nascent anti-slavery movement, and in 1788, at the bequest of the Abolition Society, published a poem attacking slavery.

In the end, the discrepancy between Bluestockings and *salonnières* reflected the existence of a more open and elastic literary market in eighteenth-century England. A relatively liberal censorship, the quantity and diversity of periodicals, the early development of lending libraries and subscription publishing – all of these created conditions favorable to male and female writers alike. The fact that salons played a less visible role in eighteenth-century English culture reflected the existence of more, not fewer, opportunities for female participation in the literary public sphere.

Salons of Vienna and Berlin

Not until the last quarter of the century did a significant salon culture emerge in the Holy Roman Empire, first in Vienna, the residence of the Habsburg emperor, and then later in the Prussian capital of Berlin. Language had something to do with it: salons presupposed a well-developed literary vernacular, for it enabled educated women who generally did not learn Latin to participate in literary culture. It is no accident that the rise of salons in Tudor-Stuart England and seventeenth-century France coincided with the rapid development of English and French as literary vernaculars. In the Holy Roman Empire, however, political and confessional fragmentation stymied this process, and only in the eighteenth century did German fully emerge as a literary language. Although scholars have long emphasized this feature of German literary history, few have explored its ramifications for women. Among other things it helps to explain why seventeenth-century Germany had no female novelists comparable to Aphra Behn in England or Madame de Lafayette in France.

A second and related reason was the dominant role of universities in German intellectual life. As elsewhere in Europe, German universities were male institutions, and although the matriculation of women was not unknown, such examples were considered exotic. More typical was the case of Luise Adelgunde Gottsched, who eavesdropped on her husband's Leipzig lectures from an adjoining chamber. The persistence of Latin in German academic discourse tended to marginalize women even further. In 1687 the philosopher Christian Thomasius scandalized his Leipzig colleagues when he announced his intention to lecture in German rather than Latin. Although Thomasius, along with his contemporary Leibnitz, championed the vernacular in academic teaching and scholarship, Latin remained the language of instruction at German universities well into the eighteenth century. In the field of philosophy it was not until Christian Wolff (1679–1754), who succeeded Leibnitz as Germany's most eminent philosopher, that the discipline developed its own German vernacular. Even then, Wolff himself continued to publish most of his work in Latin. Hence philosophical discourse and academic culture in general were even more male-centered than in France or England, and the "Cartesian women" of seventeenth-century French salons had few counterparts in Germany.

A third reason for the late arrival of the salon in German-speaking Europe is the fact that for much of the early modern period, the territories of the Holy Roman Empire lacked the kind of court life that fostered the development of salon culture elsewhere. In England and France, as seen earlier, the salon had its origins in the sixteenth-century Tudor and Valois courts. The German-speaking territories of the empire had no counterpart until the late seventeenth century, when the defeat of the Turks helped pave the way for Vienna's emergence as a major court center. Even then, the Habsburg dynasty's continued identification with the aims of the Counter-Reformation inhibited the emergence of a salon culture. The court's hostility to Protestantism tended to isolate the monarchy from wellsprings of Enlightenment culture in Protestant Great Britain, Holland, and northern Germany. At the same time, the monarchy's traditional antagonism toward France delayed the influence of French culture, including the salon. It is telling that Vienna did not emerge as a center of salon life until the reign of Maria Theresia (1740–80). Not only did the Austrian Enlightenment begin to flourish during her reign; her marriage to Francis of Lorraine, as well as the conclusion of an Austro-French alliance in 1756, heightened French influence on the cultural life of the capital.

The emergence of the Viennese salon in the reign of Maria Theresia points to yet another reason for its belated development in German-speaking Europe. While the visibility and power of women at court, whether as regents in France or actual sovereigns in England, served to foster salon culture in those countries, it was not until Maria Theresia's reign that a woman governed a major court of the empire. Biological accident had something to do with it: during the seventeenth and eighteenth centuries the major dynasties of the empire enjoyed near continuity in the male line. The Prussian Hohenzollerns and the Bavarian Wittelsbachs produced an uninterrupted string of male heirs, as did the Austrian Habsburgs up to 1740. Only then, when Charles VI died without male issue and was succeeded by his daughter Maria Theresia, was a major court of the empire ruled by a female. At this point, during the latter part of Maria Theresia's reign, salons began to play a significant role in Viennese elite culture.

The first and most fashionable salon in Theresian Vienna was that of Charlotte Greiner (*née* Hieronymus, 1739–1815). Born in Hungary, where her father was serving as a lieutenant in the Austrian army, Charlotte lost her mother just after her birth. Her father died of tuberculosis in 1744 shortly after his regiment was transferred to Vienna, leaving Charlotte an orphan. One of Maria Theresia's chambermaids reported the girl's plight to the queen, who took pity on Charlotte and ordered that she be brought to Schönbrunn palace. There she was raised by a governess to the royal princesses, and received an excellent education that included French, Italian, and Latin. At the age of thirteen she became a chambermaid to the queen, and in 1762 her primary duty became that of reading aloud to Maria Theresia in the evenings. This was at the height of the Seven Years War, and Charlotte's reading consisted primarily of diplomatic dispatches and military reports written in German, French, Italian, and Latin. Her duties thus exposed her not only to the social life of the court, but also to the wider public stage of politics and diplomacy.

With more than two decades of experience at court, Charlotte acquired the skills and qualities requisite for her future career as a salon hostess. Her court duties had left her little in the way of a private life: she never went out unless accompanied by an older chaperone, and she lived under the watchful supervision of a queen ever concerned with the morals and behavior of the women in her service. Toward the end of her court service Charlotte chafed under the restrictions placed on her, particularly since the queen habitually turned away suitors for Charlotte's hand. Overall, however, the education, poise, and extroversion acquired during her years at court schooled her well for the salon, as did the "other-directed" behavior she internalized through service to the queen. Of course, she also learned how to dress and how to prepare her toilette, while her fluency in French and Italian allowed her to converse effortlessly with foreign visitors.

In 1766 Charlotte left the queen's service to marry Franz Sales Greiner, a promising young clerk in the war ministry. She used her influence with Maria Theresia to secure for her husband an appointment to the Court Chancellery, the central administrative body for the hereditary territories of the monarchy. An enlightened and progressive bureaucrat, Greiner was noted for his advocacy of agrarian reform, compulsory schooling, and toleration of Jews. Maria Theresia valued his service, frequently granted him private audiences, and in 1771 she elevated him into the nobility.

By 1775 the Greiner household had become a gathering place for reform-minded officials, professors, writers, and musicians. Among the guests at the Greiner salon were leading figures of the Austrian Enlightenment, including the judicial reformer Joseph Sonnenfels and the poets Johann Baptiste von Alxinger, Johann Michael Denis, and Alois Blumauer. Music was an important part of the Greiner salon, where Haydn, Salieri, and Mozart performed on numerous occasions. Mozart and Franz von Greiner belonged to the same masonic lodge, "True Harmony" (*Zum wahren Eintracht*), and the Greiner salon enjoyed close ties to Viennese masonic circles.

Charlotte Greiner became one of the most literate and cultivated women in Vienna. In what was an unusual role reversal for the time, her intellectual passions were natural history and astronomy while her husband

was drawn to painting, music, and poetry. Her interest in fields traditionally reserved for men was facilitated by her knowledge of Latin, which
enabled her to read a broad range of scientific works. Charlotte also held
views on women that were, at least by Viennese standards, highly advanced. She later became an avid admirer of Mary Wollstonecraft, and
in the words of her daughter Caroline, believed that "women were originally destined by nature and providence to dominate, but they lost this
dominion through a kind of usurpation by the male sex, whose physical
strength exceeds our own."[18]

The Greiner salon was an important conduit for the literary culture
of Protestant Germany. North German *Aufklärer* like Georg Forster and
the Göttingen historian Ludwig von Spittler dropped in during visits to
Vienna. Excerpts from Goethe's *Sorrows of Young Werther* and *Götz von
Berlichingen* were read aloud there, along with the poetry of Klopstock
(with whom Charlotte corresponded) and Wieland. Her daughter recalled that "at our home all the new poetic works published here or abroad
were immediately circulated, read, and discussed."[19] As in France, the
Greiner salon was also a place where aspiring young writers could find
patronage. With their impeccable connections at court, Charlotte and
her husband were particularly well placed to promote careers. One such
case was the young poet and ex-Jesuit Lorenz Leopold Haschka (1749–
1827), a regular at the Greiner salon who served as tutor to Caroline.
Haschka jeopardized his position in the Greiner household by having an
affair with Charlotte. But the liaison ended discreetly, Hashka and Franz
von Greiner were somehow reconciled, and Hashka went on to become
curator at the University of Vienna library.

During the Josephinian decade (1780–90) the Greiner salon declined
in importance as a center of the Viennese Enlightenment. It remained an
arena of philosophical and literary discussion, and with Joseph II's relaxation of censorship, the once prohibited works of *philosophes* like Voltaire
and Helvetius were debated there. But another effect of Joseph's cultural
thaw was to render the Greiner salon merely one of a burgeoning number
of public spaces that included coffeehouses, masonic lodges, and theaters.
The popularity of the Greiner salon was in any case soon outstripped by
that of a rival, Fanny von Arnstein. Fanny was Jewish and the daughter
of Daniel Itzig, a banker to the Prussian court. Her marriage to Nathan
Adam Arnstein, son of the chief purveyor to the Viennese court, united
two of the wealthiest Jewish families in the Holy Roman Empire. That a

[18] Caroline Pichler, *Denkwürdigkeiten aus menem Leben*, ed. Emil Karl Blümml, 2 vols.
(Munich 1914), I:48.
[19] *Ibid.*, 49.

Jewess could preside over the leading Viennese salon reflected not only her wealth, cultivation and beauty, but also the liberal social climate created by Joseph's progressive policies toward the Jews. The younger generation of Viennese aristocrats was drawn to the relaxed and cosmopolitan atmosphere of the Arnstein salon (one of them, Prince Carl Liechtenstein, fell in love with Fanny and died fighting a duel over her), where they mingled with bourgeois officials and literati. An anonymous visitor from Bavaria later described the mood of the Arnstein salon: "One comes without great ceremony and goes without taking formal leave; all the tiresome etiquette of the higher circles is banned; the spirit, freed from the restraining fetters of propriety, breathes more freely here."[20]

Like Vienna, Berlin did not develop a salon culture until the late eighteenth century. This was in part because Berlin, much like the Prussian monarchy itself, was a parvenu. In 1648 the city's population was a mere 7,000 inhabitants, and by 1709 its 24,000 inhabitants made it comparable in size to a modest French provincial city. As the political star of the Hohenzollerns rose, Berlin grew rapidly during the remainder of the century. But with a population of 172,000 in 1800, the city still remained small relative to capitals like London (900,000) or Paris (550,000).

The austere atmosphere that characterized the city during much of the century mirrored the frugality of the ruling dynasty, and further inhibited the emergence of a salon culture. The courts of Frederick William I (1713–40) and Frederick II (1740–86) were parsimonious by eighteenth-century standards. Preoccupied with military and fiscal affairs, neither ruler tried to make his court a cultural magnet. Frederick William I's idea of court sociability was an evening spent smoking and drinking with his officers, and Frederick the Great, though more cultivated than his father, found receptions and dinner parties tiresome. He was usually happier in the company of his Italian greyhounds. Both in any case preferred the companionship of men, and the social life of the court and indeed of the capital was heavily masculine in tone. The expansion of the Prussian army had transformed Berlin into a virtual barracks. Visitors noted the omnipresence of soldiers, and the city's demographic profile gave credence to the quip that Prussia was the only army in Europe with a state of its own. In 1755 soldiers and their families made up more than one-quarter of the city's population, 26,325 out of 100,336 inhabitants.[21]

At the court itself, Frederick the Great's well-known dislike of women (a source of speculation that he may have been homosexual) restricted

---

[20] Quoted in Hilde Spiel, *Fanny von Arnstein: Daughter of the Enlightenment 1758–1818*, trans. Christine Shuttleworth (New York and Oxford, 1991), 174.

[21] Wolfgang Ribbe, *Geschichte Berlins*, 2 vols. (Munich, 1987), I:382.

their visibility and influence. The king's relationship with his wife, Elisabeth Christine of Braunschweig-Bevern, was cold and distant, and her own court was small and inconspicuous. At the same time Frederick had no interest in keeping a royal harem, and the absence of royal mistresses further diminished the influence of women at court. If the Berlin *Aufklärer* Friedrich Gedike was correct, Frederick's ministers and officers followed his lead. Taking a mistress was unfashionable at Frederick's court, and those who did risked royal disfavor. As a consequence, observed Gedike, women exerted little influence on court politics and society:

They give no glittering parties where princes, generals, governors or high clergy are obliged to attend. No one rushes to their antechambers, no one kneels at their couches, no bliss is occasioned by their glances, no reconciliations are wrought by their words, no wave of a hand turns the court topsy-turvy. They decide neither over appointments to state office, nor over reputations.[22]

Frederickian Berlin, then, was not a city conducive to salon culture. The main arenas of Enlightenment sociability were chiefly male preserves, such as reading societies, clubs, masonic lodges, and coffeehouses.

The death of Frederick II (1786), however, dramatically altered the tone of Berlin high society. His successor, Frederick William II (1786–97), was an amiable if indolent sovereign with little interest in political or military affairs. Beyond a faddish involvement with Rosacrucianism, his chief passion was a remarkable succession of royal mistresses. Wilhelmine Enke, the daughter of a court musician, was a woman of considerable intelligence who bore the king five children in a morganatic marriage. She remained a trusted advisor even after the king's erotic interests turned elsewhere. Two other mistresses followed, not to mention dalliances with a string of singers and courtesans, as the relative austerity of the Frederickian court gave way to an opulence and sensuality more Bourbon than Hohenzollern in style. Reinforcing this trend were the French aristocrats who emigrated to Berlin after 1789, bringing with them the softer and more rococo manners of the French court.[23] The result was a social atmosphere receptive to salon culture, as women became more visible at court and in Berlin high society at large.

But none of this explains what would be a key feature of Berlin salon life, namely the dominant role of Jewish women as salon hostesses. Not all *salonnières* were Jewish: in 1796 Wilhelmine Enke, the king's morganatic consort, began hosting a small salon, while Princess Luise Radziwill (the daughter of Prince Ferdinand) and the Duchess Dorothea von Kurland

---

[22] Friedrich Gedike, "Über Berlin," *Berlinische Monatschrift* 3 (1784), 144.
[23] Deborah Hertz, *Jewish High Society in Old Regime Berlin* (New Haven and London, 1988), 137.

hosted two of Berlin's leading salons in the early nineteenth century. But the first salons to hold sway in the cultural life of the capital were those of Henriette Herz (1767–1847), whose father was the first Jewish physician to practice in the city, and Rahel Levin (1771–1833), the daughter of a wealthy Jewish jewel merchant. The social ascendancy of Henriette and Rahel, like that of Fanny Arnstein, was partly a reflection of their assimilated backgrounds. All three received relatively secular educations from private tutors, and all defied the traditional Jewish prohibition that forbade married women from appearing in public with their hair uncovered. Rahel scandalized the local Jewish community by ostentatiously breaking the Sabbath, riding through the streets of the city in an open carriage; later in life both she and Henriette Herz converted to Protestantism.

A century of Hohenzollern immigration policy had encouraged the acculturation of this affluent Jewish stratum. Intent on repopulating territories devastated by the Thirty Years War, "the Great Elector" Frederick William (1640–88) promoted a program of religious toleration as a means of attracting settlers to his lands. These included Huguenot refugees from France, but also wealthy Jewish families expelled from Vienna. The latter settled in Berlin, followed by other Jewish refugees. The most successful earned fortunes as army contractors, manufacturers, and bankers, forming the core of the city's Jewish elite. They were still subject to various legal restrictions, and Prussian law defined them as resident aliens. But until Joseph II eased restrictions on Jews in the Habsburg monarchy in the 1780s, Berlin was the only court city in the empire that did not confine its Jewish population to ghettos.

Accordingly, public space in the capital was more accessible to its assimilated Jewish residents than in other German cities. The Herz and Levin families resided in the more fashionable districts of the city, and regularly visited its opera and theaters. The philosopher-critic Moses Mendelssohn, a leading figure in the Berlin Enlightenment and a symbol of Jewish cultural assimilation, hosted dinner parties in his home attended by gentile writers and scholars. The physician Markus Herz, Henriette's husband, was a former Kant student who during the 1780s gave lectures on natural science in his home. His audience at various times included members of the royal family, the Humboldt brothers, and Christian Wilhelm von Dohm, the enlightened official and noted advocate of Jewish emancipation.

The Herz circle was the nucleus of Henriette's salon, which enjoyed its heyday during the 1790s. Among its regular guests were literary representatives of the younger generation, such as Friedrich Schleiermacher, the Humboldts, and Heinrich von Kleist. The salon met in two adjoining rooms, one devoted to scientific and the other to literary discussion.

Henriette presided over the latter, where she championed the cause of Storm and Stress and early Romantic writers. Also attending was Rahel Levin, a close friend of Henriette who in the 1790s founded her own salon. Rahel's circle originated as a group of noblewomen she had befriended during her visits to Bohemian spas. It soon expanded into a center of the emerging Romantic movement, counting among its guests the critic Friedrich Schlegel and the poet Jean Paul. The philosopher Johann Gottlieb Fichte also found refuge there after charges of atheism had forced him to resign his professorship at Jena.

Attendance at the Levin salon was not limited to the intellectual avant garde; leading representatives of the Prussian nobility also visited regularly, including Prince Ferdinand, nephew of Frederick II, and the scions of families like the von Schlabrendorffs and von Finckensteins. Nobles in fact made up a substantial percentage of the membership in Berlin salons – approximately one-third of the men and two-fifths of the women.[24] This admixture of nobles and commoners was of course typical of salons everywhere in the eighteenth century, but in Berlin high society it was unprecedented for nobles and Jews to socialize. Why were so many nobles in the city willing to discard traditional prejudices? Financial indebtedness sometimes played a role. The Prussian nobility had never been a particularly wealthy class, and during the 1790s, with the collapse of the speculative boom in landed estates that had occurred during the previous three decades, a considerable number faced financial ruin. For those who flocked to Berlin in search of preferments, credit, or simply entertainment, the prospect of marrying into a wealthy Jewish family became an increasingly attractive option. As Hannah Arendt bluntly observed, "the impoverished junkers suddenly saw the moneylender of the *Judengasse* as the father of a daughter with a large dowry."[25] Jewish salons were an important venue for courtships between noblemen and Jewish women, which often led to marriage. And marriage strategies aside, friendships with wealthy members of the city's Jewish community – many of whom loaned money to nobles on a regular basis – also promised important access to credit.

But non-material motives also came into play. At a time when the Romantic movement had begun to sweep through the cultural and intellectual life of the city, the exoticism and foreignness of Jewish salons was alluring to free-spirited nobles of the younger generation. It must be remembered that *salonnières* like Henriette Herz and Rahel Levin,

---

[24] *Ibid.*, 115.
[25] Hannah Arendt, *Rahel Varnhagen: The Life of a Jewish Woman*, rev. ed. (New York and London, 1974), 180.

however acculturated they may have been, were still outsiders by Prussian legal standards. Indeed, their position outside the established corporate structure of Prussian society helps account for the relaxed, informal atmosphere that prevailed in their salons. (Salon regulars, whether noble or commoner, addressed each other in the familiar *Du* form.) While the wealth and cultivation of Jewish salon women helped make them "clubable" socially, their anomalous status freed them from the more rigid behavioral constraints of Old Regime society. That status at the same time helped reduce the stigma that nobles might otherwise have incurred by socializing with those beneath them. Upon entering a Jewish salon, the noble crossed a social threshold that released him from the hierarchies prevailing on the outside. In this respect the Jewish salon was a liminal space, one which, at least temporarily, dissolved the differences in rank and status that existed beyond its walls.

The Jewish salons of Vienna and Berlin inaugurated what was to be a hallmark of Central European high culture from the French Revolution to the Nazi era, namely the cultural prominence of a wealthy and acculturated Jewish stratum. These salons were places where, for the first time in the history of Central Europe, Jews and non-Jews met on terms of relative equality.

This cultural encounter, however, remained fraught with tension. This is seen above all in Berlin, where Jewish salons reached the height of their fashionability in the 1790s but then rapidly lost their allure. Berlin's Jewish salons chiefly owed their decline to the nationalistic, anti-French mood that dominated the capital in the wake of Prussia's disastrous defeat by Napoleon in 1806. Jewish salons, with their cosmopolitan or indeed French associations, were a casualty of this rising nationalist tide. More ominously, they became a target of the latent anti-Semitism that persisted beneath the polite veneer of Berlin high society. Fueling this anti-Jewish backlash was the new mood of "Christian patriotism" that gained currency in Berlin intellectual circles following the occupation of the city by the French. Men who had once patronized Berlin's Jewish salons, such as the novelist Heinrich von Kleist or the diplomat Friedrich Gentz, now shunned them. Even the relatively philo-Semitic Wilhelm von Humboldt ended his year-long friendship with Rahel Levin.

The decline of Berlin's Jewish salons also reflected a certain masculinization of the city's cultural life, a symptom of the ideological remilitarization accompanying the struggle against Napoleon. A notable example was the Christian-German Eating Club (*Tischgesellschaft*), a circle of prominent conservative intellectuals who gathered at midday every Tuesday between 1811 and 1813.[26] The club, whose members included conservative romantics like Adam Müller, Achim von Arnim, and Clemens Brentano, was nationalist and Francophobe in spirit. In important respects the *Tischgesellschaft* was an outgrowth of the Enlightenment public sphere. Its gatherings were occasions for discussion and debate, with both commoners and nobles participating. Its members also employed print media, publishing a newspaper and organizing choral groups to mobilize popular patriotism. The *Tischgesellschaft* was notable, however, in the groups it excluded. Women did not participate, and the *Tischgesellschaft* served as a kind of male counter-salon. This exclusion of women served to distance the club from the Frenchified style of the Jewish salon, which was now associated with the decay that had allegedly sapped the moral and military strength of the Prussian state. Self-consciously Christian, the *Tischgesellschaft* also did not admit Jews – even those who had converted. This exclusion pointed to a more "modern" strain of anti-Semitism, one that defined Jewishness in racial rather than purely religious terms. By the logic of this definition, neither conversion nor assimilation would ever suffice to make Jews a part of German culture.

The *Tischgesellschaft* is a reminder of the varied and multiple directions in which the Enlightenment public sphere would evolve. On the one hand, the *Tischgesellschaft* grew out of communicative practices and forms of sociability associated with the public sphere. Its members acknowledged "public opinion" as a force to be mobilized in political life, courting it through newspapers and meetings. On the other hand, its chauvinistic nationalism, anti-Semitism, and exclusion of women stand in evident contrast to the liberal and emancipatory features Habermas identified with the public sphere. The *Tischgesellschaft* and the fate of the salon in early nineteenth-century Berlin show that if the Enlightenment public sphere offered the potential for a more open political culture, it also contained the seeds of a more closed and intolerant one.

Bibliographical note
Our understanding of the rise of the salon in seventeenth-century France owes much to the pioneering study by Carolyn Lougee, *Les Paradis des Femmes: Women, Salons, and Social Stratification in Seventeenth-Century France* (Princeton, 1976). The nature of salon sociability is examined in Elizabeth Goldsmith, *Exclusive Conversations: The Art of Interaction in Seventeenth-Century France* (Philadelphia, 1988), while there is much on the salon's significance for literary and intellectual life in Joan DeJean, *Tender Geographies: Women and the Origins of the Novel in France* (New York, 1991), and Erica Harth, *Cartesian Women: Versions and Subversions of Rational Discourse in the Old Regime* (Ithaca and London, 1992).

[26] Here my discussion follows the analysis in Hertz, *Jewish High Society in Old Regime Berlin*, 271–75.

On women and sociability in Enlightenment thought, Sylvana Tomaselli, "The Enlightenment Debate on Women," *History Workshop Journal* 20 (1985), and Daniel Gordon's *Citizens Without Sovereignty: Equality and Sociability in French Thought, 1670–1789* (Princeton, 1994), are excellent on the decisive importance of the Scottish Enlightenment for views of women and the civilizing process. On the waning of civic humanism and the impact on views of women, see Vera Nünning, "Die Feminisierung der Kultur: kulturgeschichtliche Bedingungen für den Wandel der Wertschätzung in England des 18. Jahrhunderts," *Archiv für Kulturgeschichte* 76 (1994).

My own discussion of eighteenth-century Parisian salons owes much to Dena Goodman, *The Republic of Letters: A Cultural History of the French Enlightenment* (Ithaca and London, 1994). See also her "Enlightenment Salons: The Convergence of Female and Philosophic Ambitions," *Eighteenth-Century Studies* 22 (1989), and "Governing the Republic of Letters: The Politics of Culture in the French Enlightenment," *History of European Ideas* 13 (1991). For England, an interesting recent analysis of the Bluestocking salons is Deborah Heller, "Bluestocking Salons and the Public Sphere," *Eighteenth-Century Life* 22 (1998). See also Sylvia Harcstark Myers, *The Bluestocking Circle: Women, Friendship, and the Life of the Mind in Eighteenth-Century England* (Oxford, 1990) and the older study by Chauncey Brewster Tinker, *The Salon and English Letters* (New York, 1915). For comparisons with Parisian salons, see Evelyn Gordon Bodek, "Salonnières and Bluestockings: Educated Obsolescence and Germinating Feminism," *Feminist Studies* 3 (1976).

Salons in the Holy Roman Empire (as well as in France) are examined in Peter Seibert, *Der literarische Salon: Literatur und Geselligkeit zwischen Aufklärung und Vormärz* (Stuttgart and Weimar, 1993). Berlin salons have attracted considerable attention because of their relevance to the social position of German Jewry. Deborah Hertz, *Jewish High Society in Old Regime Berlin* (New Haven and London, 1988), and Petra Wilhelmy, *Der Berliner Salon im 19. Jahrhundert* (Berlin and New York, 1989), both examine Berlin's Jewish salons in detail. See also the biography by Hannah Arendt, *Rahel Varnhagen: The Life of a Jewish women*, rev. ed. (New York and London, 1974). For salons in the broader context of Jewish emancipation, readers should also consult Jacob Katz, *Out of the Ghetto* (New York, 1978); David Sorkin, *The Transformation of German Jewry, 1780–1840* (New York and Oxford, 1991); and Steven M. Lohenstein, *The Berlin Jewish Community: Enlightenment, Family, and Crisis, 1770–1830* (New York and Oxford, 1994). Outside of Hilde Spiel's, *Fanny von Arnstein: Daughter of the Enlightenment 1758–1818*, trans. Christine Shuttleworth (New York and Oxford, 1991), there is little on Viennese salons of the eighteenth century. Waltraud Heindl, "Amt und Salon – Bildung und Kultur der Wiener Beamten zur Zeit Mozarts," in Gunda Barth-Scalmani, Brigitte Mazohl-Wallnig, and Ernst Wangermann, eds., *Genie und Alltag. Bürgerliche Stadtkultur zur Mozartzeit* (Salzburg, 1994), contains a brief discussion of the Greiner salon; my own account is taken from the autobiography of Caroline Pichler, *Denkwürdigkeiten aus meinem Leben*, 2 vols., ed. Emil Karl Blümml (Munich, 1914), who was Charlotte Greiner's daughter.

7   Drinking in public: taverns
       and coffeehouses

People in the eighteenth century did much of their drinking in public. At a time when most lived in dwellings that were small, cramped, and poorly heated in the winter, taverns, wineshops, and cafés offered a warm fire and refuge from crowded and uncomfortable quarters. But taverns and coffeehouses were more than simply an escape from the discomforts of home. People frequented taverns and coffeehouses to find jobs, conduct business, exchange information, or celebrate important events of their lives. These were places where baptisms and marriages were celebrated, newspapers circulated, stock traded, crimes plotted, votes solicited, ministers attacked, laborers employed, wars debated, freemasons initiated.

Taverns and coffeehouses were in principle public space, open to anyone who could pay for their drink. This side of taverns continues to find expression in the British term "pub" (after public house), which entered common usage in the eighteenth century. The openness and accessibility associated with public-drinking establishments date back to the Middle Ages, when local statutes or custom sometimes prescribed sanctions against tavern keepers who refused to serve a patron without good cause. Such provisions were rooted in medieval traditions of hospitality, which under specific conditions obliged communities and lordships to offer food, drink, or accommodations to travelers and pilgrims. The publicness of drinking establishments in early modern Europe found expression in the often picturesque signs that beckoned those on the street to come within. The public status of taverns and coffeehouses was also reflected in their function as urban landmarks at a time when it was not yet common for buildings to bear numbers. Street addresses in eighteenth-century cities were often designated by reference to a tavern or coffeehouse. One resided "opposite the Sun Tavern"; a street crime occurred "near the "Café du Rendez-vous"; a journeyman newcomer was told he could find his employer "in the shop behind the Grenadier Arms."[1]

---

[1] Cf. David Garrioch, *Neighborhood and Community in Paris, 1740–1790* (Cambridge, 1986), 28.

But like other forms of sociability in the eighteenth century, drinking in public was circumscribed by prevailing social and sexual norms. An individual's sex, social rank, occupation, and even politics had a bearing on where, what, and when one drank. This chapter examines some of the public settings in which drinking occurred, as well as the norms and expectations that governed access to them.

Alcohol and sociability

By modern-day standards, alcohol consumption in early modern Europe was high. Poor sanitation was partly responsible, since water sources were often contaminated and beer, ale, or wine seemed a safer alternative. During his stay in Paris in 1765, the English traveler William Cole never drank the local water without first diluting it with wine. "The Seine water," he warned his readers, "is very apt to disorder strangers on their first coming to Paris, & therefore a too free use of it, without a good Deal of Wine... , is not reckoned wholesome."[2] Per capita beer consumption (children and adults alike) in sixteenth- and seventeenth-century Germany has been estimated at 400 liters a year; around 1700, the equivalent figure for wine consumption in Paris and Vienna was 160 liters. Alcohol was an integral part of the European diet and an important source of calories. In revolutionary France, where the average diet totaled 1,800 calories a day, a liter of wine yielded more than a third of the caloric intake of a man weighing 145 pounds. Beer served a similar function for the German peasant: in the countryside of northern Germany, peasants traditionally began their day with a soup made of beer, eggs, and butter.[3]

Taverns, of course, were only one place where alcohol was consumed. The relative spaciousness and comfort of their residences meant that the upper classes, aside from business or pleasure trips, had less need to drink or entertain outside the home. As for those lower down the social scale, much of the public consumption of alcohol had traditionally taken place not in taverns but in other communal contexts. The festive occasions celebrated by artisans in their guild halls, the churchyard ales held on religious holidays, the market days and fairs on the town or village square, were common settings for the public consumption of alcohol.

[2] William Cole, *A Journal of My Journey to Paris in the Year 1765*, ed. Francis Stokes (London, 1931), 167.

[3] Statistics taken from R. Sandgruber, *Bittersüsse Genüsse. Kulturgeschichte der Genussmittel* (Vienna, 1986), 28; Thomas Brennan, "Social Drinking in Old Regime Paris," in *Drinking: Behavior and Belief in Modern History*, ed. Susanna Barrows and Robin Room (Berkeley, 1991), 62; Gregory Austin, *Alcohol in Western Society from Antiquity to 1800: A Chronological History* (Santa Barbara and Austin, 1985), 272, 364. See also Wolfgang Schivelbusch, *Tastes of Paradise: A Social History of Spices, Stimulants, and Intoxicants* (New York, 1992), 22–33.

From the late Middle Ages on, however, the tavern had acquired increasing importance as a center of public drinking. Taverns proliferated in the wake of the Black Death, when labor shortages occasioned by the drop in population drove up wages and encouraged laborers to migrate in search of higher earnings. The resulting growth of a migratory labor force was a boon to taverns and inns, for it fostered an increasingly mobile population forced to seek food, drink, and lodging outside the home.[4] Paradoxically, the Protestant and Catholic Reformations may have also enhanced the importance of taverns. As a center of communal life, the parish church had traditionally been the site of festivals and celebrations where heavy consumption of alcohol was the rule. The drunken and riotous behavior of the laity on Sundays and other religious holidays came under sharp attack during the sixteenth and seventeenth centuries, when Protestant and Catholic reformers sought to ban or at least restrict public drinking on those occasions. The effect, as Puritan attempts to enforce the Sabbath in seventeenth-century England illustrate, was to heighten the importance of alehouses as centers of public drinking. Driven from the churchyard, public drinking found refuge in the tavern.

In the eighteenth century, rapid urban growth and the expansion of inland trade were a further spur to tavern keeping. Paris had almost 3,000 public drinking establishments by the mid-eighteenth century, while London had 8,000 alehouses alone.[5] As the volume of trade expanded, so did the number of taverns and inns accommodating itinerant merchants, tradesmen, and workers in the cartage trade. These establishments functioned not just as places to eat, drink, or sleep, but also as centers of commerce, transport, and communication. The more elaborate ones, like the English inn, the French *hôtel*, or the German *Gasthof*, catered to an elite clientele drawn from the landed, professional, and mercantile classes. Located in cities, larger provincial towns, and along major commercial and transportation arteries, inns usually had ten to fifteen rooms and sufficient stables to accommodate up to a hundred horses. By the eighteenth century inns had begun to replace marketplaces and fairs as places where commercial and land deals were negotiated and transacted. They were also the primary distribution centers for goods and information exchanged between city and countryside, with the innkeeper acting as

---

[4] On the development of taverns in early modern England, see Peter Clark, *The English Alehouse: A Social History, 1200–1830* (New York, 1983).

[5] Thomas Brennen, *Public Drinking and Popular Culture in Eighteenth-Century Paris* (Princeton, 1988), 89. Brennen's figure includes coffeehouses, of which there were around 600 in Paris at this time. See Ulla Heise, *Kaffee und Kaffeehaus. Eine Kulturgeschichte* (Hildesheim, 1987), 186. The figure on London alehouses is taken from Friedrich Rauers, *Kulturgeschichte der Gaststätte*, 2 vols. (Berlin, 1941), I:1127.

the local postmaster and forwarding agent. These functions explain why in Germany, for example, many of the large carrier and shipping firms of the nineteenth century had originated as inns in the eighteenth century. Throughout the week a steady stream of stagecoaches and carriers moved from inn to inn, delivering and receiving goods and information. Enhancing the importance of public houses as communication hubs was the rapid expansion of postal services in the eighteenth century. Inns and taverns were the most common depot for the post chaises that crisscrossed a region, carrying mail and passengers. Known as *messageries* in France and *Laubenkrüge* in Brandenburg (literally "arcade taverns," after the awning over the entrance that sheltered the coach while mail or passengers were unloaded), they were the equivalent of the modern-day post office.

The great majority of public drinking places were less lavish in their amenities or elite in their clientele than the inn. These were the alehouses of London, the *tavernes* and *cabarets* of Paris, the *Kneipen* and *Tabagien* of Berlin, the *Weinkeller* and *Bierhäuser* of Vienna. Much more rudimentary in their furnishings and fare, these establishments attracted patrons from more modest social backgrounds. Tavern society varied considerably as one moved from England to the continent, and these differences can sometimes illuminate important variations in the social and political environment.

Taverns and politics: the case of London

The typical London alehouse of the sixteenth and seventeenth centuries was a small, cramped, often raucous establishment catering to a distinctly plebeian clientele. Frequented by journeymen, day laborers, poor craftsmen, and domestic servants, alehouses were generally shunned by the propertied classes. Puritan opinion was of course hostile to the alehouse, and not until the Restoration did it begin to acquire a measure of respectability. By the advent of the "Gin Craze" in the 1720s, alehouses had come to seem positively benign in comparison with the gin-shop. Gin consumption in England rose from 1.23 million gallons in 1700 to 8.2 million in 1743, and by 1750, when the gin epidemic was at its height, the per capita consumption of adult males in London may have been as high as 14 gallons annually.[6] Gin became popular among the London poor owing

---

[6] Hans Medick, "Plebejische Kultur, plebejische Öffentlichkeit, plebejische Ökonomie. Über Erfahrungen und Verhaltensweisen Besitzarmer und Besitzloser in der Übergangsphase zum Kapitalismus," in Robert Berdahl *et al.*, eds., *Klassen und Kultur. Sozialanthropologische Perspektiven in der Geschichtsschreibung* (Frankfurt am Main, 1982), 184.

to its affordability, making it a target of Methodists and other moral reformers alarmed at the debilitating effects of the liquor. Supporting their campaign were alehouse keepers who feared competition from gin shops and lobbied for their tighter regulation. The gin epidemic ended in 1751, when a parliamentary tax brought an end to cheap gin. In the meantime, the lurid reputation of the gin-shop had helped to rehabilitate the alehouse. Hogarth's "Gin Lane" and "Beer Street," which contrasted the physical and moral ravages of the former with the salutary effects of the latter, graphically portrayed the respective reputations of the two.

Another reason for the rehabilitation of the London alehouse was the growing prosperity and social respectability of its clientele. Laborers and small craftsmen, whose economic position generally improved during the first half of the eighteenth century, remained an important part of the alehouse's constituency. For those seeking work, the alehouse functioned as a kind of employment agency. "Houses of call," as they were known in the eighteenth century, were drinking establishments where prospective employers could hire laborers. Some houses of call catered to a particular trade and often provided credit for food and drink while a laborer waited for work. But many alehouses also began to attract patrons from the middle class and the gentry by expanding their facilities and adding additional rooms to accommodate private gatherings. These rooms hosted the clubs, masonic lodges, mutual-aid societies, and political associations that proliferated during the Hanoverian era. London freemasons, for example, held their first annual convention in 1717 at the Goose and Gridiron alehouse.[7] The tavern was the stage on which the flourishing associational life of Hanoverian England unfolded, and helps to explain the success of urban English taverns in attracting patrons from varied social backgrounds. At a tavern in London's Foster Lane, observed the journalist Ned (Edward) Ward in 1720, "topers of all sorts frequent, from daily laborers to men styled gent, of all opinions and conditions."[8] Although one continued to encounter laborers, skilled artisans, and journeymen in the eighteenth-century alehouse, merchants, gentlemen, parsons, or barristers could also go there without jeopardizing their status. The fact that London alehouses began to be called "pubs" in the late eighteenth century suggests the growing heterogeneity of their clientele. The term was also applied to the more elite inn, which points to a narrowing of the social distance between the two establishments over the course of the eighteenth century.

[7] Clark, *English Alehouse*, 223–35.
[8] Edward Ward, *Vademecum for Maltworms* (London, 1720), 33.

That is not to say that the members of this socially diverse clientele necessarily conversed and socialized with each other. Most likely the addition of extra rooms and tables fostered the creation of more socially segregated spaces within the tavern. The radical reformer Francis Place, who himself grew up in a working-class family, recalled of London taverns in the 1780s: "It was the custom at this time, as it had long been, for almost every man who had the means to spend his evening at some public house or tavern or other place of public entertainment. Almost every public-house had a parlour . . . for the better class of customer."[9] A similar specialization of social space could be found in many German taverns, which sometimes reserved a special room for more elite patrons. A 1669 patent issued by the Prussian elector decreed that a tavern should have two rooms, one for the common people and one for its more elite clientele. Spatial divisions in taverns could serve to reinforce social ones, a fact that must be kept in mind when assessing the function of taverns as public space.

Taverns were predominantly male in their clientele, although women were sometimes tavern keepers. Taverns had traditionally enjoyed a reputation for harboring prostitutes – a notoriety not entirely undeserved, judging from contemporary accounts. Samuel Pepys describes an assignation with a prostitute in the Dog Tavern in Westminster, where in a dark corner "I did do what I did desire with her and did it backward, not having convenience to do it the other way"; roughly a century later, James Boswell's London journal of 1762–63 described similar encounters.[10] A woman covetous of her reputation did not enter a tavern alone, and one who did was considered promiscuous and risked being accosted or assaulted. A woman escorted by a man entered a tavern at less risk to her honor. Taverns were a common venue for working-class courtships, as well as a place where couples went to celebrate marriages, baptisms, and funerals. Even middle-class women visited taverns on occasion: in 1750 Samuel Johnson organized a party at London's Devil Tavern for Charlotte Lennox, to celebrate the appearance of her first novel (she attended with her husband). The otherwise male clubs and societies that met in taverns also invited female guests from time to time. Beginning in the 1770s, for example, debating societies began to admit women to their tavern meetings. In 1774 a member of the Birmingham Free Debating Society chastised some of his fellows for the slovenly garb they wore to their meetings at the Red Lion Tavern. "The Ladies are permitted

<hr />

[9] Quoted in M. Dorothy George, *London Life in the Eighteenth Century* (London, 1925), 266.

[10] Quoted in Steven C. Hahn, "Taverns and the Public Sphere: A View from the Metropolis," unpublished seminar paper, Department of History, Emory University, 1995, 10–11.

gratis," he admonished them, "and cleanliness is a compliment due to the sex everywhere."[11]

As the debating societies suggest, taverns provided a crucial forum for political expression and association during the Hanoverian era. Alehouse politics was no eighteenth-century invention: during the Civil War and Restoration, taverns were a frequent site of political organization and agitation. Nor was tavern politics a peculiarity of the English. Elsewhere in Europe, taverns traditionally served as places where opposition to a local lord or town council was publicly vented or organized. Taverns figured prominently in the German Peasants War, for example. One of the headquarters of the peasant uprising in Franconia was the Thorn Tavern in Würzburg, where in 1525 the peasant leader Florian Geyer made common cause with the town council against the bishop. That same year, in a tavern near the town of Gundelsheim, the rebellious peasants of the Neckar valley formally appointed Götz von Berlichingen their leader. In the absolutist regimes of the eighteenth century, public drinking establishments were a major source of political news and rumor for subjects who otherwise had little access to the affairs of government. The journalist Josef Pezzl called the beer halls of Vienna "temples of political gossip":

The people who frequent them want to think that they know something about the mood of the cabinet, and the less they know of it, the more they like to gossip about the great affairs of the world. The multitude of domestic servants cheerfully relate this or that anecdote, or some suggestive comment they picked up at their master's table or elsewhere ... Here one concludes alliances, launches fleets, dispatches armies, announces the deaths or travels of potentates, and so forth.[12]

Here Pezzl highlighted the dialectic of governmental secrecy and popular rumor discussed in Chapter 2. In the absolutist regimes of the continent, taverns were places where the political subject imposed meaning on the more or less opaque world of high politics. For governments, conversely, they were a vehicle for monitoring public opinion and rooting out sedition. According to Pezzl, permanent fixtures of Viennese beer halls were the lowly spies who were paid 34 Kreuzer a day by the government to eavesdrop on conversations. Parisian taverns had been a favorite haunt of government spies since the reign of Louis XIV, whose newly organized police force instituted the surveillance of taverns in every district of the city.

Tavern politics in England, on the other hand, had an overt and organized dimension that was lacking in France and the empire. As places

---

[11] Quoted in John Money, *Experience and Identity: Birmingham and the West Midlands, 1760–1800* (Montreal, 1977), 113.

[12] Josef Pezzl, *Skizze von Wien*, ed. G. Gugitz and A. Schlossar (Graz, 1923), 364.

where Whig and Tory politicians gathered to plot strategy and mobilize electoral support, taverns had been an integral part of England's emerging party system in the late seventeenth and early eighteenth centuries. Political anniversaries and celebrations provided ample occasion for the expression of party loyalties. Whig alehouses did a bustling business on Guy Fawkes Day and the birthday of Elizabeth I, when tavern celebrations by anti-Catholic and anti-Stuart crowds were likely to end down the street in a pope-burning procession. Opponents of the Whigs had their tavern celebrations, too. In early eighteenth-century London, for example, an extensive network of Jacobite alehouses could be found where Restoration Day was celebrated with toasts to the Stuart pretender and the flaunting of white roses (a mark of allegiance to the dynasty).[13] The provision of drink was a standard electoral ritual. In especially well-oiled campaigns, the candidate or local patron distributed tickets to supporters that could then be redeemed for drink, food, and perhaps a bed at a particular tavern or inn. After the election, the tavernkeeper submitted the tickets to the candidate or patron for compensation. In other cases specific taverns were reserved by one side or another, the names often appearing in handbills or newspapers, where local voters were promised drink and out-of-towners lodging. "Treating" made up a substantial part of campaign expenditures. In the Norfolk election of 1784, the rival candidates footed the bills at almost a hundred inns and taverns accommodating their supporters. Following the 1796 elections, the Sun Tavern in Shrewsbury billed a local candidate some £400 for food and drink served to voters. Expenses included 443 breakfasts, 572 plates of bread and cheese, 1,265 dinners, 1,164 gallons of cider, and 1,875 gallons of ale.[14] The custom of treating at elections found its way to the American colonies. When young George Washington stood for a seat in the Virginia House of Burgesses in 1758, he was concerned lest his election agent prove too stingy in providing drink to potential supporters: "My only fear," as he wrote his agent, "is that you spent with too sparing a hand." In the end, the 144 gallons of drink he dispensed helped yield 307 votes.[15]

Treating was not confined to elections. Even in off years, voters expected an MP or his representative to provide drinks on the house from time to time. Tavern treating was woven into the paternalistic fabric of Hanoverian social and political relations. For members of the political

---

[13] Paul Kléber Monod, *Jacobitism and the English People, 1688–1788* (Cambridge, 1989), 105–7.

[14] H. T. Dickinson, *The Politics of the People in Eighteenth-Century Britain* (New York, 1995), 44; Frank O'Gorman, *Voters, Patrons, and Parties: The Unreformed Electoral System of Hanoverian England 1734–1832* (Oxford, 1989), 153.

[15] W. J. Rohrbaugh, *The Alcoholic Republic* (New York, 1979), 152.

elite, it was a chance to demonstrate affection for and commitment to the local community; for the voters present, it was a way to establish or affirm ties of loyalty and deference.

Beyond their importance in mobilizing and sustaining electoral loyalties, taverns also provided a stage for extraparliamentary activism. In virtually every major crisis and *cause célèbre* of the Hanoverian era, taverns were a center of popular political agitation. In March of 1733, tavern crowds throughout England celebrated the defeat of Walpole's unpopular Excise Bill. In November of 1740 and 1741 riotous tavern celebrations commemorated Vice-Admiral Edward Vernon's naval victory over the Spanish, and for years after his head adorned tavern signs. Tavern politics, like the public sphere itself, were not inherently oppositionalist: as was evident during the Jacobite rebellion of 1745–46, the outbreak of war against France in 1756, and the struggle against Napoleon, taverns could also be the site of a vigorous popular loyalism. But the extraparliamentary opposition that came of age with the Wilkite movement of the 1760s and 1770s would have been inconceivable without the tavern culture that nurtured it. During the reform agitation of those years, Wilkes's core constituency of artisans and small tradesmen gathered in alehouses to collect petitions and money on his behalf. Alehouse proprietors capitalized on Wilkes's popularity by naming their taverns after him, and as with Vernon earlier in the century, the signs of countless drinking establishments sported his profile. During the 1770s and 1780s, the radical clubs and associations spawned by the Wilkite agitation continued to make taverns their organizational nuclei.[16]

Taverns played an equally important political role in Britain's North American colonies. Already in the early 1700s, taverns had become the breeding grounds for an oppositional political culture in which discussion and debate increasingly occurred outside the purview of both Puritan ministers and royal officials. Fostering this development were disaffected members of the colonial assembly who helped license or even purchased taverns as a means of building a local political base. By the eve of the Revolution, Massachusetts taverns and their proprietors were thoroughly politicized. John Adams observed this process with considerable ambivalence, noting in 1760 that taverns "are become in many places the nurseries of our legislators."[17] Tavernkeeping was by this time a common occupation among colonial politicians, as it was among leading opponents

[16] John Brewer, *Party Ideology and Popular Politics at the Accession of George III* (Cambridge, 1976), 149, 185; Kathleen Wilson, *The Sense of the People: Politics, Culture and Imperialism in England, 1715–1785* (Cambridge, 1995), 67.

[17] Quoted in David Conroy, *In Public Houses: Drink and the Revolution of Authority in Colonial Massachusetts* (Chapel Hill and London, 1995), 190.

of the crown in general. During the 1760s Boston tavernkeepers made up 20 percent of the Sons of Liberty, a hotbed of resistance to royal policy whose members met regularly in a Boston tavern to talk politics and drink rum punch from a silver bowl (commissioned from Paul Revere) commemorating John Wilkes and the 45th issue of his *North Briton.*

The centrality of the public house in Hanoverian political culture reinforced the relative heterogeneity of tavern society. English taverns were a place where disparate publics intersected and sometimes interacted. Originating as a predominantly plebeian sphere of sociability, taverns were a central part of the emerging party system, the expanding realm of popular politics, and the burgeoning associational life of Hanoverian England. As a meeting ground for political elites and local constituencies, as well as an organizational matrix for clubs, societies, and extraparliamentary politics, taverns attracted a relatively broad spectrum of English society.

Paris: from cabaret to café

The heterogeneous public often found in London taverns was less often encountered in the wineshops of eighteenth-century Paris. Parisian *tavernes* and *cabarets* were much more plebeian in their clientele, and appear to have become even more so as the century wore on. Statistics on Parisian taverns between 1691 and 1771 show a preponderance of working-class patrons, and tavern society in Paris appears to have grown increasingly proletarianized over the course of the century. Nobles and middle-class professionals rarely patronized *tavernes* and *cabarets* at all, and made up perhaps no more than 10 percent of their clientele. The most prosperous group to visit Parisian wineshops in any significant number were tradesmen and master craftsmen, and even these strata appear to have shunned taverns after the mid-eighteenth century. While those occupations made up roughly 21 percent of tavern patrons in 1752, the percentage had dropped to 10 percent in 1788. During the same period the percentage of unskilled workers rose from 5 percent to 13 percent, and that of journeymen from 20 percent to 33 percent.[18]

In the eighteenth century, then, Parisian taverns were associated with the culture of the common people and belonged to a public sphere that was more plebeian than propertied. Closely tied to the world of work and the street, *tavernes* and *cabarets* often served as the local employment office or as an extension of the workshop. Common laborers and journeymen went there to find jobs, and craftsmen lingered while wives or apprentices waited in their shops for customers. The fluid boundaries between tavern

[18] Brennan, *Public Drinking*, 145–46; Garrioch, *Neighborhood and Community in Paris, 1740–1790*, 182–86.

and street life also made *cabarets* a natural haven for prostitution, especially those located near the bustling markets and fairs of the city. These
establishments were sometimes furnished with wooden partitions that
enabled prostitutes and clients to transact their business in private. As in
England, the connection between taverns and prostitution discouraged
women solicitous of their reputations from frequenting them unattended.
Like their English counterparts, however, working-class women in Paris
did visit taverns in the company of husbands and lovers. *Guinguettes*, the
suburban taverns that grew up around Paris in the eighteenth century,
were especially popular with working-class couples. Located just beyond
the city's custom barriers, *guinguettes* were able to serve wine more cheaply
and therefore attracted a large working-class clientele. A *Guinguette* excur-
sion on Sundays and holidays was a popular plebeian pastime. Because of
their location outside the city, *guinguettes* had space for larger rooms and
gardens where games were played and dances held. The prevalence of
dancing was an indication of the *guinguette*'s more sexually mixed public.
This greater degree of sexual integration may have reflected the fact that
the *guinguette* was more divorced from the rhythms and spaces of everyday life than was the neighborhood tavern, where drinking punctuated
the work day and occurred in close proximity to one's home and place
of work. Temporally as well as spatially, *Guinguettes* were a more discrete
form of sociability. One visited a *guinguette* on weekends or holidays, usually from a different neighborhood, which may have served to suspend
or at least relax prevailing gender-based expectations and conventions.
Whatever the cause, the suburbanization of public drinking had a similar
impact on sexual sociability elsewhere in Europe. In Vienna, where the
practice of traveling just beyond the boundaries of the city in order to
drink more cheaply also became a popular pastime in the eighteenth century, suburban taverns (*Heurigen*) had a sexually more integrated clientele
than taverns within the city.[19]

The *cabarets* of Paris were notorious for their violence. Over one-
quarter of Parisians prosecuted for violent crimes in the late eighteenth
century committed them inside or directly outside taverns.[20] Since *cabarets* were primarily neighborhood establishments, most of the violence was
between individuals who knew each other. Often the altercations were an
extension of conflicts in the workplace: business rivalries, conflicts between masters and journeymen, or struggles for power within a guild
were just a few of the possible causes. By virtue of its public nature the

---

[19] On *guinguettes* see Brennan, *Public Drinking*, 168–72, and Garrioch, *Neighborhood and
Community in Paris, 1740–1790*, 190–91. *Heurigen* are briefly discussed in Sandgruber,
Bittersüsse Genüsse, 42.
[20] Brennan, *Public Drinking*, 32.

tavern served as an arena where reputations could be assaulted, affronts to honor avenged, and local power relationships affirmed or challenged. There one could assail an enemy's manhood by questioning his wife's fidelity, or malign a rival tradesman by denouncing his business practices.

The reputation of cabarets for lower-class debauchery, sexual license, and violence helps to explain why the middle and upper classes increasingly avoided them over the course of the century. Writing during the 1770s, the Parisian lieutenant general of police Lenoir observed that the bourgeoisie had stopped frequenting *cabarets* in the early eighteenth century. *Cabarets*, he wrote, had become the preserve of "soldiers, workers, coachmen, lackeys, and . . . prostitutes. A few petit bourgeois or *marchands* still went to the *guinguettes* on Sundays and feast-days; but many more of them frequented the cafés, the clubs, even houses of ill repute."[21] Here Lenoir alludes to other reasons why Parisian elites increasingly shunned tavern life. One was the growing popularity of coffee: early in the century, when elegant cafés like the Procope (which also served wine and brandy) were becoming fashionable among Parisian elites, drinking at a *cabaret* became distinctly *declassé*. Another was a general tendency among the Parisian bourgeoisie to distance themselves from the more plebeian culture of the street. This withdrawal from street and neighborhood entailed the construction of a new social identity rooted in the home and conjugal family on the one hand, and in an expanding network of professional contacts extending outside the neighborhood and throughout the city at large on the other. Hence withdrawal from the local neighborhood (and by extension the tavern) gravitated in two directions: inward, into a privatized realm of domesticity, and outward, fanning into horizontal networks of sociability based on business and professional ties. Typifying the latter direction was the growing popularity of freemasonry among the Parisian middle class. Middle-class masons tended to have ties outside their quarter of residence. In joining lodges, they entered an expanding public sphere of clubs and societies that superseded neighborhood loyalties. In the process they also distanced themselves from their lower-class neighbors, thereby constructing new cultural barriers that set them apart from *le menu peuple*. In the case of *cabarets*, the 1774 decision by Parisian lodges of the Grand Orient to prohibit their members from meeting in wineshops was illustrative of this process of cultural distantiation.[22]

Hence the "proletarianization" of Parisian tavern life was the flip side of an expanding public sphere where members of the Parisian middle class

---

[21] Quoted in Garrioch, *Neighborhood and Community in Paris, 1740–1790*, 181.
[22] *Ibid.*, 173–80.

elaborated an identity distinct from those below. Or to view it in another light, the middle-class retreat from the *cabaret* was a symptom of the emerging gulf between "popular" and "elite" culture that Peter Burke has associated with the early modern period.[23] The abandonment of taverns by the propertied classes removed an important point of contact and negotiation between elite and plebeian culture, and in the process may well have contributed to the plebeian sense of "us *vs.* them" that surfaced during the Revolution. The radicalism of the Parisian sections and the revolutionary ardor of the *enragés* flourished amidst a tavern culture that elites had abandoned during the previous decades.

As the Parisian café illustrates, however, this process of social distancing was not continuous across the culture of public drinking. Although Parisian cafés had initially catered to a relatively elite clientele, this was no longer the case by the mid-eighteenth century. As coffee became cheaper and more affordable, its popularity spread to all levels of society. The rise of coffee as an article of mass consumption tended to democratize Parisian café culture, as coffee lost the elite reputation it had enjoyed earlier in the century. A symptom of this social leveling was the fact that tavern proprietors increasingly served coffee in their establishments, which they sometimes renamed cafés in order to enhance their respectability. The effect was to blur the difference between cafés and wineshops, and after the Revolution, when the drink and victualing trades were deregulated, the distinction disappeared altogether.[24]

So if *cabarets* became less mixed in the eighteenth century, cafés became more so. Although Left-Bank cafés like the Procope retained a more upper-class clientele, boulevard expansion and the growing commercialization of the city's central districts encouraged the proliferation of cafés attracting a more heterogeneous clientele. By the 1780s, as Robert Isherwood has shown, the boulevards that now transected the city were lined with cafés where one sat amidst promenaders, acrobats, harlequin shows, and street musicians. Some cafés featured their own entertainments. At Monsieur Validin's café on the Place Louis XV (now the Place de la Concorde), blind musicians gave daily concerts under the direction of a conductor who wore a helmet adorned with donkey ears as he sat perched astride a stuffed peacock. At another café in the area, chubby nymphs sang to the patrons while dangling on a cloud over the stage. Drawn to the entertainment and spectacle, a broad range of people visited these cafés. One of the most popular, the Tambour Royal, attracted everyone from countesses and intendants to fishmongers and rag-pickers.

[23] Peter Burke, *Popular Culture in Early Modern Europe*, rev. ed. (New York, 1994).
[24] W. Scott Haine, *The World of the Paris Café: Sociability among the French Working Class, 1789–1914* (Baltimore and London, 1996), 15–16; Garrioch, *Neighborhood and Community in Paris, 1740–1790*, 181.

By the eve of the Revolution, the most important center of café life
central Paris was the Palais-Royal. This palace had once been the residence of the young Louis XIV, who later deeded it to the Orléans family.
In order to raise the money necessary for its renovation, the owner, the
duc de Chartres, decided in 1781 to lease its gardens for development
into a popular fair. These were now transformed into what could be
called the city's first shopping and entertainment mall. Flanking its public promenade were arcades lined with shops, bookstores, entertainment
stalls, small theaters, cafés, and clubs. There was no visible split between
an elite and a popular clientele – all were drawn to the spectacles, entertainments, and public spaces of the Palais-Royal. Mercier described the
crowd as a "confusion of estates," while his fellow journalist, Mayeur de
Saint-Paul, wrote that "all the orders of citizens are joined together, from
the lady of rank to the dissolute, from the soldier of distinction to the
smallest supernumerary of farms."[25] The Palais-Royal's cultural marketplace knew no sex, and its cafés, like those of the boulevard, were sexually
as well as socially mixed.

In 1789, amidst the euphoria that marked the early days of the Revolution, the cafés of the Palais-Royal were rapidly politicized. Individuals of all classes congregated there to fraternize and exchange information. "What most impressed me," wrote the revolutionary Théroigne de
Méricourt, "was the atmosphere of general benevolence; egoism seemed
to have been banished, so that everyone spoke to each other, irrespec-
tive of distinctions [of rank]; during this moment of upheaval, the rich
mixed with the poor and did not disdain to speak to them as equals."[26]
Amidst this heady atmosphere, the cafés of the Palais-Royal were transformed from places of leisure and entertainment into centers of political
sociability where politicized plebeians met radicalized elements of the
bourgeoisie. Café culture during the Revolution was a fusion of street
theater and political pamphlet, of oral and literate culture, features an
aristocratic observer observed of the Palais-Royal's cafés in 1789: "Here
a man is drafting a reform of the Constitution; another is reading a pamphlet aloud; at another table, someone is taking the ministers to task;
everybody is talking; each person has his own little audience that lis-
tens very attentively to him... In the cafés, one is half-suffocated by the
press of people."[27] As W. Scott Haine has shown, journalist-agitators
like Jean-Paul Marat and Jacques-René Hébert thrived in this atmosphere, transforming the violent language of the café-wineshop into the

---

[25] Quoted in Robert M. Isherwood, *Farce and Fantasy: Popular Entertainment in Eighteenth-
Century Paris* (New York and Oxford, 1986), 249.
[26] Quoted in Haine, *The World of the Paris Café*, 209.
[27] *Ibid.*, 209, 210 (quote).

revolutionary rhetoric of the *Ami du peuple* and the *Père Duchesne*. The cafés of Paris would remain a center of popular radicalism up to 1794, when the Jacobin-sponsored Terror resulted in the closing of almost half of them. They were further suppressed under Napoleon, although they would reemerge in the nineteenth century as centers of working-class radicalism – "parliaments of the people," as Balzac termed them.

The political culture of coffee

The first coffeehouse in Christian Europe opened in Venice in 1645. It was modeled after the coffee-shops that Western travelers encountered in the Ottoman Empire, where Islamic prohibitions against alcohol had made coffee a popular drink since the early sixteenth century. Coffeehouses subsequently made their way to England, where the first was established in Oxford in 1650. Within a few years, coffeehouses had spread to London, where their soaring popularity made them a fixture of public life by 1700. The French café dated back to 1672 when an Armenian immigrant began to dispense coffee from a stall at the Saint-Germain market in Paris. But the real prototype of the Parisian café was the Procope, established in 1686 by the Sicilian, Procopio di Coltello. The Procope was the first European café to install mirrors, and this innovation, along with elegant candelabras, marble-topped tables, and its location near the Saint-Germain fair and the Comédie Française, helped attract an elite and fashionable clientele. Coffeehouses reached the height of their fashionability under the Regency and early in the reign of Louis XV (himself a passionate coffee-drinker who had his gardeners plant coffee shrubs in the hothouses at Versailles). Paris had 280 establishments serving coffee in 1720, 600 in 1750, and 900 by 1789.[28]

Throughout most of the Holy Roman Empire, coffee was a relatively expensive and exotic drink up to the 1720s. Unlike England and France, which could import coffee less expensively from their Caribbean colonies, the territories of the empire had no overseas possessions. Coffee was therefore more expensive, and the efforts of mercantilist-minded princes to curb or prohibit coffee imports made it even more so. Eventually, however, the coffee habit caught on in the empire too. The first coffehouse opened in Hamburg (1671), followed by Vienna (1683), Regensburg (1686), Nuremberg (1686), Frankfurt am Main (1689), and Leipzig (1694). By the 1730s coffeehouses existed in most cities of the empire, and Vienna, owing to its relatively cosmopolitan population, was

---

[28] Heise, *Kaffee und Kaffeehaus*, 93, 102, 186–88; Heinrich Jacob, *The Saga of Coffee: The Biography of an Economic Product* (London, 1935), 127.

especially renowned for them. The number of Viennese coffeehouses grew from thirty-seven in 1737 and sixty-four in 1784 to more than eighty in 1791. With fourteen coffeehouses in 1750, Hamburg had a large number for a city its size. The English merchants who traded at its port doubtless helped popularize the institution. Because of efforts by the Prussian crown to restrict coffee imports, coffeehouses were few in Berlin. The first did not open until 1721, and in 1780 the Prussian capital still had only twelve. Other German princes also sought to limit coffee consumption, but prohibitions were unpopular and difficult to enforce. In the town of Paderborn, where in 1785 the prince-bishop had issued a decree restricting coffee drinking to nobles, clergy, and officials, townspeople showed their contempt for the measure by openly drinking coffee in the town square. When the prince-bishop sent troops to enforce compliance, his soldiers were met with howls of derision. The edict remained on paper, but there were no further attempts to enforce it. By the late eighteenth century, most German princes had abandoned efforts to restrict coffee consumption.

As seen in the above sketch, coffeehouses achieved their earliest and most widespread popularity in England. How does one explain the rapid proliferation of coffeehouses in Restoration and Augustan England? The political turbulence of the period was partly responsible. The coffeehouse arrived in England three years after the execution of Charles I, and its growing popularity coincided with the Stuart restoration, the Exclusion Crisis, the Glorious Revolution, the bitter partisan struggles of Anne's reign, and the explosion of political journalism that marked the Augustan era. Born in an age of revolution, restoration, and bitter party rivalries, the coffeehouse provided public space at a time when political action and debate had begun to spill beyond the institutions that had traditionally contained them.

A prototype of the coffeehouse as public sphere was the Turk's Head in London, where the arch-republican James Harrington founded the Rota Club in 1659. The club, whose other members included John Milton, took its name from Harrington's proposal in his utopian *Commonwealth of Oceana* (1656) to establish term limits for Members of Parliament. The club met around an oval table and debated political issues of the day. Samuel Pepys, a frequent visitor there, described how in the heat of debate the members would decide an issue by casting their votes in a ballot-box.[29] The radicalism and proto-democratic sociability of the Rota

---

[29] *The Diary of Samuel Pepys*, ed. Robert Latham and William Matthews, 11 vols. (Berkeley and Los Angeles, 1970–1983), I:20–21.

Club helps explain why Restoration coffeehouses came to be viewed as havens for political and religious dissent. Puritan writers reinforced this reputation by repeatedly praising the sobering virtues of coffee over the intoxicating effects of alcohol. These very qualities led royalist critics to associate coffeehouses with incessant talk, places where irresponsible chatterboxes subjected the affairs of church and king to relentless criticism. Hence *The Character of a Coffee-House* (London, 1673) called it "a *High Court of Justice*, where every little Fellow in a *Chamlet-Cloak* takes upon him to transpose Affairs both in Church and State, to shew reasons against *Acts* of Parliament, and condemn the Decrees of *General Councels*."[30] Richard Allestree, chaplain to Charles II, observed of coffeehouses in 1667: "At those tables our superiors are dissected; calumny and treason are the common, are indeed the more peculiar entertainments of those places."[31] Royalist critics of the coffeehouse lauded ale, on the other hand, for its mellowing and tranquilizing effects. One pamphleteer assured his readers (1675) that the alehouse patron "is one of the quietest subjects his Majesty has, and more submissive to monarchical government." Sir Thomas Player, a high official in London city government and himself a Whig, was nonetheless alarmed by the anti-government mood of London coffeehouses during the Third Anglo-Dutch War (1672–78): "It was not thus," wrote Player, "when we drank nothing but sack and claret or English beer and ale."[32]

Convinced that coffeehouses were hotbeds of anti-royal, anti-Anglican sedition, Charles II and his ministers launched a campaign to suppress them. In a letter to parliament (1673) Charles condemned coffeehouses as "pernicious and destructive," places where people "sit half the day, and discourse with all companies that come in of State matters, talking of news and broaching of lies, arraigning the judgments and discretion of their governors, censuring all their actions, and insinuating into the ears of the people a prejudice against them."[33] In 1675, as the earl of Shaftesbury and his Whig followers plotted opposition strategy from their headquarters at John's Coffeehouse in London, the crown issued a proclamation closing the city's coffeehouses. But the measure provoked such a storm of protest, both inside and outside parliament, that the crown was forced to revoke it ten days later.

---

[30] Reprinted in Gwendolen Murphy, ed., *A Cabinet of Characters* (London, 1925), 315–22 (quoted, p. 316).

[31] Quoted in Steve Pincus, "Coffee Politicians Does Create: Coffee Houses and Restoration Political Culture," *Journal of Modern History* 67 (1995), 827.

[32] Quotes taken from Pincus, "Coffee Politicians Does Create," 28, and Allen, "Political Clubs in Restoration London," 570.

[33] Quoted in Aytoun Ellis, *The Penny Universities: A History of the Coffee-House* (London, 1956), 91.

Despite the reputation of Restoration coffeehouses, their political culture was not inherently anti-royalist. As autonomous arenas of political sociability, they were a natural haven for any oppositional group – royalist as well as roundhead, Tory as well as Whig. Oxford, the birthplace of the English coffeehouse, was a royalist stronghold, and coffeehouses had often served as a gathering point for opponents of the Cromwell regime. Hence later, when the earl of Clarendon urged Charles II to suppress coffeehouses, Sir William Coventry reminded him that in Cromwell's time "the King's friends had then used more liberty of speech in these places then they durst in any other."[34] The coffeehouse was bipartisan: as was the case with taverns, politicians and supporters of both parties congregated there. If eighteenth-century Whig politicians met in London coffeehouses like Button's, St. James, and Arthur's, Tories had their network of coffeehouses as well. One of them, the Cocoa Tree, served as the party's London headquarters during the Tories' long period of exclusion from high political office (1715–60).

On the continent, too, coffeehouses developed into politicized spaces of public discussion. As places where affairs of government were dissected and often judged, coffeehouses were antithetical to the absolutist assumption that politics were an arcane realm whose "secrets" should be accessible to no one beyond sovereigns and their ministers. Theodor Johann Quistorp, a friend of the critic and dramatist Gottsched in Leipzig, wrote in 1743:

A coffeehouse is like a political stock exchange, where the most gallant and wittiest heads of every estate come together. They engage in wide-ranging and edifying talk, issue well-founded judgments on matters concerning the political and the scholarly world, converse sagaciously about the most secret news from all courts and states, and unveil the most hidden truths.[35]

As early as 1704, the French visitor Freschot was amazed at the brazen political commentary he heard in Viennese coffeehouses: "without the slightest discretion one discusses not only the conduct of generals and ministers, but even the personal life of the emperor himself." Apparently the tone had changed little by the end of the century, when a police report from 1787 stated that in Viennese coffeehouses one heard "more and more conversations that are as insulting to the sovereign as they are to religion and morals." By this time the coffeehouses of Vienna swarmed with police spies in the hire of Joseph II's notorious police minister, Count

[34] Quoted in *ibid.*, 90.
[35] Quoted in Hans Erich Bödecker, "Das Kaffeehaus als Institution aufklärischer Geselligkeit," in Étienne François, ed., *Sociabilité et société bourgeoise en France, en Allemagne, et en Suisse, 1750–1850* (Paris, 1986), 73.

ohann Anton Pergen. Even the Prussian crown, known for running a
politically tight ship, could not banish political chatter from coffeehouses.
Von Münchow, a Prussian minister in Breslau, complained of subaltern
officials who "dare in the public coffeehouses to speak about royal matters
known to them through their office and to express an opinion on the state
of affairs."[36]

Coffee, capitalism, and the world of learning

Coffeehouses also belonged to the world of commerce, which is another
reason why coffeehouses had become so popular in London by the early
eighteenth century. The decades between 1680 and 1720, when coffeehouses reached the height of their popularity in England, coincided
with the triumph of a commercial and imperial Britain. In an age that
witnessed a rapidly expanding colonial empire, the establishment of the
Bank of England (1694), and the creation of the London Stock Exchange
(1698), the widening circle of individuals with a financial stake in Britain's
imperial expansion fueled a tremendous demand for commercial information. As places where information could be obtained or exchanged,
coffeehouses helped meet this demand. Taverns remained important as
venues for business transactions, but the coffeehouse was particularly well
suited to the speculative and commercial boom of the early eighteenth
century. Unlike alcohol, after all, coffee was a stimulant that induced activity and alertness. The mental stimulation it provided allowed business
to be transacted in a more brisk and efficient manner, an advantage noted
by the anonymous author of *Coffee Houses Vindicated* (1745):

It is grown, by the ill influence of I know not what hydropick stars, almost a
general custom among us, that no bargain can be drove, or business concluded
between man and man, but it must be transacted at some publick-house ... where
continual sippings ... would be apt to fly up into their brains and render them
drowsy and indisposed ... whereas, having now the opportunity of a coffee-house,
they repair thither, take each man a dish or two ... and so, dispatching their
business, go out more sprightly about their affairs, than before.[37]

Investors had to be quick and alert in the stock-jobbing world of Augustan England, where the sudden outbreak of war, the fall of a minister, or a storm at sea could make or break one's fortune. One also
needed ready access to news, and the role of coffeehouses as informational
clearinghouses does much to explain their popularity. The early history

---

[36] Quotes are from Gustav Gugitz, *Das Wiener Kaffeehaus* (Vienna, 1940), 21, 78; *Acta
Borussica. Denkmäler der preussischen Staatsverwaltung im 18. Jahrhundert*, Abteilung 1:
Die Behördenorganisation und die allgemeine Staatsverwaltung Preussens im 18. Jahrhundert,
ed. Preussische Akademie der Wissenschaften (Berlin, 1894–1936), VI/2: 830.

[37] Quoted in Ellis, *The Penny Universities*, 57.

of London coffeehouses was inseparable from that of English journalism, and far more than taverns, the culture of the coffeehouse was literate as well as oral. Coffeehouses throughout Europe usually made newspapers available to their customers. Writing of Parisian cafés in the 1780s, Louis-Sébastien Mercier observed that "the chatter... revolves incessantly around the gazette"; a French visitor to Vienna in 1704 observed that "the city... is full of coffeehouses, where those desiring the latest gossip or newspapers come together, as in other places, to read the gazettes and discuss them with one another." Complaining in 1750 of the "false and wicked newspapers" being sold in Viennese coffeehouses, Maria Theresia prohibited their further sale; when the measure proved ineffective, the prohibition was limited to Sundays and holidays. Joseph II's liberalization of censorship (1781) lifted all restrictions on coffeehouse newspapers, so that Friedrich Nicolai could describe the Viennese coffeehouse in 1781 as a place "filled with large numbers of people reading newspapers." Newspapers were commonly read aloud. In 1733 Zedler's lexicon declared that German coffeehouses provided "an occasion to read or to hear the latest newspapers."[38]

Coffeehouses became important not only for distributing news but collecting it. In Button's Coffee-house in London, the journalist and essayist Joseph Addison installed a letter-box designed by Hogarth in the shape of a lion's head with a large mouth. The box served as a receptacle for any news and information the public might want to contribute to Addison's weekly *Guardian*. By 1729 the connection between coffeehouses and journalism had become so self-evident that London coffeehouse owners petitioned Parliament for a monopoly on the publication of newspapers. Parliament rejected their plan to replace existing newspapers with a "Coffee-house Gazette," but the incident does illustrate how closely the worlds of journalism and the coffeehouse were intertwined. Again, one finds parallels on the continent. The Hamburg *Patriot* (1724–26), which enjoyed the largest circulation of any periodical in Germany, originated in a coffeehouse. It was published by the Hamburg Patriotic Society, whose members met once a week in a local coffeehouse to discuss political, economic, and constitutional issues.

Owing to their role in the collection and dissemination of information, coffeehouses occupied a prominent position in the business culture of Augustan England. The London Stock Exchange originated in Jonathan's Coffeehouse in Change Alley, while Lloyd's of London dated back to 1688, when Edward Lloyd opened a coffeehouse in Tower Street that

---

[38] Quotes are from Louis-Sébastien Mercier, *Tableau de Paris*, 8 vols. (Amsterdam, 1782–83), I:159; Gugitz, *Das Wiener Kaffeehaus*, 21; Friedrich Nicolai, *Beschreibung einer Reise durch Deutschland und die Schweiz im Jahre 1781* (Berlin, 1783), V:236; Zedler, "Caffée-Hauss," V:112.

catered to underwriters in the shipping industry. He also published a newspaper, *Lloyd's News*, which provided his patrons with ships' lists, meteorological reports, and other information useful to shipping interests. England's oldest fire insurance company was established at Tom's, a London coffeehouse, and at some coffeehouses one could even purchase slaves. A 1728 issue of the London *Daily Journal* advertised the sale of a "Negro Boy, aged about 11 years. Inquire at the Virginia Coffee House in Threadneedle Street, behind the Royal Exchange."[39]

Linked as it was with the expanding world of print, the coffeehouse also played a key role in London's expanding literary public sphere. London's moral weeklies (see Chapter 3) drew much of their readership from coffeehouses, many of whose proprietors subscribed to periodicals like the *Tatler* and the *Spectator* in order to lure patrons. The coffeehouse public not only read periodicals but talked about them. At Bedfords's Coffeehouse, wrote the London *Connoisseur* in 1754, "every branch of literature is critically examined, and the merit of every production of the press, or performance at the theaters, weighed and determined." On the continent, too, the coffeehouse functioned as a literary tribunal. Louis-Sébastien Mercier wrote of Parisian literary cafés in the 1780s: "There one judges authors and plays; there one assigns their rank and value."[40] Mercier's observation was accurate in a literal sense, in so far as the actual editing of literary journals sometimes took place in coffeehouses. In Leipzig, for example, the editors of the *Bremer Beyträge* (1745–48) gathered daily in a Leipzig coffeehouse to read, edit, or evaluate submissions. Enlightenment coffeehouses also served as a kind of literary clubhouse, where established authors held court and aspiring young writers sought their patronage. In the Parisian world of letters, successful "networking" in the city's fashionable literary cafés could mean the difference between Grub Street and an academy membership. Youthful writers on the make dreamed of gaining an introduction to Voltaire at the Café Procope, or dropped in regularly at the Café de la Régence in the hopes of meeting Grimm or Rousseau. Haunting the Parisian cafés following his arrival from Besançon in 1751, the eighteen-year-old Jean-Baptiste Suard managed to gain an introduction to the Abbé Raynal at the Café Procope. Raynal, a well-connected *philosophe*, became his chief patron, launching a career that would ultimately include the editorship of the *Gazette de France* and membership in the Academy of Sciences.[41]

Like the salon, the coffeehouse could provide a base of support for one's literary ventures. There an author met with friends and supporters

[39] Quoted in Ellis, *The Penny Universities*, 115.
[40] Quotes taken from *ibid.*, 176; Mercier, *Tableau de Paris*, I:159.
[41] Alan Charles Kors, *D'Holbach's Coterie: An Enlightenment in Paris* (Princeton, 1976), 24–5.

to mobilize acclaim for a forthcoming poem or play, or more insidiously, to poison the reception of a hated rival's work. The theater claques hired to applaud or damn a theatrical piece were often organized in coffeehouses, and the lesser literary cafés of Paris were especially notorious for their cabals. Mercier describes their cutthroat atmosphere:

> Ordinarily the poets who have yet to make their debut are the ones who speak the loudest, along with those whose careers were cut short by catcalls and who are now ordinary satirists. The failed author is always the harshest critic. The cabals, for or against a work, are formed [in the cafés].[42]

Coffeehouse sociability

Contemporary descriptions of coffeehouse society emphasized its inclusiveness. Noting the social heterogeneity of the coffeehouse, Montesquieu observed: "It is an advantage of the coffeehouse that one can sit the entire day as well as night among people from all classes."[43] Coffeehouses were also places where foreigners and natives, visitors and locals, traded news and gossip about the outside world. The out-of-town visitor found the coffeehouse a congenial point of entry into local society. During a visit to Leipzig in 1785, Friedrich Schiller wrote that "up to now my most pleasant pastime has been to visit Richter's Coffeehouse, where I can always find half the Leipzig social world together and can expand my circle of native and foreign acquaintances."[44]

The mood of the coffeehouse, like that of the tavern, was informal and spontaneous. One could enter and leave at any time, and the presence of newspapers provided endless subjects of conversation. The early coffeehouse typically consisted of one room, with a long table where customers were seated on benches. This arrangement served to attenuate distinctions in rank as well as foster conversation. Unlike the tavern, where tempers fueled by drink could flare up at any time, the informality of the coffeehouse was more sedate and hence less threatening to the outsider. Coffeehouse sociability had all the spontaneity of the tavern, with none of its raucousness and violence. Embodying a synthesis of liberty and order, the culture of the eighteenth-century coffeehouse foreshadowed norms later associated with nineteenth-century liberalism and its attendant model of civil society.[45] Coffeehouse conversation was free and unregulated, yet

---

[42] Mercier, *Tableau de Paris*, I:159–60.

[43] Quoted in Heise, *Kaffee und Kaffeehaus*, 127.

[44] Quoted in Bödecker, "Das Kaffeehaus als Institution aufklärischer Geselligkeit," 74.

[45] On this point, see Woodruff D. Smith, "From Coffeehouse to Parlour: The Consumption of Coffee, Tea, and Sugar in North-Western Europe in the Seventeenth and Eighteenth Centuries," in Jordan Goodman, Paul E. Lovejoy, and Andrew Sherrat, eds., *Consuming Habits: Drugs in History and Anthropology* (London and New York, 1995), and Lawrence

also civil and orderly. Unlike taverns, coffeehouses were not associated with crime and violence and they did not require the frequent intervention of the authorities to restore order. In this respect the coffeehouse anticipated the liberal faith that society could function in an orderly way without the constant need for intervention by an authoritarian state.

But like the latter-day liberal state, the coffeehouse was not a democracy. Although visitors often commented on its social openness, there were limits to its inclusiveness. One was sexual: some German cities (e.g., Leipzig in 1704) actually had ordinances that prohibited women from frequenting coffeehouses, and while it was not unknown for a woman to enter a London coffeehouse, the clientele seems to have been largely male. The ribald *Women's Petition against Coffee* (London, 1666?), purportedly a petition by the women of London to close the city's coffeehouses (the actual author is unknown), implied as much in complaining that they kept husbands away from home. Among its other claims, the pamphlet also declared that coffee made husbands impotent and warned that men who frequented coffeehouses "run the hazard of being cuckolded by dildos." On the other hand, Parisian cafés appear to have been less segregated sexually. Women were a common sight in the cafés that lined the boulevards and the Palais-Royal, where the carnivalesque atmosphere that characterized these commercial centers of Parisian entertainment served to relax prevailing gender norms. It was also common for affluent women to frequent more elite and expensive cafés, such as the Procope in Paris or Wiegand's in Vienna. In general, however, most women who drank coffee or tea in the eighteenth century did so at home. Women's teas became common in English bourgeois households during this period, as did the coffee-klatsch (Kaffeekränzchen) among upper-middle-class German housewives.

Another limit to the social mixing that reputedly occurred in coffeehouses was their often specialized clienteles. London proprietors, like tavernkeepers, began to expand their facilities in the early eighteenth century. Rooms were added and individual booths began to replace the open tables. Space within the coffeehouse became more private and intimate even as it expanded, which in turn made the coffeehouse an ideal place to talk business or politics. Often a coffeehouse came to be associated with a particular profession: Nando's was popular with barristers, Child's with clergymen, Jonathan's with stockbrokers, and the New York with colonial merchants. In Paris the Café des Armes d'Espagne was frequented by army officers, the Bourette by men of letters, and the Anglais by actors

Klein, "Coffeehouse Civility, 1660–1714: An Aspect of Post-Courtly Culture in England," *Huntington Library Quarterly* 59 (1996).

and actresses. Hamburg's Dresser Coffeehouse had a chiefly literary clientele, while those in the shipping business gathered at the Tostbrücke. As the century developed, some coffeehouses became private clubs in order to maintain their more elite clientele. In 1764, Tom's Coffeehouse in London became a private club with almost 700 members, each of whom paid an annual subscription fee. White's at first charged a 6 pence admission fee to keep out undesirables, but when this strategem proved insufficient its affluent clientele bought the establishment themselves and hired its former proprietor as their servant. Other London coffeehouses, including political ones like St. James (Whig) and the Cocoa Tree (Tory), had also evolved into exclusive clubs by the late eighteenth century. A similar process appears to have occurred in Germany, where the private club displaced the coffeehouse as a preferred center of elite sociability. In Berlin, for example, the Scholar's Coffeehouse became a club for the members of the Berlin Academy of Sciences; to enter it one had to pay a steep 2 Taler per week. Noting the waning popularity of commercial coffeehouses among the upper classes of northern Germany, the Hanoverian statesman Ernst Brandes claimed that "clubs are the chief reason that public coffeehouses are rarely or not at all visited by the higher ranks (*guter Gesellschaft*)."[46]

Hence coffeehouse society, like other arenas of the Enlightenment public sphere, was not classless. Indeed, in England and Germany it appears to have been more segregated in 1800 than it had been a half century earlier. In France the situation was somewhat different. The convergence of café and tavern as well as the upheavals of the revolutionary era made public drinking in Paris a somewhat special case, though there too, as in England and Germany, tavern drinking would become somewhat declassé in the nineteenth century. Throughout Europe the rise of the temperance movement, modeled on the anti-alcohol associations that became popular in the United States beginning in the 1820s, certainly played a role. Ideals and practices of bourgeois domesticity also contributed to the declining respectability of taverns. The heightened value placed on domestic life, and a general tendency to socialize more selectively and discriminately at home or in private clubs, served to discourage tavern going among the middle classes. For the laboring classes, on the other hand, the importance of taverns as a center of sociability rose in the nineteenth century. This was in part a by-product of the crowded housing conditions wrought by rapid urbanization. The decline of guild associations, around which much of the social life of early modern artisans had been organized,

---

[46] Quoted in Bödecker, "Das Kaffeehaus als Institution aufklärischer Geselligkeit," 79.

also enhanced the significance of the tavern as a venue of working-class sociability.

All in all, then, the sharpened social contours of public drinking that were evident by the early nineteenth century attest the Janus-faced character of the Enlightenment public sphere. In some respects inclusionary, especially where the mixing of middle class and noble were concerned, the public sphere also showed a tendency to delineate sharper cultural boundaries between propertied and unpropertied, educated and uneducated. Chapter 8 will explore this process further.

Bibliographical note
On public drinking from a broader cultural and anthropological perspective, see Mary Douglas's introduction to *Constructive Drinking: Perspectives on Drink from Anthropology* (Cambridge, 1987), and Wolfgang Schivelbusch's engaging if sometimes idiosyncratic *Tastes of Paradise: A Social History of Spices, Stimulants, and Intoxicants* (New York, 1992). For basic information on alcohol consumption in history, see Gregory Austin's *Alcohol in Western Society from Antiquity to 1800: A Chronological History* (Santa Barbara and Austin, 1985).

For English alehouses and taverns, I have relied above all on Peter Clark's *The English Alehouse: A Social History, 1200–1830* (New York, 1983). The political import of taverns in colonial America is examined in David Conroy, *In Public Houses: Drink and the Revolution of Authority in Colonial Massachusetts* (Chapel Hill and London, 1995), and in the earlier chapters of W.T. Rohrbaugh, *The Alcoholic Republic* (New York, 1979). On London coffeehouses, Aytoun Ellis's *The Penny Universities: A History of the Coffee-House* (London, 1956) is semi-scholarly but detailed. Steve Pincus, "Coffee Politicians Does Create: Coffee Houses and Restoration Political Culture," *Journal of Modern History* 67 (1995). On coffeehouse sociability, I have benefited from Lawrence Klein, "Coffeehouse Civility, 1660–1714: An Aspect of Post-Courtly Culture in England," *Huntington Library Quarterly* 59 (1996), and Woodruff Smith, "From Coffeehouse to Parlour: The Consumption of Coffee, Tea, and Sugar in North-Western Europe in the Seventeenth and Eighteenth Centuries," in Jordan Goodman et al., eds., *Consuming Habits: Drugs in History and Anthropology* (London and New York, 1995).

On public drinking in Paris, see Thomas Brennen, *Public Drinking and Popular Culture in Eighteenth-Century Paris* (Princeton, 1988) and W. Scott Haine, *The World of the Paris Café: Sociability among the French Working Class, 1789–1914* (Baltimore and London, 1996); also Thomas Brennen, "Social Drinking in Old Regime Paris," in Susanna Barrows and Robin Room, eds., *Drinking: Behavior and Belief in Modern History* (Berkeley, 1991). Vivid descriptions of Paris's boulevard cafés can be found in Robert M. Isherwood, *Farce and Fantasy: Popular Entertainment in Eighteenth-Century Paris* (New York and Oxford, 1986). Cafés are also discussed in David Garrioch, *Neighborhood and Community in Paris, 1740–1790* (Cambridge, 1986).

On German taverns, see Friedrich Rauers, *Kulturgeschichte der Gaststätte*, 2 vols. (Berlin, 1941); Hasso Spode, *Die Macht der Trunkenheit. Kultur- und Sozialgeschichte des Alkohols in Deutschland* (Opladen, 1993); and R. Sandgruber,

Bittersüsse Genüsse. Kulturgeschichte der Genussmittel (Vienna, 1986). Coffeehouse sociability in Germany is discussed in Hans Erich Bödecker, "Das Kaffeehaus als Institution aufklärischer Geselligkeit," in Étienne François, ed., *Sociabilité et société bourgeoise en France, en Allemagne, et en Suisse, 1750–1850* (Paris, 1986). See also Ulla Heise, *Kaffee und Kaffeehaus. Eine Kulturgeschichte* (Hildesheim, 1987) and Gustav Gugitz, *Das Wiener Kaffeehaus* (Vienna, 1940). On princely efforts to suppress coffee drinking in eighteenth-century Germany, I have consulted Peter Albrecht, "Kaffeetrinken. Dem Bürger zur Ehr' – dem Armen zur Schand," in Rudolf Vierhaus, ed., *Das Volk als Objekt obrigkeitlichen Handelns* (Tübingen, 1992).

8   Freemasonry: toward civil society

Coffeehouses and masonic lodges were similar in important respects. Both flourished first in Great Britain and later spread to the continent. Both were at times associated with sedition, although freemasons repeatedly insisted on the nonpolitical aims of their lodges. And as places where individuals from diverse social and occupational backgrounds intermingled, both tended to dissolve distinctions of rank and foster the more egalitarian style of sociability characteristic of the Enlightenment public sphere. In the process, each contributed to the formation of new social identities distinct from traditional corporate and hierarchical norms of Old Regime society.

Membership in a lodge was voluntary, not ascribed, and was defined by criteria that were independent of the individual's formal legal status. Lodges cut across boundaries of occupation, confession, and class. They created or expanded networks of communication and sociability, and encouraged contacts between individuals from varying social backgrounds and regions. For these and other reasons, scholars like Margaret Jacob have emphasized the ways in which freemasonry anticipated the forms of associational life characteristic of modern civil society. Freemasonry was the first secular, voluntary association ever to have existed on a pan-European scale. It was also the largest, at least in the eighteenth century. In France, for example, freemasons may have comprised as much as 5 percent of the urban, adult male population on the eve of the Revolution.[1] Adolph Freiherr von Knigge, a Hanoverian aristocrat and for a time an important figure in the Illuminati movement (see below), noted in 1788 the spread of masonic lodges and other secret societies in the Holy Roman Empire: "Nowadays one meets few men, regardless of their estate, who have not for at least a time been a member of a secret brotherhood, whether out of a search for knowledge, a need to socialize with others, or sheer curiosity."[2]

[1] Daniel Roche, *La France des lumières* (Paris, 1993), 392.
[2] Knigge, *Über den Umgang mit Menschen* (Hanover, 1788), 382 (in Knigge, *Ausgewählte Werke*, ed. Wolfgang Fenner, Vol. VI).

The cultish, quasi-religious quality of freemasonry seems on the face of it at odds with the norms of accessibility and openness characterizing other institutions and practices of the Enlightenment public sphere. Freemasonry was a secret organization: members swore an oath to uphold the mysteries of their order, and they routinely referred to nonmembers as the "profane." The masonic preoccupation with secrecy appears strangely antithetical to the transparency demanded by enlightened journalists and publicists – all the more so since many of the very writers who condemned the opacity in which absolutist ministers and cabinets shrouded their actions were themselves freemasons, sworn to protect the mysteries of their order.

This paradox points to the ways in which freemasonry looked backward as well as forward. At one level, masonic secrecy and opacity were appropriate to absolutist political cultures where politics was considered an arcane affair understandable only to a privileged few. Not for nothing was the "privy council," with its connotations of secrecy, an administrative fixture of absolutist cabinets. Yet in other respects the masonic cult of secrecy ran counter to the premises of absolutism. By seeking to guard the secrets of their order, masons were not merely protecting a body of esoteric knowledge; they were also claiming a sphere of autonomy *vis-à-vis* the state and its institutions. As the Hamburg founders of the first German lodge declared, secrecy and silence were the armor that shielded them from the profane: "The secrets and the silence are our principal means of self-preservation, and of preserving and strengthening our enjoyment of Masonry."[3] Freemasonry's affirmation of its own inviolability and autonomy expressed an idea that was basic to the emergence of the enlightened public sphere: the idea of civil society as a realm of association whose members defined and asserted their interests separately from the state.

Yet freemasonry was neither politically nor socially inherently subversive. Like the associations of nineteenth-century civil society it foreshadowed, freemasonry spanned a broad political spectrum. English freemasons included Wilkite opponents of crown in the 1760s, but also its loyalist supporters in the 1790s. If many French lodges were passionately republican after 1789, others remained resolutely royalist. If the revolutionary Illuminati in Germany illustrate the radical directions in which freemasonry could develop, the large number of princes and nobles in the empire who joined lodges also shows that freemasonry could be quite compatible with the existing absolutist order. And even where freemasonry fostered modes of sociability that dissolved the boundaries between noble and bourgeois, this blurring of social distinctions was as

---

[3] Quoted in Reinhart Koselleck, *Critique and Crisis: Enlightenment and the Pathogenesis of Modern Society* (Cambridge, Mass., 1988), 73.

apt to reconcile middle-class masons to the society of the Old Regime as it was to alienate them from it. At the very least, freemasonry established new criteria of social distinction that accentuated the gap between the propertied and the unpropertied even while it reduced the distance between the nobility and the middle classes.

The rise of freemasonry

The origins of freemasonry are shrouded in colorful myths dutifully passed down by generations of masons. In their constitution of 1723, English freemasons traced the history of their order back to Prince Edwin, the son of the tenth-century Saxon king Athelstan. Viennese freemasons dated their order back to the Templars, the knightly crusading order of the twelfth century, while other masons claimed the builders of Solomon's temple as their ancestors. Masonic genealogies were sometimes politically colored: in France the more aristocratic lodges linked their origins with Charles I of England and his Stuart descendants, while their less noble counterparts claimed Oliver Cromwell as their founder.

Legends aside, most historians now agree that the masonic lodges which dotted the urban landscape of Enlightenment Europe originated out of the stonemason guilds of seventeenth-century England and Scotland. Master stonemasons were highly skilled craftsmen who had traditionally occupied an elite position within medieval and early modern guilds. They were often prosperous and literate businessmen whose craft demanded a fairly sophisticated knowledge of architecture and engineering. Taking pride in their craft, stonemasons developed over the centuries a rich repository of legends and rituals highlighting their history as the builders of palaces and churches. Their myths and ceremonies also attracted the attention of individuals outside the guild, often gentlemen with esoteric philosophical and scientific interests who saw masonry as a means of gaining access to the wisdom and secrets of the ancients. Around 1700, masonic guilds began to admit these and other fellow travelers as members, so that by the 1720s, for example, fellows of the Royal Society had become a major presence in the London lodges.

As masonic lodges evolved in the early decades of the century from craft guilds into fraternal lodges, they increasingly shed their identity as occupational associations. Out of the roughly one hundred men who belonged to one London lodge in 1730, for example, not a single one was a working stonemason.[4] Lodge membership had by this time expanded to include a high percentage of merchants, who were to become

---

[4] Margaret Jacob, *Living the Enlightenment: Freemasonry in Eighteenth-Century Europe* (New York, 1992), 40.

a core constituency of freemasonry. The geographical mobility of merchants does much to explain freemasonry's appeal to this stratum, in Great Britain as well as on the continent. Lodges gave merchants a social and communicative network that provided valuable support during their extensive travels. For the merchant traveling far from home, the familiarity and camaraderie he found in a lodge helped to ease the loneliness and isolation he otherwise felt as a stranger. No matter what town he visited, he could usually expect a warm reception from his fellow masons. Through his masonic contacts he often received food, lodging, or even credit in the event of a mishap. As one Hamburg freemason observed in 1746, a merchant "can find [financial assistance] from his brothers in the event of an unforeseen misfortune, such as a robbery, a shipwreck, and the like."[5]

Masonic lodges varied in size from ten to fifteen members in the smaller lodges to several hundred in the larger, more established ones. Freemasonry was an urban phenomenon. It flourished not only in major capitals but also in smaller provincial towns, as the statistics below on English freemasonry illustrate (see Table 3):

Table 3 *Freemasonry in England, 1721–1775*

	London lodges	Provincial lodges
1721–25	37	37
1736–40	114	60
1756–60	129	114
1761–65	142	185
1766–70	184	200
1771–75	167	216

Source: John Money, "Freemasonry and the Fabric of Loyalism in Hanoverian England," in Eckhart Hellmuth, ed., *The Transformation of Political Culture: England and Germany in the Late Eighteenth Century* (Oxford, 1991), appendix.

The popularity of London freemasonry reached its peak during the 1760s and leveled off after 1770, while in English provincial towns its growth continued unabated into the nineteenth century.

Freemasonry's urban, mercantile, and geographically mobile base explains how it could spread so swiftly to the rest of Europe. One first finds evidence of a Parisian lodge around 1725, although it is not clear whether

---

[5] Quoted in Norbert Schindler, "Freimaurerkultur im 18. Jahrhundert. Zur sozialen Funktion des Geheimnisses in der entstehenden bürgerlichen Gesellschaft," in *Klassen und Kultur: Sozialanthropologische Perspektiven in der Geschichtsschreibung*, ed. Robert M. Berdahl *et al.* (Frankfurt am Main, 1982), 220.

this was indeed the first established in France. Up to the mid-eighteenth century, at any rate, the earliest and densest concentration of French lodges was not in Paris but Bordeaux, whose international port and commercial ties with England hastened the importation of freemasonry. As in Britain, merchants were heavily represented in French freemasonry and made up a third of its membership.[6] Military officers were also a major presence: "L'Anglaise," the first lodge established in Bordeaux, was founded in 1732 by three British naval officers stationed in the city. Freemasonry appealed to members of the military profession for some of the same reasons it attracted merchants. Highly mobile, transferred from one urban garrison to another with relative frequency, officers appreciated the ready-made social life and friendship networks that freemasonry supplied.

Official hostility, political as well as ecclesiastical, at first impeded the spread of French masonry. The ministry of Cardinal Fleury (1726–43) distrusted freemasonry as a subversive English import, while Pope Clement XII's condemnation of the order in 1738 rendered the movement suspect in the eyes of the church. During this period freemasonry was officially banned and police routinely raided lodge meetings. By the 1750s, however, freemasonry had acquired respectability as lodges multiplied throughout Paris and French provincial capitals. Seventy new lodges were established in France between 1750 and 1759, another 182 were founded during the 1770s, and by 1789 there were an estimated 600 lodges in the monarchy. In 1770 Paris alone had some 10,000 freemasons, and by the eve of the Revolution the masonic population for the monarchy as a whole was somewhere between 50,000 and 100,000.[7]

The first lodge in German-speaking Europe was founded in a Hamburg tavern in 1737. Here as in France, connections with England proved decisive: Hamburg enjoyed close commercial ties with England, and the lodge was founded under the aegis of the London Grand Lodge. (The tavern where the first Hamburg masons met was named, appropriately enough, "The English Tavern.") From Hamburg the order spread to other cities of the empire, where (excluding Austria) some 450 lodges were founded between 1737 and 1789. Berlin, where forty-three lodges cropped up between 1740 and 1781, became an important center of German freemasonry and the seat of its umbrella organization, the Grosse Landesloge.[8] In 1738 Crown Prince Frederick of Prussia (later Frederick

---

[6] Daniel Roche, *Le siècle des lumières en province: académies et académiciens provinciaux, 1680–1789*, 2 vols. (Paris, 1978), I:265–67.

[7] Figures taken from *ibid.*, II:257, and Jacob, *Living the Enlightenment*, 74, 205.

[8] Winfried Dotzauer, "Zur Sozialstruktur der Freimauerei in Deutschland," in Helmut Reinalter, ed., *Aufklärung und Geheimgesellschaften: zur politischen Funktion und Sozialstruktur der Freimauerlogen im 18. Jahrhundert* (Munich, 1989), 110; Horst Möller,

the Great) joined a lodge, an event that helped make freemasonry not just respectable but positively fashionable among nobles throughout the empire. Frederick was introduced to freemasonry during a visit to the Rhineland in 1738, when Count Albrecht Wolfgang of Schaumberg-Lippe aroused his interest in the order. The count, the first German mason whose actual identity is known to historians (he became a member around 1723), then personally arranged for Frederick's induction. The following year Frederick himself founded a lodge in the Prussian town of Rheinsberg. His involvement with freemasonry was relatively brief, and his interest in the order quickly faded following the outbreak of the Silesian wars in 1740. Frederick's flirtation with freemasonry has been viewed as a latent act of rebellion against his tyrannical father, Frederick William I, who disapproved of the order. Freemasonry may also have facilitated the crown prince's break with organized religion, and probably also strengthened the tolerant attitudes that later became the hallmark of his religious policies.

Freemasonry also took root in the territories of Frederick's archrival, Maria Theresia of Austria. The Habsburg ruler had been hostile to the order since the papal condemnation of 1738, although her husband, Francis of Lorraine, became a mason in 1731. Her son and successor, Joseph II, also joined a lodge and encouraged the movement during the first part of his reign. By 1784 there were sixty-six lodges in the monarchy, eight of them in Vienna. In a move symbolic of Austro-Prussian rivalry, Austrian masons seceded from the Berlin-centered Grosse Landesloge in 1784 and formed their own national lodge.[9]

Inclusion and exclusion

In her wide-ranging and stimulating study of British, Dutch, and French freemasonry, Margaret Jacob argued that masonic lodges served as a conduit for the diffusion of British political culture on the continent. "By their own admission and by their meeting records," she writes, "the European lodges emerge as societies organized around British constitutional principles, around elections, majority rule, and representative government."[10] The analogies between masonic organization and British constitutional principles are indeed striking. Masons referred to the rules of their lodges as "constitutions," and proto-parliamentary themes pervaded masonic

"Enlightened Societies in the Metropolis: The Case of Berlin," in Eckhart Hellmuth, ed., *The Transformation of Political Culture: England and Germany in the Late Eighteenth Century* (Oxford, 1991) 222–23; Norbert Schindler, "Freimaurerkultur," 208.

[9] Edith Rosenstrauch-Königsberg, *Zirkel und Zentren: Aufsätze zur Aufklärung in Österreich am Ende des 18. Jahrhunderts* (Vienna, 1993), 259–60.

[10] Jacob, *Living the Enlightenment*, 15.

texts and rituals. In electing their officers and members, masons practiced the principle of majority rule. In debating issues of membership and lodge organization, they learned how to speak in public or listen tolerantly while others did the same. In imposing fines on members who used foul language or who drank to excess, freemasonry inculcated civility and decorum in its members. Masons learned how to take minutes on debates, keep records of meetings, and pay "taxes" in the form of lodge dues. Such obvious parallels between masonic practices and those of parliamentary regimes also point to freemasonry as an antecedent of modern political parties.

There was also a distinctly egalitarian tone to masonic sociability and ceremony. Masonic meetings, where titles were dropped and members referred to each other as "brother," suspended differences in social rank. Initiation ceremonies were similarly egalitarian in their implications. Norbert Schindler has described how in certain German ceremonies of induction, the (male) initiate's jewelry was removed along with any clothing outside of the shirt and pants. His left arm was then removed from the shirt, exposing the breast as far down as the heart. Here the ceremony symbolically stripped away the accidents of birth, rank, and privilege to disclose the universal humanity the initiate shared with his brothers. Joseph Sonnenfels, a freemason and a leading figure of the Austrian Enlightenment, invoked this image of removal, of stripping away, when he wrote in 1784 that "at the threshold of our temple the prince puts aside his crown, the noble dispenses of his rank, and within our fraternal circles they rejoice in their humanity." A German mason asserted in 1744 that "as soon as we are all assembled, we are all brothers ... Prince and subject, noble and burgher, rich and poor, each is as good as the other. Nothing distinguishes one from the other, nothing separates them, all are equal in their virtue."[11]

As with other institutions of the Enlightenment public sphere, however, exclusionary practices could belie the egalitarian language. Masonic lodges were predominantly male in composition and in Great Britain women were banned from becoming members altogether. One obstacle to the admission of women was the masonic requirement that a member be independent in status. The masonic constitution of 1723 declared that a mason had to be "his own master," subject to no lord, and some masonic writers considered a woman's state of subjection in marriage to be incompatible with this autonomy. As one French mason put it in 1769, "The first quality of a mason is to be free, and liberty is never

---

[11] Quotes taken from Rosenstrauch-Königsberg, *Zirkel und Zentren*, 285, and Schindler, "Freimaurerkultur," 210.

the allotment of women."[12] As seen in Chapter 6, some have viewed the growing popularity of freemasonry in late eighteenth-century France as a masculinist reaction against the cultural influence exercised by women in Enlightenment salons. It has been argued that even where women were allowed to join the order, as in the so-called lodges of adoption, their role was passive and marginal. Salon women had stood at the center of Enlightenment culture; in the lodge they moved to the periphery.

Janet M. Burke and Margaret Jacob have challenged this contrast between an earlier, female-centered salon culture and the male-centered world of French freemasonry. Not only were French lodges distinctive in their occasional admission of women, a practice that dated from the 1740s and spread as the century developed; women, far from occupying a marginal and subordinate position in mixed lodges, acquired an increasingly prominent role in masonic organization and ritual. By the 1770s mixed lodges were led by a grand mistress as well as a grand master, both of whose presence was required at meetings. Female masons participated in the election of officers, and a part of the ritual noted the error lodges had made in excluding women from membership. The ritual of one adoptive lodge enjoined "sisters" to emancipate themselves from male domination by studying the natural sciences. In the last quarter of the eighteenth century, mixed lodges also began to employ in their rituals images of women who were anything but passive: Judith was invoked, as was the queen of the Amazons. Hence the mixed lodge did not end but sustained the kind of female participation in Enlightenment culture that the salon represented. Indeed, Jacob and Burke viewed the mixed lodge as a forerunner of the women's republican clubs that emerged in the early years of the French Revolution. Already in the 1780s, in fact, some mixed lodges had become outspoken advocates of sexual equality and defended the right of women to higher education and even to bear arms.

Although these examples serve to qualify views of freemasonry as inveterately masculinist, there is little question that the vast majority of European lodges were male in composition. Masonic membership was socially circumscribed as well. Freemasonry was in practice the preserve of the propertied, and while well-to-do artisans were not uncommon, the unskilled laborer was relatively rare. Literacy, a formal prerequisite for membership in a lodge, was doubtless one obstacle to plebeian membership. Another was the initiation fee and membership dues masons were required to pay. Induction into an English lodge, for example, cost several pounds, while dues came to several shillings a month. The silk and taffeta robes worn by masons were also costly, as were the frequent, sometimes

---

[12] Quoted in Jacob, *Living the Enlightenment*, 136.

sumptuous banquets they held. Taken as a whole, these incidental expenses required a level of disposable income well beyond what the laboring poor could have afforded. At a deeper level, the masonic conviction that only the individual who was "his own master" possessed the moral and legal autonomy necessary for membership militated against the membership of economically dependent wage earners. This belief prefigured arguments employed by liberals in the nineteenth century to justify confining the franchise to those with sufficient property to be independent.

In the British case, the social profile of eighteenth-century freemasons did in fact coincide with that of the "political nation," the roughly 20 percent of adult males who owned sufficient property to vote. Membership lists from early eighteenth-century British lodges show a diverse lot – merchants, fellows of the Royal Society, journalists, Whig aristocrats, government ministers – but the possession of property and education was common to them all. The same was true in France, where the social composition of lodges ranged from bourgeois merchants, bankers, lawyers, and officials to noble officers and aristocrats. Statistics show that 15 percent of the members in provincial lodges were nobles, 36 percent were merchants, bankers and manufacturers, and 33 percent bourgeois officials, lawyers, and architects.[13] This noble–bourgeois mixture also characterized German and Austrian freemasonry, although nobles appear to have been more heavily represented than in Great Britain or France. Of the 111 members who made up the Viennese lodge "Crowned Hope" (Zur gekrönten Hoffnung) in 1780, 65 were nobles; of that number more than a quarter were counts, members of the upper nobility. A breakdown of membership in another prominent Viennese lodge, "True Concord" (Zur wahren Eintracht), from 1783 shows a similarly high proportion of nobles:[14]

lords (upper nobility)	15 percent
knights (lower nobility)	40 percent
teachers, professors, officials	32 percent
clergy	8 percent
other	5 percent

In smaller states of the empire like Bayreuth, Weimar, or Braunschweig-Lüneburg-Wolfenbüttel, the territorial prince himself took the lead in establishing a lodge. In those cases a lodge was almost indistinguishable

[13] Statistics are from Jacob, Living the Enlightenment, 47–48, and Roche, Le siècle des lumières en province, I:265–67.

[14] Eva Huber, "Zur Sozialstruktur der Wiener Freimaurerlogen im josephinischen Jahrzehnt," in Reinalter, ed., Aufklärung und Geheimgesellschaften, 175–79.

from the prince's court, with masonic ritual serving as a variant of court
ceremonial.

Even as freemasonry fostered an egalitarian, meritocratic spirit among
its noble and bourgeois members, it could also underscore the distance
between these groups and those lower down the social scale. As mentioned earlier, the spread of freemasonry in eighteenth-century Paris was
tied to changes in middle-class sociability that enabled the Parisian bourgeoisie to create horizontal, city-wide ties. By contributing to the formation of these new and more extended social networks, masonic lodges
enabled the Parisian middle class to distance itself from the local forms
of sociability oriented toward street and neighborhood. In the process,
middle-class masons constructed a social identity that defined itself negatively *vis-à-vis* the less propertied and educated.[15] Further attesting to
the social and cultural distance that could separate masons from the lower
classes were the so-called "mock-masons" of London, rabble-rousing plebeians in the 1740s who disrupted the solemn processions organized by
regular lodges. Led by a "grand master" perched astride a donkey, mock-
masons marched in counter-processions that travestied masonic ritual.
When a 1744 procession ended in brawling and arrests, London masons
discreetly decided to curtail their public processions.

Mozart's *Magic Flute*, perhaps the most renowned masonic work ever
produced, also illustrates the social divide that separated freemasonry and
plebeian culture. Mozart and Emanuel Schickaneder (the author of the
libretto) were both masons, although Schickaneder's Regensburg lodge
expelled him for his allegedly disreputable behavior. Many in the audience
who attended the Vienna premier of the opera in 1791 were undoubtably
masons as well. They would have recognized Sarastro, the High Priest of
the Temple of Wisdom, as a masonic master, and his consecrated band
as a lodge. *The Magic Flute* is packed with masonic symbols and themes,
and since choral singing was an integral part of lodge sociability (masonic
choirs have been credited with popularizing the musical refrain), it was
fitting that Mozart made freemasonry the subject of his *Singspiel*.

The behavior of Tamino, the princely hero of the opera, and of Papageno, his servant, illuminates the social parameters of freemasonry. At
the opening of Act II, Sarastro and his followers debate whether Tamino,
who is of royal birth, is sufficiently virtuous to endure the trials necessary
for his initiation. "Consider well!" warns one priest: "He is a prince!" To
this Sarastro replies, "More than that! He is a man!" For the High Priest
Sarastro, the question of Tamino's birth is irrelevant; what is important

---

[15] David Garrioch, *Neighborhood and Community in Paris 1740–1790* (Cambridge, 1986),
    180, 202–8.

is his intrinsic merit as a man. Tamino then embarks on a series of initiatory ordeals and is accompanied by his servant, Papageno, who is also to undergo the trials of induction. Papageno was modeled on the figure of Hanswurst, the comic figure of the Viennese stage whose plebeian ways were pointedly and often humorously contrasted with those of his social betters. Here the respective attitudes of Tamino and Papageno toward their impending ordeal typify this contrast. When the priests ask Tamino, "Thou wilt undergo every ordeal?", the prince replies without hesitation: "Every one!" But when the priests then turn to the plebeian Papageno and ask, "Wilt thou also do battle for wisdom's love?", the servant hesitates: "Fighting's not for me. Really and truly, I yearn not after wisdom!" "I'm a simple man; sleep, food and drink are enough for me; if I could only get me a woman . . . " The needs of Tamino and Papageno are clearly of a different order. One yearns for wisdom and love, the other for the fulfillment of his simple sensual desires. Both survive their ordeals and win the object of their love, as Tamino rejoins his beloved Tamina and Papageno finally wins his Papagena. But only Tamino is granted the priestly vestments of membership in the Temple, only he is capable of Wisdom. Wisdom is beyond the reach of his affable but simple-minded servant, who is too dominated by his material and sensual needs to ascend to a higher cultural plane.

Here *The Magic Flute* depicted the social and cultural gulf that distinguished freemasons from the laboring classes. Freemasonry, like other institutions of the Enlightenment public sphere, was a meritocracy, but it was a meritocracy of the propertied and educated. While blurring the distinctions between noble and bourgeois, it accentuated differences between the educated and noneducated, literate and illiterate, cultured and uncultured. In this respect, freemasonry was simultaneously egalitarian and elitist.

Freemasonry and politics

This side of freemasonry must be kept in mind in light of a long historiographical tradition that has viewed freemasonry as a proto-democratic, egalitarian, and even revolutionary movement. The earliest example of this interpretation was the Jesuit Abbé de Barruel's anti-masonic history of the French Revolution (1787), which interpreted 1789 as the product of a masonic plot. Conspiracy theories surrounding the masons or their offshoots (e.g., the German Illuminati) have continued to flourish since Barruel's day, partly because the oath of secrecy sworn by freemasons tended to breed them, and partly because nineteenth-century conspiratorial movements like the Carbonari in Italy and the Decembrists

in Russia did in fact model themselves on freemasonry. Although professional historians have generally tended to dismiss these theories as the
work of crank amateurs, more recent scholars have reaffirmed the relationship between freemasonry and the democratic revolutions of the later
eighteenth century. Building on the earlier work of the Catholic royalist historian Augustin Cochin, François Furet saw the abstract moralism
and egalitarianism of freemasonry as foreshadowing the Jacobin quest for
ideological purity and unity, while Margaret Jacob emphasized freemasonry's contribution to the formation of a liberal-democratic political
culture. Furet and Jacob differ in their interpretations – the former emphasizes the Jacobin legacy of freemasonry, the latter its liberal and constitutional one – but both see freemasonry as fundamentally antagonis-
tic to the traditional social and political structures of the Old Regime.
Furet described the organizational and ideological parallels between the
lodges of the Old Regime and the post-1789 Jacobin clubs, while Jacob
noted how the language of freemasonry anticipated the constitutional
rhetoric of 1789. The Austrian Grand Lodge used distinctly constitutional language in its charter of 1784: "Masonry, in its constitution
as well in the relationship between the individual lodges, is a democratic union and each lodge is a democracy."[16] Prescribing a multina-
tional structure that granted official recognition to the provincial lodges
of Austria, Hungary, Transylvania, Galicia, Bohemia, and Lombardy,
this constitution envisioned the sort of federalist solution that moderate
liberals in the Habsburg monarchy would champion in the nineteenth
century.

But to highlight these dimensions of freemasonry risks taking a somewhat teleological view of its history. If, instead of viewing 1789–93 or
1848 as the *terminus ad quem* of freemasonry, one disjoins the order from
the liberal and democratic movements that followed it, freemasonry appears less subversive of the existing order. Freemasonry looked to the
past as well as to the future, and its ceremonial, hierarchical, and mystical elements were deeply embedded in the symbolic universe of the
Old Regime. On the continent, at least, masonic secrecy was in some
ways the natural outgrowth of an absolutist political culture in which
politics was deemed an arcane and necessarily secret affair. The Janus-
faced character of freemasonry is especially evident in its quasi-religious
features. Lodges had much in common with traditional religious orders
and confraternities: they provided their members with conviviality, hospitality, mutual aid in times of need, and an outlet for charitable work.

---

[16] Quoted in Helmut Reinalter, "Freimauerei und Demokratie im 18. Jahrhundert," in
Reinalter, ed., *Aufklärung und Geheimgesellschaften*, 43.

Their elaborate ceremonies and esoteric symbolism provided a sense of spiritual solemnity and mystery. Like a church, freemasonry fostered in its members the belief that they enjoyed access to a higher wisdom denied to the "profane." Part of freemasonry's appeal lay in its ability to bridge the secular and sacred, filling the void left among those whose attachment to organized religion had waned. Thus Maurice Agulhon has linked the rise of freemasonry in eighteenth-century Provence to the decline of Counter-Reformation lay confraternities, which local office-holders and merchants increasingly abandoned to join masonic lodges. In the Habsburg monarchy, where numerous ex-Jesuits entered lodges following the dissolution of their order in 1773, one finds a similar relationship between the waning of the Counter Reformation and the rise of freemasonry. In these instances freemasonry occupied an intermediate position between the lay organizations and religious orders traditionally sanctioned by the Catholic Church, and the more secular voluntary clubs and societies associated with an emerging civil society.

The transitional nature of freemasonry also explains its ability to attract both noble and bourgeois adherents. Especially on the continent, as we have seen, nobles made up a sizable proportion of lodge membership. What attracted them to freemasonry? One answer is the fact that despite its egalitarian features, freemasonry had its own hierarchy with internal gradations in some ways redolent of Old Regime distinctions of rank. The rungs of the masonic ladder were "degrees," and advancement from one to another was marked by a formal ceremony that bestowed honor and status on the recipient. The master of a lodge was installed in ceremonies that imitated elevation to knighthood or the coronation of a king. At the same time, however, masonic hierarchy was based on principles fundamentally different from those of the Old Regime. Status was acquired, not ascribed: masons advanced from a lower to a higher degree through service to the order and mastery of its secrets, not by virtue of social rank. In this regard freemasonry was indeed meritocratic in its implications, since distinction within the order rested on service rather than birth.

This blend of hierarchy and meritocracy could appeal to disparate elements within the nobility. With its hierarchical structure, arcane symbols and emblems, and elaborate rituals and processions, freemasonry evoked the aristocratic "representational publicness" of the Old Regime. But its meritocratic ethos of service at the same time resonated on the continent among an expanding stratum of bureaucratic nobles who owed their titles to state service and not to their blood-lines. For nobles of older lineage, on the other hand, masonic membership was a mark of moral and cultural merit that could complement and bolster claims to nobility based on birth. Such a distinction was all the more desirable in a century when the spread of luxury, once a visible index of noble status, had made it increasingly difficult to divine or exhibit nobility of birth through outward dress.

Finally, this blend of hierarchical and meritocratic norms gave freemasonry a social and ideological elasticity that enabled it to bridge the worlds of noble and bourgeois. This synthesis was not always a stable one, and it sometimes unraveled in the face of conflicts over admission to or advancement within the order. Resentment toward the gentry-dominated Grand Lodge in London led to a schism (1751) in English freemasonry, when the "Ancients," a network of lodges whose members came more from the middling ranks of society, seceded to form their own organization. In France, too, freemasonry was occasionally rent by social divisions. After 1770, the aristocratic leadership of the Grand Lodge in Paris was periodically embroiled in disputes with local lodges over admission policies and the awarding of higher degrees.[17] Social tensions within German freemasonry also existed. After the mid-eighteenth century, the branch of freemasonry known as the Strict Observance began to make its way into Germany from France.[18] Observant lodges were more esoteric and mystical in their rituals than the other, more rationalistic forms of masonry borrowed from Great Britain that had up to then prevailed in Germany. Observant lodges claimed to have originated as a knightly order and not as a guild (they traced their origins back to the Templars), and their internal hierarchy was more calibrated (Observants created additional degrees of advancement). Hence some scholars have attributed the spread of Observant lodges to a "refeudalization" of German freemasonry, an attempt to establish more hierarchy and social differentiation within the order.[19]

Although it is tempting to view these developments as harbingers of revolutions to come, one should not overinterpret the internecine struggles that afflicted eighteenth-century freemasonry. These conflicts were often occasioned by personal rivalries, and were to some extent inevitable given freemasonry's relatively loose organizational structure. Moreover, too great a focus on lodges as a site of class conflict obscures the repeated claims by masonic writers of the period that freemasonry served to dissolve – not widen – the social and cultural boundaries between noble and bourgeois. Andreas Georg Friedrich Rebmann, a German freemason, wrote that the order "succeeded in removing, at least within its

[17] Jacob, *Living the Enlightenment*, 60–62, 184, 203–14.
[18] See Ludwig Hammermayr, *Der Wilhelmsbader Freimaurer-Konvent von 1782* (Wolfenbütteler Studien zur Aufklärung, V/2, 1980), 9–20.
[19] See, for example, Manfred Agethen, *Geheimbund und Utopie: Illuminaten, Freimauerer und deutsche Spätaufklärung* (Munich, 1984), 65–66.

fraternal circle, the walls which cold etiquette and convention constructed to separate individuals from each other, and in accepting human beings purely as human beings."[20] There is no reason to assume that the middle-class mason who mixed on an equal footing with his aristocratic brother would thereby have favored the abolition of rank and privilege. Indeed, socializing with those of a higher station may have made the formal distinctions of rank more tolerable to the non-noble. The Austrian mason and *Aufklärer* Joseph Sonnenfels, himself the son of a Jewish businessman who had converted to Catholicism, suggested as much in a 1784 essay. Through the intermingling of noble and bourgeois that occurred in lodges, wrote Sonnenfels, "he who holds a lower rank is accorded a kind of compensation that maintains his spirits and helps him bear with equanimity differences in estate, rank, and fortune."[21] Had freemasonry been inherently revolutionary, it is doubtful whether it would have attracted so many aristocrats, high officials (like Sonnenfels), clergy, and others with a stake in the existing social and political order.

In the case of Great Britain, it is hard to deem subversive an organization that the Church of England viewed with approval. The influx of Anglican clergy into lodges after the 1750s attests to freemasonry's social and political respectability. To be sure, British freemasonry was not immune to the surge of popular radicalism wrought by John Wilkes and his supporters in the 1760s. The schism of 1751, when the "Ancients" broke with the gentry-dominated Grand Lodge to form their own national organization, had in fact foreshadowed Wilkes's movement as a symptom of the growing political dissatisfaction of small merchants and tradesmen who felt disenfranchised by a closed and corrupt parliamentary regime. When the participation of freemasons in the campaign to seat Wilkes in Parliament threatened to belie the order's avowed abstention from politics, some masonic leaders began to express their alarm. In 1769, for example, a Newcastle freemason warned his brothers that "riot and disorder cannot correct errors that arise in government."[22] During the 1770s, leaders of both branches of English freemasonry sought to distance their organization from the popular radicalism of the previous decade. Their efforts may explain the attrition in membership suffered by London lodges during this decade, when attempts by masonic leaders to depoliticize the order might have driven its more radical members out of freemasonry and into more overtly political clubs and associations. At any rate, by the 1790s English freemasonry had become thoroughly

---

[20] Quoted in *ibid.*, 57.
[21] Quoted in Rosenstrauch-Königsberg, *Zirkel und Zentren*, 285.
[22] Quoted in Jacob, *Living the Enlightenment*, 62.

domesticated. The rhetoric of liberty and brotherhood that had hitherto dominated the language of the movement gave way to a conspicuously patriotic discourse, one that stressed respect for national tradition and loyalty to church and king.[23] By 1800 almost all members of the royal family were masons, and the Prince of Wales himself served as a grand master from 1790 to 1813. Here the loyalist tone of British freemasonry mirrored more broadly the patriotic mood that pervaded British political culture at the end of the eighteenth century.

As for German and Austrian freemasonry, one must likewise doubt the alleged subversiveness of an order whose members included Frederick the Great, the Austrian Emperor Francis I, or the Elector Karl Theodor of Bavaria. Freemasonry in the Holy Roman Empire was an integral part of Enlightenment culture, which had to a large extent developed within the institutional framework of territorial absolutism. Accordingly, German and Austrian freemasons accommodated themselves to the goals and language of enlightened absolutism with relative ease. The masonic ethos of service, which neatly dovetailed with enlightened absolutist conceptions of the ruler as "the first servant of the state" (Frederick the Great), helped ease the process of adaptation. An anonymous mason expressed this convergence of masonic and absolutist ideals of service when he declared in the *Berlinische Monatschrift* (1786): "Whoever fails to serve the state and the king with loyalty and sincerity, whoever violates one's sacred duties as a member of mankind, as a citizen, as a spouse, or as a father...is an unworthy mason."[24] That Prussian lodges commonly named themselves after Frederick II (a Königsberg chapter founded in 1769 called itself "Frederick's Golden Scepter") was telling evidence of masonic royalism, as was the substantial proportion of princely officials in lodges throughout the empire.

The 1780s witnessed a proliferation of other secret societies throughout the empire, some of them secessionist offshoots of freemasonry, which were deeply mystical in outlook and represented a reaction against the rationalism of the late Enlightenment. The most prominent of these was the Rosicrucians, a pansophical, alchemical sect claiming miraculous powers of healing along with the ability to transmute base metals into gold. Arising in southern Germany around 1760, the Rosicrucians gained a brief ascendancy at the Berlin court following the death of Frederick II in 1786. Two of their number, Johann Rudolf von Bischoffswerder and Johann Christian Wöllner (both of whom had attained high degrees in

---

[23] John Money, "Freemasonry and the Fabric of Loyalism in Hanoverian England," in Hellmuth, ed., *The Transformation of Political Culture*, 262–64.

[24] Quoted in Rüdiger Hachtmann, "Friedrich II. von Preussen und die Freimaurerei," *Historische Zeitschrift* (1997), 48.

Berlin freemasonry), became leading advisors to Frederick William II.
As friends of the young crown prince, Bischoffswerder and Wöllner had
persuaded Frederick William to join the Rosicrucians in 1781. Following
his accession they embarked on a campaign to tighten censorship and
purge the church of rationalist theologians. These efforts culminated in
Wöllner's Edict on Religion (1788), signed by the king, which attempted
to impose stricter standards of orthodoxy on Prussian Protestant clergy.

Despite this brief period of influence, Rosicrucianism proved little more
than a passing fad and by 1800 the order had faded into obscurity. But it
illustrates the ability of freemasonry to bear progeny that were anything
but revolutionary or even "liberal." In the nineteenth century Prussian
freemasonry itself became a conservative force, a shift already evident in
1833 when Frederick William III praised masons as his most loyal subjects. During the Berlin Revolution of 1848, the counter-revolutionary,
ultraconservative "Loyal Alliance with God for King and Fatherland"
(*Treubund mit Gott für König und Vaterland*) was modeled organizationally on freemasonry and included prominent Prussian masons among its
members.

By its very nature, however, the secretive character of freemasonry and
its offshoots in the empire could arouse official distrust or outright pro-
scription. The Illuminati were a notable example. The Illuminati order
was founded in 1776 by Adam Weishaupt, a professor of law at the University of Ingolstadt and a former Jesuit. The aims of the Illuminati, unlike
those of freemasonry, were avowedly political. Their admittedly vague
program envisioned the establishment of a utopian world order without
states or rulers. The Illuminati hoped to bring about this transformation
not through revolutionary upheaval – conspiracy theories to the contrary,
Weishaupt himself was an opponent of the French Revolution – but by assuming strategically important positions in the absolutist state. This was
to entail a gradual process of moral education and improvement in which
members of the society slowly gained control over the highest positions in
the state, the church, schools, and universities. Here the Illuminati bore
more resemblance to the Jesuits, Weishaupt's former colleagues, than
to freemasonry. The society in fact enjoyed its greatest influence in the
Catholic territories of Austria and Bavaria, where it managed to attract in
a remarkably short time the support of prominent figures in government.
Ten of the twelve councillors on the Bavarian censorship commission
belonged to the society in 1780, and in the Habsburg monarchy members likely included Joseph Sonnenfels and Gottfried van Swieten, the
minister of education and censorship.[25] Just how seriously one should

[25] Agathen, *Geheimbund und Utopie*, 335; Rosenstrauch-Königsberg, *Zirkel und Zentren*,
146.

take the participation of such high-level governmental figures is difficult to say, nor is it clear whether their involvement was a matter of serious engagement or simply a momentary fad. In any case the Illuminati never had more than a thousand or so members, and the autocratic structure of the organization soon disillusioned many erstwhile adherents. The Illuminati had none of freemasonry's democratic features. Officers were not elected but appointed by the head of the order, who was unknown to most of its members. The clandestine character of the society, as well as its professed goal of creating a cosmopolitan republic, fueled fears and rumors of subversion that ultimately led the Bavarian elector to outlaw the organization in 1784.

In the Habsburg monarchy, mainline freemasonry would also be suppressed on account of fears aroused by its secretive nature. The Habsburg ruler, Joseph II, originally sympathetic to freemasonry, eventually tightened his government's supervision over the order. Joseph's reversal was largely due to concerns that freemasonry's international orientation jeopardized the secrecy of his foreign policy, especially since so many government officials were masons. His freemasonry patent (1785) tightened surveillance over the order by prohibiting the establishment of lodges outside of Vienna and provincial capitals, and by permitting no more than three lodges in each city. Lodges also had to report to the authorities the time and place of their meetings, as well as submit their membership lists. These measures struck at the heart of masonic secrecy, and although some masons hailed the patent as a means of halting the proliferation of unauthorized lodges, Joseph's patent had a chilling effect on the organization. Within a year the number of masons in Vienna fell from 706 to 547.[26] As governmental fears of conspiracy and subversion mounted with the accession of the archconservative Francis II in 1792, freemasonry became even more politically suspect. The discovery of a Jacobin "plot" in 1794 seemed to confirm government anxiety when it was discovered that several of the accused were also freemasons. The investigation exposed only a few dozen conspirators, most of whom were guilty of little more than loose (and sometimes drunken) talk or indiscreet renditions of the *Marseillaise*. A recent treatment concludes that "most were not Jacobins at all, but merely frustrated Josephinians."[27] Indeed, one is tempted to view the conspiracy as largely the invention of a frightened government intent on launching a broader campaign of repression. Be that as it may, the fact that a clandestine group of Innsbruck conspirators modeled their

---

[26] Eva Huber, "Zur Sozialstruktur der Wiener Logen im josephinischen Jahrzehnt," in Reinalter, ed., *Aufklärung und Geheimgesellschaften*, 186; Rosenstrauch-Königsberg, *Zirkel und Zentren*, 20, and, *Freimaurerei im josephinischen Wien: Aloys Blumauers Weg vom Jesuiten zum Jakobiner* (Vienna and Stuttgart, 1975), 59–64.

[27] Charles Ingrao, *The Habsburg Monarchy 1618–1815* (Cambridge, 1994), 225.

organization on a masonic lodge, or that Andreas Riedel's circle of French sympathizers called itself a "substitute lodge" (*Logenersatz*), was enough to persuade Francis II to outlaw freemasonry in 1794.

These connections do suggest the ways in which masonic organizational structures could be employed as a vehicle of opposition, however tame. The point is not to deny such connections, but rather to emphasize that freemasonry was a protean form of association that could be appropriated for very different political ends. Its social and ideological elasticity enabled freemasonry to accommodate a broad spectrum of political attitudes, ranging from royalist celebrations of absolute monarchy to Jacobin assaults on it. Even in France, the link between freemasonry and revolution is more ambiguous than Augustin Cochin once contended. In revolutionary Toulouse about a third of the 250 individuals who can be identified as freemasons were of royalist sympathies, and there were Parisian lodges that were hostile to the Revolution from its very inception.[28] To the extent that one can establish a statistical correlation between masonic affiliation and membership in revolutionary clubs, the results are skewed by the large segment of French urban society in general that belonged to lodges on the eve of the Revolution. By 1793 at any rate, many lodges (including the Grand Lodge, one of the two national masonic organizations) had stopped meeting. After 1789, pro-revolutionary masons had tended to desert their lodges to join more overtly political clubs and associations, and with the growing radicalization of the Revolution, freemasonry came to be viewed with suspicion owing to the aristocratic leadership of many lodges.

Bibliographical note
On masonic lodges and their importance in eighteenth-century political culture, Margaret Jacob's *Living the Enlightenment: Freemasonry in Eighteenth-Century Europe* (New York, 1992) is a tour de force that covers France and Holland as well as Britain. Like Jacob, Reinhart Koselleck's *Critique and Crisis: Enlightenment and the Pathogenesis of Modern Society* (Cambridge, Mass., 1988) emphasizes freemasonry's role in the emergence of modern civil society; unlike Jacob, who highlights the liberal features of freemasonry, Koselleck sees the movement's utopian dimensions as having been ultimately totalitarian in their implications. On the arcane question of the origins of freemasonry, I have relied chiefly on Jacob's account; detailed studies also include David Stevenson, *The Origins of Freemasonry: Scotland's Century, 1590–1710* (Cambridge, 1988) and Stevenson, *The First Freemasons: Scotland's Early Lodges and Their Members* (Aberdeen, 1988). My source on the mock masons is W. J. Crawley, "Mock Masonry in the Eighteenth Century,"

---

[28] Rolf Reichardt, "Zur Sozialität in Frankreich beim Übergang vom Ancien Régime zur Moderne: Neuere Forschungen und Probleme," in Étienne François, ed., *Sociabilité et société bourgeoise en France, en Allemagne et en Suisse, 1750–1850* (Paris, 1986), 263.

Transactions of the Quatuor Coronati Lodge 18 (1905). John Money, "Freemasonry and the Fabric of Loyalism in Hanoverian England," in Eckhart Hellmuth, ed., *The Transformation of Political Culture: England and Germany in the Late Eighteenth Century* (Oxford, 1991), is informative on the movement's loyalist turn in the late eighteenth century.

In addition to Jacob's work, Ran Halévi, *Les loges maçonniques dans la France d'Ancien Régime: Aux origines de la sociabilité démocratique* (Paris, 1984) offers a good analysis of the movement and detailed maps showing its diffusion. The movement's importance in French Enlightenment culture is also emphasized in Daniel Roche, *Le siècle des lumières en province. Académies et académiciens provinciaux, 1680-1789*, 2 vols. (Paris, 1978), and Roche, *France in the Enlightenment*, trans. Arthur Goldhammer (Cambridge, Mass., 1998). On the links between French freemasonry and older confraternity traditions, I have consulted Maurice Agulhon, *Pénitents et Franc-Maçons dans l'ancienne Provence* (Paris, 1968). François Furet's *Interpreting the French Revolution*, trans. E. Forster (New York, 1981) builds on the work of Augustin Cochin, *Les sociétés de pensée et la Revolution en Bretagne* (1788–89), 2 vols. (Paris, 1925), in arguing for the role of freemasonry in the evolution of Jacobin ideology. On women and French freemasonry, Janet M. Burke and Margaret C. Jacob, "French Freemasonry, Women, and Feminist Scholarship," *Journal of Modern History* 68 (1996) challenge the notion that freemasonry was a masculinist phenomenon.

Freemasonry's importance for the development of German associational life is emphasized in Richard van Dülmen, *The Society of the Enlightenment: The Rise of the Middle Class and Enlightenment Culture in Germany*, trans. Anthony Williams (New York, 1992). See also Thomas Nipperdey, "Verein als soziale Struktur in Deutschland im späten 18. und frühen 19. Jahrhundert," in Nipperdey, *Gesellschaft, Kultur, Theorie. Gesammelte Aufsätze zur neueren Geschichte* (Göttingen, 1976), and Otto Dann, "Die Anfänge politischer Vereinsbildung in Deutschland," in U. Engelhardt *et al.*, eds., *Soziale Bewegung und politische Verfassung. Beiträge zur Geschichte der modernen Welt* (Stuttgart, 1976) On the cult of secrecy in German lodges, see Norbert Schindler, "Freimauererkultur im 18. Jahrhundert," in Robert M. Berdahl *et al.*, eds., *Klassen und Kultur: Sozialanthropologische Perspektiven in der Geschichtsschreibung* (Frankfurt am Main, 1982). The social composition of various German lodges is analyzed in Winfried Dotzauer, "Zur Sozialstruktur der Freimauerei in Deutschland," in Helmut Reinalter, ed., *Aufklärung und Geheimgesellschaften. Zur politischen Funktion und Sozialstruktur der Freimauerlogen im 18. Jahrhundert* (Munich, 1989); in the same volume, Eva Huber, "Zur Sozialstruktur der Wiener Freimauerer Logen im josephinischen Jahrzehnt," investigates the social backgrounds of Viennese masons. On freemasonry in Vienna see also Edith Rosenstrauch-Königsberg, *Zirkel und Zentren. Aufsätze zur Aufklärung in Österreich am Ende des 18. Jahrhunderts* (Vienna, 1993), and Rosenstrauch-Königsberg, *Freimauerei im josephinischen Wien: Aloys Blumauers Weg vom Jesuiten zum Jakobiner* (Vienna and Stuttgart, 1975). Berlin lodges are discussed in Horst Möller, "Enlightened Societies in the Metropolis: The Case of Berlin," in the Helmuth volume cited above. On the relationship of Frederick II of Prussia to the movement, I have used Rüdiger Hachtmann, "Friedrich II. von Preussen und die Freimauerei," *Historische Zeitschrift* (1997).

The Illuminati are treated in Eberhard Weis, "Der Illuminatiorden (1776–1786): unter besonderer Berücksichtigung der Fragen seiner sozialen Zusammensetzung, seiner politischen Ziele und seiner Fortexistenz nach 1786," in Reinalter, ed., *Aufklärung und Geheimgesellschaften* (cited above). On the Rosicrucians see Horst Möller, "Die Gold- und Rosenkreuzer: Struktur, Zielsetzung und Wirkung einer anti-aufklärischen Geheimgesellschaft," in Peter Christian Ludz, ed., *Geheime Gesellschaften* (Wolfenbüttel, 1979).

Conclusion

Like other institutions of the Enlightenment public sphere, freemasonry symbolized an emerging civil society that was increasingly coming to view itself as autonomous from the state. At the same time, the vicissitudes of eighteenth-century freemasonry show that this nascent civil society was politically protean and not inherently liberal or oppositional. Liberal and democratic movements were to be a part, not the whole, of the civil society spawned by the Enlightenment public sphere. Nineteenth-century civil society would give birth to liberal, democratic, even socialist and feminist movements and associations, but it also produced nationalist, racialist, and militaristic ones, foreshadowings of which were already visible in the precociously developed political public sphere of eighteenth-century England. By the end of the nineteenth century, the ambiguous offspring of civil society were much apparent. From, say, Imperial Germany, where right-wing populist associations like the Pan-German League and the Navy League produced a steady stream of chauvinistic and imperialistic propaganda, to the anti-Semitic diatribes of anti-Dreyfus newspapers and associations under the French Third Republic, it was obvious that the public sphere of nineteenth-century civil society could take forms that were anything but liberal.[1]

Curiously, Habermas himself had little to say about nationalism and its role in the structural transformation of the public sphere. This silence is all the more paradoxical owing to the fateful historical role of nationalism in his native Germany, and Habermas has in fact distinguished himself as a vocal advocate of postwar Germany's need to come to terms with

---

[1] On these and other nationalist associations see David Blackbourn, "The Discreet Charm of the Bourgeoisie: Reappraising German History in the Nineteenth Century," in David Blackbourn and Geoff Eley, *The Peculiarities of German History: Bourgeois Society and Politics in Nineteenth-Century Germany* (Oxford and New York, 1984), 159–292; Geoff Eley, *Reshaping the German Right: Radical Nationalism and Political Change after Bismarck* (New Haven, 1980); David Blackbourn, *The Long Nineteenth Century: A History of Germany, 1780–1918* (New York and Oxford, 1998), 424–40. On anti-Dreyfus newspapers and associations see Robert Gildea, *France 1870–1914* (London and New York, 1996), 56–58.

the darker side of its nationalist past.[2] Habermas's failure to address the relationship between the rise of the public sphere and the development of nationalism stems in part from his idealized depiction of the former: for him the public sphere was an arena for reasoned and critical debate, not of national or racial self-exultation, which only manifested themselves after the institutions of the public sphere had succumbed to the social and economic imperatives of capitalism. Yet the rise of the public sphere and the rise of nationalism were inextricably bound up with one another. The institutions of the Enlightenment public sphere forged networks of communication and sociability that transcended locally embedded identities and thereby made it possible for people to imagine themselves as members of a larger political community.[3] The integrative effects of this process were evident in eighteenth-century England in the nigh-xenophobic popular patriotism fanned by newspaper accounts of war and empire, while institutions of the public sphere in France were cultivating proto-republican ideals of the nation well before the momentous events of 1789. Even in the more politically and confessionally fragmented territories of the Holy Roman Empire, newly created networks of print had begun to break down the cultural and religious divide separating Protestant north and Catholic south. In short, the rise of the public sphere can no more be separated from the origins of nationalism than it can be divorced from the development of capitalism.

Hence the institutions of the Enlightenment public sphere were from their inception far more ambiguous than Habermas's liberal and rational model implies. They produced different kinds of audiences and different sorts of political outcomes. "The public" was a heterogeneous and elusive entity, as the enlightened critics who invoked or sought to direct it usually found out. Feminist critics have been most attuned to the ambiguous legacy of the eighteenth-century public sphere, highlighting its gendered assumptions and inconsistencies. But an insistence that the public sphere was intrinsically masculinist, like the assumption that the public sphere was inherently liberal, obscures its multiple guises and narrows the range of attitudes and outcomes it could generate.

In the end the institutions of the Enlightenment public sphere were the product of an information revolution, and information revolutions – like the one we find ourselves amidst today – are invariably ambiguous in their implications. Elizabeth Eisenstein made this point some two decades ago

[2] See Charles S. Maier, *The Unmasterable Past: History, Holocaust, and German National Identity* (Cambridge, Mass., 1988), 34–65.

[3] Cf. Benedict Anderson, *Imagined Communities: Reflections on the Origin and Spread of Nationalism* (London and New York, 1983), 39, who especially emphasizes the role of print culture in creating a sense of membership in a particular nation at a particular time.

in her magisterial study of the print revolution in early modern Europe.[4] The information revolution heralded by print, as Eisenstein argued, drove the production of knowledge but also the proliferation of error. It hastened the circulation of ideas but also created new ways of controlling and manipulating them. It forged communities but also divided them, it challenged traditions but also helped stabilize them. So too with the eighteenth-century public sphere. The enshrinement of "public opinion" as a principle of legitimacy could be an antidote to political oppression, but it could also be used to justify terror at home and aggressive war abroad. Commercialized cultural institutions and literary markets created new publics for books, plays, and art, but this also destabilized standards of aesthetic taste that critics have bemoaned from the eighteenth century up to our own day. The Enlightenment public sphere assigned new importance to women as producers and consumers of culture, but often on the basis of values that served to justify their subordination. Its norms of openness and inclusion created new kinds of association, but also new forms of exclusion. For all this ambiguity, however, we continue to invoke the norms of openness and transparency preached by the Enlightenment public sphere even as we criticize its failure to live up to them. For that reason its legacy is more enduring than it seems, whatever its vicissitudes from the Enlightenment to our own day.

[4] Elizabeth L. Eisenstein, *The Printing Press as an Agent of Change: Communications and Cultural Transformations in Early Modern Europe*, 2 vols. (Cambridge and New York, 1979).

Index

absolutism: French theories of, 45–8; and
fiscal policy, 58–61; and freemasonry,
253, 260–1, 263, 267, 269–70; and the
press, 33; and public opinion, 12,
55–63, 66–71; and secrecy, 8–9, 47, 59,
68, 74–5, 243–4, 253; and the theater,
166–71, 187–91
academies, 105, 130, 136
Adams, John, 234
Addison, Joseph, 95–8, 116, 165,
171, 175, 245
Adorno, Theodor, 9
Agulhon, Maurice, 264
alehouses, see taverns
Alexander, William, quoted 14, 204
Allestree, Richard, 242
almanacs, 87–8
Alxinger, Johann Baptiste von, 217
American Revolution, 33–4, 37, 39, 58,
71–2
Anabaptists, 83
Anne, queen of England, 33, 126, 171,
211, 241
Anne of Austria, queen of France, 103
Arendt, Hannah, 222
Argenson, René Louis de Voyer de Paulmy,
marquis d', 53
Aristotle, 6, 119
Arnim, Achim von, 224
Arnold, Matthew, 118–19
Arnstein, Fanny von, 218–19
Assembly of Notables (1787), 60
Association movement, 31, 37–8, 40
Aubin, Penelope, 156
Augustine, St., 164
Austen, Jane, 149
Austria: book trade in, 144–6; coffeehouses
in, 243–5; and the Enlightenment, 216;
freemasonry in, 257–8, 260–4, 266–70;
salons in, 216–19; schooling and literacy
in, 84–5; taverns in, 232; theater in, 165,
167, 184–5, 188–91

authorship: and copyright, 137–48; in
England, 124–9, 136; female, 148–57; in
France, 123, 125, 128–32; in the Holy
Roman Empire, 123, 132–6; humanist
ideal of, 124–5, 137–48; and patronage,
125, 130–31, 136–7
autobiography, 101

Bachaumont, Louis Petit de, 68
Bad Karlsbad, 153
Bad Pyrmont, 1, 153, 163, 170
Baker, Keith, 47
Balzac, Honoré de, 240
Bank of England, 244
Bank of France, 58
Barruel, Abbé de, 262
Bath, 1, 107, 153, 162, 170, 211–12
Beaumarchais, Pierre Augustin Caron de,
101, 180
Becker, Rudolph Zacharias, 145
Behn, Aphra, 99, 148, 215
Bell, David, 51, 53, 55
Beulwitz-Walzogen, Friederike von, 152
bibliothèque bleue, 88–9
Bischoffswerder, Johann Rudolf von,
267–8
Bluestockings, 152–6, 212–14
Blumauer, Alois, 217
Bolingbroke, Henry Saint-John, viscount,
27–8, 36, 45, 70, 203
Bonhote, Elizabeth, 154
Bossuet, Jacques Bénigne, bishop of
Meaux, 46
Boswell, James, 213, 231
boulevard theaters, 179–81, 184
bouquinistes, 107
Brandes, Ernst, 249
Brentano, Clemens, 224
Brienne, Loménie de, 60–1
Brissot, Jacques-Pierre, 53, 131
Brothers of the Christian Schools, 84
Bürger, Gottfried August, 134